James M. Landis

James M. Landis
Dean of the Regulators

Donald A. Ritchie

HARVARD UNIVERSITY PRESS
Cambridge, Massachusetts
London, England   1980

Copyright © 1980 by Donald A. Ritchie
All rights reserved
Printed in the United States of America

Library of Congress Cataloging in Publication Data

Ritchie, Donald A   1945-
  James M. Landis, dean of the regulators.

  Includes bibliographical references and index.
    1. Landis, James McCauley, 1899-1964.   2. Lawyers
— United States — Biography.   3. Law teachers —
United States — Biography.   I. Title.
KF373.L33R58   340'.092'4 [B]   80-12828
ISBN 0-674-47171-7

Designed by Mike Fender

To my parents,
Arthur V. Ritchie
and
Jeannette M. Ritchie

Preface

The story of James M. Landis, I discovered early in my research, was really that of two men. One was a prominent public official, successful at tackling problems of national and international scale; the other was a private man, somehow less sure of himself and less competent to deal with his own problems. The public man advanced remarkably, from a brilliant law school career to a position of influence in Washington and an eminent law practice in New York, while the private man lived perilously close to the edge of self-destruction. Eventually, the private recklessness of one destroyed the public reputation of the other, leading to prison, disbarment, and disgrace. My interest in James M. Landis began with the public man and his role in the development of the federal regulatory process. But to explain his public successes I increasingly felt the need to unravel his private failures, to understand the interaction between the two, and to present a portrait of the whole person.

Landis left behind a substantial body of papers. His collection at the Library of Congress numbers over two hundred boxes, although for the most part they are the papers of the public man: official correspondence, memoranda, and speeches. Supplementing them are the extensive National Archives files of the various federal agencies in which he served, and the records of the Roosevelt, Truman, and Kennedy administrations, in their respective presidential libraries. The Harvard Law School and Harvard Archives contain accounts of Landis' progress from student to professor to dean. Filling in many of the gaps in these collections is an interview that

Neil Gold conducted with Landis for the Columbia University Oral History Collection, transcribed into seven hundred pages of text. The interview was a remarkable occasion in which Landis recalled and interpreted the highlights of his career, but despite his retrospective mood he revealed little of his private life other than his childhood.

For the private man I turned to his family, friends, and associates. Most helpful were Landis' widow, Dorothy Landis Fenbert, and his daughters, Ann Landis McLaughlin and Ellen Landis McKee, who opened personal letters, diaries, poetry, and memorabilia in their possession and consented to many hours of interviews. Mrs. Fenbert lent me several hundred letters that James Landis had written to her, a rich and revealing collection which she subsequently deposited in the Library of Congress. For a deeper understanding of Landis' childhood, I benefited from the reminiscences of his sister, Eleanor Landis Walker, and brother, George Landis. In addition, at the Presbyterian Historical Society in Philadelphia I found the records of the East Japan Mission, which contain the letters of his parents, Henry and Emma Landis, discussing their children and the environment in which they grew up. Others who graciously shared their insights into different areas of Landis' life, through personal interviews, were Benjamin V. Cohen, Wallace Cohen, Thomas G. Corcoran, Justin Feldman, Stanley Gewirtz, Erwin N. Griswold, Nicholas D. Katzenbach, Frances G. Knight, Agnes Maher, John B. Martin, Austin Wakeman Scott, Jean P. Smith, George Solomon, Mary Walker Taylor, Telford Taylor, and Allen Throop.

I owe a special debt of gratitude to Lawrence C. Kolb, former director of psychiatric service at the Columbia Presbyterian Hospital, for access to records and correspondence dealing with James Landis' psychiatric analysis and treatment during his last years. Convinced that a miscarriage of justice had occurred, and acting with the permission of Landis' family, Dr. Kolb offered his professional evaluation of his troubled patient for this study.

Many others provided valuable assistance. Carolyn Hoover Sung of the Library of Congress first introduced me to the Landis Papers, which she had arranged and catalogued, and freely shared her own interpretations of Landis' life. The Eleanor Roosevelt Institute came to my aid with a grant to fund a research trip to the Franklin D. Roosevelt Library, where William J. Stewart and the rest of the staff made my stay particularly rewarding. Dean Albert M. Sacks of the Harvard Law School allowed me to examine the deanship papers of Landis and Roscoe Pound. The Harvard Corporation opened the papers of President A. Lawrence Lowell, about which Harley P. Holden of the Harvard Archives offered a most useful discussion. Paul A. Freund gave permission to use the Felix Frankfurter papers at the Harvard Law School; and Erika S. Chadbourn, Curator of

Manuscripts and Archives at the Harvard Law School, was exceedingly cooperative with my research. Many archivists at the Truman and Kennedy libraries and at the National Archives, particularly in the Social and Industrial Branch, not only made records available but offered experienced advice as to other collections and record groups to examine.

I also want to thank Martha Ross, who first directed me to the field of oral history. Louis M. Starr and Elizabeth B. Mason assisted me in my research at the Columbia Oral History Collection and granted permission to quote from "The Reminiscences of James M. Landis" (copyright 1975 by the Trustees of Columbia University in the City of New York), "The Reminiscences of Bernard Gladieux" (copyright 1975), "The Reminiscences of Gardner Jackson" (copyright 1972), and "The Reminiscences of Chester T. Lane" (copyright 1972).

Two journals have extended permission to republish material which originally appeared as articles: "The Legislative Impact of the Pecora Investigation," in *Capitol Studies* (now *Congressional Studies*), Fall 1977; and "Reforming the Regulatory Process: Why James Landis Changed His Mind," in *Business History Review*, Autumn 1980.

Horace Samuel Merrill, my advisor and good friend at the University of Maryland, set the standards for researching and writing that I have tried to reach. Others who read all or portions of the manuscript and offered helpful criticism were James Baughman, Herman Belz, Wayne S. Cole, Richard P. Hallion, Stuart B. Kaufman, Keith Olson, Ronald Ranald, and J. Samuel Walker. Roger Newman made suggestions based on his studies into the mysteries of law, history, and Felix Frankfurter. My wife, Patricia Cooper, was always ready to interrupt her own doctoral work in history to smooth out obscure passages in the text, to discuss difficulties in interpretation, and to cheer my spirits.

My colleagues at the Senate Historical Office, Richard A. Baker, John O. Hamilton, Elizabeth Hornyak, Kathryn A. Jacob, and Leslie Prosterman, provided advice, assistance, and encouragement during the last stages of preparation, when I needed it the most.

Donald A. Ritchie

Washington, D.C.

Contents

*A man's fate often depends on far
greater risks than he will estimate.*

— FELIX FRANKFURTER
Williams v. North Carolina, 1945

Introduction

At the apex of the Federal Triangle, between the White House and the Capitol, stands the Federal Trade Commission, one of the oldest of the independent regulatory commissions. The building is laden with symbolism, from the hulky art deco statues of men wrestling trade, in the form of balking horses, at its entrances, to the long interior corridors lined with photographs of obscure faces from the commission's past. One face among them is especially striking, that of a young, unsmiling man whose lean, angular features the photographer shot out of focus to highlight his dark eyes and intense gaze. James M. Landis, as a thirty-three-year-old federal trade commissioner, never worked in the neoclassical limestone edifice at that prestigious address. During his New Deal service the commission operated out of a World War I stucco and tarpaper structure far down the Mall. Landis entered the regulatory process during its years of "lusty youth," with its temporary buildings and procedural innovations, and watched over its development for the next thirty years as it moved to permanent quarters and bureaucratic incrustation. Around the city of Washington other portraits of Landis hang in the halls of the commissions in which he served, and a bronze bust stands in the anteroom of his former law office. They remain the few tangible signs of his long and influential career. His legacy is more lasting, if less visible.

Before the New Deal, the federal regulatory commissions played only a minor role in overseeing the American economy. The industrial turmoil of the late nineteenth century, which saw the emergence of giant corporate monopolies, spurred on the first regulatory attempts on the state level.

1

When court rulings overturned state regulation of the railroads, farmers, businessmen, and others irate over the inequities of railroad rates and routes took their complaints to Washington, where they brought about the establishment of the Interstate Commerce Commission in 1887.

Creation of the new independent agency was an admission on the part of Congress that it could not devote sufficient long-range attention to the complex shifts and circumstances of industrial growth, nor could it find the time to meet each crisis separately. Acknowledging the need for action, yet refusing to concede to the executive branch its constitutional authority to regulate interstate commerce, Congress adopted the independent commission as its solution. The movement toward federal regulation proceeded slowly. Congress took another twenty years to grant the ICC the essential power to set railroad rates. By then, Progressive reformers had given new impetus to the designation of independent panels of experts to handle problems of trade, tariff, currency, and consumer protection, outside of the political arena. The regulatory commissions they initiated survived the demise of the Progressive era, but conservative appointees hobbled the commissions and rendered them incapable of controlling the business and banking excesses of the 1920s.

The depression and the coming of the New Deal revived the regulatory process. Although Franklin D. Roosevelt distrusted the commissions' independence, he accepted them as expedients and presided over their period of greatest flowering. The commissions were essentially compromises between the differing objectives of Congress and the chief executive, each jealously guarding its own prerogatives. The presidents would appoint the commissioners, Congress would define their authority, and the courts would review their decisions. The independent commissions provided the means of recognizing the legitimate grievances of labor and other interest groups perennially excluded from business-oriented administrations. As quasi-judicial bodies they would moderate the disputes between producers and consumers, management and labor, large and small industry. The New Dealers conceived of the independent agencies both as policemen to patrol the private sectors of the economy and as planners to promote industrial recovery and expansion in the public interest.[1]

When the young Harvard law professor James M. Landis arrived in Washington during the early days of the New Deal, the regulatory commissions were just beginning to acquire authority over vast areas of the economy. Landis became enamored with the basic concept of the commissions, their ability to combine the powers of the executive, legislative, and judiciary branches of government to concentrate on a single economic area, whether it be stock trading, air transportation, or collective bargaining. Over the years he helped draft regulatory legislation, served as a federal trade commissioner and chairman of the Securities and Exchange Commission and the Civil Aeronautics Board, participated in regulatory reorganizations, defended clients before the commissions, and analyzed the entire process in his books, articles, and speeches. These diverse roles gave him a multifaceted perspective, and he came to see the regulatory commissions as an efficient method of handling economic problems in modern society and an essential mechanism for checking the abuses of private enterprise without resorting to government ownership.[2]

American society, from Landis' New Deal vantage, was a composite of interest groups, diverse and competitive, whose demands liberal government needed to keep in equilibrium. In such a pluralistic society, he believed, regulatory commissions should serve less as advocates than as mediators. His sympathies lay with neither the consumer nor the producer, the "people" nor the "interests," but rather with the healthy balance between them. "Low rates are desirable," he argued in one case, "but when they are established at such a level as to threaten the economic health of the industry or destroy the desires of people to become part of the industry because of restraints imposed upon its growth, the public interest is not served." Regulatory decisions, in his "umpire theory," were simply wise compromises between conflicting claims.[3]

James Landis' contemporaries regarded him as a "phenomenally brilliant man," but for all his "brain-truster" image he disdained ideologies and philosophies and concentrated on the practical and the attainable. As a law professor, he interpreted law not as a restrictive set of rules but as a process, a means to other, larger ends. The highest role of the lawyer was that of "mediator of human affairs." As a regulatory commissioner, Landis demonstrated the practical application of his theories. He was a shrewd bargainer and negotiator, whether dealing with politicians or lobbyists, industry executives or diplomats. He approached each case separately, refusing to adhere to any preconceived position or tradition. His maverick style, however, often made him appear unpredictable and eccentric. By the time of his death in 1964, the *New York Times* noted, Landis had "achieved the rare distinction of being regarded as a conservative by liberals and as an extreme liberal by conservatives."[4]

In truth, much consistency threaded through Landis' work. He wholeheartedly accepted the capitalist system. "I've been called everything, including a Socialist and a Communist," he observed, "but my theory is a simple one. My desire was to take this system of capitalism and make it live up to its pretensions. Certainly not to overturn it." As a law clerk and follower of Justice Louis D. Brandeis, Landis cherished Brandeis' vision of economic diversity, business competition, and decentralization of power. Yet, Landis was sophisticated enough to recognize that large and uncompetitive institutions would be unavoidable in some fields. It became the duty of the regulatory commissions to determine whether or not such growth served the public interest. Unregulated growth would only foster abuse of power and encourage massive government intervention. "If regulation fails," he warned, "there's only one answer. Socialism. Government ownership. And that's something I don't want to see."[5]

As the singularly most positive defender of the regulatory process, Landis had his critics. They accused him of overestimating the abilities of the commissions because of his New Deal experiences. The unusual political circumstances of the depression and the Roosevelt administration, critics charged, blinded young administrators like Landis to the inherent inactivity of the bureaucracy. They criticized Landis for placing too much faith in the expertise of commission staffs and for encouraging broad delegation of power to the agencies without sufficient standards and safeguards. The pluralistically-minded commissions, in their view, were incapable of effective planning, and merely settled disputes through bargaining between economic interest groups, a system of "legitimatized privilege" in which the strong prevailed.[6]

Such criticism reflected a general disappointment with the post-World War II development of the regulatory process which even Landis shared. Increasingly, the commissions became more responsive to the industries they regulated than to the general public. They tended toward inaction and excessive caution. Consumers complained that the commissions failed to protect them, while producers objected to costly interference in their businesses. Conservatives feared dangerous delegation of power to the independent bodies outside the three traditional branches of government, while liberals often found the same agencies weak and ineffective. By the 1950s, critics from all sides of the political spectrum were recommending everything from overhaul to abolition of the regulatory process. Though dissatisfied, James Landis did not give up hope. "The administrative process is, in essence, our generation's answer to the inadequacy of the judicial and legislative process," he had written, and "our effort to find an answer to those inadequacies by some other method than merely increasing executive power." In the independent commissions he believed the nation had found the basic mechanism, if given broad enough powers and competent personnel. "Good men can make poor laws workable," said Landis, "poor men will wreak havoc with good laws." Such was the message of his final contribution, the major regulatory reforms he proposed as special assistant to President John F. Kennedy, a coda to his career as controversial and stormy as ever.[7]

What predisposed Landis to the regulatory process? Why did he not share the traditional preference of lawyers for judicial procedure, or continue his specialization in statutory law as Harvard's first professor of legislation? Partly it was education: his exposure to Felix Frankfurter as professor of law expounding on the commissions as laboratories for governmental experimentation, and his fascination with the legal realists who were building new pragmatic theories of law and society. Partly it was chance: his year with Brandeis at the Supreme Court during a critical case affecting the independence of the commissions, and his unexpected invitation to aid the New Deal in drafting legislation for securities regulation. And partly it was personality: his admiration of the potentials of independence, assertion, and authority in the commissions, qualities which he sought to achieve for himself but often found so lacking in his own personal life.

Personality was the least evident but not the least significant factor in Landis' association with the commissions. Outwardly he presented himself as a stern, self-confident administrator who missed no detail and mastered every situation. In reality, he suffered a lifelong crisis of self-esteem which led him to develop dependencies on strong personalities, from his own remarkable father to such surrogates as Felix Frankfurter and Joseph Kennedy. He grew to resent his dependencies and sought to extract himself from them, often causing him to rebel against conventional thinking and behavior. He needed constant recognition for his accomplishments and always had to prove himself to others and to himself. At heart a romantic and emotional man, he suppressed his emotions as weaknesses and devoted himself to the coolly impersonal routines of administration. The regulatory commissions, as he envisioned them, were not to be havens of faceless bureaucracy but creative forums for innovative commissioners. He urged other commissioners to write signed opinions like judges, to identify themselves with issues and interpretations, but they would be freer than judges to seek out evidence, initiate legal proceedings, and plan for future economic development. As instruments of government, the commissions would thrive on economic and legal expertise rather than political skill and influence. In short, he idealized the process which fit his talents and satisfied his needs.

James Landis, a friend once wrote admiringly, "gave the administrative process, usually so dull and pedestrian, a spark which is challenging."[8] From the New Deal to the New Frontier, the successes and failures of his career closely paralleled the growth, deterioration, and search for regeneration of that process. The dean of the regulators by dint of service and contribution, he significantly shaped the evolution of the federal regulatory commissions which in turn influenced nearly every aspect of American economic life.

1 | A Demand for Excellence

A Broadway production of *The Winslow Boy* once brought forty-nine-year-old James Landis to tears. Regaining control of himself, Landis explained to his surprised wife that the "father" in the cast had reminded him terribly of his own father. Not only had the actor physically resembled the late Reverend Henry Mohr Landis, with his lean frame, angular features, and walrus mustache, but the two men were hauntingly similar in their single-minded pursuit of causes, mindless of personal consequences. On stage, the character of Arthur Winslow obsessively fought to clear his son from charges of theft, and imperiled his family's finances and reputation in the process. While Winslow defended his action as a quest for simple justice, those around him ascribed it to "just plain pride and self-importance and sheer stubbornness." For James Landis, the characterization triggered memories of deep affection but also of abiding resentment for his relentlessly demanding father. The play's triumphant curtain also left a final sting, for Arthur Winslow's vindication contrasted sadly with Henry Landis' frustrations. Sitting in the theater, experiencing a rare mood of introspection, the son reflected on how powerful his father's influence had been upon his life.[1]

A hard-driving man, Henry Mohr Landis was the descendant of Mennonites who had fled from Switzerland to the Netherlands and then to Pennsylvania for religious freedom. Born in 1857 on a farm in Bally, Pennsylvania, Henry worked his way through Princeton, graduated cum laude, and won a scholarship to study mathematics and physics in Germany. While a student at the University of Berlin, he experienced a religious call-

6

ing and returned to Princeton to enroll in the Theological Seminary. Then while tutoring in the nearby schools to support his studies, he met and fell in love with Emma Marie Stiefler, a young German graduate of the Royal Academy of Dresden who had come to the United States as tutor-governess for a wealthy German-American family. In 1887 Henry was ordained in the Presbytery of New Jersey. That same year a missionary arrived at Princeton to recruit ten men to teach in Japan. "I was one," an old missionary later told James Landis, "and your father was the other nine." On his way to the mission field, Henry returned to Germany, where Emma had gone back to teach. In 1888 they married and together made the journey across Europe to Venice and the forty-day sea voyage to Yokohama.[2]

Once in Japan, Henry and Emma were quickly swept up in the work of the small, understaffed Meiji Gakuin school, a joint venture of the Presbyterians, Northern Baptists, and Dutch Reformed in Tokyo. Henry Landis confined his activities largely to the classroom. Except for a Sunday School class and an occasional visit to preach at a leper colony, he chose the role of teacher over that of evangelist. "He taught everything, literally everything," his son later remembered. "Everything" included algebra, physics, psychology, logic, elocution, political economy, geology, astronomy, English, Greek, and the New Testament. At his peak he taught twenty-nine periods of instruction a week, while studying the Japanese language on the side. His farmboy experiences made him skillful enough with tools to repair watches, tune pianos, and design and construct mission buildings. He also edited a Sunday School magazine, compiled statistics, and prepared the first missionary map of Japan, ruining his eyes in the process. Constitutionally unable to turn down a request for help, he would work through the night on his projects, regularly delaying family meals while he tinkered.[3]

Energetic, eclectic, and visionary, Henry Landis pursued scores of "careers" within the confines of missionary life, but the more diverse his work became, the more he suspected that his talents went unappreciated. He found his outlet in his students and later in his children, for whom he set rigidly high standards. Partly because of his disturbingly slow progress in Japanese, he taught in English and used long, complicated sentences which his students found difficult to follow. They admired him for his wide-ranging interests and knowledge but feared him just the same for his severity. Basically a kind man, Henry compensated by opening his home to his students, and in that atmosphere they found him warm and friendly. "Outside the classroom," one student reminisced, "Mr. Landis was to us a father who was ready to do anything in his power for us." They honored him as a man who had sacrificed his ambitions and prospects as a scholar, scientist, and theologian "for the sake of his spiritual country." It was in such a setting of self-sacrifice and dedication, intellectual curiosity and rigid discipline, strictness and warmth, that the Landises raised their own children.[4]

A year and a half after Henry and Emma reached Japan their first son, Fritz, was born, followed over the next decade by Eleanor, Paula, George, and Charlotte. The birth of their last child took place on September 25, 1899, and they baptized the boy James McCauley, in memory of the family doctor at the mission. The youngest and the brightest child in a talented family, Jim Landis grew up feeling the glow of his parents' pride as well as the sting of their disapproval whenever he slackened in any pursuit. From his mother he found favor, encouragement, and a great sense of security. From his father, the always-demanding teacher, he learned English, Greek, and Latin and received a strong religious indoctrination. Every morning the family read verses from the Bible and knelt together in prayer. On Sundays they read only the Bible or stories about it.[5]

Life was simple and spare. When a shipment of apples arrived from Korea, Emma sternly instructed her children to eat the bruised ones first to prevent undue waste. Yet, as a German who enjoyed card playing and other minor pleasures from which her husband abstained, she saved the family from becoming entirely puritanical. A man of little playfulness, Henry could relax only during the summer months when Meiji Gakuin classes had recessed. In 1893 the Landises had lost their eldest boy, Fritz, to tubercular meningitis, and ever after they sought escape from the "malarial climate" of Tokyo each summer by taking their children to a cabin in the cool mountains at Karuizawa. There Jim would walk with his father in the hills and gather flowers, which Henry Landis used to explain botany and biology to his children. At night he would set up a telescope to teach them the rudiments of astronomy. "There was very little he didn't know," his son would recall admiringly.[6]

In time the hectic pace grew too great for Henry Landis. For years the Board of Foreign Missions had warned him to conserve his energy and "work more consecutive years than to labor under such a pressure and run the risk of health." But too much remained undone for him to heed the advice. In January, 1896, while in great pain from gall stones, he suffered a "general nervous breakdown" and the mission allowed him to go home on furlough. Afterwards, other illnesses plagued him. Then on a frosty morning in 1904, as he supervised construction of the Meiji Gakuin chapel, Henry slipped off the scaffolding and fell head first into a pile of broken bricks. Unconscious for over a week, and feared near death, he never completely recovered from the blow. In later years it produced lapses into unconsciousness, hallucinations, and epileptic seizures. Recovering slowly, he contracted erysipelas, an acute and feverish skin inflammation around his face and head. Frantically, Emma reported that his "mind wandered off," and she pleaded for another furlough.[7]

The Presbyterian Board of Foreign Missions in New York had a limited budget and more limited patience. Reluctantly, it agreed to the furlough but adamantly refused to pay for family visits to both Germany and the United States. Henry Landis planned to return to Pennsylvania for medical treatment and to see his family. Emma, an only child, believed it equally her right and duty to visit her own parents. After much correspondence, the board finally paid the family's way to Germany, but only Henry's expenses to the United States. Furious over the need to beg for funds, Emma scathingly replied that "missionaries ought to be rich so the humiliating fact to ask the Board for extra pay would be avoided." But at a salary of $1,500 a year the Landises were far from rich, and so Emma settled in Germany with her five children while Henry traveled on without them.[8]

A year later he returned and made plans for the trip back to Japan. Their two oldest daughters, Eleanor and Paula, would remain in Germany to study music. German music training impressed Henry and Emma, although they both considered American schools superior in most other fields. When their son George later showed an interest in science, they sent him to the University of Cincinnati to study engineering. Their youngest son, Jim, attended the Tokyo Foreign School for children of missionaries and visiting businessmen. A fiery Irishman presided over polyglot classes of American, British, Siamese, and Dutch students, and kept standards high with a free use of corporal punishment. The number of students enrolled was never very large, and when Jim's class shrank to four, his parents decided it was time to send him to the United States, where he could prepare for entrance into his father's alma mater, Princeton.[9]

In the summer of 1913, the thirteen-year-old James Landis set out alone on the voyage to San Francisco. Anticipation of at last seeing his homeland helped lessen the pain of separation from his parents. As a missionary child in an insular community, he had grown up conscious of being a foreigner in a strange land. A sensitive and imaginative boy, he developed an exaggerated sense of patriotism for his father's birthplace. His childhood love of his country, he later suggested, was even stronger than his love for his own family.[10]

America came as a rude shock to him. San Francisco's harbor was surrounded with the signs of industrialism. Having grown up in the Orient, the boy could not believe his eyes when he saw white men doing manual labor on the docks and living in depressing waterfront buildings. From California he viewed the West from a train window as he traveled to Holland, Michigan, to live with family friends. In 1914 Jim moved to Ohio and stayed in his brother's fraternity house on the University of Cincinnati campus. Later that year his parents returned to the United States on furlough and rented an apartment in Cincinnati. Soon after, his sister Paula arrived, having narrowly escaped from Berlin at the outbreak of World War I. In Cincinnati Jim attended Hughes High School, where he found himself academically far ahead of the rest of his class. Already having read Cicero and been through solid geometry, he became bored with the slow pace of the public school. Before returning to the mission field, Henry and Emma registered their son at the Mercersburg Academy, a religious-oriented preparatory school in south central Pennsylvania.[11]

At Mercersburg, where most of his classmates came from more privileged backgrounds, Jim waited on tables in the dining room to help pay his tuition. The busboy job put him under the "sternest disciplinarian" he ever met. "If your table was not set right," he recalled, "if you swiped an extra dessert, and Jim Walker found out, there was certainly the very devil to pay." The other students teased him about his Japanese upbringing, nicknamed him Banzai, and sometimes made him sit on the floor to eat his meals "to keep in tune for a possible return to the land of cherry blossoms." But his excellent grades and missionary zeal helped him win social acceptance. He became editor-in-chief of the school literary magazine, served on the editorial board of the newspaper, made the debating team and scrub football team, and was class president and valedictorian, winning medals in Greek, Latin, and Bible history. "He had a chance to graduate this year and is only 15 years old," his mother proudly reported, but since he was too young to enter college, he waited at Mercersburg for another year.[12]

After graduation in 1916 Jim Landis took a summer job with a West Virginia coal mining company in Keystone. He earned fifty dollars a week as a scrip clerk, issuing the certificates the miners used to buy groceries and supplies at the company store. The practice bound the miners to the company and disturbed young Landis deeply enough to make him transfer to an engineering crew which surveyed the mines. The rough and bawdy life of Keystone, with its notorious red-light district and Saturday night shootings, served as a startling introduction for him to the world outside of Mercersburg, as well as to the conditions of American workers.[13]

That fall he enrolled in Princeton, determined to pursue his father's profession and return to Japan as a missionary himself. Soon the excitement of the war in Europe disrupted his studies. In November 1916, when Woodrow Wilson concluded his "He Kept Us Out of War" campaign and returned to the Princeton campus to vote, Landis followed him about in admiration for his progressive program but rooted for the more bellicose Republican candidate to win. Wilson's reelection seemed to signal continued American neutrality. Despite his mother's German birth, Landis despised the German war effort and was determined to find some way to participate in the war on his own. Underage and unable to drive, he was rejected as a Red Cross ambulance driver. His parents shared his distaste for the Kaiser, but they considered their seventeen-year-old son too young to leave school and refused to sign the necessary waiver for a minor. His sister Paula, who watched over his affairs while Henry and Emma were in Japan, also vigorously disapproved. Then, like his father before him, Jim Landis succumbed to the persuasive oratory of a visiting missionary. Sherwood Eddy arrived at Princeton to raise volunteers for the British Young Men's Christian Association. Lying about his age, Landis volunteered and waited until he boarded the ship before sending his sister news of his decision.[14]

The wartime sea voyage promised to be a great adventure. Landis patrolled the decks in search of "one of those fabulous German raiders" but ended up watching whales instead. In his cabin he avidly read melodramatic war novels. One that especially inspired him was Mary Shipman Andrews' *The Three Things,* which he found a "simple, beautiful story of heroism in the war, coupled with a young American finding social democracy, God, and love for his enemies." Back on deck, the realities of the voyage were more mundane. The ship's passengers consisted of French wine merchants, American YMCA secretaries, businessmen, and ambulance drivers who did "nothing but drink beer and play poker." His ambivalence between missionary plans and secret dreams of military glory tore at his conscience. He was repelled by the "cheap moral character" of one ambulance driver, yet could not help but admire his *medaille militaire.* When the ship docked at Bordeaux, he visited the city's cathedrals, where the sight of women dressed in mourning, mingled with the blue uniforms of the soldiers, fired his patriotic emotions. As he listened to the slow chant of the priest, he caught himself uttering a prayer "for the conquest of French arms."[15]

After the initial exhilaration came disillusionment and depression. Too young to fight, he had to content himself with YMCA work, occasionally observing artillery practice and once visiting terrifyingly close to the battlefield at Ypres. The tired, frightened, and badly wounded young men he saw at the battlefield hospitals shattered his shipboard fantasies of military glory but increased his guilt as a noncombatant. With the arrival of American troops in Europe, Landis switched from the British to the American YMCA. By then an experienced hand, he took command of a canteen at Winchester which handled all soldiers disembarking at Liverpool. As thousands of troops passed through his facilities, he worked to entertain them by sponsoring boxing matches, ball games, and other sporting events. From London, YMCA headquarters urged the Winchester canteen to hold more prayer meetings and hymn sings. Landis rebutted that he would not force religion onto soldiers who came in for coffee and doughnuts. He felt further disgust over the YMCA's emphasis on profits in the canteens. "If a guy needed a pack of cigarettes and didn't have it, you gave it to him," he insisted as he regularly fell short in his accounts.[16]

The horror and futility of the war threw into doubt his childhood beliefs in God. Feeding those flames, less reverent friends introduced him to Hindu philosophy and other literature from which the Meiji Gakuin and Mercersburg schools had sheltered him. He became an agnostic and lost his faith in the "traditional religion" of his father. In 1917 Landis expressed his emotional turmoil in a poem, "Despondency":

> Night after night remembrance holds me thrall
> With longing for unnumbered days since dead
> Mere dreams! Bitter as wormwood and the gall
> More bitter since their night of hopes has fled.
> And ghostly shadows whisper that there lies
> No newborn stars amid the ancient sky.[17]

Much to the disappointment of his father, who gloried that "James is out trying to save rather than to kill," Jim Landis quit the YMCA and returned to the United States to enlist in the army. By then, the months of agonizing indecisiveness caused his health to collapse, both physically and emotionally. He registered for the draft but gained a temporary deferment through the political influence of a Cincinnati friend. Landis made his way to the West Coast and sailed for Japan to recuperate.[18]

With his health shattered and his beliefs in chaos, he returned to Meiji Gakuin only to find that his strong and dominating father could no longer offer guidance or support. By 1918 the serious head injuries Henry Landis had sustained had taken their toll. His son found him forgetful and suffering "transient hallucinations." He had also become obsessed with the cause of Romanji, the transliteration of the Japanese language into the Roman alphabet. "The question *is* an important one," the president of the Meiji Gakuin School admitted, "but it is hardly too much to say that for a good while Mr. Landis has been almost *possessed* by it." His classroom lectures, conversations, and letters to his children concentrated solely on that issue. Student dissatisfaction rose and the other teachers concluded that he could no longer carry out his duties. Since the Presbyterian Mission Board had no pension provisions, the mission appointed Henry and Emma Landis "missionaries-at-large," in effect a paid retirement. When Jim arrived home, he found his father confused and resentful over his forced retirement. "I think you know that Mr. Landis is a disappointed man," the president of the school explained to the Mission Board. "He feels that his coming to Japan deprived him of a career that might have been his; and also that he has never been appreciated in Japan. For a long time this has been the condition of his mind."[19]

Jim Landis returned to the United States almost as depressed as he was when he left. The Armistice cut off his acceptance into Officers Training School and sealed his chances for military service and distinction. Tired of all crusades, he reentered Princeton, where he joined F. Scott Fitzgerald's disillusioned generation, "grown up to find all Gods dead, all wars fought, all faiths shattered." No longer having any desire to enter the ministry or become a missionary, he had little idea of what else to do. While he maintained his faith in "Woodrow Wilson's concept of social justice," 1919 was the year of Wilson's stroke, the Red Scare, and national retrenchment from social reform. Even at Princeton, Wilson's social reforms had not survived. While president of the university, Wilson had fought to abolish the exclusive eating clubs for undergraduates, but the clubs endured and the campus remained a place of "tight and secure little communities." Those who failed to join the clubs ate their meals with the "non-club pariahs" in the class commons. Equally nonchalant about social status and personal appearance, Landis shunned the more prestigious eating clubs and joined the informal Cloister Inn. Its members affectionately, if ethnically confused, nicknamed him "Chink" for his Far Eastern background and his "spare, tight-skinned skull that mildly suggests the Oriental."[20]

Something of a loner with few close friends, Landis still won campuswide attention for his academic record. When called on to answer in class, he sounded "as if he had written the textbook." He rarely seemed to study and generally waited until a few nights before his exams to lock himself in his room with his books and pots of black coffee. At other times he could play poker the entire night and go straight to an 8 a.m. exam. Either way, he scored the highest grades in the class and was elected to Phi Beta Kappa. In four years at Princeton his only grade less than an A was a B+ in German, the language he had spoken at home with his German mother and had therefore not bothered to study. But when Henry Landis visited Princeton, only the B+ concerned him. He would accept no excuses; his children had to be the best.[21]

Academic excellence freed Jim Landis from waiting on tables by earning him a reputation he could turn to profit. Each term thirty or forty of his wealthier but duller classmates paid a dollar and a half an hour to hear him second-guess the professors in pre-exam tutorial seminars. "You are going to get all of the following questions in some form or another," he would say, "and if you know the answers to these questions you will get a passing mark." Expanding those services, he went into partnership with an upperclassman, George Silbey, to form the Princeton Syllabi Company. From their class notes, Landis and Silbey wrote and sold course syllabi and textbook briefs for $25 to $200 apiece. Despite steep prices, the business boomed. Within a short time Landis became affluent enough to purchase an automobile, the ultimate symbol of student success.[22]

In 1920 his fame spread off campus when members of the Cloister Inn ran him for Princeton's justice of the peace. Landis had gone to New York over the preelection weekend and knew nothing of the write-in campaign his clubmates launched in his behalf. Five dollars bought enough posters to spread around town, and for added measure they flashed Landis' name on the screen at the local movie theater. By the time he reached the campus on election night, he had won election by three times the vote of his nearest competitor. Cheering undergraduates greeted him at his dormitory room and marched him to the university auditorium for a victory speech. The job carried no salary and involved nothing more than performing marriage ceremonies, which he promised to conduct free for any student. Flushed with surprised success, he startled even his most boisterous boosters by predicting that the new office was only the first of many honors destined to come his way, and joked that it might be a stepping stone to the office that Warren G. Harding had won that same night.[23]

Neither business nor politics disturbed his studies. In 1921 he graduated first in his class, read the Latin salutatory at graduation, and received medals in debating, the Class of 1876 Memorial Prize, and the Class of 1869 Prize in Ethics. His classmates elected him the "most brilliant" and "most scholarly" among them. Capping those successes, the *Michigan Law Review* accepted his undergraduate paper on "The Commerce Clause as a Restriction on State Taxation" for publication, an auspicious beginning for his newly chosen career in law.[24]

Landis had mixed feelings about his future. Identifying his father's disappointments with his versatility and lack of specialization, he determined to concentrate his own energies into a single field. "He was a jack of all trades," he said of his father. "He never wrote anything that was significant . . . there's not anything that's left of him except extremely pleasant memories." Like many another Princetonian, Jim Landis imagined himself a future F. Scott Fitzgerald. But in spite of the number of awards his essays had won, he realized that his family was too poor to support him until his writing could earn him a living. At the same time he had become romantically attached to a wealthy young woman from the Princeton area and felt the need to make himself worthy of her. In hopes of "quick rise to money and position," he applied for and won a scholarship to the Harvard Law School. Law held some intellectual interest for him as well, since he ranked the courses in constitutional law and public administration he had taken from Professor Edward S. Corwin as his most satisfying experiences at Princeton. His prime motive, however, evaporated when the girl rejected him. "It's the common story of someone who was rich and someone who was poor," he told friends. Afterwards, the wounds of unrequited love kept him from returning to Princeton for a number of years and reduced his once strictly monetary interest in the law.[25]

The month that James Landis entered the Harvard Law School, his father died in Japan. Shortly after he had returned from his last visit to his children in the United States, Henry Landis had a paralytic stroke. While recuperating at the family's summer home in Karuizawa, he suffered a series of seizures and died on September 6, 1921. He was buried in the Temple Grounds at Meiji Gakuin. To his widow he bequeathed a modest estate. To his children he left as his legacy only a demand for excellence.[26]

2 | Frankfurter and Brandeis, Mentors

The Harvard Law School was under siege in 1921. That May a group of prominent alumni had petitioned for the removal of Professor Zechariah Chafee, Jr., and questioned the fitness of other faculty members, including Dean Roscoe Pound and Professor Felix Frankfurter. Their crimes had been to criticize wartime restrictions on free speech, to challenge court rulings in espionage cases, and to request executive clemency for the convicted. Harvard's Board of Overseers regarded the charges as serious enough to investigate, and at the "Trial of the Harvard Club," academic freedom survived the storm by only a vote of six to five. The war, the Russian Revolution, the Red Scare, and the reactionary politics of "normalcy" were promoting a more narrow-minded, restrictive, and materialistic society. Professor Frankfurter, in particular, worried what effect the "general corrupt atmosphere" would have on the new students entering the school. Their aspirations seemed no higher than the financial reward of a Wall Street corporate law firm. What the future leaders of the nation needed was "the discouragement of material ambitions and the instilling of spiritual concerns that really matter," an assignment that belonged to his colleagues and himself, Frankfurter decided. "The law and lawyers are what the law schools make them."[1]

When James Landis entered the law school that September his own concerns were limited to academic survival. An annual attrition rate of one-third the class hung heavily over all first year men, and faculty members exploited those statistics to spur on their studies. "Turn and look at the man on your left and the man on your right," professors taunted them on the

16

first day of classes. "A year from now one of you three men will not be here." Fellow Princetonian Adlai Stevenson complained that "all we've heard since we arrived were gruesome tales of disaster from our friends and staggering stories of astonishing hours of work when the big reviews begin in March." (Stevenson eventually dropped out of the school.) Another law student of the era, Archibald MacLeish, marveled that the school "made young men who had never used their minds before use their minds until they forgot to eat or sleep."[2]

Harvard served James Landis well. As he wished, it channeled his wide-ranging mind into a single field, one in which he clearly excelled. "He was the strongest man I ever had under me," Dean Roscoe Pound commented, "a man of keen mind, very brilliant, steady, quiet, an exceptional student in every way." Landis stood out from among his classmates; his retentive mind enabled him to excel in every subject. To Professor Austin Wakeman Scott, it seemed as if legal concepts came to him by instinct. He proved himself a hard worker, a tireless researcher, and a clear and precise writer. Landis promised himself that he would leave and try something else if he disliked law after one year's study. "Fortunately or unfortunately, at the end of the first year I headed the class," he noted. "I couldn't quit after that."[3]

By the end of the first year he won a place on the *Harvard Law Review* staff, the school's most prestigious honor. The extra work from the *Review* helped carry him through what he considered the excessively dull Bills and Notes, Sales, and Wills courses of his second year. He was a natural candidate for editor of the *Review,* but during the balloting for the post he tied with Warren S. Ege. The tie broke when Professor Frankfurter lobbied backstage for Ege's election. The loss came as a terrible blow to Landis, who could not tolerate personal failure. That night he walked the streets of Cambridge in disgrace, not wanting to see anyone. Later, in the sober light of day, he accepted Ege's offer of the next highest *Review* post, case editor, with W. Barton Leach as note editor. The three men decided to take up living quarters near each other and Leach moved into Landis' cramped garret apartment.[4]

Gregarious Bart Leach puzzled over Landis' lack of social life. When Leach arranged double dates with Radcliffe women, Landis showed no particular interest. "He lives for classes, the *Review* and bridge at Lincoln's Inn," his roommate concluded. Bridge was particularly serious business for Landis, who supplemented his scholarship with his winnings at the tables. Each day he spent three hours in class, six at the *Review* office, and the rest at bridge or studying. At night, when he had collected as much as he could from the card tables, he would return to his apartment and, as Leach observed, "lie down on the floor, face down with pillows under elbows, reading his cases for the next day's classes. When he fell asleep he would

17

simply turn his head right or left on one of the pillows until he wakened and then continued reading the casebooks." The method worked well enough. By the end of his three years Landis had no grade other than an A, graduated first in his class, and attained what was reputedly the highest average at the school since Louis Brandeis had graduated in 1878.[5]

Ironically, his only setback, failure to become editor of the *Harvard Law Review,* came at the hands of the man who ultimately would do most to further his legal career. In 1923 Frankfurter had not really noticed the quiet, hard-working law student, J. McCauley Landis (as he briefly listed himself). The professor's interference in the voting for *Review* editor had been a serious breach of tradition, which had wounded Landis greatly. During his third year he enrolled in Frankfurter's public utilities class to confront the professor and prove himself in his eyes. As it turned out, the two men profoundly impressed each other.

Frankfurter excited him. He could bring to life the Supreme Court justices whose portraits covered the classroom walls, and seemed able to prove "how great issues of history lay embedded in apparently any legal doctrine." Landis had no use for professors who merely sat and lectured. He admired Frankfurter's socratic approach, forcing students to dig out material, quarreling with their analyses, making them seriously rethink their basic assumptions. While slower students found Frankfurter aloof and frivolous, Landis and the brighter students worshiped him as if "the sun rose and set down his neck." On Saturday evenings Frankfurter would open his home to selected students to argue constitutional law. He dominated every gathering, throwing out provocative questions and waving his arms in fervent debate. Landis generally took an opposite stance, sitting back and saving his comments until they counted most. Once into a topic, however, both were quick-witted and filled with nervous energy.[6]

When Landis led the class of 1924, winning the Fay diploma for the student who showed the greatest promise, Frankfurter offered him a $2,000 research fellowship to stay and earn his doctoral degree. It was a newly created fellowship for a newly created degree. A group of Frankfurter's friends, including Louis D. Brandeis and Julian Mack, had just agreed to make annual contributions to provide a fellow to work with him in administrative law. Describing the new arrangement to Harvard President A. Lawrence Lowell, Dean Pound made it clear that Landis was the obvious candidate: "He is one of the ablest men we have had in the school in many years, and we are rejoiced at the prospect of his staying for a fourth year." The new degree of doctor of juridical science, first offered in the 1924-25 term, was designed to prepare men for law teaching. Landis was accepted into the program despite a warning in the law school register that candidates should have at least three years of experience in practicing or teaching law before applying for admission. As for Landis, he made his choice because he could think of nothing more enticing than to follow his mentor into a career in the classroom.[7]

Having completed three years of intensive study, Landis rewarded himself with a summer vacation before beginning his graduate program. As a student, he had talked vaguely and romantically about "spiritualistic economics—some call it communism," and he wanted to take the opportunity to see the Marxist experiment in the Soviet Union at first hand. To the American left in the 1920s, postrevolutionary Russia represented a creative national social program. Robert La Follette, Sr., and Lincoln Steffens had journeyed there in 1923, and their reports encouraged a steady stream of socially conscious activists, including John Dewey, Rexford Tugwell, Paul Douglas, Stuart Chase, and Sidney Hillman, to make the pilgrimage to Moscow. Domestic politics also influenced Landis' decision to make the trip. Calvin Coolidge's Republican administration appeared likely to triumph in November despite the Teapot Dome scandals. The Democratic candidate, John W. Davis, offered no alternative, and Frankfurter's candidate, La Follette of the Progressive Party, seemed doomed to defeat.[8]

Officially, Landis made the trip as a reporter for the *Baltimore Sun,* although the paper gave him only accreditation as a journalist and would not pay him until after he filed his stories. Withdrawing his entire $500 savings account, he sailed for England. Since the United States maintained no diplomatic relations with the Bolshevik state, Landis sought out Frankfurter's friend Harold Laski for help in obtaining a visa. When Laski succeeded, Landis sailed for Latvia. On the train from Riga to Moscow, he chanced to meet a Russian-born American businessman whose brother was director of the State Bank of Russia and who could assist him in making contacts with Russian officials. Further help came from Walter Duranty, the *New York Times* correspondent. Duranty's apartment in Moscow served as a meeting place for many Russian leaders, and there Landis caught glimpses of Leon Trotsky and other Politboro members.[9]

As a law school graduate, he wanted most to witness the judicial system under the new regime. Hiring a translator, he sat for days in a courthouse on Tverskoi Boulevard observing courtroom proceedings. The building had once housed the governor of Moscow and was still hung with faded wall decorations and incongruous paintings amid the propaganda placards. Landis' attention riveted on the chief judge, Smiroff, a "one-time baker's assistant, anarchist, and student." Dressed in a peasant blouse, Smiroff sat behind a crimson-covered table. His deep-set eyes fixed in an intense gaze that impressed Landis "with the fact that the majesty of the law needs neither gowns nor wigs, but simply an unflinching desire to do justice."

19

Cases varied widely and the untrained judge relied heavily on a legal advisor, but Landis admired Smiroff's pragmatic approach and make-shift improvisations. After all, he asked himself, was the goal efficiency or justice?[10]

Because of his regular attendance in the court, Landis came to meet Smiroff, and on their last meeting the judge presented him with a bound copy of his decisions and a volume of the Russian Criminal Code inscribed: "In Memory of the Visit of an American Citizen to the Proletarian Court of Moscow. I know you disagree with our ideals, but do us the honor to appreciate them." Those words proved more helpful than Landis suspected. Even as early as 1924, a sense of paranoia had settled over Soviet life. The police seemed everywhere. Once at a railway station in Moscow the authorities suddenly arrested him. The worst possible fears rushed through his mind: "I've talked too much!" Instead, they reprimanded him for tossing his cigarette butt on the platform and fined him one ruble. At the Latvian border, as he left Russia, he met with more serious harassment. Guards questioned him about his activities and rifled through his books and papers. Here the inscription from Smiroff helped clear him from suspicion. But as Landis waited for the endless red tape to unravel, he paced the station with his businessman friend, each talking furiously without listening to the other "just to release ourselves from all the kinds of restraints we'd been under for weeks."[11]

His uneasiness over civil liberties spoiled any romantic notions of the Soviet system, but the six weeks he spent in Russia helped shape his nascent views on governmental responsibility toward workers and toward general social betterment. Landis had to admire the zealousness of the Russian workers who held boat races between factories after their shifts, or students so eager for an education that they slept in the streets when rooms were unavailable. Traveling back overland through Europe, he could see obvious contrasts. Russian conditions appeared immensely better than those in Berlin, which he found a starving city, rampant with unemployment, crime, and prostitution. To Landis, Russia was a "civilization trying to pull itself together, to lay the foundations for technological improvement, industrial output and the like. And they were certainly doing it."[12]

His capacity for exaggerating and dramatizing the trip expanded the further away from Russia he traveled. On board the *Saxonia,* crossing the Atlantic, he entertained Jean Smith, a young American woman he met, with tales of his adventures in the Soviet Union, claiming he had escaped "with a price on my head and with only the clothes on my back." When he discovered she was an English literature major from Stanford and Oxford, he dropped the dialectics and regaled her for hours with poetry he had written or memorized. Jean Smith found him a "slight, wiry, intense, idealistic, and often cynical young man with piercing blue eyes, brilliant smile and frayed collar."[13]

Once back at Harvard for his doctoral studies, Landis began writing articles about his Russian experiences. While the *Baltimore Sun* printed a few, most of his essays were returned with rejection slips for not emphasizing the "utter failure" of Russian Communism. At the same time, he found himself caught in the middle of campus political debates. Disagreeing with the arguments of Communist students but defending them from what he considered mindless attacks from the right, he came under fire from both sides. During the autumn of 1924 he finally took up the cause of Robert La Follette's Progressivism and devoted much of his spare time to the third-party campaign. "I should say that it is his fight against the organized power of finance that appeals to me," Landis explained to skeptical friends. He did not oppose capitalism, any more than did La Follette. Rather, he favored a more pluralistic division of power within the capitalist system. "We want to give a fair share of representation to other interests that have so far been warped out of their place under the control of government by the present parties."[14]

During that period Landis began to follow the Teapot Dome trial of oil magnate Edward Doheny. Through Frankfurter's influence, he covered the trial for the *New Republic* and supplied the editor of the New York *World*, Walter Lippmann, with memoranda for editorials on the subject. Out of the assignments grew his interest in the congressional investigation of Attorney General Harry Daugherty's brother Mally, which Landis chose to research for his dissertation. He threw himself into these studies with his customary passion, proud of his participation in national events, and only occasionally regretful over "the savagery of consistent work." "I just seem to have the habit of working in this fashion," he wrote, "extending myself to the utmost of time and letting the future take care of itself."[15]

Much of his fatigue, as well as his stimulation, came from Frankfurter, who constantly embarked on new projects and monopolized Landis' time. Perpetually busy, Frankfurter divided himself among classes, government, and his burgeoning "placement service" for law school graduates. He absorbed the lives of his students and guided them from the law school to law firm to government service. As he himself cultivated the friendship of such influential older men as Henry Stimson, Oliver Wendell Holmes, Jr., and Louis Brandeis, so he played the role for his younger followers, gaining in power as they did and sharing vicariously in their triumphs. Handling an enormous correspondence, and involving himself in numerous causes, Frankfurter found it nearly impossible to set aside time for serious scholarly writing. More and more he turned to Landis to co-author his journal articles, for the *New Republic* and the *Survey* as well as the *Harvard Law Review*.

Early in 1925 Frankfurter proposed to Landis that they collaborate on a series of articles concerning the mechanics of the federal judiciary and the impact of the recent judicial reform act. The series would eventually form a book entitled *The Business of the Supreme Court.* [16]

To his research fellow, Frankfurter assigned the tedious responsibility of ferreting out court cases and legislation and tracing the history of the American judicial system. Soon other law students noticed Landis' "rapid movements about the stacks" as he collected volume after ponderous volume. For his part, Frankfurter sifted through the material and memoranda Landis had compiled. The professor would often spend hours talking about a subject before dictating a single word on it, but Landis always found conversation with Frankfurter to be bright and stimulating. The writing that emerged from their collaboration resembled Frankfurter's style, although Landis participated in every stage. They struggled over each sentence and idea until neither could distinguish his own contributions from the other's. Still, Landis modestly admitted that most of their joint work "could not be done without Frankfurter and most of it could be done with anybody substituted for me."[17]

In June 1925, shortly after the first article in the series appeared in the *Harvard Law Review,* Frankfurter left for Ithaca to teach a summer session at Cornell. Landis accompanied him to continue their research and writing. That summer the bond between the two men grew into warm and mutual affection. The childless Frankfurter had never found a more congenial companion among his students and adopted the fatherless Landis as an intimate confidant, amusing him with anecdotes about the famous men he had known and facilely tossing about new ideas with him. "It's a marvellous gift," Landis recounted. "I satisfy myself with an idea; he's hungry for its expression in the ultimate finesse of words." The two read to each other, played tennis and swam together, and shared picnic suppers. In the evenings they walked in the countryside, by the lake and nearby waterfalls, with the ebullient professor talking endlessly "about law and life." Frankfurter developed a deep admiration for Landis' "extraordinary capacity for work, his penetrating imagination, in mysterious fields of law and affairs, his fruitful curiosity. All rooted in a devotion to the integrity of an adventurous life." As for Landis, he admitted, "I suppose I'm nearing more and more each day the brink of pure idolatry."[18]

While at Ithaca, Landis also sent an extraordinarily florid note to the vacationing Marion Frankfurter, who passed it on to her husband. "Isn't this letter of Jim's the strangest ever?" she asked. "I think it's too funny how the Japanese have colored his insides and his outsides too. This has the lack of simplicity, the saying too much because of ignorance of how to say just enough and no more, the overdoneness of the inability to be natural

—which comes from extreme reticence, plus the flowery ornateness of the Oriental." Frankfurter, who had noticed the young man's "occasional glances" at his wife, cautioned her to be more understanding with Landis. "Apparently, he's had hard luck with women," he suggested.[19]

After their vacation together, Landis returned not to Cambridge but to Washington, for Frankfurter had awarded him one of his highest accolades, an appointment as law clerk to Justice Louis Brandeis. Landis approached the elderly justice with admiration and trepidation. "Here was not only a Supreme Court Judge," he thought, "but the greatest of them excepting perhaps Marshall and Holmes." His new duties required him to serve Brandeis as legal secretary at the Court and then as social secretary at his Monday afternoon teas and evening dinner parties at home. At Brandeis' apartment gathered the *illuminati* of Washington's liberal community: Monsignor John A. Ryan, Judge Benjamin Cardozo, editor Norman Hapgood, Interstate Commerce Commissioner Joseph Eastman, and Senator Thomas Walsh, among many others. Landis delighted in their intellectual sparring and regretted only his duty of seeing that all guests departed promptly at ten (since the justice's workday would begin at five the next morning).[20]

To his dismay, Landis soon found that hero worship made for a poor law clerk. His most important task was to review the justice's handwritten drafts of opinions. At first he dared not change a word or phrase in the drafts and had them printed and circulated among the other judges exactly as Brandeis had written them. The result was a traumatic experience for the young clerk. Holmes returned his copy first, pointing out an obvious proof error. Then came Pierce Butler's copy, noting a miscitation. When the third corrected a lower court citation, Brandeis penciled a note across it: "We must be more careful." Landis felt sick and ashamed. After the next three arrived with more criticism, the justice appeared at the door and asked if his law clerk had checked the draft for accuracy. No, Landis replied, he had assumed the justice had already done so. "Sonny," Brandeis corrected him, "we are in this together. You must never assume that I know everything or that I am even correct in what I may say. That is why you are here. Don't let's have it happen again." Embarrassed but reassured, Landis felt that he had been "accepted more through my errors than my virtues into a junior partnership with the greatest Justice of the Supreme Court.[21]

The year that James Landis spent with Brandeis came at a juncture when he was admittedly "most impressionable." Brandeis profoundly believed in the powers of man to achieve. "This was his appeal," Landis said, "particularly to the young men who see visions." The people surrounding Brandeis, those whom Landis met at the teas and dinner parties, sought not merely to make a living but to accomplish significant things with their lives.

It was Brandeis' encouragement of their desires that brought them together, "and to spend time with him was to have your faith regenerated," Landis explained, "to throw off the sense of frustration and quietly become young again." In the heart of the materialistic 1920s, Landis revered a man who preached moderation of life and abjuration of all excess.[22]

From Brandeis, Landis learned to distrust concentration of power and to admire economic freedom, both for the individual and for the nation. However, Brandeis' philosophy was more than a singleminded attack on economic bigness. The "People's Lawyer" was also a former corporate lawyer and careful investor who believed essentially in free enterprise. He had no desire to see massive federal control of the economy, but wanted the government to prevent corporations from growing powerful enough to eliminate competition from their own markets. In 1914, as President Wilson's advisor, Brandeis had first urged enactment of strong antitrust legislation to outlaw all forms of "restraint of trade." When the drafting of a comprehensive bill in congressional committee proved impractical, Brandeis was flexible enough to join those who were encouraging Wilson to endorse a federal trade commission to set long-term guidelines for business. Although Wilson's weak appointees, and those of Harding and Coolidge, made the FTC largely ineffective for its original purposes, Brandeis continued to support the concept of "regulated competition." From his seat on the Supreme Court he worked to prevent the conservative chief executives of the 1920s from dominating the independent commissions.[23]

It was Brandeis' dissent in the case of *Myers v. United States* in 1926 that first involved Landis with the federal regulatory commissions. Seemingly, the case concerned only a Portland, Oregon, postmaster whom President Wilson fired without the consent of Congress. Chief Justice William Howard Taft, a former president, seized upon the case as a vehicle for settling once and for all the long-standing constitutional question of a president's power of removal, and also for placing the Progressive era's regulatory commissions more directly under presidential authority. "Congress," Taft wrote privately, "is getting into the habit of forming boards who really exercise executive power." The trend had produced a "hydra-headed Executive," perpetuated by the commissioners' lengthy terms in office, which overlapped changing administrations and stripped a new president of "much of his capacity to determine and carry out his legitimate policies."[24]

For two years Taft worked on the case, hearing and rehearing arguments, constantly rewriting his majority opinion. Finding in favor of the government and against the deceased plaintiff, Frank S. Myers, Taft argued that the framers of the constitution intended the President to have absolute power to remove executive appointees, regardless of their rank.

To those appointees, he gratuitously added the commissioners of the independent regulatory commissions, noting that even though the President could not influence or control their quasi-judicial decisions, he could use the voting record of each commissioner as a reason for removal, "on the grounds that the discretion regularly entrusted to that office by statute has not been on the whole intelligently or wisely exercised."[25]

Believing that Taft's conclusions would undermine the independent commissions, Justice Brandeis vigorously struck out against him. The Court faced the "narrow question" of whether a president could remove a postmaster without the consent of Congress, Brandeis insisted, "and this only." As Taft had done, Brandeis buttressed his argument with historical data, surveying legislation and cases since the Civil War to prove that a president's power of removal came from Congress and therefore could be restricted by Congress, particularly for offices whose terms of service Congress had set by statute.[26]

Starting with a page and a half of text for his dissent, Brandeis assigned Landis to investigate the *Congressional Record* and lower court rulings for supporting evidence. Enthusiastically, Landis produced enough documentation to swell the opinion to over forty pages, leaving Brandeis' text floating above his massive citations. A ruffled Chief Justice Taft, on reading the dissent, complained of its "enormous number of fine-print notes and . . . citations without number." Landis felt justly proud of his efforts. "I paged, literally paged every one of the Senate journals from the time of the passage of the Tenure of Office Act," he related, "just in order to determine what the practice was." Brandeis' dissent, he boasted, exhibited "more research than any other opinion in the law books."[27]

His prodigious work on the *Myers* case made Landis familiar with the laws relating to the regulatory agencies and stimulated his thinking about their role in the government. From Brandeis he also developed an appreciation for "expert determination of the new and complex industrial claims by administrative commissions, supervised but not throttled by the courts." The case inspired his lifelong fascination with the regulatory process.[28]

Away from the Supreme Court, Landis' year in Washington exploded with academic and social activity. The *Harvard Law Review* regularly published chapters from *The Business of the Supreme Court,* although Landis' position with Brandeis prevented his name from appearing as co-author. Frankfurter, nevertheless, made certain that the other members of the law faculty understood Landis' contribution to the articles. Whenever free from his court duties, Landis would wander upstairs from the Court chambers in the Capitol and sit in the Senate galleries to cheer on Senator Tom Walsh and "Young Bob" La Follette against the "Mellon-Reid gang." His evenings were spent discussing law and politics at the home of Dean Acheson, another Frankfurter protégé, or reading poetry at the "Robert Service Filling Station," an informal gathering of literary-minded friends. Other times he joined with members of the National Liberal Club for dinner, dancing, and political debates at the Penguin Club on I Street.[29]

For the most part, the "boiled-shirt" society of Washington bored Landis. He felt older than his generation and uninterested in its fixation on "cars, liquor, shows, gossip." What drove him out into social nightlife so frequently was an intolerable homelife. After years of complete independence, he now shared an apartment with his mother. Emma Landis had remained in Tokyo, working with the Presbyterian Mission after her husband's death. On September 1, 1923, a great earthquake struck that city and the fires of its aftermath consumed her home and all of her possessions. She lost thousands of dollars worth of goods, but the Mission Board offered her only $250 in recompense. Her bitter disappointment, together with a growing sense of isolation as younger missionaries replaced old friends on the field, persuaded her to retire. By then Jim was her only unmarried child and she expected she could settle with him, keep house, and feel useful. "I hope he won't get married for a few years yet," she confided to her daughter Paula.[30]

Emma arrived in San Francisco in July 1925 and set out to visit each of her children. When she reached Ithaca, where Landis and Frankfurter were working, her son realized that their seven years of separation had made them almost strangers to each other. Out of a sense of duty he invited her to live with him in Washington, but then spent as much time as possible away from their apartment. Since Emma knew almost no one in the city, she was lonely and miserable, which further soured relations between mother and son.[31]

One evening in January 1926 Jim Landis noticed a tall, slender, raven-haired woman with a southern accent at the Penguin Club. "Mistaking" her for someone else, he asked her to dance. She was Stella Galloway McGehee of Mississippi, a graduate of Millsaps College and a literary secretary to the journalist E. W. Scripps. She had just returned from a year-long cruise around the world on Scripps' yacht, and the two fell into conversation over the exotic places they had both visited, their love of sailing, and their mutual passion for poetry. Stella intrigued him with a "perfectly uncanny habit of quoting fragments of lines forgotten long before and eyes that in Lord Dunsany's phraseology (which she, of course, knew) 'smiled beautifully.' " The next day he invited her to lunch and the conversation continued. Stella McGehee was five years older than James Landis. She had had her share of unhappy romances and was busily pursuing an ambition to become a writer. While flattered, she tried to cool off the ardent young man. That afternoon, Landis went back to his office and wrote "Madrillon — A Restaurant":

26

How was it that you brought me back to these —
Far yearnings and the nameless love one writes
In tears? Why should I think to see the peace
Of hurricanes and stormy starless nights,
And lonely watches through the dark of day;
Of heat and canvas steaming in the rain,
And decks awash and choking, blinding spray,
And fevered eyes and blood athrob and pain.

You talked of Thursday Isle and Java Head,
Old names that beat like trumpets in my ear,
Of youth and hope and hearts that have no fear
For aught save lack of further fears ahead.
And then you went; but somehow, left a trace
Of dawn winds blowing fresh upon my face.[32]

For two weeks he consigned the poem to a desk drawer. "I'm black — just as black-mooded as I can be," he reported. "I've given up going to parties, begun to say nice things about my friends, and all in all wondered just what this buzzing was about." Finally he typed the poem on Supreme Court stationery and sent it to Stella (mispelling her name "Magee") at her *Washington Daily News* address. "When again are you going to be free for luncheon!" he added.[33]

The poem reunited them and their relationship warmed steadily. In the evenings, Landis would leave work and rush to Stella's apartment. On Sundays he drove her out into the Virginia countryside. He ordered a new suit, bought theater tickets, and wrote pages of poetry. The romance worried Emma Landis, who held much higher social ambitions for her brilliant son. Stella came from an old Southern family, once prominent but now financially hardstruck. For years she had worked to meet the family's mortgage payments.[34] Emma Landis looked down upon her working girl status and instead promoted the charms of a wealthy young woman in Philadelphia. "She is a bright girl and has something to say," Emma asserted on behalf of her candidate. "She would not only look at a man and admire him, like Stella does." Landis' favorite sister, Paula, also opposed the match. "Will exchanging a mother for a wife bring back freedom, if it is freedom that you want?" she asked. If he wanted to be rid of mother, then the other children would take her in, Paula promised. "You are not married to your mother."[35]

Over his family's objections, James Landis proposed to Stella McGehee and married her on August 28, 1926, less than eight months after they had met. Among his family, only his mother and sister Eleanor, visiting from the mission field on furlough, attended the small wedding. Thwarted and hurt, Emma Landis suffered a nervous collapse. "I don't wonder that my nerves have gone back on me," she wrote as she packed her bags and prepared to leave Washington. Although she soon became reconciled with Stella, Emma retained a lasting resentment for her "selfish" son. Similarly, Landis never quite forgave his mother. "When someone fails you at a most critical moment, the lack that failure demonstrates is always there," he explained to Paula. "In my case, it turned for a while to almost hatred and then later you neglect it, save you never again can put yourself in a place of real understanding." The incident further isolated him from his geographically separated family.[36]

Married and with his time at the Supreme Court drawing to a close, Landis faced an uncertain future. In the past he had turned down offers to join prestigious law firms, making it clear that he wanted no "raccoon coats and chauffeurs." The previous December he tentatively had accepted an offer to teach at the Harvard Law School. The school was still in the throes of a rapidly increasing postwar enrollment and had a pressing need for new faculty. Dean Pound, at Frankfurter's insistance, had asked Landis to return as an assistant professor at a salary of $4,000, four hundred dollars more than he earned as Brandeis' clerk.[37] But with almost no money in the bank and new family obligations, Landis reassessed his prospects. Undecided, he approached Justice Brandeis. The justice, who had made his own fortune in corporate practice, advised him to go back to Harvard. No other vocation, he counseled, afforded the challenges of teaching and the leisure time for learning and thinking. When Landis left his office, Brandeis wrote to Frankfurter and offered secretly to lend his law clerk $2,000 to establish himself in Cambridge.[38]

The recommendations of Frankfurter and Brandeis, the two men he most respected, convinced Landis to return to Harvard in September 1926. Jim and Stella settled in a small white frame house on Remington Street, a few blocks from the law school. Within months, Stella's "Southern charm" had infiltrated the tight New England community of scholars, and Landis' classroom performance had launched his reputation as a skillful and popular teacher. "If I could always instill energy of that type and get them to test their mettle," he said of his first experience before a class, "I think I could enter into work of this kind with a great deal of enthusiasm."[39]

3 | Harvard Law and the Making of a New Dealer

When James Landis stepped in front of his first class, he faced one hundred and fifty disappointed students. They expected the popular Professor Samuel Williston to teach their first-year course in Contracts, but because enrollment grew too large, Dean Pound split off one section and assigned it to Landis. As they scrutinized the new assistant professor, the students were unimpressed. Only twenty-six years old, five-foot-seven, hawk-like in appearance, wearing a slightly rumpled three-piece suit, he projected none of Williston's personal charm or classroom mastery. He was not much of an orator, and lectured so softly that they had to strain to hear him. Students described his style as the "School of the Furrowed Brow," nervously intent, hands stuffed in his pockets, pacing back and forth across the dais. But Landis had learned his lessons from Felix Frankfurter. He copied his mentor's method of teaching by questioning and challenging his class with hypothetical cases that sent them into "agitated knots of discussion." After a few weeks his wit and intelligence, lucid arguments, and elaborately prepared lectures converted the class. On the final day of the term the students rewarded their new professor with an ovation. In Washington Justice Brandeis was delighted to learn that "the boys who were not assigned to Williston's section thought they had missed something; but find they haven't."[1]

Success in the classroom helped tie Landis to Harvard, and for the rest of the 1920s his career orbited in a path never far from the law school. Intellectually, the law school set him apart from the prevalent conservatism of government and business during the decade and provided him with a

29

dynamic environment. The leading schools were grappling with innovative concepts of law, changes which often brought discord to their faculties but produced a new generation of lawyers steeped in the theories of "sociological jurisprudence" and "legal realism." By 1933 Landis and other students of the era would take to Washington a more pragmatic concept of law than any other group of lawyers and administrators had ever before carried with them. They would give a framework of legal realism to the New Deal, which would free it from the inhibitions of legal traditionalism and would perfectly fit the flexible administrative approach of Franklin D. Roosevelt.[2]

Harvard figured prominently in the debates over legal theory. A half century earlier its dean, Christopher Columbus Langdell, had introduced the case system. Abandoning the law school's habitual textbooks and memorized recitals, Langdell applied the principles of Darwinism to law and began to collect judicial precedents as if they were scientific facts. Langdell and his followers compiled massive casebooks which arranged and catalogued significant court cases. From these volumes his students traced past doctrinal developments in the opinions of judges, in search of principles of law which they could apply to contemporary problems. The casebook method quickly spread throughout American law schools, but left some scholars dissatisfied with its emphasis on the mechanical and formalistic nature of law. During the "revolt against formalism" of the early twentieth century, another Harvard man, Roscoe Pound, challenged Langdell's assumptions. Pound perceived the law as an evolutionary process rather than a set of rules, and related it more closely to the social sceinces than the natural sciences. His writings on "sociological jurisprudence" called for the incorporation of sociology, economics, and political science into the curricula of law schools to supplement the volumes of judicial decisions.[3]

In 1916 Pound became dean of the Harvard Law School, and from that prestigious position he watched his proposals dramatically alter American legal education. Where law professors previously stressed the narrow nature of law, they now began to speak of its limitless qualities. Able practitioners of Pound's sociological approach, among them Felix Frankfurter, expanded traditional course material to encompass the whole host of the social sciences. In their classes the morning newspaper assumed equal rank with the case book. Outside of Harvard, Pound's pragmatism generated newer and more ambitious methods of education. Young teachers, particularly at Yale and Columbia, developed far more radical theories than Pound could accept. They attempted to strip the law of all fixed and fundamental principles, and came to see it as a means to an end, rather than as an end in itself. To the group loosely known as "legal realists," the law was really the aggregate of judicial and administrative actions. "What these officials do about disputes," said Karl Llewellyn bluntly, "is, to my mind, the law itself."[4]

Where Pound pictured law as a constant struggle between social stability and flexibility, the legal realists were fascinated with flexibility. They were political liberals who rejected the conservative image of a mechanical legal system as irrelevant to the new industrial and technological society. The legal process, they argued, should be a means to achieve positive social and economic improvements. During the decade of Harding, Coolidge, and Hoover they stressed state and regional experimentation, but were willing to use the federal government to obtain their goals, if ever possible. Always at heart a Republican, Roscoe Pound could not go that far. The legal realists, he feared, were abandoning the government of law for a government of men. Under their train of thinking "there is nothing to law but force," he wrote. "Whatever is done by those who wield the force of politically organized society is the law."[5]

The debate divided law schools and set scholar against scholar, both philosophically and personally. James Landis, who had abandoned all "best or true faiths" during the war, was able to draw from both schools of thought without siding completely with either. As a student and young professor, he studied Pound's theories together with Frankfurter's emphasis on the "fluid tendencies and tentative traditions" of administrative law. Simultaneously, he read and agreed with many of the more radical theories of the legal realists and became one of their strongest advocates at Harvard. Even without committing himself wholeheartedly to any side, he acquired through these debates a flexible concept of the law that shaped his thinking for the rest of his life.[6]

The new assistant professor was beginning to draw some attention for his own work. In the fall of 1926, he completed the requirements for his S.J.D. degree with a dissertation entitled "Constitutional Limitations on the Congressional Power of Investigation." Landis strongly defended the Senate's subpoena of Mally Daugherty, brother of President Harding's attorney general, and presented the case for Congress' unfettered freedom to investigate.[7] As he wrote, the case was pending at the Supreme Court, and Justice Brandeis urged him to finish before the Court reached a decision. The dissertation's publication as a *Harvard Law Review* article in December 1926 came a month before the Court upheld Daugherty's subpoena and Landis' arguments. Disappointingly, Justice Willis Van Deventer's majority opinion made no reference to Landis' research. But legal scholars in courts and law schools across the country praised the article, and editorials endorsed it in several newspapers. "A very fine and valuable piece of work it is," wrote Benjamin Cardozo, while John Dickinson commented jovially

31

on the "felixity" of its style.[8]

Dickinson's gentle ribbing touched on what some thought the most serious problem facing Landis. One Frankfurter student, Henry Friendly, who decided to enter private practice, warned Landis against becoming too dependent on any single individual. Frankfurter loved his protégés, the wife of another one commented, "but he also owned them." Stella Landis warily observed Frankfurter's continued influence over their lives. "I don't think he likes you to do anything he hasn't a hand in," she told her husband. But Frankfurter's enthusiasms were infectious, and Jim still talked about his mentor "by the hour."[9] During the 1920s, a decade so frustrating for American liberals, Frankfurter refused to cloister himself in the law school. He served as legal counsel to the American Civil Liberties Union and the National Association for the Advancement of Colored People, he wrote briefs to uphold minimum wage laws and abolish child labor, and he actively supported the presidential candidacies of Robert La Follette, Sr., and Al Smith. As often as possible, Landis joined in Frankfurter's causes.[10]

Most of their activities were limited to writing magazine articles, but occasionally their crusading moved beyond the pen. In 1926, when Frankfurter threw his limitless energies behind the defense of Nicola Sacco and Bartolomeo Vanzetti, Landis went along to help with "a little polite rabble rousing." As Frankfurter exposed the injustices of the Sacco-Vanzetti trial in an *Atlantic Monthly* article, Landis took the "glorious fight" to the podium. In April 1927 he addressed an assembly at Smith College and declared the two men "guilty of the crime of radicalism, not of murder." Stressing the reasonable doubt in the fairness of their trial, he called upon the assembly to petition the Massachusetts governor for a review of the case. Instead, the meeting dissolved into near riot when irate townspeople from Northampton shouted down the college women from Smith and prevented passage of the resolution.[11]

Open and undisguised hostility met the supporters of Sacco and Vanzetti both in Boston and at Harvard. In the pages of the *Boston Evening Transcript* John Henry Wigmore, dean of the Northwestern School of Law, chastised Frankfurter for his interference in the Sacco-Vanzetti case and defended the court proceedings as entirely proper; Frankfurter responded and their charges and countercharges ran on for the next two weeks. Dean Pound, who considered Sacco and Vanzetti innocent and their trial a miscarriage of justice, thought Wigmore's letters were "a disgrace to legal scholarship." Normally Pound objected to his law professors speaking out on cases still pending before the courts, but he was willing to see that rule broken because of the great amount of prejudicial material already printed against the two Italian immigrants. Yet for the most part Pound remained silent on the case, despite urgings from friends of the school that he come to

Frankfurter's defense. Not the least reason for the dean's silence was his fear that controversial publicity would endanger the law school's endowment-raising campaign. Diminishing alumni contributions and violently anti-Frankfurter mail confirmed the validity of his fears. The controversy helped drive a wedge between Frankfurter and Pound that split the school into factions. Landis remained a Frankfurter loyalist, feeling "less afraid of radicalism than of the smug complacent satisfaction of our institutions and among the leaders of them."[12]

Then the university's president, A. Lawrence Lowell, put Harvard's ultimate imprimatur on the case through his signature on a "Lowell Committee" report finding no fault with the convictions of Sacco and Vanzetti and sealing their doom. Frankfurter was furious with Lowell and "his crowd, the Yankees," for their bias against the two immigrants. Lowell, for his part, considered Frankfurter "first rate in intelligence, but defective in character," and wished there was only some way to convince the controversial professor to leave the school voluntarily. He realized that he could not dismiss or even censure Frankfurter for his outspokenness. "Oxford did not for a couple of centuries recover the effect of the expulsion of Wycliffe," Lowell explained to one angry alumnus who wanted Frankfurter removed. "No doubt a great temporary injury may be done to a university by inconsiderate publications, but not in the long run anything so fatal as restricting the freedom of the professor."[13]

Frankfurter's willingness to remain at Harvard, despite his distrust of Pound and Lowell, heightened the tensions with which Landis had to deal. Although Frankfurter had once championed Pound for the deanship and had joined the faculty with a "sympathetic outlook" for his theories on sociological jurisprudence, he came to see the dean as a "timid creature." For Lowell he reserved a harsher judgment. Frankfurter never forgave the Brahmin president for his leadership of a movement to limit the enrollment of Jewish students at Harvard in 1922. Fighting against the proposal, Frankfurter had lost a chance to sit on the school's admissions committee because of Lowell's persistent objections. The outraged professor also held Lowell personally responsible for overriding the law school's recommendations and blocking the teaching appointments of two of his more gifted students, simply because the young men were Jewish. Yet, for twenty years Frankfurter willingly "breathed the atmosphere" of an institution headed by a man he called "a refined Adolph Hitler."[14]

Harvard meant too much to Frankfurter for him to abandon his career there over any personality dispute. As an Austrian immigrant and a child of New York City's tenements, he clung to the Harvard Law School with a self-confessed "quasi-religious" devotion to its traditions. "A great history, like that of this law school," he insisted, "is an important source for creative power." His reverence for the institutions of the law school and the United States Supreme Court created a barrier that steadily separated him from the more iconoclastic legal realists, at the same time that it slowly transformed his crusading liberalism into cautious judicial conservatism. While James Landis never lost his own pragmatic liberalism, he associated with Frankfurter long enough to feel uncomfortable with the more experimental realists. Caught between the two forces, he set out to chart a course in legal theory for himself.[15]

Which way could he go? As a new assistant professor, he drew all first-year classes, none of which offered much room to maneuver nor lay near enough to his real interest in public law. Frankfurter monopolized the third-year course in public utilities, while "labor law and administrative law were luxuries for only those with esoteric interests unconcerned with the bread and butter of the practicing world." Landis wanted no part of teaching the history of law or of Roman law, which he dismissed as "so dead beside the *living issues* that challenge us daily here." Legislation was more to his liking. After his stint with the Supreme Court, and his hours in the Senate galleries, Landis had become fascinated with the chaotic nature of legislation in the United States. Legal training, he decided, concentrated "to the extent of 99 44/100 percent" on judicial decisions and placed too heavy an emphasis on judge-made common law. Such rigidity had been responsible "for that very legal conservatism which has barred lawyers as a class from every imaginary utopian state." Law students needed to move beyond case law to see the law system as a way "of realizing aims and desires rather than simply inhibiting arbitrary action." Training in interpreting and drafting legislation would enable students to become better practitioners, judges, administrators, and legislators. Although a few schools already offered courses in legislative draftsmanship, Landis conceived of the study of legislation on a broader level. He lobbied for the appointment of a professor of legislation, and envisioned himself in the post, where he could collate the haphazard federal and state statutes and prepare them for "scientific treatment."[16]

Offer of that desired post came not from Harvard but from the University of Pennsylvania. In April 1928 Professor Francis Bohlen had had his fill of Cambridge's "stuffiness" and was preparing to return to the Pennsylvania Law School. He suggested that Landis come with him, and arranged for the school to offer him a full professorship, a $7,500 salary, and freedom to teach anything he wanted. Landis could emerge from under Frankfurter's shadow, Bohlen coaxed him, and also be better able to support his family.[17]

Although he felt intimately attached to Harvard, the Pennsylvania job was far too attractive for Landis to ignore. Over lunch, he broached the subject to Frankfurter and read off the litany of his complaints: the "starva-

34

tion" wages of an assistant professor; the academic rigidity he felt settling in at Harvard; his heavy teaching load and surfeit of first-year classes; his desire to get into public law; and his absolute inability to converse with Dean Pound. Landis could recall one of his painful first encounters with the dean. As a second-year student he had taken to Pound a note on equity he was writing for the *Review*. Pound disagreed, lost his temper, and began throwing pencils from his desk out the window, one by one, as he made his points, in part to distract and befuddle Landis in his arguments. Afterwards, Pound took him outside to help collect up the pencils. As a faculty member, Landis still felt somewhat intimidated each time he entered the dean's office, distrusting his temper and his word.[18]

Disturbed at the prospect of losing his favorite protégé, Frankfurter brought his case to the faculty. Landis was an outstanding scholar and a popular teacher with a flair for public law, he said, whom the school could not afford to let go. The faculty agreed unanimously and offered the twenty-eight-year-old Landis a new research professorship of legislation. The promotion would carry a raise in salary to $6,000 and a reduction in teaching load from handling an average of 750 undergraduates to teaching only one graduate seminar, with the rest of his time free for research.[19]

His rise would be "meteoric, almost unheard of," Dean Pound remarked with dissatisfaction. The dean preferred a "picture card" appointment for the new professorship, someone with more experience. Pound was less than grieved, therefore, when President Lowell ignored the faculty's recommendation and offered the legislation professorship to a prominent Boston politician and attorney, Henry L. Shattuck. "What is the faculty," Frankfurter demanded, "a deliberative body of scholars, or a lot of German privates *before the war?*" Behind the scenes, Frankfurter enlisted the aid of professors Zechariah Chafee and John M. Maguire, who went to the dean and threatened to resign if Landis did not receive his promotion. Fearful that a showdown would "disrupt the faculty," and mindful of a recent mass resignation at the Columbia Law School, Pound offered Landis a chair in judicial organization. But for Landis it was legislation and nothing else, so he refused the offer. Shattuck finally settled the matter by announcing that he could not abandon his practice and politics and could devote only two-fifths of his time to the law school. Finding that proposition unacceptable, President Lowell permitted Landis' appointment to go through just as Felix Frankfurter had planned.[20]

Young, ambitious, and a full professor, Landis plunged into the field of legislation with great dreams of scholarly contribution. As the first professor of legislation at Harvard, he had no established procedures to build on, and doubted that any real work had been done in the field since the days of Jeremy Bentham, the early nineteenth-century British jurist. Landis' strengths as a researcher made him a strong and imaginative teacher. To achieve a comparative treatment of statutes, he presented his seminars with such topics as narcotics legislation, or field and game legislation, and then assigned each student to handle the subject from the standpoint of a different state. That way they could discuss amendments, administrative organization, delegation, and enforcement in concrete form. By the end of the term each student drafted a statute with an accompanying committee report, and the rest of the class reviewed the product as a legislative body. In November 1929 the *Harvard Law Review* instituted a new section on legislation, which Landis' students conducted. Students in the seminar also helped draft actual statutes, preparing pharmacy legislation for Nebraska and proposing birth control legislation for Margaret Sanger. Landis himself volunteered his services drafting model legislation for the National Conference of Commissioners on Uniform State Laws.[21]

His efforts in legislation culminated in the most important article of his academic career, "Statutes and the Sources of Law." Writing a broad historical survey, he deplored the wide scope of judicial review which had reached its apogee during the Gilded Age, when state legislatures drafted laws to correct the social and economic abuses of industrialism, only to watch the conservative courts strike them down as interference with the existing economic system. Legislatures responded by improving the quality of their statutes through more expert draftsmanship and use of the committee system. In the twentieth century the sheer volume of legislation made it difficult for the courts to ignore. The time had come, Landis wrote prophetically, for the courts to apply statutes in the same broad fashion as they did judicial precedents. Economic power should shift from the courts back to the legislatures, which could supervise its development more democratically. His trail-breaking article, Professor Erwin Griswold acknowledged, "would surely be included in a collection of the great legal essays of all times."[22]

The very newness of his legislative work isolated Landis from the rest of the Harvard law faculty. His interests more closely paralled the work then going on at Yale, Columbia, Chicago, and Johns Hopkins. Deans Robert M. Hutchins and Charles W. Clark at the Yale Law School and Young B. Smith at Columbia had put together eager and imaginative faculties that were experimenting with psychology, medicine, and criminology within their law courses. Like the legal realists, Landis read John Dewey and sought a more pragmatic approach to law. From his year with Brandeis he had realized that law was more than a game of wits; "instead it became the instrument for the realization of the hopes of men and women intent on fuller and happier lives." That realization opened his mind to the ideas of the realists, who reminded him of Robert Browning's poem, "Fra Lippo

Lippi." Like Browning's artist the realists had broken away from earlier traditions and were portraying people and institutions realistically as they saw them. "The common ordinary things of life, as a whole," he paraphrased Browning, "pass mankind by until someone puts them before us so that we must look at them."[23]

The legal realists, in turn, thought Landis out of place on the Harvard law faculty. Yale's Dean Clark wondered "whether it would not be better for his own future development that he accept some of the very flattering offers he has had elsewhere and obtain other points of view, at least for a time." Columbia's Dean Smith felt similarly, and in April 1929 he opened negotiations with Landis to accept a position there. Teaching at Columbia during the summer, Landis had formed a favorable impression of its law faculty, which included such realists as Karl Llewellyn and Underhill Moore. He saw a career there as "offering much, especially to those whom youth made eager enough to grasp for much." Columbia had that "electric atmosphere of drive and ambitious courage" which might stimulate him to more daring and brilliant work than would be possible at Harvard.[24]

But Landis' responsiveness to the realists had its limits. He could not completely escape the aloof attitudes of the Harvard Law School. The sociological approach in the hands of small men, he feared, "degenerates into an attempt to collect and interpret volumes of fact." At times he became thoroughly discouraged with that method, for it seemed to bring him "no further along the road to wisdom." Felix Frankfurter further prevented him from making alliance with the realists. Outwardly, Frankfurter applauded their innovations, but privately he took upon himself the task of defending Harvard from their criticisms. If the realists detected at Harvard an attitude of condemnation for their experiments, Frankfurter insisted that his school was open-minded and advocated "no creeds, no dogmas, no disciples." He carried that spirit of tolerance to the extreme of defending even the most reactionary of his Harvard colleagues, earning himself the realists' scorn for "gross institutional parochialism." In return, Frankfurter questioned whether the realists' programs would water down legal education with too many courses, too many research undertakings, and too many second- and third-rate teachers. Law schools must "limit the range of what we do," so that "everything we do will be of first-rate quality." And Harvard, for Frankfurter, epitomized first-rate quality.[25]

It irritated Landis when the realists charged him with harboring the typical "Harvard attitude." "I refuse to admit the existence of any Messiah," he rebutted, "whether they stalk under the names of Pound, Ames, and the real though not corporate entity of Harvard, or under the names of Oliphant, Cook, Marshall, Clark, or anyone else." If Harvard emphasized anything it was the law "as a method of ordering social activity to meet social needs," and method and process interested Landis more than did any particular philosophical viewpoint. He finally rejected the Columbia offer, although the school had a "sound gospel" of legal realism, and chose to remain at Harvard. "All I want is freedom for myself and freedom from 'true faiths,' " he explained to Frankfurter, "and despite the many things we lack we do individually get that from Harvard." Perhaps equally weighing on his decision was his legislation course. He had invested a year of work in it with "nothing thus far to show," and felt an obligation to stay with the course and make it succeed.[26]

With renewed effort he resumed his labors to accomplish "something significant." His students noted that his light in Austin Hall "shined at all hours of the night" as he prepared course material and wrote legal articles. The rigor of his labors affected his health, and colleagues worried that his face had become sallow and emaciated. Still, the pace did not satisfy him. The Harvard community was too small to contain his energies.[27]

In 1931 Landis came close to escaping into government service. Through Frankfurter's connections he traveled to Wisconsin for an interview with the new governor, Philip La Follette. La Follette offered him a tempting post on the state's Railroad Commission, but uncertain finances held Landis back. As a professor he earned $6,300 a year, to which he added his earnings from summer school teaching, lecturing, book royalties, and writing assignments for the *Encyclopedia Britannica,* boosting his annual income to $8,500. From that he estimated his yearly expenses at $7,500. He carried $30,000 in life insurance and was paying off an $8,000 mortgage on his home. His savings were modest, and Stella frequently overdrew on their accounts, but they maintained membership in the Harvard Club and the Cambridge Boat Club and kept up their position in society. The Wisconsin job would pay only $5,000 a year. After exploring and failing at the possibility of a sabbatical leave at half-pay to add to that income, Landis sadly rejected the post. "It would mean a sacrifice of almost $7,000. That would more than sweep away my small savings after five years of teaching," he wrote La Follette. "I wish that I were so situated that I could devote my means to the public service," but that was impossible for the time being.[28]

The financial pinch sometimes made for a rough time at home. At first Landis kept the family budget himself, making entries in his ledger in two colors of ink, but before the year was out he became preoccupied with his classes and left family finances to Stella. After the birth of their two daughters, Ann in 1928 and Ellen in 1930, money problems became more pressing. Landis still owed a $125 tuition loan to Princeton, and went so far as to offer to cash in an insurance policy to pay it off. Settling his father's small estate took over a decade, and providing an income out of it for his mother remained a persistent family problem until her death in 1935. In financial matters Landis generally advised caution and prudence and rejected materialism. "The possession of things is to me of such slight moment that I can't arouse any feelings over a matter of such a nature," he wrote to his sister. He often lost his temper, however, when Stella misbudgeted their resources. His furious lectures on finances to her may have reflected inner fears of inadequately providing for his family, but she bore the brunt of his fury. "Just sometimes," Stella asked, "tell me things I don't do so badly — even if you have to lie — and know I know it. Don't make me hate myself so."[29]

Unexpectedly, the Great Depression improved the Landises' financial standing. During the prosperous 1920s Harvard professors had suffered a severe decline in their standard of living. A concerned President Lowell determined to raise faculty salaries to a level where they could "live comfortably, in a style reasonably appropriate to their position and duties." The university initiated a $15 million endowment fund drive, with the result that Landis' salary as a full professor rose from $6,000 to $9,000, towards a possible ceiling of $12,000. The new wage scale came at a time of dramatically falling prices, due to the depression, and gave the Harvard faculty a sixty percent increase in their real income. Since Landis owned few stocks and deposited his small savings in a stable bank, the stock market crash and wave of bank failures left him unharmed. In 1931 he and Stella felt secure enough to begin looking for a larger home. They considered building one, but then took advantage of low prices and mortgage rates to purchase a handsome house on Gray Street for only $11,500. There was money enough left to hire a maid to care for the children and cook and clean. "Your family and home in the environment of Harvard and Cambridge make and visualize achievements of which you are justly proud," Landis' brother-in-law wrote. "It is all very healthy and solid."[30]

He possessed all the trappings of a comfortable and happy life: a family, a prestigious job, a place in the community, and financial security. Why was that not enough? The lure of government service still haunted him. He looked for new challenges and an opportunity to have a greater impact on his times. After rejecting the Wisconsin job offer, he turned to Massachusetts politics, advising various local politicians, from Republican Christian Herter in the state legislature to Democratic Mayor Richard Russell in Cambridge. Russell, a reform mayor, designated Professor Landis to reorganize the city government, and before long Landis announced his intention of running for the City Council himself, as a Democrat. Once again, however, Felix Frankfurter intervened.[31]

For years Frankfurter had kept his eye on the political career of Franklin Delano Roosevelt, a fellow veteran of the Wilson administration. In 1928, when Roosevelt won the governorship of New York, Frankfurter saw visions of the presidency for him. Landis usually followed Frankfurter's lead in politics, but he found it difficult to develop any enthusiasm for the governor. Once, Frankfurter had driven Jim and Stella to Hyde Park to meet the great man whom he believed could pull the nation together. They arrived late on a hot summer afternoon and found Roosevelt stretched out on a small bed, his leg braces propped up against a nearby wall. The governor was tired and waved them away without a noticeable effort to be sociable. Both the Landises came away convinced that Roosevelt was a sick man who would never have the strength to serve as president. Landis had also been disappointed by the governor's evasiveness on the issue of nonpartisan selection of judges in New York. In the 1932 Massachusetts primary, Landis endorsed Al Smith over Roosevelt; and when Roosevelt won the nomination, Landis despaired of any hope of a Democratic victory that November.[32]

Roosevelt's landslide election proved Landis a poor political pundit, while it thrust Frankfurter into the forefront of national affairs. The new President drafted Frankfurter as legal advisor and "recruiting officer" for the New Deal. Only a month after the Inauguration in March 1933, Frankfurter received a call for help on the administration's securities reform program. One Thursday after classes, Frankfurter boarded the train to Washington, taking along with him James Landis, since "it would be a very valuable experience for our professor of legislation." En route they stopped in New York to pick up another former Frankfurter student, Benjamin V. Cohen. Ahead of all three men lay long, turbulent, and fruitful associations with the federal government.[33]

Landis' transformation from law professor to government advisor came not without its difficulties, but as usual Frankfurter smoothed the way. The major obstacle was President A. Lawrence Lowell, who disapproved of the spectacle of Harvard faculty running off to Washington at the call of the New Deal. Soon to retire, Lowell seized upon the law professors' absence from their classes as his last opportunity to discipline the errant Frankfurter. Lowell's approach was to apply a new rule which the Harvard Corporation had enacted in December 1932 at the request of Dean Pound, who had complained of law professors postponing or missing their classes because of outside assignments — an offense for which Pound considered Felix Frankfurter "absolutely incorrigible." The new rule required faculty members to seek permission for leave in advance of any absence, no matter how brief and no matter for what cause.[34]

Then in the spring of 1933, when Frankfurter's appearances in Washington became a matter of newspaper coverage, Lowell employed several students to spy on his delinquent faculty. Soon these student agents reported back that Professor Frankfurter had rescheduled several classes, while Professor Landis had missed his classes and a doctoral examination. Armed with that evidence, Lowell marched upon the law school and confronted Dean Pound in his office. The dean, no ardent defender of either man, confirmed the charges and agreed to put them in writing in a long memorandum: Landis had indeed missed an important oral examination, and although Frankfurter had appeared as Landis' substitute, his contribution had been "casual" and he had left early. With only one graduate class to teach, Landis had missed it "without asking leave of anyone." As for Frankfurter, he had left his students confused over conflicting notices which he posted rescheduling his classes for later dates. "This sort of thing is very demoralizing and ought to be stopped," wrote Pound.[35]

Lowell sent a copy of Pound's memorandum to each member of the Harvard Corporation, with a reminder that the two professors had violated the new regulation on absences. If the corporation supported him, Lowell would be in an ideal position to embarrass Frankfurter, perhaps leaving his nemesis no alternative but to submit his resignation once and for all. But the response of the corporation tempered Lowell's enthusiasm. Agreeing that on the surface the behavior of the two professors seemed inexcusable and that they should be "made to behave," the members were unwilling to accept Dean Pound's accusations at face value and expressed interest in conferring directly with Frankfurter and Landis. Some members suggested that the root of the problem was Pound himself; the dean could not handle the law faculty (although one noted that Frankfurter did his best to make the dean's job more difficult). Of the two professors charged with violating the rules, Landis seemed more at fault for having actually missed his classes, and the members thought he deserved some form of reprimand. Frankfurter, however, had merely rearranged his schedule and "incommoded" his students, hardly grounds for serious reproach.[36]

As Lowell prepared to call Frankfurter in for a personal confrontation, one corporation member, Grenville Clark, met with Frankfurter for lunch at the Faculty Club and leaked the contents of Pound's memorandum to him. Indignantly, Frankfurter explained how he had gone to Washington at President Roosevelt's request and how he had brought Landis with him. When they discovered that their stay in Washington would take longer than expected, they had telegraphed Dean Pound. Returning to Cambridge alone, Frankfurter had informed the dean that Landis would have to continue on the project for another week, and that he would cover all his classes. According to Frankfurter, Pound had replied, "Sure, that's all right. I'm glad Landis is doing that — it's good for him."[37]

Clark assured Frankfurter that he stood behind him and had warned him of the charges only because he was "a little afraid if they were jumped on you suddenly by Lowell you might get so damned mad that you might tell him to go to hell." Frankfurter replied that he could take care of himself, but was concerned about the discouragement the incident would arouse in Landis. "He's a moody temperament and very unhappy here as it is, under the present situation." The next day, Frankfurter advised Landis to petition the dean in writing for a few days' leave of absence to finish the securities bill. Landis, who by then had returned to Cambridge, personally carried the note to Pound and heard the dean blame the whole affair on President Lowell. That afternoon, Lowell sent Frankfurter a note requesting a meeting for the following morning.[38]

When Felix Frankfurter entered Lowell's office, he knew exactly what to expect. "You are giving the Corporation some concern," Lowell began, and handed him a copy of the corporation's rule on unauthorized absences. Frankfurter read it over, handed it back, and replied that he was entirely familiar with the regulations and certain that he had kept within them. Sanctimoniously, Lowell dismissed whatever had happened in the past, with the implication that the professors had erred but now knew enough to sin no further. But Frankfurter refused to allow the aging president to score a single point against him. He insisted upon detailing the entire story, particularly with regard to Landis, since he had been "responsible for entangling him in this situation." By the end of his presentation, Frankfurter had demonstrated that he could present an able defense for himself and his protégé. With the knowledge that the members of the corporation were unwilling to accept Dean Pound's complaints without first interviewing Frankfurter and Landis, Lowell had no choice but to retreat. That afternoon he confirmed to the dean that Professor Landis had complied with the rules of the corporation, and endorsed his request for a leave of absence. There would be no reprimands and no resignations.[39]

Lowell's note set Landis free for service in the federal government, which in varying degrees dominated the rest of his professional life. In years following, the lessons he learned at the law school significantly shaped his actions in the government, and the flexible stance he exhibited towards law grouped him among the many legal realists who populated the Roosevelt administration. Law was a means to an end for Landis, an end which he came to identify with the social and economic goals of the New Deal.

4 | The Happy Hotdogs

In the early hours of Friday morning, April 7, 1933, Felix Frankfurter, Ben Cohen, and James Landis arrived at Washington's Union Station on board the Federal Express. They had come to salvage President Roosevelt's securities legislation, then badly bogged down in Congress. Landis, envisioning only a short trip, planned to work through the weekend and leave in time to teach his Monday classes; but his stay in Washington lasted four years. Once he began drafting the Federal Securities Act, he became enmeshed in the whole New Deal regulatory program; and through appointments to the Federal Trade Commission and the Securities and Exchange Commission, he abandoned the role of law professor for that of Wall Street expert, to battle the nation's most powerful bankers and stockbrokers. For a relative novice in financial and political affairs, he established an entirely creditable record.

Journalists soon singled out Landis, Cohen, and Thomas Corccran as the "Happy Hotdogs" and "Sorcerer's Apprentices," chief lieutenants of Professor Frankfurter's army on the Potomac. The labels irritated Landis, who wanted to earn his own reputation, but teamwork accounted for his initial successes in the federal government. No one from the administration had asked him to come to Washington; Frankfurter had simply thought to bring him along. Not many politicians would stop to listen to an earnest thirty-two-year-old professor, except for his mentor's White House connections. Frankfurter gained fame through his sponsorship of a legion of eager, ambitious, and intelligent young lawycrs throughout the government. For Landis, they were contacts he met in conference or after work over drinks, who reported on news of other agencies and lent their talents to his own projects.[1]

The Happy Hotdogs were united only in their relationship with Frankfurter. They claimed no common ideology, although most, like Landis, admired Brandeis and his economic theories. Few thought solely in terms of bigness or littleness in industry, but they shared Brandeis' desire to preserve economic diversity in its fullest. They also lacked the power of a political constituency, which they compensated for with their sheer intellectual and personal persuasiveness inside the administration. To the Frankfurter group, the New Deal represented a profusion of theories and interest groups all vying for power. As Corcoran noted, the administration seemed to take on its different colorations "almost completely from those human beings whom the Skipper has at hand and on whom he relies as his advisors." They were determined to gain access to Roosevelt's side and affect that coloration themselves.[2]

Securities regulation accidently provided for their entrance onto the political stage. Far from being their idea, the bill already had a lengthy and confused heritage. That Roosevelt would impose some form of stock regulation was a foregone conclusion, even on Wall Street. The 1929 crash, while not the sole cause of the depression, had been its igniting spark, and was irrevocably linked in public opinion with the current hard times. Beginning in February 1933, daily headlines on the Senate Banking Committee's expose of Wall Street malpractice provoked nationwide indignation. Under forceful examination by the committee's chief counsel, Ferdinand Pecora, a parade of influential bankers admitted to market manipulations that were clearly unethical, if not illegal.[3]

In that setting, President Roosevelt counted securities and exchange legislation among the ten "must" items of his first hundred days' program. He assigned the bill to Samuel Untermyer, counsel for the Pujo "Money Trust" hearings of 1912. But the aging Untermyer could produce nothing newer than a twenty-year-old proposal for Post Office supervision of stock and bond sales. Without removing Untermyer, the President turned the task over to Huston Thompson, a former Federal Trade Commission chairman and author of the 1932 Democratic plank on securities reform. Tall, distinguished, with great courtroom presence and a soaring ego, Thompson had dearly wanted the post of attorney general in the new Cabinet, and Roosevelt hoped to placate him with another job. Thompson's intrusion in the field annoyed Untermyer, but at a White House meeting Roosevelt waved away all objections and denied that any real conflict existed. He instructed Untermyer to handle the regulation of stock exchanges, while Thompson would write the bill to prevent fraudulent stock sales.[4]

Unfortunately, Thompson proved equally inept. Influenced strongly by Louis Brandeis' 1914 tract entitled *Other People's Money* and by the various state "blue-sky" laws (designed to protect investors from unscrupulous stock salesmen who would sell everything including the blue sky above), Thompson proposed the filing of all stock sale information with the Federal Trade Commission. His bill also would have pushed the FTC into the dubious area of judging whether stock-issuing corporations were of "unsound condition or insolvent." When he appeared before the House Committee on Interstate and Foreign Commerce to defend his proposals, Thompson came under attack from both Democratic and Republican members for the bill's loopholes, misuse of words, and vague concepts. Chairman Sam Rayburn appealed to Raymond Moley, who agreed that Thompson's draft was a "hopeless and unintelligible confection" and called on Felix Frankfurter for help.[5]

At the Carlton Hotel, Frankfurter assembled three of his most outstanding students, whom he chose for their diverse but complementary abilities. Benjamin V. Cohen, a lanky, quiet, thirty-eight-year-old New York lawyer with a talent for technical detail, had specialized in corporate reorganization and made a small fortune investing in stocks. The flamboyant Thomas G. Corcoran, thirty-two, had spent five years in the New York law firm of Cotton & Franklin, handling stock promotions, pools, and blue-sky legislation problems. For the past year, Corcoran had been assistant counsel to the Reconstruction Finance Corporation, where he learned to find his way through the labyrinth of Washington's bureaucratic and political structure. James Landis' participation stemmed more from his legislative drafting skills than from any financial experience. Later, he would joke about Frankfurter's making him "overnight, an authority on finance." He owned only a few inherited stocks and although his legislative seminars often used state blue-sky laws as examples, as late as October 1932 he declined to work on a uniform sale of securities law, claiming he knew "too little about the subject." But Frankfurter believed that Landis' research into the legislative process would prove valuable in preparing the bill, especially for meeting the eventual court challenges.[6]

After describing their general objectives, Frankfurter confidently left to spend the weekend at the White House. His absence led to a far stronger bill than he expected. Only a month before, Frankfurter had addressed Landis' legislative seminar and warned against "over-specialization," the attempt to ennumerate and bar every possible unwanted action through legislation. He preferred to grant wide discretionary powers to administrative agencies and then let them make their own policy decisions. Of the three protégés, Landis tended most toward Frankfurter's flexible approach. Cohen and Corcoran, from their New York experiences, had acquired greater suspicion of financiers and their lawyers. Cohen also reflected an earlier training under Professor Ernst Freund at the University of Chicago, who lectured against "unstandardized power." Freund had warned that regulatory commissioners too often were influenced by economic and political pressures and that discretionary power "should be avoided as far as possible." Landis, Cohen, and Corcoran additionally worried that Republican appointees had given the Federal Trade Commission a decidedly pro-business bias, and they wanted to define its responsibilities "in such a detailed manner as to make administration almost a matter of mechanical and compulsory routine."[7]

Drafting of the important liabilities and enforcement provisions fell largely to Landis, who was eager to apply his law school ideals. Regulatory agencies traditionally had issued subpoenas to bring in witnesses. If a witness failed to appear, the agency had to go to court for an order to enforce the subpoena. Landis solved that delay by making noncompliance a penal offense, forcing the burden of the court case on the witness rather than the agency. In another novel development, he devised the "stop order," which set specific time limits for the commission to investigate newly filed stock registrations. If the FTC discovered irregularities, it could issue a stop order and freeze the stock's sale until after it completed a more extensive study. If not, the issuer would have speedy assurance of the government's approval of the sale. His most daring contribution was to strip away corporate facelessness by imposing fines and prison terms on all those involved with preparing fraudulent stock sales, from the board of directors to the underwriters, accountants, appraisers, and lawyers handling the issue.[8]

On Sunday night Frankfurter returned to the hotel, read over the bill, listened to their reasons for its more stringent provisions, and agreed to defend it before Rayburn's committee the next day. Monday morning the four men had breakfast with Huston Thompson to assure him they were "simply perfecting amendments" to his bill. Characteristically, FDR had never bothered to tell Thompson he had replaced him, but had merely shifted him to another assignment. When Landis later visited Justice Brandeis, he asked how Thompson could have written such a poor bill. "Huston Thompson has every quality that makes a great lawyer, except one," said Brandeis. "Brains."[9]

Before the House Commerce Committee, Frankfurter made a masterful presentation of the new draft, and by five o'clock that afternoon the committee adopted their version as the basis for the legislation. Chairman Rayburn requested that Landis and Cohen remain for another week as special consultants for the final revisions. Pleased with the smoothness of their operation, Frankfurter promised Landis to look after his classes and returned to Cambridge alone.[10]

In Frankfurter's wake, the burden fell on Landis and Cohen. The two men worked steadily in the musty basement office of the House legislative draftsman Middleton Beaman, and at night in their seventh-floor hotel room. After spending his own day at the Reconstruction Finance Corporation, Tommy Corcoran would join them at the Carlton, where he tossed himself on the bed, "drank coffee laced with sugar, memorized the ceiling patterns," and tried to keep peace between his companions. High-strung and abrupt, Landis too easily lost his temper under the daily pressures and frequently resorted to "blowing off." Cohen, a more sensitive man, was offended by Landis' brusqueness as well as by his habit of trying to do everything himself. Their sharpest disagreement came over Cohen's proposal to add a specific list of stock registration requirements in the text of the bill. Landis, thinking that would open the door to congressional tinkering, recommended leaving such details to the regulatory commissioners. In frustration, Cohen telephoned Frankfurter that their teamwork had broken down and that he was withdrawing from the project. Frankfurter could sympathize, recalling "past experiences" with Landis' volatile temper, but he insisted that Cohen remain on the job. From Cambridge, he telegraphed both Roosevelt and Moley to urge that the itemized registration data remain in the bill, and asked Moley to keep an eye on Landis, "who in his intensity has not been wholly wise in his relations with Ben."[11]

Eventually, Middleton Beaman settled the controversy by putting Cohen's list in a separate schedule attached to the bill. He predicted that Congress would exhaust itself over the body of the bill and more than likely would gloss over the schedules. Beaman reasoned correctly. Neither the committee nor the full House paid much attention to the schedule, although, as Landis later acknowledged, "the schedule had the guts of the bill in it."[12]

During the redrafting, Wall Street became uneasy. At first, the financial community had reacted apathetically to Roosevelt's securities regulation message, interpreting it as a recovery program to restore public confidence in the markets. The longer that financiers and their lawyers had to examine the Thompson bill, and the more rumors they heard about the Landis-Cohen "amendments," the more worried they grew. Through Raymond Moley they pressed Rayburn's committee to hold new hearings, and a trio of skillful corporate lawyers—John Foster Dulles, Arthur H. Dean, and Arthur I. Henderson—arrived in Washington to testify. On his way to the hearings, Landis felt himself trembling. Despite all his recent efforts, he had to admit that he knew relatively little about the intricacies of investment banking, and he suspected that the Wall Street attack could shred him to pieces. John Foster Dulles served as spokesman for the group, but he soon revealed that he had not bothered to examine carefully the distinctions between the Thompson and Landis-Cohen versions. In his rebuttal, Landis exploited Dulles' errors. "Technically I had him way out in left field, and he never got back to home base," he gloated. Later that day Rayburn called Landis to his office, where in a burst of obscenities he asked why Dulles had bothered to appear when he obviously knew so little about the bill. "I've been told by Chambers of Commerce and other outfits like this what I should do for years," he reassured Landis, "and I've gone ahead and done whatever job I thought was right to do."[13]

On May 2, after a month of deliberation and revision, Rayburn's committee presented the Landis-Cohen bill to the House. With Ben Cohen sitting by his side to advise on technical matters, a stern Sam Rayburn shepherded the bill through six hours of debate, prevented any amendments, and won unanimous approval. "Everything went on schedule," Cohen wrote to Landis, who finally had returned to his classes in Cambridge. "When it was over, Rayburn remarked that he did not know whether the bill passed so readily because it was so damned good or so damned incomprehensible."[14]

Landis returned to Washington briefly to help in the expected struggle at the joint Senate-House conference committee, but again Rayburn held complete control of the situation. The Senate Banking Committee, still deep in its Wall Street investigations, had accepted the Thompson bill and the Senate had passed it. As conference chairman, Rayburn called first for a vote on using the Senate bill as their basic working draft. When that produced the tie vote he expected, Rayburn declared the motion defeated and adopted the House bill by default. The senators then made only minor changes in the Landis-Cohen bill. By May 27 Congress had enacted the Federal Securities Act and Roosevelt had signed it, reading from a speech Frankfurter prepared for the occasion. "If this country is to flourish, capital must be invested in enterprise," the President declared. "But those who seek to draw upon other people's money must be wholly candid."[15]

Exhausted yet exhilarated, Landis returned home, settled down with his family, and graded his final examinations. His first New Deal experience brought him enthusiastic congratulations and a reputation as a brilliant legal technician. Sam Rayburn wrote warmly of him to Frankfurter, "I have not known a man for the same length of time for whom I have a higher personal regard and whose character and ability I have more unstinted admiration." The victory gave Landis a great boost to his self-confidence and a thirst for more action. Shortly afterwards, the Federal Trade Commission wired a plaintive message asking him to come back to prepare the complicated regulations needed for registration. Although the agency lacked funds to pay him, it hoped he would freely contribute his "patriotic service." By then Landis had become too emotionally involved to refuse. As Ben Cohen observed, they might have been better off if the act had not passed so closely to their original draft. "That gives us too much parental interest in the darned thing." Abandoning his family for the summer, Landis left to shoulder those new parental responsibilities.[16]

Back in Washington, he quickly realized that the FTC was "pretty weak" and its staff "really knew nothing about securities at all." Most threatening was the presence of Commissioner William E. Humphrey, an arch-reactionary who had helped doom any hope of the FTC acting as watchdog over industry. Under his leadership the agency had prohibited other government departments from using its records, ceased prosecution of "insignificant" charges, and permitted corporations under investigation to attend "informal" hearings to negotiate with the FTC before it went into open hearings. As far as possible, Landis worked to keep the obstructionist Humphrey away from the new Securities Division. When Commissioner Raymond Stevens asked Landis, as a law professor, whether the President had the power to fire Humphrey, Landis gladly volunteered that he was "probably the greatest authority on that point." Relating how he had assisted Brandeis in his *Myers* opinion, Landis explained how Chief Justice Taft had specifically stretched the ruling to include presidential authority over the independent commissioners. "If that had not been put in there, I doubt whether some of the dissents would have been as bitter as they were." Stephens communicated that legal justification to the President, who responded by demanding Humphrey's resignation. "Humphrey is out!" Landis jubilantly announced to his Harvard colleagues, taking full credit for the coup.[17]

Humphrey fought back through the courts. "It is stating the obvious that if the Commissioners are to be entirely at the will of the President, the independent commissions will be destroyed," he lectured Roosevelt. Two years later, the Supreme Court overturned Roosevelt's action, in *Humphrey's Executor (Rathbun) v. United States,* and left Landis with a peculiar ambiguity over the decision. He was chagrined that his advice had turned out so wrong, but was pleased that the court had finally endorsed the principles of Brandeis' dissent. Later, as he mused over the turn of events, he decided that "if I had an independent opportunity to look at the situation, I would have been on the side of Humphrey." But in 1933, as a political and legal realist, he shaped his advice to fit the immediate needs of the New Deal.[18]

The Humphrey matter had been only a diversion from the real headaches of that summer. Within a month's time the FTC had to examine every new stock issued in the country, prepare the legal mechanism for hearings and investigations, and convince investment brokers that it sought to prevent fraud, not to interfere in their normal business. In June the commission chose Baldwin B. Bane to head its Securities Division. Landis worked closely with Bane in the sweltering stucco-and-tarpaper temporary FTC building from early morning to late into the night. By July 7, when the law went into effect, they had completed everything but the printing of the appropriate forms. Still, the prospectuses, summaries, and exhibits, which issuers filed in triplicate on that first day, covered the floor of Bane's office in towering stacks. Among the first to file was Huston Thompson, who proudly registered three small reports for common stock in an automobile devices corporation. By the end of the day, forty-one companies had filed statements and collectively paid $8,000 in registration fees, for which they could issue $80 million in stock after twenty days.[19]

The largest registration amounted to $10 million in shares of a Boston investment trust, but most of the others represented far smaller issues in investment trusts, breweries, and gold mines. It augured a disturbing trend, for the large industrial corporations and investment houses made no move to cooperate with the new law. Uncertain of their liabilities and unwilling to publish their finances publicly, they refrained from issuing new shares of stock while their lawyers pored over the Securities Act. In the meantime, the absence of larger stock issues reduced the Securities Division's tasks to minor policework against small-time fraud.[20]

By autumn Landis was finished with his work at the FTC, but temperamentally was unprepared to return to scholarly life. He could not decide between his commitment to teaching and his desire for public service. Earlier that year, when Frankfurter toyed with accepting the post of solicitor general, Landis wrote that he hated "to see men fall for the lure of doing things instead of thinking them." But he also admitted that "Roosevelt is tremendously in need of doers who also know how to think." In September Tommy Corcoran passed on word that an FTC commissionership would soon be vacant and urged him to take the post if Roosevelt offered it. Landis "bumbled about," mentioning his duties at Harvard, but Corcoran sensed that he really wanted the job. "He had his fingers in it and he'd love to go through."[21]

When the telephone call and offer from President Roosevelt came at last on a Saturday morning in October, Landis unhesitatingly accepted. He hurried to inform the dean, but as usual Roscoe Pound was too busy to see him. By contrast, he found Harvard's new president, James B. Conant, available and receptive. The depression was like wartime, Conant agreed, and the university needed to do all it could to aid the government. When Pound finally heard the news, he demanded that Landis resign, but Conant overruled him and granted Landis a one-year leave of absence.[22]

James Landis turned from Harvard to the FTC because his "heart was in the business of securities administration," and because he believed the Securities Act needed a champion to prevent Wall Street from emasculating it by way of new amendments. Also joining him on the commission was George C. Mathews, a La Follette Republican from Wisconsin, who became his closest ally. Appointment of the two commissioners to defend the Securities Act coincided with a rising chorus of denunciations against it. At the Investment Bankers Association convention in Hot Springs, Virginia, President Frank M. Gordon proclaimed the act a hindrance to national recovery. "All over the United States corporations are ready to undertake necessary financing," he asserted, "but no corporation director is going to risk existing resources by putting his name on financing under a law that makes him personally liable for the next ten years." When Gordon suggested that the Securities Act used bankers as scapegoats for all those who made bad investments, the delegates jumped to their feet cheering and passed a resolution calling for amendments to the act.[23]

Financiers like Gordon, who had expected only a loose federal recognition of trade association self-regulation, were astonished by the tough liability provisions of the Securities Act. Corporate directors who held largely ceremonial posts suddenly were legally responsible for errors or omissions in the registration statements they signed. Investors who lost money on improperly advertised stocks could sue to recover their entire investment. Even accidental errors might bring fines and jail terms. "The civil liabilities are so severe and out of proportion to individual responsibility," the president of the New England Council warned ". . . that securities houses will hesitate to risk their existence on new issues." Arthur Dean became the act's most outspoken critic, charging that long-term credit was evaporating because investment bankers were afraid to underwrite issues, and large corporations were bogged down compiling and verifying registration data. Dean launched a vigorous campaign to "educate" Congress on the need to revise the Securities Act.[24]

Lack of activity in the capital goods market—in such industries as coal, steel, and lumber, which provided the means of production for other manufacturing—seemed to bear out Dean's prophecies. The FTC's own list of registrations showed that no major industry had registered any new securities during 1933. From October through the end of December only 129 registrations became effective, amounting to $173 million in new securities, a paltry sum when compared to the estimated $1.2 billion needed just to refund corporate obligations during the next year. Without those funds the capital goods industry could neither revive nor provide the increased employment the New Deal so desired. "Business is beginning to bubble over in the pot," the editor of the *Atlantic Monthly* warned Frankfurter, "and the kettle runs the risk of bursting if the lid is clamped down." Turner Catledge and Arthur Krock of the *New York Times* and Walter Lippmann of the *New York Herald Tribune* wrote that the Securities Act was naive and inconsistent with the planning policies of the National Recovery Administration. Yale law professor William O. Douglas dismissed it as "a nineteenth century piece of legislation" that relied on small units of production rather than on "constructive planning between big business and government" (although ultimately, Douglas conceded, such planning would "run to fascism or socialism").[25]

Echoes of Wall Street's wailing soon reached the White House. Roosevelt's long-time friend, the New York banker and Progressive-era reformer Henry Bruere, relayed word that businessmen did not object to full disclosure of stock information, but were extremely uncertain over the law's liabilities provisions. Throughout the autumn of 1933, Roosevelt wavered. His acting Secretary of the Treasury, Henry Morgenthau, Jr., favored amending the Securities Act, while Attorney General Homer Cummings recommended standing firm against the "strike" of capital. On December 9 Adolf A. Berle, Jr., reported to the President a conversation he had held with Lewis Strauss of Kuhn, Loeb and Company. Strauss admitted to Berle that the leading securities houses had reached a tacit understanding to float no issues pending revision of the act. "That talk you had with L.S. confirmed my guess," Roosevelt responded; he then publicly announced that Congress should clarify the Securities Act to dispel confusion and build business confidence in federal regulation.[26]

"There's no way of telling where the President stands," Tommy Corcoran wrote sadly to Frankfurter. Adding to the confusion was a revival in the administration's interest in exchange regulation. During the summer of 1933 the "New Deal Market," a brief boom following the repeal of Prohibition and creation of the National Recovery Administration, had unexpectedly burst. Over only one week in July, the markets suffered their greatest setbacks since the 1929 crash and 1931 business failures. Liberal critics who blamed the depression on business saw no hope for recovery until they had reformed the economic system, and placed their hopes on the continuing exposés of the Pecora investigation to lead to a tough stock exchange bill. Businessmen and economic planners who supported the NRA looked to the administration for a more sympathetic hearing. The planners were encouraged when Roosevelt appointed Assistant Secretary of Commerce John Dickinson to head an interdepartmental committee (which also included Arthur Dean) to propose new exchange legislation. "The right hand knoweth not what the left hand doeth," Ben Cohen complained when he learned of the Dickinson committee, fearing that it would also propose amendments to the Securities Act.[27]

At that critical moment Landis, Cohen, and Corcoran lost their strongest asset, when Felix Frankfurter sailed for England to serve as a visiting professor at Oxford for a year. In his absence, Raymond Moley promised to look after his "children" in Washington and to continue Frankfurter's role as their advocate in the White House. Moley soon found the task more demanding than he had bargained for. "I wish, Felix, that you were here, because the day-to-day grind is pretty exhausting on all of us," he wrote. "Tom, Ben, and Jim are doing well, but they need more leadership. The little that I can give is not enough."[28]

With Frankfurter gone, Landis as an FTC commissioner moved to develop his own contacts with the President. Remembering all the years at Harvard when he fretted over visits to the dean and rarely saw the university's president, he was amazed at how easily he could arrange a meeting with the President of the United States. Minutes after their first interview started, Landis found himself talking informally with Roosevelt, "as with an equal." The President's gracious style and his seemingly sincere interest in Landis' problems won his complete allegiance. Once, when Landis became ill, two dozen roses and a message of concern arrived from the President. "You don't forget a thing like that," Landis remembered long afterwards. Cohen and Corcoran reacted suspiciously to his White House intimacy. Their friend was "an easily flattered man," Corcoran surmised, and the President's smooth talk could distract him and leave him with a "rosy glow of false optimism." Cohen worried that FDR had convinced Landis to back down on the Securities Act. "All of which is quite amusing," he wrote to Frankfurter, "in view of the way Jim used to carry on about you not getting to the Skipper frequently enough and wishing he had a direct approach."[29]

Landis was subtly drifting away from his partnership with Cohen and Corcoran, partly because of personality differences and partly because of his marital status. Cohen and Corcoran, both bachelors, had moved into a "grand house" in Georgetown, which became a center of legislative drafting for other young New Dealers. Landis, however, had finally brought his wife and children down from Cambridge to join him.[30]

"Do you realize that we have hardly lived together for six months?" Stella wrote him. "Do you look forward to matrimony again?" In November she gave up her own political work with the Cambridge League of Women Voters to move herself, her husband, and their children into a small rowhouse in Alexandria, across the Potomac from Washington. The move hardly reunited them as a family. Landis worked overtime at the FTC and often spent the night on a cot in his office. On those evenings that he made it home, Stella generally was already in bed. By the light of the bed lamp, she could see his face, "too weary, too hollow cheeked, too gray! I could scream with nervous impatience at having to watch him work like this and helping so little." His compulsion for work left him practically no time for social engagements or personal relationships. "Sometimes I think in my low

53

moments he'd be better off if we were not here to bother him," Stella wrote in her diary. "Then I think if it were not for us he'd turn into a machine and nothing else—He almost is now."[31]

Never realizing how much he neglected his family, Landis was basking in his newly won reputation as "the outstanding figure on the Federal Trade Commission," and was involved in preparing both the exchange bill and amendments to the Securities Act. When the President had appointed the Dickinson committee, Landis had telephoned the Harvard Law School graduate John Dickinson to ask to join his committee. After Dickinson consented, Landis commenced a campaign of working by day with the business accommodationists on the committee and by night with the determined reformers on Pecora's staff. He hoped to play each side off against the other in an effort to shape the eventual compromise. It was a delicate balancing act, which would earn him suspicion from both sides.[32]

The Dickinson committee's report, completed in January 1934, reflected its chairman's moderate views. Forty years old, known for his bald head, corn-cob pipes, tweedy suits, and what *Fortune* magazine called "a professorialism such as has rarely been seen outside a satirical novel," Dickinson served as a liaison between business and the New Deal. Although he too had been a Frankfurter law student, he had spent his years as a Wall Street attorney defending corporations against antitrust suits. Professing disinterestedness, he shuddered at Landis' "moral earnestness." Dickinson's "middle way" philosophy severely restricted the committee's recommendations. Instead of drafting a bill, the committee made only suggestions for federal licensing of exchanges under the supervision of a "Federal Stock Exchange Authority," one of whose members would be a representative of the stock markets. The report also advised against any specific prohibitions of pools, short selling, and other controversial market devices, and advocated a vague enabling act, similar to that of the NRA, which Dickinson had also helped to draft. "The thing to be avoided," the report emphasized, "is the placing of this complex and important machinery in a strait jacket."[33]

Although Landis signed the report, he personally had wanted a tougher approach. He disliked the plan for licensing exchanges and was "not yet ready to give up the idea that the government has a direct place in the day to day regulatory activities of the exchanges." He did agree with Dickinson on the desirability of granting discretionary power, but, unlike Dickinson, he wanted that power placed solidly in the hands of a regulatory agency. The Dickinson report gratified Wall Street as much as it dismayed the Senate Banking Committee investigators. Ferdinand Pecora termed it "inadequate" and threatened to ignore it when he drafted his own bill. When Landis showed an early copy of the report to Pecora's aide Max Lowenthal, he gasped at the compromises and urged Landis not to sign it. "But evidently it was not his idea of strategy," Lowenthal ruefully concluded. Landis kept his strategy to himself until a weekend visit to Cambridge, when he admitted, "under the mellow influence of cocktails," that he had been trying to keep the Dickinson committee busy while Cohen and Corcoran drafted their own version of the bill. Capitalizing on the jealousies between the Dickinson committee and Pecora's staff, Landis encouraged each "to think it was their bill" being created.[34]

Since the Pecora investigation was still in progress, Max Lowenthal (another former Frankfurter student) had approached Landis, Cohen, and Corcoran to prepare the Banking Committee's exchange legislation. Landis' duties at the Federal Trade Commission prevented him from taking a direct role, but he assigned his legal secretary, I. N. P. Stokes III, and Telford Taylor, both recent Harvard law graduates, to write the preliminary draft. The two younger men produced a dozen versions before Cohen and Corcoran could take leave of their regular government posts during the Christmas holiday to shape the bill themselves. They had almost finished when Roosevelt sent the Dickinson report to Congress.[35]

After so many months of delving in the sordid story of Wall Street, Pecora found the Cohen-Corcoran bill too lenient. One member of Pecora's staff, John T. Flynn, passionately distrusted all bankers and securities dealers and warned that shrewd corporate lawyers would exploit any ambiguities in the bill to subvert its intent. As a result of their prodding, the final draft of the exchange bill set high margin requirements, outlawed all pools, and enumerated other illegal stock manipulations. Landis, whose views had been embodied in the earlier Stokes and Taylor drafts, heatedly argued for a more flexible measure, but Cohen and Corcoran felt they were working for Pecora and had to adhere to his wishes.[36]

Confronted with the widely differing versions of proposed exchange legislation, President Roosevelt chose to remain neutral. In private White House talks with Landis, Pecora, and congressional leaders, he urged them to go ahead with the Cohen-Corcoran draft, but kept a free hand for himself by declining to endorse the bill officially. Roosevelt knew that considerable opposition to the bill existed in the Treasury Department, Federal Reserve Board, and National Recovery Administration, not to mention on Wall Street. The financial press exuded hostility for the bill. *Business Week* charged that it went about regulation "in ruthless and clumsy fashion. It lays hands on delicate machinery with all the finesse of a Russian peasant." The *Wall Street Journal* described the bill as part of a pervasive movement towards "social control." Both journals encouraged hope that the administration had purposely exaggerated its proposals to leave room for "hoss trading" with Congress.[37]

New York Stock Exchange President Richard Whitney appeared in

Washington to take personal charge of the lobbying against the bill. He first sought a meeting with the President, but Roosevelt asked Landis to handle the confrontation. Well aware of Whitney's arrogant and aristocratic manner, Landis made a little performance of the occasion by inviting Whitney for a 45¢ lunch, brought up from the FTC basement cafeteria and served on his crowded desk. That humble meal represented one of the few amusing episodes in the bitter fight over the exchange bill. The "truly despicable" tactics of the financiers amazed Landis. "I really thought that they were essentially decent though somewhat misguided people," he wrote to Frankfurter, "but I have my doubts now."[38]

At the Willard Hotel, Whitney organized what Sam Rayburn called "the biggest and boldest, the richest and most ruthless lobby Congress had ever known." Fired by Whitney's warnings that the bill would enable the FTC to "dominate and actually control" their business, hundreds of bankers, brokers, businessmen, and their employees telegraphed and petitioned Congress in protest. Landis and other proponents of regulation had no reason to suspect that the intensity of Whitney's campaign might also have personal motivations. But periodically, since 1926, Richard Whitney had been embezzling money from funds entrusted to his firm to cover bad investments. Most of Whitney's loans came from the Harriman National Bank, which had failed in March 1933, sending its president to prison for mishandling its funds. As Whitney's financial standing crumbled, the demand for federally filed financial reports threatened to expose his dealings.[39]

"The Stock Exchange bill is receiving a terrific beating," Landis reported to Frankfurter. "My office for the last three weeks has been a general reception room for brokers, bankers, and the like who come in and tell me their troubles. I listen honestly and conscientiously, and always reaffirm my confidence that both Congress and the President will see to it that a good and fair stock exchange bill will eventually be written." Wall Street's pressure was inexorable. John Dickinson, who resented Landis' "double dealing" toward him, icily testified that the bill's high margin requirements would have a deflationary impact, "diametrically opposed to President Roosevelt's policy of maintaining values." Word leaked out of the White House that the President favored simplifying the bill and that congressional leaders concurred.[40]

By mid-March the bill had undergone considerable change. After lengthy negotiations with Treasury Department and Federal Reserve Board officials, Landis, Cohen, and Corcoran agreed to a more elastic margin system. The Federal Reserve Board would have power to raise and lower margin requirements, while the Federal Trade Commission would administer the rest of the act. To prevent the same fears that followed the Securities Act, they also reduced the bill's liability provisions. "The boys did a magnificent job of drafting," Raymond Moley congratulated Frankfurter, "and since the process of amending has been underway, they have been tactful and skillful in handling the obvious necessity of yielding certain unimportant aspects in the interests of holding to the essentials." Meanwhile, letters of opposition poured into Congress. Despite Roosevelt's assurance that the mail bore "all the earmarks of origin at some common source," the volume of the protest had its effect. Members of the congressional committees revolted against the bill's more stringent sections. Landis and Corcoran appeared before the House committee but failed to convince a majority that the rewritten draft was the most effective compromise they could reach. House members wanted lower margin rates, and to prevent committee disharmony Rayburn agreed to further revisions.[41]

In the Senate, Carter Glass led the opposition to the bill, aiming to protect his own creation, the Federal Reserve Board, from "being mixed up with stock market gambling." In two close committee votes he won amendments to eliminate fixed margin provisions and to establish a Securities and Exchange Commission to administer the entire act. Thus the conservative Senator Glass became the "father" of the SEC.[42]

When debate opened on the floor of Congress, the months of preliminary fighting had put each side in a testy mood. Sam Rayburn led the administration forces with an impassioned attack on the New York Stock Exchange for spearheading the massive propaganda campaign against the bill. Evading his charges, the opposition concentrated its fire on the authors of the legislation. Republican Representative Fred Britten of Illinois denounced the bill as the work of "the scarlet fever boys down in the little red house in Georgetown." Heaping scorn on the "Prof. Felix Frankfurter cheer leaders," Britten pointed out that Benjamin Cohen was right then sitting next to Rayburn in the House chamber as an advisor. "I am sorry I caused all this," Britten sarcastically apologized as an embarrassed Cohen departed, "because I truly believe that no one on the floor understands this legislation as does the boyish Mr. Cohen." Britten charged that the Frankfurter group had "kidnapped" the exchange bill and used it "to Russianize everything worthwhile under the unqualified and unprepared Federal Trade Commission."[43]

Cohen and Corcoran watched the harangue from the gallery and heard Britten admit that they worried him far less than did FTC Commissioner Landis and his power over industry. "James McCauley Landis probably had more to do with the writing of all these various bills than any other individual," Britten warned, adding, "It is understood, Mr. Chairman, that Judge Landis has no sympathy whatever with the stock exchanges." (The title "Judge Landis" indicated that Britten had confused James Landis with Judge Kenesaw Mountain Landis, a Chicago jurist and first commissioner of baseball. It was a common, recurring, and undoubtably most annoying error.) Sam Rayburn then rose in Landis' defense. "There has been a great deal said around this Capitol and whispered throughout about Mr. James M. Landis, a so-called 'member' of the 'brain trust.' I say this about Jim Landis — that if there is a 'brain trust' in this government he is entirely capable of being a member of it." (There followed a burst of applause from the House.) The President was a "man of sanity," Rayburn reasoned, who would surely appoint both Landis and Mathews to any commission Congress might designate to administer the act.[44]

Over the bitter attack, the House passed the exchange bill 280 to 84. The Senate passed a similar bill but made significant changes, chief among them a last-minute rider amending the Securities Act of 1933. By prearrangement with the Senate Banking Committee's chairman, Duncan Fletcher, Landis wrote the amendments and Fletcher introduced them in the Senate to avoid further aggravating the House debates. If he had had dictatorial powers, Landis mused, he could not have arranged the situation any better.[45]

The new amendments proved that Landis could learn from his mistakes. The second time around he consulted extensively with brokers and bankers on how to break Wall Street's psychological barrier against the act. Essentially, his new amendments concentrated on modifying penalties, limiting the underwriter's liabilities to no more than the original cost of the stock offering, and reducing the statute of limitations on fraud cases. Finally, to eliminate fears that contentious investors would "blackmail" underwriters by suing them for every investment loss, the amendments granted courts power to assess trial costs to the plaintiffs if their cases had no merit. "They were good amendments," Landis was confident. "We had been too tough in some places, much too tough . . . But we didn't accept the idea of weakening amendments that had originally been pushed."[46]

The Senate overwhelmingly accepted his amendments, and all that prevented its final passage was the joint conference committee. Rayburn dominated the House delegation, and Senator Fletcher sought a sympathetic Senate delegation by passing over two senior members of his committee, Carter Glass and Robert Wagner, who supported a separate SEC, in favor of Alben Barkley and James Byrnes, who leaned toward continued administration through the FTC. In a furor, Glass loudly resigned from the Banking Committee. Majority leader Joseph Robinson refused to accept his resignation, and the move embarrassed Barkley and Byrnes into declaring that they were honor-bound to support the Senate's version of the bill. The final compromise in some ways disappointed all sides. To Landis' regret, the conference committee endorsed Glass's plan for a new five-member Securities and Exchange Commission. But to Glass's dismay, they undercut his primary objective by placing margin requirements under the Federal Reserve Board's control. Pecora and his staff were angered because the bill left all decisions on reforming such practices as floor trading, short selling, and pool operating to a new commission of unpredictable membership and direction. Nevertheless, Senator Glass reluctantly agreed to support the bill, Landis gave it his endorsement, and Pecora termed it "a happy compromise." Cohen and Corcoran, who had suffered through all of the redrafts, were the most pleased with the outcome. After writing the original bill in a form much tougher than they had really wished, to meet Pecora's specifications, they suspected that they could never have gained as much authority for the new commission if the first draft had not been so strong.[47]

On June 1, 1934, Congress passed the Securities and Exchange Act without bothering to call for roll-call votes. Wall Street accepted the inevitable. "I am truly hopeful that if wisely and judiciously administered the Act will be a constructive measure," Richard Whitney conceded. Franklin Roosevelt signed the bill on June 6. Landis had gone to Chicago to deliver a speech, but Cohen, Corcoran, Rayburn, Fletcher, and Pecora all stood proudly around the President's desk during the signing ceremony. Handing the last of the pens to Pecora, Roosevelt asked, "Ferd, now that I have signed this bill and it has become law, what kind of a law will it be?" Taking the pen, Pecora answered gravely, "It will be a good or bad bill, Mr. President, depending upon the men who administer it."[48]

Knowledgeable observers were already second-guessing the President and calling it "Landis' New Commission." *Business Week* put forward a list of financiers as candidates but admitted that "the force of 'Cocksure' Landis as he is known on the hill, will stand out even in that impressive company. He will continue to smite the wicked in high places and protect the lowly with the aid of his fellow commissioners — or in spite of them if necessary." *Time* named him as "the brilliant young leader of the small minority of New Dealers who are true economic radicals." Others saw him as "fanatical, radical, and inclined to be vindictive." Former Secretary of State Henry L. Stimson privately called James Landis "the most dangerous man in the United States."[49]

Meanwhile the Happy Hotdogs were busy trying to influence the choice of appointees to administer the hard-earned act. Their "official ticket" included Landis, Mathews, FTC counsel Robert Healy, and Ben Cohen. Corcoran especially wanted to see his legislative partner appointed, pointing out that Cohen had done the most work on the bill and received the least credit. Raymond Moley recommended the ticket to Roosevelt, noting that Cohen was "as able as Landis and more experienced." But Moley returned with distressing news: the President feared an anti-Semitic reaction to Cohen's appointment. From England, Frankfurter counseled that the real opponents were Wall Street operators, both Jew and Gentile. "I don't have to tell you," Frankfurter wrote to Corcoran, "that the leading Jewish bankers and leading Jewish Wall Street lawyers feel about Ben Cohen's influence and the myths of my own influence in the administration precisely as their non-Jewish colleagues in finance and at the bar." But, as Roosevelt wavered, Cohen took himself out of contention for the job.[50]

Roosevelt delayed making his nominations until after Congress adjourned for the summer. On June 30 he called Landis, Mathews, and Healy to his office to give them the nod. For the other two commissioners he told them he had chosen Pecora and Joseph P. Kennedy. The President would not dictate their choice of a chairman but suggested that they "take a good look at Kennedy," to whom he had assigned the longest term of office. If the idea of Kennedy, a financier and market operator, as chairman disappointed Landis, who wanted the post himself, it scandalized Pecora and his staff. "I say it isn't true. It is impossible. It could not happen," cried John Flynn. Other critics found more amusement in the event: "Four grave men and true, reformers and purgers of business by natural slant and experience, are led by a jovial master of the quick money-making art, a consummate product of the era they would bury." On the whole, however, Kennedy's appointment was a shrewd gambit. Not only had Roosevelt paid off a long-standing debt to an affluent campaign contributor but he had found the ideal man to win business support for the new commission and break the strike of capital. "Joe is able, loyal, and will make good," Roosevelt chortled. "What more can one ask?"[51]

On July 3 Kennedy arrived from Massachusetts and went directly to Landis' FTC office. Forty-five years old, robust, self-confident, anxious to begin his new job, Kennedy took care to show proper respect for Landis' talents. "After that morning," Landis commented, "I came out with the conclusion that . . . he was the best man." Mathews and Healy agreed, but Ferdinand Pecora held out. That afternoon he appeared minutes before their scheduled 3:00 p.m. swearing-in ceremony and made it clear he would either be chairman or not accept appointment. With Pecora in Landis' office and Kennedy in Mathews', Landis shuttled back and forth for an hour negotiating between the two. Then Kennedy accompanied Landis to a face-to-face meeting with Pecora, where they debated the policy and patronage demands he set as conditions for membership.[52]

Finally, after 5:00 p.m., when the FTC building was deserted of all but the designated commissioners and a handful of tired reporters, Landis, Kennedy, and Pecora emerged smiling and walked in step back down the hall to Mathews' office. There they took the oath of office, unanimously elected Kennedy chairman, and posed for photographs. The new SEC chairman had nothing but praise for James Landis and Ferdinand Pecora.

"I'm no sucker," he told reporters. "They know more about this law than I ever hope to know. They put their blood into it."[53]

5 | Wall Street's Policeman

When the first Securities and Exchange commissioners were sworn in, Wall Street and Pennsylvania Avenue traded rumors over how they would proceed. Nothing was clear. The new commission had no staff, no headquarters, no program, and no accumulated precedents, only five diverse personalities. They would be the policeman on the stock market beat that Otto Kahn had anticipated in his testimony before the Pecora investigation. "We were all sinners," repented Kahn, the patriarch of the investment house of Kuhn, Loeb and Company. "If we indulge again in practices that are socially, economically, and from the point of view of the country undesirable, I think the policeman ought to be ready to step in." Not all investment bankers and stock dealers shared Kahn's contrition. Their deep-rooted suspicion of any government intervention into the exchanges lingered on long after the congressional battles ended. The capital market remained stagnant, and some major corporations talked of removing their stocks from the American exchanges before submitting to federal regulation. Would the policeman disrupt honest business in his pursuit of a few malefactors?[1]

Business Week underscored those fears by placing on its cover for that week the stern face of James M. Landis, rather than the new SEC chairman, Joseph P. Kennedy. While the journal hoped that Kennedy could exert a conservative influence on his agency, it suspected that he would find it difficult to "get anything past the militant New Dealers who complete the membership of the commission." Such analysis underestimated Joe Kennedy's persuasiveness and Jim Landis' pragmatism. Friction between the millionaire stock market operator and the spartan law professor failed to materialize. Kennedy and Landis worked smoothly together, drawing upon each other's talents to shape the SEC into a remarkably conciliatory policeman.[2]

After a year and a half of jousting with Wall Street, Landis believed it wise statesmanship to proceed gently until the commission had won the confidence of the exchanges and the business community. The Securities and Exchange Commission tried to adopt a spirit of business-government cooperation reminiscent of the early National Recovery Administration. Under the successive chairmanships of Kennedy and Landis, the SEC emphasized the "guidance and supervision of the industry as a whole," rather than the "mere proscription of abuses." They would police the exchanges to prohibit all fraudulent activity, Landis explained, but their greater aim lay in "evolving a better harmony between the operations of these institutions and the goals of restoring sound economy."[3]

At first the SEC operated out of Landis' and Mathews' offices at the Federal Trade Commission. In the sweltering heat of Washington's summer, Kennedy and Landis set out to locate a new building and organize a staff. The rapidly growing bureaucracy that was needed to serve the New Deal put a premium on office space in the capital, but after some negotiation they finally acquired several floors in the old Interstate Commerce Commission building on Pennsylvania Avenue, two blocks from the White House. After his career as a financier and Hollywood producer, Joe Kennedy was visibly dismayed with the starkly functional government building, as he surveyed its dark halls, beaverboard walls, and greasy windows. "That building had not been cleaned," he grumbled, ". . . for at least ten years."[4]

Next they went into combat with the Civil Service Commission for special authorization to hire legal and financial experts equal to the commission's tasks. Ethical questions further complicated matters. Felix Frankfurter wanted Landis to establish a two-year prohibition against former SEC employees appearing before the commission in defense of clients, which would prevent them from exploiting inside knowledge for personal profit. Landis had been dangling just such advantages before his prospective staff as a means of attracting talented young lawyers to the commission. "If I'd insisted that they would be debarred from practicing, and that I wanted them to stay with the government their entire lives," he demurred, "I wouldn't have gotten these people."[5]

Filling one post caused Landis the most anguish. Tommy Corcoran was lobbying for Ben Cohen's appointment as the SEC's chief counsel. "In a sense, he was entitled to it," Landis acknowledged, but Chairman Kennedy wanted Judge John Burns of Massachusetts for the job. For a time, the commission considered appointing two chief counsels, until Frankfurter warned them that such an "unnatural" division inevitably would cause internal conflict. At that point, Landis switched his support to Burns, reasoning that the chairman ought to have a counsel of his own choosing. Unexpectedly, the story reached the public through the distorted medium of Drew Pearson's "Washington Merry-Go-Round" column. Pearson charged that anti-Semitism had denied Cohen a well-earned appointment as commissioner, and enabled Landis to seize the role of "supreme importance" on the SEC. "Ben must understand," Pearson had Landis saying, "that he will be an employee of the commission and will take orders from me." Moreover, Pearson accused Landis, "that great liberal and one time enemy of Wall Street," of stalling commission decisions and complaining that Wall Street was not getting "a fair break." Publicity had gone to his head, Pearson wrote. "After all, he is barely 35."[6]

An angry Landis immediately suspected Ferdinand Pecora of being the story's source. When, as Ben Cohen described it to Frankfurter, Landis "threatened to make a scene" in the commission, Joseph Kennedy took him aside and "handled him extremely well, sternly, but sympathetically, like a father." By the next day, Landis had calmed down and felt somewhat contrite. He admitted to Cohen that "it probably was a good thing that it happened as it had brought him to his senses." Cohen responded that he hoped the incident would encourage the commissioners to put aside their personal differences and work together. As soon as the mails would allow, Frankfurter sent his advice to Landis not to allow "brickbats" to get under his skin. But a letter made a poor substitute for personal contact during a crisis. At the same time, *Fortune* magazine published a laudatory biographical article on "The Legend of Landis," which annoyed Jim and Stella Landis because of its emphasis on Frankfurter's influence on his career. They both felt that the habitual "Happy Hotdog" references detracted from Landis' individual achievements. Neither Jim nor Stella could hide their resentment from Frankfurter, and the professor became increasingly aware of his protége's reliance on the "fatherly" Kennedy.[7]

Never before had Landis met anyone quite like Joe Kennedy. The husky Irishman possessed the kind of imperious nature that only great wealth and complete self-confidence could bring. Beneath the surface of the aggressive, self-made man, the speculator and the wheeler-dealer, however, Landis could see a strong "national consciousness." Above everything else, Kennedy was a family man whose concern for the future of his country and concern for his children were strongly linked. It was also an easy step for Kennedy to take a paternalistic interest in his high-strung SEC associate. He forced Landis to take time off on weekends, induced him to go out on the golf links, and invited him to his Rockville, Maryland, estate. Despite their wealth, the Kennedys avoided ostentatious luxury and they presented a "very homey atmosphere" which greatly appealed to Landis. He joined them in sailing, conversation, or a game of Chinese checkers with their highly competitive children.[8]

Both Kennedy and Landis shared a Harvard background, and Kennedy was intrigued and impressed by Landis' intellect. At the SEC he listened intently whenever Landis lifted commission discussions from technicalities to higher levels of social and economic theory. The chairman gave him a free hand in developing legal procedures and administrative practices, delegations of power which never detracted from Kennedy's own authority. In his fourteen months as chairman, Kennedy left an indelible impression on both the SEC and his successor, James Landis.[9]

Chairman Kennedy viewed the commission less as a prosecutor than as a promoter of restored prosperity. "We do not start off with the belief that every enterprise is crooked and that those behind it are crooks," he assured businessmen. It was Kennedy's objective to convince both brokers and his fellow commissioners that the SEC could operate best once it had the co-operation of Wall Street. Realistically, he weighed the magnitude of the securities trading business against the budget and staff of the SEC. Successful regulation, he argued, depended primarily on the exchanges themselves. "In a large measure we would have the exchanges do their own policing," he explained. "They are in much better shape to do this than to have the government send in a staff."[10]

Throughout the summer and autumn of 1934 Kennedy met with exchange leaders, brokers, and accountants to plan new registration requirements and to quiet corporate fears about the SEC. The fruits of his efforts soon became evident. The SEC demanded that all exchanges, and all corporations listing their stocks on the exchanges, register by September 15 if they wished to continue operation, or list their stocks, after October 1. In registering, each exchange had to agree to enforce SEC rules and punish or expel members who violated them. Twenty-five exchanges filed under the act, while fourteen asked for exemption on the grounds that their volume of business was too small. Over three thousand securities, including those of all major corporations, received temporary registrations. The filing was so heavy that Landis ordered cots moved into the SEC offices so his staff could stay around the clock to complete their work. The New York Stock Exchange cooperated by helping its member firms prepare the necessary forms, acting as a clearing house for registration information, and promising to discipline all those who missed the deadline. Richard Whitney himself carried a large suitcase full of registrations to the SEC headquarters.[11]

Of the twenty-five exchanges that registered, the SEC ordered four to close their doors permanently and persuaded others, such as the New York Produce Exchange, to abandon their securities operations. Under SEC direction, the Boston Curb Exchange went out of business for listing illegal stocks on its board. The New York Mining Exchange, once known as the "penny stock market" for its fleecing of the poorest investors, closed forever.[12]

That kind of police action gave the SEC a crusading image, but Chairman Kennedy was more interested in stirring up the "torpid waters of American finance" by encouraging new stock issues. On the speakers' trail he belittled business hesitancy, and in Washington he ordered revisions in the SEC's registration forms to help entice businessmen out of their hibernation. Some young liberal economists on the staff scoffed at Kennedy for "rushing out on Pennsylvania Avenue and nabbing all prospective registrants," but the chairman pursued his goal of attracting new money into the markets with all seriousness. He and Counsel John Burns "packed their suitcases like traveling salesmen" and criss-crossed the country to assure business leaders of the safety and wisdom of issuing new securities. Finally, in March 1935, Kennedy persuaded Swift and Company to register with the SEC a $43 million bond issue for refinancing. "The logjam in the capital market is broken," he proclaimed. And as he hoped, company after company came forward with new bond issues, to take advantage of the lowest interest rates since the World War. Afterwards, large new stock issues also appeared.[13]

Publicly, the other members of the commission adopted Kennedy's conciliatory message. Behind the commission's closed doors, less harmony prevailed. Landis and Mathews consistently supported Kennedy's policy of easing regulations to win business support, while Pecora and Robert Healy stood in opposition. The dissenters had both conducted lengthy investigations into business practices, Pecora at the Senate Banking Committee, Healy at the Federal Trade Commission, and neither would tolerate any laxity. Healy, in particular, believed that the SEC should hold firm to its rules and force the exchanges to bend to them. At commission meetings he argued against simplifying registration forms and demanded reforms in corporate accounting practices. Landis often led the majority against him. Although he admired Healy's force of conviction, Landis viewed the dour Vermont judge as an old-fashioned common-law lawyer, more concerned with form than substance, and unwilling "to sacrifice certain ideal qualities and take the chance of making things work." Voting with Healy in the minority, Ferdinand Pecora became so frustrated with the commission's tendency to compromise, and so bored with its bureaucratic routines, that he began missing commission meetings and after only six months resigned to accept a seat on the New York Supreme Court.[14]

Joseph Kennedy was also ready to quit. Unlike Pecora, he was entirely satisfied with the direction of the SEC. He enjoyed the politics and publicity of Washington life, but the great bulk of his commission's work dealt with detailed technical issues, tedious memoranda, and bulky reports. Kennedy also missed his family and was tired of commuting so frequently to Palm Beach, Florida, to join them on weekends. Shortly after the Swift and Company announcement, Kennedy determined that his task had ended and he could leave. On the same day as he prepared his resignation, the Supreme Court handed down its stunning decision declaring the National Recovery Administration unconstitutional. Out of loyalty to President Roosevelt, he tore up the letter.[15]

He had hoped to get out before becoming entangled in the President's pet project for a Public Utility Holding Company bill, which was sure to explode in Congress. The bill's "death sentence" clause, outlawing all holding companies whose subsidiaries were not geographically and economically integrated, threatened to disrupt the rapport he had carefully established between financiers and the SEC. To the Congress, Kennedy communicated his view that the "death sentence" would place impossible burdens on the SEC. In August, after the bill passed, he decided that its administration would require a continuity of leadership for at least a full year, of which he wanted no part. Under those circumstances, he formally resigned as SEC chairman on September 20, 1935.[16]

Few observers doubted that Landis would succeed Kennedy as chairman. The liberal choice for the post only a year before, Landis had since then won business confidence. "Two years ago," the *New York Herald Tribune* commented, "if the financial community had been told that regulation of the securities business was to be entrusted to James M. Landis, young disciple of Justice Brandeis and protégé of Felix Frankfurter, it would have thrown up its hands in horror." Yet now, the paper admitted, "by his own open-mindedness he has allayed its fears, by his capacity and his intellectual honesty he has earned its sincere respect." Why such profuse praise from the conservative camp? That question disturbed many of Landis' liberal supporters. The *Nation* worried that its slayer of financial dragons had "doffed his plume and armor" to "lean backwards to give business the fairest and squarest deal possible." John T. Flynn, financial columnist for the *New Republic,* added that the SEC "must be managed by men who are willing to choose boldly from which side they wished their applause to come." Flynn prayed that Landis would "be spared the humiliation of having regulated Wall Street to its entire satisfaction."[17]

Another dissenting voice came from Felix Frankfurter. The estranged mentor displayed his unhappiness with his prodigal son by supporting John H. Fahey, of the Home Owners' Loan Corporation, for the SEC chairman-

67

ship. It was a futile, but meaningful, gesture.[18]

On September 24, 1935, with Kennedy's endorsement and Roosevelt's blessing, James Landis became chairman of the Securities and Exchange Commission, a day before his thirty-sixth birthday. At his first press conference Landis made clear his intentions of upholding his predecessor's program of cooperation and exchange self-regulation. "Mr. Kennedy's policies are the commission's policies and there is no reason for changing them," he declared. At the same time, he vowed to prosecute all stock frauds and to establish effective regulation over the vast public utility holding companies. As Landis was holding forth before the press, gathered in his office, Joe Kennedy suddenly appeared at the door. "Good-bye, Jim boy," he said as he grasped Landis' hand. "Good luck to you. Knock 'em over." He was gone as quickly as he came, leaving Landis speechless.[19]

Newsmen could not help notice the difference between the two chairmen, who agreed so thoroughly on policy but contrasted so sharply in personality. Joe Kennedy was tall, athletic, well-groomed, and colloquial as he wise-cracked with reporters. Jim Landis was short, thin, indifferent to dress, soft-spoken, and always careful in his choice of words. When Kennedy left on a trip, his SEC aides held the elevators for him, had his car waiting at the curb, and had his plane ready at the airport. Landis would pack his own bags and casually mention to his secretary, "See you tomorrow, I've got to go up to New York." The differences in style were apparent even to Landis, who admitted some "serious doubts" about his ability to handle the rough political and financial responsibilities ahead.[20]

Of all the problems his predecessor had bequeathed him, none was as pressing as the regulation of public utilities. Where Kennedy hedged his support of the Holding Company Act, Landis strongly endorsed it. The act's emphasis on breaking down the powerful utility pyramids with their excessive rates, unsupported bond issues, absentee management, financial draining of subsidiaries, and acquisition of political influence represented the Frankfurter group's greatest affirmation of the ideals of Brandeis. The group aimed less against size than against the abuse of power, and worked to create an orderly and efficient national utility system. Cohen and Corcoran had drafted the act; Frankfurter had contributed the crucial compromise on the "death sentence"; and Landis as chairman of the SEC would administer it.[21]

Since he believed that the government had won its major victory with the passage of the act and since the SEC would need several more years to develop a comprehensive program for dealing with the unwieldy holding companies, Landis saw no reason to adopt a hard-line approach. Instead he recommended that the utility companies begin the process of simplification by voluntarily divesting themselves of their "non-integrated" affiliates. But the conciliatory approach that worked so well for Kennedy had no impact on the utility companies. After waging an extensive battle against the bill in Congress, they were literally prepared to fight to the death in the courts before registering with the SEC.

As a test case, the bankrupt American Public Service Company petitioned the courts in Baltimore to review the Holding Company Act's constitutionality. One of the utility company's bondholders entered the case to "protect" his holdings, and secured the prestigious Wall Street lawyer and former presidential candidate John W. Davis as his counsel. Another creditor entered the case in favor of the act's constitutionality, while employing as counsel a utility company lawyer well known for his opposition to the act. With all parties representing the utilities, the SEC could intervene only as a "friend of the court," and not as a participant in the case.[22]

Making his first radio address as chairman, Landis attacked the Baltimore case and demanded a fair test involving all interested parties. "By doing so," he said, "the major portion of the industry could be left free to take advantage of the opportunity, which we gladly offer, to cooperate with us in fashioning the mechanics of regulation." Meanwhile, his staff busily prepared for the utility companies' registrations. "We seem to be drowning in the administrative burdens of the holding company act," Landis reported. By the November 1 deadline they could all relax. Only fifty-eight small companies registered. The rest either filed for exemption or ignored the law. On November 7, 1935, Judge William Coleman in Baltimore ruled the Holding Company Act "unconstitutional and invalid in its entirety." Emboldened, dozens of utility companies filed similar suits.[23]

With neither the budget nor the staff to meet all those challenges, the SEC requested the courts to hold all pending cases in abeyance until it could prepare a single test case. For their battleground, Landis, Counsel John Burns, and Ben Cohen selected the Electric Bond and Share Company, reputedly the world's largest electric utility holding company. Landis opened negotiations with the company to persuade them to register, but by the final deadline of December 1, 1935, Electric Bond had not acted. On the morning of December 3 the company's president personally informed Landis that Electric Bond planned to initiate its own suit against the SEC. As the utility president strolled out of his office, Landis picked up the phone and called his agent in New York to file a prearranged suit in Judge Julian Mack's expectedly sympathetic court. His quick action caught Electric Bond completely off guard.[24]

In January 1937, when Judge Mack ruled that the holding companies must register with the SEC, Landis climbed out of a sickbed, called reporters to his office, and launched into a "brilliantly bitter tongue lashing" against the utilities. For twenty minutes he let loose all of his pent-up emotions over the case. One reporter described him "smacking his knuckles on the table, choosing his words with surgical preciseness, presenting his statement with the gusto and dramatic power of a prosecuting attorney sending a killer to the scaffold." Electric Bond and Share and other companies, Landis declared, had "cut their own throats." "We have no worry about its going to the Supreme Court," he said of the case. Despite the Court's conservative leanings, he had faith in the justness of the act and in the competence of Ben Cohen and Assistant Attorney General Robert Jackson, who would argue for the SEC. But it was not until 1938 that the Supreme Court unanimously upheld the constitutionality of the Holding Company Act, and the long years of litigation prevented the Securities and Exchange Commission from regulating the nation's utility system during Landis' chairmanship.[25]

The turn of events allowed him to concentrate on his own "first and real love," the securities markets. There he believed he could avoid the "type of cat and dog fight" with the exchanges that the utility companies were waging. His optimism derived from the "revolution" within the financial community that had occurred shortly before he became chairman. Richard Whitney, who had continued to dredge up every device he could find to stall SEC regulation, had lost his bid for renomination as president of the New York Stock Exchange. "It's a matter of public relations," the nominating committee chairman had told Whitney. The presidency went instead to broker Charles R. Gay, who had the support of the commission houses, but in the ensuing elections Whitney's "Old Group" won a clear majority of the board of governors and promised a check on any reforms that Gay might attempt.[26]

As a result, Gay's administration could not assist the SEC as fully as Landis had hoped, although their relations remained cordial. By the end of 1935 the SEC was handling an investigatory load that averaged four hundred cases a month. Many of those cases dealt with allegations against exchange members, which the commission could turn over to the exchanges' business committees for "self-regulation." For those complaints concerning nonmembers, the SEC conducted its own hearings, often carrying them through to the courts.[27]

Although policing duties consumed only a small portion of the SEC's time, they drew the most publicity. The commission adopted a deterrent policy of going after those it regarded as the most flagrant stock manipulators, in the hope of intimidating smaller operators by example. Two prime targets of the commission's attention were Michael J. Meehan and J. Edward Jones. No matter that Meehan, a prominent speculator and onetime "boy wonder of Wall Street," had been a close personal friend of Joe Kennedy's and a heavy financial contributor to Al Smith and Franklin Roosevelt; those attributes only made him a better target. Meehan's expulsion from seats on three major exchanges gave widespread notice of the SEC's power and determination.[28]

For conservatives, the proceedings of the Meehan case were more shocking than its outcome. The SEC refused to make public its bill of particulars against Meehan, arguing that the circumstances of the case made that impossible. Meehan had used a "matched sale" technique of boosting Bellanaca Aircraft stocks by buying and selling in different markets through different agents, thus raising the price and luring other investors to the stock before he sold his own shares at enormous profits. His elaborate subterfuge presented a tortuous path for SEC investigators to follow, and a full bill of particulars would only allow Meehan's lawyers to prime the government's key witnesses before they could take the stand. When Meehan's lawyers demanded the accused's traditional right to know the nature of the charges against him, Landis responded that an administrative agency was not bound by judicial technicalities and had "inherent flexibility" over its procedures. Besides, he claimed, Meehan's lawyers could always get a recess in the hearings to prepare against any surprise witnesses.[29]

Even more unsettling to traditionalists was the SEC's case against J. Edward Jones, chairman of the National Petroleum Council. The commission issued a stop order against Jones' issuance of new shares in an oil royalty venture and ordered him to appear at a public hearing.[30] Jones simply withdrew his registration of the oil royalties and refused to attend the hearing. The Securities and Exchange Commission's Counsel Burns argued that his maneuver would enable swindlers to "go right up under the gun of a stop order" and then retreat if the SEC discovered their deception. So the commission continued its prosecution of Jones. In April 1936 the Supreme Court ruled six to three in Jones' favor, with the majority, in the words of Justice George Sutherland, finding the commission's actions "unreasonable and arbitrary" and likening them to "those intolerable abuses of the Star Chamber." Benjamin Cardozo, writing the dissenting opinion for Brandeis, Harlan Stone, and himself, noted that the SEC lacked the coercive powers of arrest or imprisonment. "Historians may find hyperbole in the sanguinary simile," said Cardozo of the "Star Chamber" reference.[31]

Chairman Landis assured President Roosevelt that the Supreme Court had struck down only an administrative device and had not challenged the SEC's constitutionality. The ruling's only effect was to compel the SEC to allow all registrations to become effective *before* it issued a stop order. The ruling did not even stop further prosecution of J. Edward Jones. "When wrongs such as these have been committed or attempted," Landis announced, "they must be dragged to light and pilloried." The commission won an indictment against Jones for mail fraud, but after another year of court battles Jones won acquittal on all counts. The SEC could only take comfort from a Better Business Bureau report that oil royalty fraud had sharply declined during the Jones litigation.[32]

The type of heavy-handed tactics involved in the Jones case stirred up much criticism of the administrative process. Conservatives distrusted the independent agencies' vague discretionary power, with its potential for turning arbitrary or capricious. A defendant before the SEC generally had no choice in the location of his hearings, no subpoena power to call witnesses, and no preliminary warning of the bill of particulars against him. As one critic charged, "these hearings at which the commission is at once the accuser, prosecutor, judge and jury are not due process, are un-American and constitute a reversion to procedures wholly foreign to American jurisprudence." To Landis, who helped initiate the procedures in question, such rhetoric was merely a cloak to conceal political enmity to the New Deal and federal regulation. If a commission committed legal errors, defendants could always appeal their cases to the courts. In fact, he believed that the courts were overusing their power of judicial review against the commissions. "If the courts in their early stages of development," he wrote to Frankfurter, "had had all their procedural developments subjected to the scrutiny of a jealous superior, what kind of development would there have taken place in the common law?"[33]

The debate over administrative powers became both abusive and murky. Landis focused so narrowly on the New Deal that he rarely addressed himself to the question of how subsequent administrations might use those powers. Those who opposed the New Deal reacted more to an anticipation of regulatory malpractice than to concrete evidence and saw any discretionary power as dangerous in the hands of Roosevelt and his appointees. They suspected Landis, especially after his strong reaction to the Jones case, of being a modern-day Savonarola out to purify the stock exchanges. In their ire they conveniently ignored the attack on the SEC chairman coming from the left.

Liberal reformers called on the SEC to take stronger actions to protect investors, but Landis worried that more cumbersome regulations might endanger economic diversity. A ruling to abolish some troublesome aspect of the giant New York Stock Exchange could destroy many smaller exchanges or drive smaller brokerage houses out of business. Landis' identification with Brandeis led him to temper his dealings with the more powerful exchanges in order to preserve the weaker ones. His encouragement of exchange self-regulation alarmed the more dogmatic reformers, who accused him of accepting "self-control *by* Wall Street rather than government control *of* Wall Street." The release of a series of SEC market studies and legislative recommendations, which Congress had requested, further disenchanted the political left. Far from being academic exercises, the studies represented major policy disputes inside and outside the Securities and Exchange Commission.[34]

The most controversial of these reports was the SEC's study on segregating broker and dealer functions. Landis took the position that brokers and dealers with lucrative businesses on the New York exchanges might successfully separate their activities, but that the smaller volume of trading on other regional exchanges would not support the division. Fearing further centralization of securities trading, he pointed out that fewer than twenty-five brokerage firms dominated the national investment market. Landis' most outspoken opponent on the separation issue, and on so many other issues, was the *New Republic's* John T. Flynn, who defined the problem more in moral than economic terms. "I lay it down as a truism," Flynn wrote, "that no man whose primary function is a fiduciary one—that of an agent—should be permitted to enter the market in which he appears as an agent for others to trade in that market for himself."[35]

Inside the SEC, Flynn's most avid supporters were Chief Economic Advisor Kemper Simpson and Chief of Special Studies Willis J. Ballinger. They prepared the commission's report and adopted Flynn's arguments for unequivocally separating brokers and dealers. Considering their position impractical, Landis rewrote the report. Both sides agreed on some form of separation. A quarter of all exchange transactions involved members trading for their own accounts, with the temptation always present for unloading their own stocks onto their clients. Landis' revised report called for members of the exchanges to register either as brokers or as dealers. Off the floor, brokers could still trade for themselves, as could their firms. He declined to recommend any specific legislation on the subject, assuming that the SEC already possessed sufficient power to "suggest" that the exchanges adopt those rules. By avoiding the rigidity of a statute, he hoped to protect dealers on the smaller exchanges while more strictly regulating activities on the New York Stock Exchange.[36]

Even his more moderate report fell as a bombshell on Wall Street. Brokers defended their dual functions as the only way of keeping a constantly liquid market and assuring their clients of "a reasonably fair price" in declining markets. Landis interpreted liquidity as "a fetish," the cry of professional speculators seeking to "justify their profession." From the opposite corner, Ballinger and Simpson leaked copies of their original draft to the *New York Herald Tribune* and the *New Republic*. John Flynn responded by denouncing the Landis version as "a futile gesture of regulation. Its recommendations are hardly creditable coming from practical men."[37]

By then, Flynn had gotten under Landis' skin. Appealing to Frankfurter, who had once been a contributing editor to the *New Republic*, Landis begged him to intercede with the editors over Flynn's "unfriendly attitude" toward the SEC. In a paragraph that he scratched out before sending the letter to Frankfurter, Landis complained, "I sit here every day, taking it on the chin, psychologically speaking, from the group that hate every effort for general reform in the field of finance, and to find that those who may really be more liberal, more radical—and perhaps be right in being so—weaken the strength that needs not only to be conserved but needs to be built up, is an extraordinary bit of irony." No longer associated with the *New Republic,* Frankfurter could only console him with the thought that attacks from the left would help persuade Wall Street that the SEC's reforms were not all that radical. (In a later twist of fate, during the 1940s John T. Flynn shifted his politics from radical to reactionary and came to see the Securities and Exchange Commission as having far too much power over the stock exchanges.)[38]

Despite his fury with Simpson and Ballinger for leaking their report, Landis kept both men on as employees of the commission and made no public rebuttal to the *New Republic.* He did abolish their independent posts and reassign them elsewhere in the commission. Ballinger resigned with rancor, but since he was assured a position at the Federal Trade Commission, he made no public statements. Later, when Kemper Simpson resigned, he leveled a blast at the SEC's moderate stance. Reviewing the grievances and tensions within the commission, Simpson denounced its leadership as "dominated by those interested in technical detail and legal phraseology," rather than in real economic reform.[39]

Eventually, the criticism and internal struggles began to weary Landis, and the excessive hours he devoted to the SEC showed their strains on him and his family. "The light in my office still shines as late as it ever did back at Austin [Hall]," he told Cambridge friends. When he returned home, tense and tired, Stella would sit with him, playing bridge or working crossword puzzles, until he could unwind. Then he would often go to his study with more work he had brought home with him. Generally, he slept only four or five hours a night. His work kept him away from most social functions in Washington, and once Stella, when asked to bring her husband to a friend's party, replied, "What husband?"[40]

Given his work habits, the Landises tried to stabilize family life as best they could. In the summer of 1934 they rented a much larger house further into the countryside, with two and a half acres of land and formal and informal gardens. Stella adjusted herself to gardening, afternoon teas, and her husband's irregular hours. As chairman of the SEC, his status had risen, while his salary remained fixed at $10,000. Rent, however, was cheap during the depression, and impressive automobiles were available at low prices. Landis had first driven to Washington in a 1926 Ford coupe. While at the FTC he purchased a used 1932 Buick sedan, and at the SEC bought a still newer Buick. Even after he became SEC chairman, he was still driving an old, weather-beaten Ford roadster to work until one morning when the front bumper fell off and snarled traffic on Memorial Bridge. After that incident he purchased a used 1935 LaSalle, more commensurate with his position.[41]

The punishment of work he inflicted upon himself steadily eroded his health. During the winter of 1936 he suffered a series of bouts with influenza and once fainted at a dinner at the home of Treasury Secretary Morgenthau. His doctors warned him to reduce his workload. But with two other commissioners ill, another absent on leave, and a fourth immersed in legislative preparation, Landis' responsibilities actually increased. To add to his lot, President Roosevelt named him to the National Power Policy Commission, which meant more meetings to attend, more memoranda to digest, more issues to decide. At that low ebb of resistance, Landis received a flattering offer to return to Cambridge — not just as a professor but as dean of the Harvard Law School. The time had come for him to make a choice between government service and legal scholarship. "There are scores of men who can do the job you are now doing," acting dean Edmund Morgan urged him; "there are hundreds who can do what you would do in practice; there are mighty few who can equal you in law school work." Without much hesitation, Landis accepted.[42]

Looking forward to returning to "the old days of life," he still hated to leave the Securities and Exchange Commission. As chairman, he was in full control of its activities. Commissioners George Mathews and James D. Ross (who had succeeded Pecora) voted with him on nearly every issue. William O. Douglas (who had taken Kennedy's place) often joined Robert Healy in dissent. Douglas was a man of strong opinions, but he also hoped to succeed Landis as chairman and remained relatively quiet in commission discussions, without confronting Landis' authority. In decision writing, the other commissioners deferred to Landis. When he sent a copy of the first volume of SEC decisions to the Harvard law library he could boast, "It really ought to be bound in red, because I think I wrote most of it."[43]

He would also miss the New Deal. The press of work and the feeling of power and influence created a fraternal atmosphere in the administration. The young lawyers who had flocked to the capital with almost wartime fervor considered their government employment as only temporary, until the emergency passed, and were willing to sweat out long hours at low pay. Often at night they gathered in favorite taverns to pass on information about what was happening in each other's agencies. Landis loved the "cross-fertilization" of those after-hour discussions with men like Rexford Tugwell, Jerome Frank, and Harry Hopkins. To keep up his congressional relations, once a month he also attended the Sunday night gatherings at Sam Rayburn's Dupont Circle apartment. President Roosevelt furthered the communal spirit, and Landis, as SEC chairman, saw the President on a regular basis.[44]

Every meeting with "the Skipper" was "quite an experience." Landis would arrive at the White House for an 11 a.m. appointment, only to be kept waiting in the anteroom for another hour and a half. There he would join agency heads, Cabinet secretaries, and other officials waiting to see the habitually behind-schedule President. Talk in the anteroom impressed him with the scope of problems the President faced daily, and by the time Landis entered the Oval Office he would be asking himself whether his own problem was all that important. Usually, Roosevelt would be seated behind his desk, with his coat off, and would wave him into the room, calling him by his first name. "Have a cigarette, Jim," he would offer, leaning forward to add, "You know what Jesse was telling me?" For the next fifteen minutes, Landis would listen to what Jesse Jones or some other visitor had come for, interspersed with bits of gossip and stories about Roosevelt's Dutchess County. Before Landis would have a chance to bring up his own business, appointments secretary Marvin McIntyre would appear at the door and announce that his time was up. "Oh, look, Mac . . ." Roosevelt would object and give Landis three more minutes to state his problem. "He might not have helped you at all," Landis later recalled. "He might have just thrown the problem right back at you. But you went out of there as if you were walking on air. The feeling of joviality that he gave you, the stimulation . . . then you'd go back and solve the damn problem yourself."[45]

Not wanting to lose Landis, Roosevelt offered him the post of undersecretary of the treasury. The President went so far as to write James Conant at Harvard personally to try and win another extension of his leave of absence. But the law school wanted its new dean that September. As a measure of Landis' respect for Roosevelt and of his reluctance to leave Washington, he stayed on at the SEC for another eight months after announcing his plans to resign. It was a costly mistake. William Douglas, with his own expectation of the chairmanship, interpreted Landis' delay as a personal slight. Actually, FDR had asked Landis to remain on the job until after Congress adjourned for the summer. Acceding to the President's wishes, Landis sacrificed not only a large part of his much needed vacation but much of his friendship with Douglas as well. The eight months as lame-duck chairman also drew him back into one last fight with the stock exchanges.[46]

Erratic stock selling and the New Deal's antibusiness rhetoric caused great uncertainty within the financial community during 1937. In August, when industrial activity unexpectedly collapsed into a severe recession, the president of the New York Stock Exchange, Charles Gay, denounced SEC regulations as the root of the problem. In September, as Landis prepared to resign, the market went into a spiral down to its lowest levels since 1931. At his last press conference Landis fired back at Gay and other critics who pinned the recession on the SEC. He blamed the sudden decline on speculators who had returned to the markets to take advantage of New Deal prosperity, whereas the "small man" had not lost confidence and was still buying stocks in volume. Where Gay had argued that SEC regulations created "narrow, illiquid markets," Landis countered that retraction of those regulations would create instability rather than liquidity. No one, he said, wanted to return to the unregulated market conditions of 1929. His comments brought a chilly response from such previously enthusiastic supporters as the *Wall Street Journal* and the *New York Herald Tribune,* which condemned his "feeble valedictory" and "unusual piece of demagoguery."[47]

The more dramatic accomplishments of his successor soon overshadowed Landis' contribution to the SEC. The differences between James Landis and William O. Douglas were mostly those of style and personality. It had been Landis, in 1934, who advised Chairman Kennedy to invite the Yale law professor to carry out an SEC investigation into bankruptcy reorganization. Douglas, and his assistant, Abe Fortas, performed outstandingly in that job, and the next year when a vacancy occurred on the commission both Kennedy and Landis recommended him. Landis was sitting in the President's office when FDR placed the call to offer Douglas the spot. When he resigned, however, Landis remained neutral over the choice of a successor, and it was Joe Kennedy who campaigned at the White House and the commission for Douglas' elevation.[48]

A week after Landis stepped down, William O. Douglas became SEC chairman. Like his predecessors, Douglas endorsed the commission's emphasis on exchange self-regulation, although he had "no sentimentality for the New York Stock Exchange nor for Charlie Gay" and was less patient with the SEC's conciliatory attempts to gain its objectives. "Under Joe the gains made toward protecting the rights of investors through President Roosevelt's legislative program were consolidated. Under Jim we were taught how to get things done," Douglas explained. "And now we're going to go ahead and get them done."[49]

To Douglas' side came the Wall Street commission houses, whose support Kennedy and Landis had cultivated for the SEC. Angered over Gay's attack on the SEC, they volunteered to help reorganize the New York Stock Exchange. With their backing, Douglas confronted the exchange's leaders. "All you've been doing is give us the run-around," he told them bluntly. "If you'll produce a program of reorganization, I'll let you run the exchange. But if you go on horse-trading, I'll step in and run it myself." In the face of his threats, the exchange capitulated. With only Richard Whitney abstaining, the Board of Governors endorsed the entire SEC rules revision, including public representatives on the board and a paid president and technical staff for the exchange. The rules changes represented the ultimate victory of the self-regulatory policies that Kennedy, Landis, and Douglas had advocated.[50]

Symbolizing their triumph were the public exposure and disgrace of Richard Whitney. The new SEC information requirements brought to light Whitney's secret history of embezzlement. In March 1938 the former president of the New York Stock Exchange admitted his insolvency, and the exchange suspended his firm from trading. A few days later New York District Attorney Thomas E. Dewey brought criminal charges against Whitney, who pleaded guilty and was sentenced to five to ten years in Sing Sing. As a final indignity, the government auctioned off Whitney's estate, limousine, and other property to pay his debts. His imprisonment removed the heart of the conservative opposition and strengthened a new partnership between the New York Stock Exchange and the Securities and Exchange Commission.[51]

James Landis retired "pretty well satisfied" with the development of securities and exchange regulation in the years since he, Frankfurter, and Cohen had first arrived in Washington. The nation's stock exchanges were no longer private clubs but semipublic institutions with an independent federal commission monitoring their activities and providing guidelines for the protection of investors. As an administrator, Landis had been a careful draftsman and a patient planner rather than a dramatic activist. Always a realist, he recognized that he had not solved every problem, that many of his programs would not work smoothly and would require frequent revision. But he always considered regulation a process, flexible and responsive to actual conditions, avoiding rigid centralization and striving to preserve economic diversity — in short, his vision of reformed capitalism. Cleaning up stock frauds and policing other aspects of the market, Landis advised one young SEC lawyer, was "a matter of eternal vigilance and one that can become bad any day when that vigilance relaxes and consequently is one for which no permanent cure can be effected." His contribution had been to help build the mechanism for future treatment of those ills. "To me," he concluded, "it is one of the boldest experiments that has ever been undertaken by our nation."[52]

6 | Dean of the Harvard Law School

The night that Harvard announced appointment of its new law dean, James Landis stole the show at the annual White House reception for the judiciary. When he and Stella arrived, well-wishers surrounded them. Stella beamed as her husband "held a regular court" for the Supreme Court justices, Cabinet secretaries, congressmen, and Washington lawyers who crowded around to congratulate him on his ascension to the preeminent post in American legal education. At thirty-seven, he was the youngest dean in the law school's history, and yet, the *Boston Herald* judged, "more conspicuous than any of his distinguished predecessors had been at the time of their elevations."[1]

On Wall Street, bankers and brokers praised his appointment, which caused the always critical John Flynn to sneer, "Suppose J. Edgar Hoover, if he should resign, got resolutions of recommendations from gangsters. It would be just as appropriate." But those conservatives who misread Landis' record at the SEC, thinking they had gained a new ally in the formerly "radical" professor, soon discovered their error. During his years as dean, for the next decade, Landis proved his unwavering allegiance to the New Deal and its most liberal causes. The return to Harvard freed him from the "mediator" role he had assumed as a regulatory commissioner. At both the Federal Trade Commission and the Securities and Exchange Commission he had interpreted "public interest" to include all economic groups, from investors to brokers, consumers to producers, labor to capital, and had sought a just equilibrium between them. Now he could discard that mantle and pursue more partisan and ideological causes. Nationally, he revealed

79

his favoritism for organized labor. Locally, he demonstrated his pluralistic view of society by supporting proportional representation in Cambridge. Above all else, his resumed academic career afforded him time to sort out his experiences and opinions on the independent regulatory commissions and their place in modern government and society. As an administrator, theorist, and partisan, Landis before long became the most controversial dean at the "citadel of conservatism" on the Charles.[2]

His resurgence of aggressive liberalism surprised no one more than Harvard President James B. Conant, who had chosen Landis as dean to reduce tensions in the law school. The selection had not been without forethought, but was rather the product of a long and careful search. Since 1933 Conant and several law professors had gone through the ritual of questioning Landis on his intentions of returning to the school, and each year they had heard more elaborate excuses for his continued stay in Washington. In 1936, for instance, he argued that crucial SEC cases before the Supreme Court required his presence and that even as a "minor piece" in the administration he could not abandon the President during an election year. To Frankfurter, Landis confided his great sense of satisfaction with his work in the federal government, contrasted to the psychological disadvantage of his limited influence at Harvard. "I am afraid we have lost him to the law school," Professor Calvert Magruder observed. "He is really having a swell time and the experience will be invaluable to him. Indeed he has acquired a great deal of self-confidence, almost cockiness."[3]

The resignation of Roscoe Pound as dean, announced on the same day that Landis became chairman of the SEC in 1935, added a new dimension to his return. A giant in legal education, Pound increasingly ruled the law school as a petty tyrant. With age he grew more intolerant of any criticism of his theories or his authority. Fanatically he clung to every administrative detail, down to allotting toilet paper to the washrooms. Once famous for his advocacy of sociological jurisprudence, he used his position as dean to block moves to revise the Harvard curriculum toward new trends in business and public law. Younger members of the faculty resented the lid he placed on innovations and tended to align themselves behind Felix Frankfurter and Thomas Reed Powell. Pound blamed their opposition on Frankfurter and bristled at his independence and outspokenness, which the dean believed had impaired the school's fund-raising drives. In addition, Pound disliked Franklin Roosevelt and was irritated at Frankfurter's raids of the law school to provide the New Deal with administrators. The two men clashed most often over faculty appointments, with Pound opposing many of Frankfurter's protégés. Regarding the dean as a "pathological liar," Frankfurter responded by accusing him of using "all sorts of untruths and chicanes" to pack the faculty with his own supporters. By the mid-1930s their warring

80

had become so intense that President Conant decided to preside personally over the law school's weekly faculty meetings, an assemblage he described as "the most quarrelsome group of men I ever encountered."[4]

As Harvard approached its tercentenary in 1936, Conant was determined to end the disruptive fighting by removing Dean Pound. He accomplished his goal by establishing the university's first mandatory retirement age. Pound acknowledged that the time had come for him to step down. He was troubled over the "entirely new spirit" in the law school, with younger faculty members coming in late, complaining about teaching loads, and demanding such frills as having their rooms air-conditioned. He wished his successor well, for whoever took the job would find it difficult and wearisome. "You may remember that Langdell went blind, that Ames died close to sixty, and Ezra Thayer after five years," Pound wrote as he left his administrative headaches to become the first University Professor and begin another thirty years of legal scholarship. "I have managed to keep in vigorous health during nineteen years of the job, but it has developed a naturally bad temper to an acute stage."[5]

For Pound's replacement, Conant had no intention of elevating Felix Frankfurter, despite his intellectual preeminence and national reputation. Frankfurter's espousal of liberal causes had made him anathema among the fund-giving alumni. At one alumni gathering an elderly graduate of some nineteenth-century class had startled Conant by jumping up and shouting: "I want you to know that I and my friends *hate* the Harvard Law School!" Another alumnus offered the school a large sum of money if it would fire Professor Frankfurter. Conant wanted a distinguished dean, one who would soothe tempers while remaining out of the headlines. He looked first outside the school for prominent lawyers with experience as practitioners rather than as teachers, but was embarrassed when his two leading candidates declined the offer. "Harvard Law School was in a ridiculous position," Barton Leach commented, "hunting the hills and dales for *someone* who would by any outside chance agree to accept the post of dean." Returning to the traditional practice of choosing a dean from within, Conant polled the faculty and found the names most frequently suggested were those of professors Austin Scott, Edmund Morgan, Barton Leach, and James Landis.[6]

Personally, Felix Frankfurter preferred any of those men over Landis. Insisting that he had no desire to become dean himself, Frankfurter wanted no one else in the position who would challenge his authority. He demanded, as one disillusioned admirer recalled, "a kind of devotion, a kind of acceptance of him as all-wise, all-loved." Landis had played that role as a student and a novice professor, but his successes in Washington had made him too self-sufficient to assure Frankfurter his loyalty. Besides, Frankfurter considered him temperamentally unsuited for the deanship. Remembering his penchant for acting alone, his outbursts at Ben Cohen and others, Frankfurter doubted that Landis possessed the tact to handle men. He envisioned the dean as the "Legal Education Minister for the United States," and wanted someone who would devote himself full-time to the post. Landis, he suspected, was too ambitious to tie himself to any one position for long. Frankfurter made no effort to hide his feelings and campaigned actively with Conant and the faculty against his former protégé.[7]

To the rest of the faculty, however, Landis easily met the high standards the post required. His intellectual abilities and scholarly productivity were unchallengeable. His newly developed executive talents and financial skills could also help the depression-troubled law school. On their advice, therefore, in December 1936 Conant took the "calculated risk" of offering the post to Landis. "The wisdom of others overruled me," Frankfurter wrote graciously to Landis. He admitted his opposition to the appointment, but promised Landis full support in the future. "You also know what the school means to me," he added, "and how deeply I care for your welfare."[8]

Justice Brandeis registered his own disapproval and belief in decentralization. On the day Conant offered him the deanship, Landis rushed to confer with the elderly justice. Brandeis looked up when he heard the news. "You mean the Harvard Law School?" he asked.

"Yes," Landis replied.

"Why do you want to take that?"

"Well," he stumbled for an answer, "it's a great position."

"Anybody can be a good Dean of the Harvard Law School," Brandeis advised. "Why not take some smaller school and do something with it?"[9]

Letters of congratulation from legal scholars, businessmen, bankers, and alumni attested to the overwhelming support for Landis' appointment, but then, without warning, political events shattered the consensus. On February 5, 1937, President Roosevelt rocked the nation and exploded the postelection calm with a request for sweeping federal court reforms. Ever since "Black Monday" in May 1935, when the Supreme Court had declared war on the New Deal by overturning the National Recovery Administration, political observers had expected the President to retaliate. Instead of using his landslide reelection mandate as a weapon to confront the Supreme Court's obstructionism openly, Roosevelt disingenuously chose to argue that the justices' advanced age retarded their work. He proposed an improved retirement system along with an injection of "younger blood" to "vitalize the courts." For every justice over the age of seventy he would add another appointee, until the Supreme Court contained as many as fifteen members. Shock and furor followed the proposal, and many of the conservative protestors held Harvard law degrees.[10]

Landis agonized over whether to support the President. As the designated dean, silence would have been his safest course. Since he disagreed with the President's methods he could have maintained public neutrality, as did Felix Frankfurter. Moveover, in their book, *The Business of the Supreme Court,* Frankfurter and Landis had praised the efficiency of the Court, and now a decade later their words could be quoted in opposition to expansion. But Landis supported the President's ultimate goals. The Court's decision against the NRA had infuriated him and had left his staff at the SEC "stunned and gloomy," suspecting that their own agency would fall next. At a Washington party Landis cornered Judge Learned Hand, who had ruled against the NRA in a lower court proceeding, and waved his finger vigorously in the judge's face while denouncing "old school judicial legalists" who were blind to contemporary economic problems. As a legal realist of sorts, Landis interpreted the Court's anti-New Deal rulings as politically motivated. The dominant septuagenarians on the Supreme Court, he decried, had made "longevity" the major principle of modern law.[11]

Slowly, Landis began to speak out in favor of the "court packing" plan. At first he approached the topic indirectly, noting in a speech to the Federal Bar Association that "the law should be the handmaiden of progress, not an obstruction." A few days later, at the Swarthmore Club in Philadelphia, he denounced court interference with the administrative agencies. The courts, he complained, were overturning the decisions of impartial experts and were hindering effective regulation. The problem was one "of practicality, not of doctrine; an issue of procedure." As a result of those speeches, the Fourth Annual Woman's Conference in Chicago invited him to debate Senator Burton K. Wheeler, one of the leaders of the anti-court-packing movement. During their debate, Landis ignored the President's arguments on the ages of the justices and aimed his barbs at the political and economic effects of the Court's recent decisions. Tracing the history of the Court's intervention into social legislation, he predicted that the President's proposals would stop reactionary judges from placing "a strait-jacket on our national life."[12]

Reaction to his performance was mixed. Charles Michelson, publicity director for the Democratic National Committee, bemoaned that Wheeler had "put it all over" Landis and that he would have to repair the damage. But Attorney General Homer Cummings, a major proponent of Roosevelt's court reform plan, congratulated Landis for his "grand speech." The President, who had already discovered his political blunder and started changing tactics, invited Landis to assist speechwriter Samuel Rosenman in preparing a new line of attack, based more on the court's abuse of power than on its "inefficiency." Applause also came from the legal realists. "Thank God that American legal education is to have as its leader one with such a combination of intelligence, courage, and adaptability," Jerome

Frank wrote. Thurman Arnold praised Landis' self-sacrifice, noting that "you would have been more available for appointment on the Supreme Court had you kept silent."[13]

Before the court fight wound down, Landis became embroiled in still another inflammatory issue. On March 20, 1937, he addressed a conference of law students at the Catholic University in Washington and, almost as an aside, referred to the recent wave of sit-down strikes in the mass-production industries. While the sit-down strikes were widely considered violations of property rights, Landis suggested that "the history of our law is replete with illustrations of the creation of new rights." He hinted that the students should not be very surprised if the courts reinterpreted property rights one day and found the sit-down strike legal, and praised "the capacity of our law to devise new concepts and mechanisms to meet the needs out of which this type of economic pressure has been born." The next day, newspapers carried notice that "Landis Envisions a Legal Sit-Down." The columnists David Lawrence and Walter Lippmann berated the speech and warned of the destruction of all private property. "You are inviting, abetting and encouraging *bloody revolution* by intimating a 'sit down' on another man's property *may be legal*," charged one of the hostile letters that inundated Landis' office.[14]

The new dean's association with such radical causes offended many Harvard alumni. In April he received a decidedly chilly reception from a Harvard Club audience in New York, and President Conant felt the need to rise in his defense. "Mr. Landis and I publicly took different positions on a current issue in which he favored a proposal and I opposed it," Conant said, alluding to the court fight. "I want to remind this Harvard audience that dissent and even heresy have been the essence of Harvard history." Despite Conant's plea, some alumni could not tolerate the new dean's outspokenness. The May issue of the *Harvard Alumni Bulletin* published a letter from a member of the class of 1910 denouncing Landis' "ill-tempered and unlawyer-like" activity. "Harvard Law School is going to lose lots of money on account of your being Dean!" another letter taunted. Fund raisers verified those warnings and complained about the closed doors that Landis' public utterances had caused. He voiced his regrets but would not retract his statements. "The importance of being allowed to disagree and express disagreement — the thing we call academic freedom — is tremendous," Landis explained to one fund raiser. "For the school to pay a few thousand dollars to maintain it is really a cheap price."[15]

No matter the furor at Harvard, Landis had begun to look forward to academic life. His work in the commissions had convinced him of their vital importance, and he wanted time and freedom to write about his experiences. Back in December 1935 the Yale Law School had invited him to deliver their prestigious Storrs Lectures. He accepted readily, without realizing how much his government position would restrict his preparations. "Even in my rough drafts I always have to think of the relationship of what I am saying to the work of the Commission," he wrote while still SEC chairman. He felt especially frustrated that he could not use the lectures to rebut recent attacks on the regulatory agencies from within the administration.[16]

For all his admiration of Franklin D. Roosevelt, Landis had some fundamental disagreements with the President over federal regulation. Landis the commissioner saw himself as an impartial judge, weighing the evidence between stock dealers and stock purchasers and searching for equitable solutions to promote the national economic welfare. Roosevelt saw the commissioners not as judges but as representatives of the people, who must act "definitely and directly for the public." With a passion for administrative flow charts and chains of command (which he was equally liable to ignore and disrupt), the President chaffed at the independence of commissions that influenced so much economic activity. From the start of his administration he expressed hope that he could eventually bring their functions under the supervision of his Cabinet secretaries. Instead, events and expediency forced him to preside over the creation of new commissions. To counter that trend, Roosevelt appointed a Committee on Administrative Management, under Louis Brownlow, which echoed his opinions and denounced the independent commissions as "a 'headless fourth branch' of the Government, a haphazard deposit of irresponsible agencies and uncoordinated powers." Roosevelt waited until after the 1936 presidential election to release the report, and for similar "political reasons" Landis felt he could not respond to its charges until after he had left public office. Yale agreed and postponed the lectures until 1938.[17]

As his lectures evolved, it became clear how significantly his experiences in the Roosevelt administration had caused him to reevaluate his earlier assumptions. He no longer placed his faith in state and regional initiative but accepted massive federal intervention into American society as permanent and beneficial. To Landis, the independent commissions represented the most practical response of the federal government to contemporary economic problems. Congress had neither the time nor the patience to supervise a diverse national economy on a day-to-day basis, and of necessity had delegated large shares of its power to the commissions. The judicial process was also inadequate, since it could only evaluate evidence that the immediate parties in each case submitted and could not conduct its own independent investigations into industrial problems. Finally, the commissions could prevent the inordinant expansion of executive authority. It excited Landis that each commission combined executive, legislative, and judicial functions in one unit. If administered wisely and vigorously, they could give direction to the economy rather than merely police its excesses.[18]

The planning and promotional duties of the regulatory commission required professional expertise, and during his four years in Washington Landis developed a great deal of faith in the expert, whether commissioner or civil servant. Unlike his "jack of all trades" father, his Jeffersonian professors of political science at Princeton, and even Felix Frankfurter, who worried over the "limitations of the expert," Landis relegated the casual office seeker to the obsolete past. Only the expert, "bred to the facts," could respond quickly and assertively to the technical details, shifts in economic conditions, and frequent emergencies of modern industrialism. "Efficiency in the processes of government regulation is best served by the creation of more rather than less agencies," he wrote. "And it is efficiency that is the desperate need."[19]

That was the message Landis expounded in his Storrs Lectures in January 1938. Taking direct aim at the Brownlow committee report, he dismissed its shrill defense of the traditional tripartite federal government as mere "numerology" rather than a realistic appraisal of regulation "against a background of what we now expect government to do." Speaking in an age of Hitler, Mussolini, and Stalin, he was not blind to the concentrations of power that the "pressures of efficiency" had caused elsewhere, nor was he deaf to the complaints of those who charged that the administrative agencies violated traditional "rules of law." He sought instead to place regulatory powers into reasonable perspective. The agencies had evolved through the democratic process, he maintained, and the other branches of the government continued to guard their own prerogatives jealously and to place restraints on the agencies' activities. Legislative limitations, executive excursions, and judicial review would all reduce the chance of arbitrary administrative power. The real danger, he predicted, lay not with the regulatory commissions' excessive zeal, but with their potential for inertness and inactivity, either from poor appointments or lack of centralized responsibility in strong chairmen. But the independent agencies were still at a stage of "lusty youth," and James Landis became their most eloquent spokesman.[20]

That same year, Yale University Press published the lectures as *The Administrative Process,* for which Landis won substantial acclaim. On the spur of the moment he dedicated the book to Sam Rayburn, "whose quiet desire to serve his country has fashioned so greatly the development of the administrative process." While the gesture disappointed Stella, who had thought he would dedicate the book to her, it genuinely touched Rayburn. The book would be a "prized possession," Rayburn wrote, and the dedication "an honor that I will appreciate to my last day."[21]

Less partial reviewers praised Landis' candor, insight, and unique position as "a philosopher who had himself labored in the vineyards." They by no means accepted all of his premises. In the 1930s critics of the regulatory process could not dispute that the commissions tackled their tasks eagerly and successfully. Rather, they worried that the regulators acted far too thoroughly. One reviewer for the *Yale Law Journal* preferred "less of the alleged expertness and 'efficiency' of the administrative tribunal, with its indefensible combination of powers, and more of the simple and wise restraint in the constitutional concept of the separation of powers." The *Harvard Law Review* ran a friendly but decidedly critical review by Landis' colleague and sailing companion George K. Gardner, who warned that the commissions were "very good things to work for us — provided we can afford the expense of them — but that they are very bad things to rule our lives."[22]

The Administrative Process went on record as the most optimistic prognosis of federal regulation, a "celebration" of Landis' New Deal experiences and his hopes for the commissions' future. Later critics would charge its author with exaggeration of the agencies' abilities to plan economic development and with blindness to their many handicaps. One of Landis' own students and his assistant at the Securities and Exchange Commission, Milton Katz, raised these same questions when he asked if Landis was not describing "an ideal as a present fact." In reply, Landis admitted that he had overstated the commissions' tendencies to promote the well-being of the industries they regulated. "I did this rather intentionally," he explained, "partly for the purpose of cajoling some of the administrative agencies into pursuing more of that role than they do now. That, of course, is a politician's and not a scholar's excuse." But in the field of regulation the author was both politician and scholar. In either role he had no doubt of the inevitable trend toward federal regulation of the economy.[23]

Beyond lecturing and writing, Landis used his position as dean to modernize legal education. New social complexities, he believed, demanded "the mastering of new techniques and new disciplines by any student who chooses to pursue the law as a calling rather than as a trade." Harvard Law School needed to broaden its base of instruction to cover wider areas of corporate and public law, and to introduce a more diverse choice of related subjects in economics, psychology, and anthropology. New lawyers required a broad cultural background and a greater sense of public responsibility. "After all," said Landis, "the best lawyer, probably, is the most civilized person." However, he had no intention of weakening the traditional core of legal education or relaxing the school's emphasis on technical skills, warning that "you cannot make good reformers out of poor lawyers."[24]

His moderation appealed to the philosophically divided Harvard law faculty. For years they had been arguing with Pound and among themselves over how to introduce the social sciences into the curriculum without sacrificing the "basic fundamentals." Before Landis became dean, a faculty committee had launched an investigation into proposals for increasing the three-year course of study to four years, adding new courses, and limiting the number of incoming students. Landis wholeheartedly agreed with their findings. He particularly favored elimination of the "unnecessary human tragedy" involved in the law school's low entrance standards and ruthless flunking of one-third of each first-year class. Under the new plan, the school set more stringent entrance requirements and sharply reduced the number of new students to only the most qualified applicants. He also favored compression of the first two years of required courses to give students a wider choice of electives in their third year. To solve the contentious question of a four-year program, he suggested a compromise. On an experimental basis the law school admitted Harvard juniors who would complete two years of legal training before returning for advanced study in economics and social science at the undergraduate college. While the program seemed a bit tepid beside the experimentation at Yale and other centers of legal realism, the Landis plan was a reform which the more cautious Harvard Law School could abide.[25]

Harvard deans needed time and tact to guide the selection of new faculty members and to persuade the others toward new programs. While the law dean was more than "first among equals," he had no power to coerce his colleagues. The post required diplomatic skills, which Landis possessed, however much the need to use them annoyed him. The only group he refused to bend for was the alumni. The opponents of the New Deal among them were as much of a nuisance to him as he was poison to them. When he advocated expansion of administrative law instruction, the "old-line lawyers" complained bitterly. "The don't want the Harvard Law School to emphasize these points," Landis explained. "They want the boys to have the same old common-law education that they had." The were dead wrong in believing that administrative law would decline once the New Deal had ended. "It is not going to make any difference who controls the government in Washington," he warned them. "They can be Democrats, Republicans, Socialists, or whatnot—the pervasive character of government will continue." He would see that Harvard law students prepared for the future, not for the past.[26]

The faculty shared none of the alumni's misgivings and, according to Professor Arthur Sutherland, they found Landis' tenure a "pleasant and wholesome era of good feelings." The new dean was an active, energetic administrator and scholar who stimulated the younger instructors and won the confidence of the older men, many of whom had been his own teachers only a decade earlier. Faculty meetings quieted down to the point where

President Conant no longer felt the need to attend. "Our faculty meetings don't have quite the irritating quality that they had when you were here," Landis wrote to a former professor, "but I like to make people mad on occasion." More than anything else, he won the confidence of Conant and the faculty by his grappling with the school's financial problems. Faced with an annual income of $740,000, which included only $31,646 in alumni contributions, he found that the law school still owed $1.5 million for Pound's reconstruction of Langdell Hall. At the end of his first school year, Landis was able to pay an installment of $42,472 on the building debt and still place a $26,000 surplus in the bank. He refused to allow an austerity budget to create stagnation, and under his direction the school inaugurated a new building program for social and dormitory facilities, expanded the library, and built the Elihu Root Room in Langdell Hall. As a talent hunter, Landis attracted to the faculty Paul Freund in constitutional law, Lon Fuller in jurisprudence, and Milton Katz to teach "Problems in Regulation of Business Enterprise." Dean Acheson and Benjamin Cohen, however, turned down his offers.[27]

During those years Landis resumed friendly relations with Felix Frankfurter, although the two men could never become as close as they once had been. Now they were competitors. In August 1937, when Justice Willis Van Devanter retired from the Supreme Court, President Roosevelt discussed possible candidates with his treasury secretary, Henry Morgenthau, Jr. As a Harvard graduate, Roosevelt expected to make at least one Harvard appointment, but with two Jewish justices then serving on the Supreme Court, he had to rule out Frankfurter. Turning to Morgenthau, the President asked, "If Brandeis resigns, whom do you think I should appoint — Landis or Frankfurter?" Morgenthau considered Landis "by all means" the best choice, but could see quite clearly that Roosevelt preferred his old friend Frankfurter. "Well," the President sighed, "I think I would have a terrible time getting Frankfurter confirmed." Then, in January 1939, following the unexpected death of Justice Benjamin Cardozo, Roosevelt nominated Frankfurter to the Court. Landis applauded the Frankfurter appointment, but could not disguise his disapproval of William O. Douglas' nomination to succeed Louis Brandeis two months later. Always competitive, he resented the elevation of the man he had helped bring to Washington and establish at the SEC. From then on, Landis renounced any judicial ambitions and described his deanship at Harvard as an equally high honor as a seat on the Supreme Court.[28]

Following Frankfurter's resignation to join the Court, the Harvard law faculty elected Landis to his chair as Byrne Professor of Administrative Law. Now, in addition to his courses on labor law, he could offer seminars in all phases of the regulatory process that so fascinated him. Erwin Griswold taught the classes in legislation, and Landis indicated no interest in returning to the field in which he once pioneered. His experiences in Washington made legislation appear "insufficient" to him, since the legislative process could only set policies in the broadest sense. "One cannot expect legislatures to prescribe variant minimum wage standards for industry upon industry, to particularize the manner of trading on stock exchanges, or to evolve the thousand and one other detailed rules," he said. The agencies, which he called "sub-legislatures," were more creative and more challenging to him as a scholarly subject.[29]

"I'm a teacher," Landis described himself, and he clearly excelled in the classroom. *Life* magazine ran a full-page photo of Landis in front of his class, his hands gripped across his chest, his face creased in concentration as he spoke. "No man could be a better model of the fierce intellectual effort which the Law School expects of its students," *Life* proclaimed. As a teacher he set high standards and devoted his attention to the best students in the class. Sometimes, when he suspected them of not giving their all, his manner could turn abrupt. Although some students complained, most found him reasonable and just. Stanley Gewirtz recalled the May morning in 1938 when one hundred and fifty worried first-year men stumbled out of Langdell Hall after their examinations in contracts. Standing almost inconspicuously on a side path, Dean Landis greeted them sympathetically, saying, "I hope you felt the questions were tough but fair."[30]

Outside the law school, the Cambridge years were happy ones for Landis. As dean he earned a yearly salary of $14,000, on which his family could live quite comfortably. He also spent more time at home than his regulatory posts had ever allowed. The family settled into a rambling, brown-shingled house on Francis Avenue and unpacked Landis' Japanese prints and screens, books, and Washington memorabilia (including a bronze bust of FDR). The deanship required them to entertain frequently, and Mississippi-born Stella Landis turned their home into "an island of the South." Always quiet, soft-spoken, and externally calm, Stella charmed Cambridge. Each year she would pore over the law school yearbooks, trying to associate names and faces so she could greet students by name at parties and receptions. Her knack for bringing people together helped expand the dean's circle of acquaintances and took the edge off his sometimes abrasive personality.[31]

The Landises were riding "on the crest of the wave" during those years. Their lives became more ordered than in Washington, and the children saw more of their father than ever before, or ever after. In 1940 Landis bought a large old country house and twenty acres of land at Newbury, near the Atlantic Coast north of Boston. There on weekends and during summer vacations he could unwind from his Harvard duties. Ann and Ellen enjoyed his exuberant efforts at gardening, his impulsive expeditions to the florist and the beach, and his ambitious if awkward carpentry, which resulted in cupboard doors that could not close and tables too massive to move. He taught his daughters to sing and act out "Joe Hill" and other labor songs, adding in a few verses from the Spanish Revolution. The New-bury house was filled with his singing, his laughter, and his happy rough-housing with the dogs. Sometimes the girls resented their father's spending more time romping with the family pets than with them. Landis could always unwind more thoroughly with animals than with people; he never had to prove himself to them.[32]

With its nearness to the sea, Newbury also enabled Landis to indulge his passion for sailing. For years he had taken off once each summer to sail the New England coast on a friend's schooner, to return a week later, bearded, bronzed, and relaxed. In 1941 he bought his own "little knockabout," and was a competent enough sailor to take the boat out during one hurricane to protect it from a battering at the dock. Sailing he described as poetry, "not only on our lips but in the foreland and wave, everywhere the wind seemed to sing at us. It's this that was once boyhood and it was that which I recap-tured."[33]

Long after he left Newbury, the house and the good times there lingered in his memory. He often made the journey back in his mind. "I drive that road out and back many times in the stillness of the night," he told Stella. "Finally you come to the gate, let the dogs out and drive slowly up the hill. Do you remember the night we first drove up the hill with the lights on in the house? And the time we drove Ann up for a surprise? And a thousand other things?" But calls from Washington drew him away from his haven. Not for years would he comprehend how much he had given up.[34]

7 | Freelance New Dealer

Once he returned to Cambridge, Landis took it for granted that he had finished with full-time government service. "The job I'm taking usually is good for ten to thirty years," he said at the law school, "pending good behavior." But part of him always remained with the New Deal. "I'll keep in step with the parade," he promised when he left Washington, "and perhaps do a little work if I'm called on." As dean it would have been wisest for him to ignore all outside calls and to concentrate his energies on the school's perennial problems with finance, faculty, and curriculum; but his ambitions and his loyalty to President Roosevelt constantly diverted his attentions from Harvard. The President exerted a magnetic attraction on Landis which, no matter how controversial the assignment, he could not resist. In a succession of difficult political issues he would "take it on the chin" for the Skipper.[1]

The dean's extracurricular activities began modestly enough with some local volunteer work for civic reform. Harvard University stood essentially as a community in itself, socially and politically isolated from the city of Cambridge. By 1938 the academic community's dissatisfaction with the moss-bound city government spurred a citizens' committee to lobby for the establishment of a city manager and proportional representation system. Known as "Plan E" for its last-place position on the upcoming municipal ballot, their program appealed to Landis because of his admiration of "efficient management" and his pluralist conviction that "vast groups in the city, allied in aim and purpose, have no one to espouse their cause." He not only joined the movement but became its leader.[2]

As he circulated through Cambridge speaking in behalf of Plan E, the dean of the Harvard Law School provided a prominent target for opponents of the plan to attack. Incumbent members of the heavily Irish city council condemned him personally and passed resolutions to expel Harvard from the city's jurisdiction. They drew exaggerated pictures of Plan E as a plot to enable "Marxist" students of public administration at Harvard to tinker with the city as a guinea pig. "Plural voting encourages voting along racial and religious lines," opposition newspapers warned. "The idea is Un-American." In November 1938 Plan E lost by 1,767 votes, with over 4,000 blank ballots cast in the referendum.[3]

The large number of blank ballots showed that the failure had been one of voter education, but the *Boston Post* also blamed the defeat on Dean Landis' "intemperate speeches." When he handed in his resignation as chairman, members of the citizens' committee refused to accept it and begged him to lead the fight in 1940. So, for the next two years Landis worked to build a more sophisticated organization with updated political techniques and better public relations. By 1940 he led his forces to a 7,500-vote victory for proportional representation, and the *Cambridge Chronicle* named him the city's "Man of the Year."[4]

The campaign for Plan E devoured Landis' spare time and turned his home into a campaign headquarters. He enjoyed the challenge, the sense of accomplishment, and the acclamation. On the other hand, local politics gave him only fleeting gratification, and he regularly interrupted his Plan E activities to head for Washington for a day, a week, or an entire summer, to tackle the latest federal problem. Landis' name ranked high on the President's list of reliable troubleshooters, and while most of his assignments were on the technical-consultancy level, he also dealt with some highly inflammatory labor issues. In those cases his activities all but obliterated the conservative image he had acquired at the SEC.

Landis' interest in labor problems dated back to his schooldays' experiences in the West Virginia coalfields, his journey to the Soviet Union in 1924, and his studies in labor law. While a law student he had published articles against labor injunctions and compulsory arbitration and had taught courses on labor law to the members of the Boston Central Labor Council. Later, as a professor, he compiled a widely used casebook on labor law (from which the Federal Theatre Project drew its "Living Newspaper" production on labor injunctions).[5] Although by no means a Marxist, Landis came to interpret labor disputes as a clash between classes, in which labor generally was "manhandled by the employer." He believed that the government must act as a referee between the conflicting claims of labor and capital. The United States, he said, "must give a promise of decent living to the lettuce workers in California just as much as it does to the investment bankers."[6]

In 1938 President Roosevelt gave him the chance to prove the sincerity of his words. At issue was a threatened national railroad strike. Hard hit in the depression, many railroads had survived bankruptcy in 1932 only when their employees voted to accept an across-the-board cut in wages of ten percent. Not until 1937 did the railroads raise wages again, and then the recession struck. Citing loss of revenue and increased operating costs, the managers of 139 railroads met in Chicago and voted to request a new fifteen percent wage cut. The railroad brotherhoods balked. They blamed the latest crisis on "railroad bankers" who lacked operating experience and fostered costly, inefficient, and top-heavy management on the lines. The companies would have to declare bankruptcy and go "through the wringer" of receivership before the brotherhoods would accept another wage reduction. In September 1938 railroad workers voted for a nationwide strike. President Roosevelt quickly utilized his option under the Railway Labor Act to delay the strike while an emergency fact-finding committee studied the problem. For the three-member panel, Roosevelt selected North Carolina's Chief Judge Walter P. Stacey, former University of Chicago economics professor Harry A. Millis, and Dean Landis.[7]

Landis' initial response was to turn the offer down. He had enough to do at the school and in the Plan E campaign, and had almost no first-hand knowledge of the current railroad situation. Roosevelt brushed away those objections with a comment that the tie-up of the nation's transportation system outranked any Harvard obligations. The Labor Department believed that the dean's legal expertise more than compensated for his lack of railroad familiarity. Without much of a fight, Landis gave in and traveled to Washington.[8]

Provisions of the Railway Labor Act suspended all strike threats for thirty days while the committee held hearings and reached a decision. On September 30 hearings opened in the ornate House Caucus Room. Railroad spokesmen testified that "the general level of railroad wages is unreasonably high in the light of existing conditions." The unions responded that their wages were "in fact, inadequate compensation for the services rendered." A long parade of witnesses appeared, including Missouri's Senator Harry Truman, who defended the unions' position. Throughout the hearings, Landis directed his sharpest questions at management, whose fumbling answers left him unimpressed. As he read through the thick stacks of government and industry reports, Landis concluded that the wage issue was relatively minor when compared to the basic weakness of the nation's railroad system. Working capital had reached a low ebb, maintenance was curtailed, and equipment had deteriorated badly. A long-term goal was needed; but the committee had to face the wage settlement as its immediate problem.[9]

All during the hearings the three committee members held hopes that labor and management would reach a settlement on some wage reduction less than fifteen percent. By the end of the hearings, however, they realized that the unions would not compromise and that they would have to act independently of the warring parties. Having made up his own mind, Landis convinced Millis and Stacey of the merit in the unions' cause. In fact, Landis had so steeped himself in railroad statistics and technical reports that he overwhelmed the others, and they delegated him to draft their report. On Monday, October 24, he secluded himself in his temporary office at the Labor Department, where he remained for the rest of the week, having his meals sent in and sleeping in the office until he finished the report. Friday night he handed it to the printer, and Saturday morning he read proofs before heading to his hotel to wash and change clothes. That afternoon the three committee members delivered the report to the White House.[10]

They had recommended no reduction in wages, and apprehensively awaited the railroads' reaction. The committee believed that the lines' losses were only short-term and already on the rebound from the depression, and they were unwilling to inflict long-term burdens on the workers again. Past record demonstrated how slowly the railroads would restore a wage cut. Roosevelt endorsed the committee's report, but also promised the railroads extensive federal aid if they would rescind their wage-cut demands. When the railroads agreed, the President beamed that "everybody in the nation is happy." Liberals like Gardner Jackson congratulated Landis on the victory as a "tremendous success, not only for labor, but for the nation as a whole." But the report, Landis surmised, "didn't increase my popularity in certain circles," and he shuddered when he thought of alumni reactions.[11]

Within a year Landis had made himself even more controversial as a result of the Harry Bridges deportation case, the most politically dangerous assignment of his career. Officially, the request came from the Labor Department, but Landis felt he was taking his marching orders from the White House. In May 1939 Labor Secretary Frances Perkins asked him to take charge of the proceedings against Bridges, the president of the International Longshoremen's Union and west coast director of the Congress of Industrial Organizations (CIO). The labor leader had immigrated to the United States from Australia in 1920 but had never completed naturalization. He now faced expulsion on the nebulous charge of communism, an offense for which the Immigration and Naturalization Service had deported seventy-six other aliens during the previous four years. Since the Immigration Service operated under Labor Department jurisdiction, the case caught Secretary Perkins in a vise between congressional demands for ridding the nation of a radical agitator and her own department's fear of alienating a powerful labor leader.[12] In Landis she saw the chance for escaping the dilemma. As an independent jurist, his record commanded wide respect in Congress as well as within the labor movement.[13]

By the time Landis entered the scene, organized activity against Harry Bridges had been under way for five years, ever since Bridges had publicly collaborated with the Communist Party during the maritime strike of 1934. The shippers, the American Legion, and the Federal Bureau of Investigation had tagged Bridges as a party member, and for years the American Legion's Radical Research Committee in California directed a network of infiltrators and informers to collect data against him. By the fall of 1937 they convinced the Seattle and Portland branches of the Immigration and Naturalization Service that they had enough evidence for deportation. At the Labor Department Frances Perkins viewed those rumblings with suspicion. "Confidentially," one department memorandum cautioned her, "there is a lineup between the Teamsters, A.F.L., shippers and business organizations in general to crush Bridges."[14]

The longer the Labor Department delayed any action, the louder the congressional protests sounded, until finally several congressmen initiated a drive to impeach Secretary Perkins. In March 1938 her department capitulated and issued a warrant for Bridges' arrest. The next month, before the hearings could begin, the United States Circuit Court of Appeals in New Orleans overturned another deportation case on the grounds that past membership in the Communist Party was not a deportable offense. That decision suspended the Bridges hearing for another year, until the Supreme Court upheld the lower court ruling, declaring that only current membership in the Communist Party could serve as a basis for deportation. The Labor Department altered Bridges' warrant to cover the technicality and arranged for hearings to take place in San Francisco in July. Dean Landis would serve as hearings examiner.[15]

Early on the morning of July 10, 1939, a small group gathered on Pier 5 on the San Francisco waterfront. Landis, Bridges, members of the prosecution and defense teams, and reporters all boarded a small ferry for a thirty-minute ride to the Angel Island Immigration Center in the bay. The prosecution chose the isolated setting to insure that their witnesses could testify in safety and without disturbance. It was supposed to be a short trial. The Labor Department promised Landis that the whole case would take two to three weeks at the most, and so he brought his family with him in the hope of combining the assignment with a vacation and leisurely drive back across the country. Instead, the hearings lasted eleven weeks, called fifty-nine witnesses, and produced seven thousand pages of testimony. The Bridges case became the longest and most publicized deportation proceeding in Labor Department history.[16]

Harry Bridges was only a shadowy figure to Landis before the hearings started. But before long Landis concluded that the government had built a terribly weak case against the labor leader. The prosecutor, an amiable government lawyer named Thomas Shoemaker, lacked all signs of court-room shrewdness. On the defense side, Bridges had an able staff of lawyers, who had compiled an elaborate index of union officials, shippers, and anyone else known to hold a grudge against Bridges. The index proved vital to the case, since Shoemaker refused to provide any information concerning who would testify or what charges he would make except that of membership in the Communist Party.[17]

In time, the unreliability of the government's witnesses demolished Shoemaker's advantages. One after another, a Runyonesque assortment of characters appeared to swear they had seen Bridges at a Communist Party meeting or had heard him declare his allegiance to communism. Under cross-examination the first major witness, a police undercover investigator and *agent provocateur* in the labor movement, admitted that he had committed perjury in an earlier trial. Another, a former Communist Party candidate for Congress whom the party had expelled as "unreliable and irresponsible," spun a story so replete with evasions, qualifications, and contradictions that Landis found it "pathological in character." A third key government witness was a man whom Landis remembered from earlier years as a reputable labor lawyer. On the stand, however, the lawyer admitted to having been indicted and disbarred for unethical practices and to having lawsuits pending against Bridges for libel and for failure to pay legal fees.[18]

Finally, the prosecution called Bridges to the stand to force him to admit his communist leanings. It was a futile effort, for Bridges as a witness spoke with such passion and conviction (and at such interminable length) that he impressed nearly everyone in the courtroom. Landis frequently interrupted the prosecutor's questioning to debate Bridges on labor history and tactics. When the prosecution rested, Landis launched his own cross-examination, leading Bridges through an array of questions "trying to see how accurate his testimony was and how it fitted in with what the government had produced." The hearing examiner and defendant sat facing each other, their knees almost touching, and their profiles facing the audience. In the courtroom Landis' daughter Ann could not help but notice the striking similarity between the two men, with their small, lean bodies, sloping foreheads, hawk noses, and intense expressions.[19]

When September came, Landis had to return to Cambridge. Calling the proceedings to a halt, he commandeered the reserve launch and "gayly, like a boy released from school," piloted the ship back to the San Francisco docks. At Pier 5 each of the participants shook his hand. When Bridges stepped up, an onlooker watched Landis' face. "It was a poker player's smile," he noted. "Was it friendly? Was it a mask under which lurked aversion? It was impossible to tell."[20]

Hurriedly, with his wife and children in tow, Landis made a hectic drive back east. With Secretary Perkins, Congress, and pro- and anti-Bridges forces all waiting for his decision, he planned to complete his report in a month. But as he reviewed the lengthy transcripts, he stopped to evaluate again and again each side in the case. For three months he went over the record repeatedly.[21]

On December 30, 1939, newspapers reported Landis' decision: Harry Bridges was not a member of the Communist Party. "That Bridges' aims are energetically radical may be admitted," Landis wrote, "but the proof fails to establish that the methods he seems to employ to realize them are other than those that the framework of democracy and constitutional government permits." Easily Landis' most colorful writing, the 152-page report read like a police novel. His intricate examination of the shady witnesses and their contradictory testimony, and his bold assertion of illegal police tactics, persuaded Secretary Perkins not to issue a deportation order for Bridges. President Roosevelt nodded approvingly, although he labeled the Landis report a "Scotch verdict," politically sound if not altogether conclusive. The report failed to convince any of Bridges' enemies. "Everybody knows Harry Bridges is a Communist," steamed American Federation of Labor President William Green.[22]

In Congress conservative forces moved to accomplish legislatively what Landis had denied them administratively. Their effort to pass a bill specifically ordering Bridges' deportation ended only when Attorney General Robert H. Jackson reopened the case. In a reorganization shuffle the Justice Department wrenched control of the Immigration Service away from the Labor Department. It also made use of the new Smith Act, which declared advocacy of overthrowing the United States government illegal. FBI agents combed the west coast in search of new evidence, and in December 1940 J. Edgar Hoover announced that his agents had confirmed charges of Bridges' communism.[23]

In his haste to convict Bridges, Hoover took a swipe at discrediting Landis' role in the case. Testifying before a congressional subcommittee, the FBI director suggested that Landis had lacked legal authority as a hearing examiner to swear in witnesses and that therefore no one had testified under oath. "It means that practically the whole first proceeding was not conducted in accordance with the law," Hoover added. Incensed, Landis contacted Hoover and carefully defined his legal powers as a Labor Department hearing examiner, which most certainly did enable him to swear in witnesses. He demanded that Hoover retract his accusation, lest it prejudice any new proceedings against Bridges. But Hoover shifted the blame to an erroneous Justice Department memorandum and refused to make any retraction. In a furious exchange of letters, Landis charged that such conduct was "a serious reflection upon those standards of fairness that should characterize the administration of your office." Writing of Hoover's "disgraceful" tactics to the solicitor of the Labor Department, Landis added that he had "rarely seen a better illustration of the characteristics that make for smallness of mind and spirit."[24]

The Bridges case dragged on for five more years, until the Supreme Court upheld Landis' arguments in a six to three decision in *Bridges v. Wixon* (with Felix Frankfurter voting in the minority). William O. Douglas wrote the majority opinion that Bridges' conduct revealed "cooperation with Communist groups for the attainment of wholly lawful objectives." Justice Frank Murphy concurred with a ringing statement that "seldom if ever in the history of this nation has there been such a concentrated and relentless crusade to deport an individual because he dared to exercise the freedom that belongs to him as a human being and that is guaranteed to him by the Constitution." Landis was pleased with how strongly Douglas' opinion relied on his own report; "it is plain that that affected the majority view." Three months later Harry Bridges became a United States citizen. Over the years Landis remained friendly with Bridges, whom he regarded as "an intelligent fellow—prejudiced, biased largely by the way of life that he's had," but a worthy man and effective labor leader. Despite the unfavorable publicity he received, Landis always felt immense satisfaction over his own role in the case.[25]

Long before the final settlement of the Bridges case, other events had captured Landis' attention. In September 1939, as he was concluding the hearings, war had broken out in Europe. When he arrived back at Harvard he found the university divided. The faculty generally supported the Allies, while an "extraordinary amount of anti-war sentiment" prevailed among the students. As an ardent nationalist, Landis favored a strong defense, which he identified with the extension of all possible aid to Great Britain and France short of war. In October he joined William Allen White's Non-Partisan Committee for Peace through Revision of the Neutrality Laws, and drafted the New England chapter's policy statement endorsing repeal of the arms embargo and establishment of a "cash and carry" policy in international trade. "The pursuit of American interest for American ends," he said, "is not only patriotic doctrine but the essence of neutral action."[26]

His nationalism never slid into jingoism; if anything, he was troubled over the trend toward national disunity and intolerance. At a meeting of the Harvard Defense Council he defended the pacifist editors of the *Harvard Crimson* from attacks on their loyalty. What he sought was "a real common denominator of idealism that ought to bring together rich and poor alike . . . We are ideologically at war — a kind of war which, if it isn't won, will defeat any other effort."[27]

In June 1940 he volunteered his services to the President for any war-related job. Having studied English war preparation, he thought he might be useful as a consultant to United States administrators facing wartime problems. Then again, recalling Felix Frankfurter's role as chairman of the Labor Policies Board during the First World War, he suggested that he could tackle wartime labor disputes. The response from Washington was hushed and cautious. With the President running for reelection, defense preparations had to proceed discreetly and indirectly. The only calls for Landis were for consulting work with the Treasury Department, the Civilian Conservation Corps, and the Advisory Committee to the Council of National Defense. He accepted them all.[28]

That autumn, he campaigned for Roosevelt in Massachusetts and the rest of New England. His admiration for the President knew no limits, not even the two-term tradition. "For my part, I distrust generalizations," he said of the third term. "I would rather pin my faith on men." Besides, he considered the Republican candidate, Wendell Willkie, a flagrant hypocrite. Recalling Willkie as a utility company executive who fought against the Public Utility Holding Company Act back in 1935, he doubted the candidate's sincerity in supporting collective bargaining, stock exchange regulation, or social security. "I can remember the days when we were fighting for these things," he commented, "and I do not remember once during those long days one word of encouragement or even sympathy coming from Mr. Willkie." During the campaign, Landis published "I Vote for Roosevelt" in the *Atlantic,* which brought renewed criticism from the Harvard alumni and further threats of financial reprisals against the school.[29]

Roosevelt's reelection in November 1940 enabled the administration to focus more sharply on problems of war and defense. Landis was still waiting for an assignment when the Treasury Department put in the first bid. Henry Morgenthau, Jr., was seeking a replacement for Under Secretary Daniel Bell, then moving to a new post. Morgenthau had first consulted with Justice Frankfurter about the possibility of acquiring Landis for the job, but Frankfurter no longer boosted his one-time protege. The justice had lectured Landis about accepting so much outside work and neglecting the law school, and was appalled at the suggestion that the dean take a leave of absence. Frankfurter warned Morgenthau that Landis was still "kind of a child," whose temper, poor handling of people, and terrible sense of public relations would make him a bad risk. In his place, Frankfurter recommended Wisconsin Law School Dean Lloyd Garrison. But Roosevelt vetoed Garrison because of his antiwar statements, and Morgenthau turned again to his first choice.[30]

Landis ached to accept the post, but with the approach of the war, the draft, and mounting financial problems at the law school, he decided that his first loyalty belonged to Harvard. As he sat writing his letter of refusal, Morgenthau telephoned from Washington. The Treasury secretary spared no effort to shame or seduce him into accepting the offer. "The world is crying out, Jim, for people like you, and they're damn rare." He needed a Democrat who understood finances, which narrowed the field "almost to an infinitesimal." If Landis did not accept, Morgenthau would have to draft another "dollar-a-year man" from Wall Street, someone who might later try to exploit his relationship with the Treasury. Dangling the potentials of wartime policy making, he warned that "the rest of this year will settle what kind of a world it will be for the next one hundred." As Landis weakened, Morgenthau aimed at his patriotism: "Don't you worry about me, you worry about the U.S.A."[31]

Morgenthau promised to "say a little prayer tonight," and Landis responded, "Yeah, I'll have to say half a dozen." As he hung up, Landis sat perplexed. His family resisted another move to Washington; Felix Frankfurter indignantly warned against leaving Harvard; members of the faculty, President Conant, and the Harvard Corporation had already expressed some annoyance over the time he spent away from the school. Two days later, Landis called Morgenthau back to accept the post. "I only wish I had two lives to live," he exclaimed.[32]

Ironically, a political enemy saved him at the last moment. Massachusetts' Democratic Senator David I. Walsh notified Morgenthau that he would block Landis' nomination in the Senate. Walsh could not forgive Landis for not supporting his reelection, and even worse for recommending his unsuccessful Republican opponent, Henry Parkman, for a post at the War Department. Because he disapproved of Walsh's anti-British attitudes and opposition to the President's foreign policy, Landis remained neutral in the Massachusetts senatorial election, despite appeals from local and national Democratic leaders. The senator got his revenge by blocking the confirmation of both Parkman and Landis. Treasury Secretary Morgenthau tried every possible means of dissuading or circumventing Walsh, but was "embarrassed, chagrined, and heartbroken" when he failed. Landis conceded more gracefully. "In one sense," he wrote Morgenthau, "Senator Walsh has unwittingly done me a favor rather than a hurt." Instead of the Treasury job, Landis devoted himself to a less prestigious part-time consultancy to the War Department, helping to create a new insurance program for its defense-building projects.[33]

By the spring of 1941 Landis had become so convinced that the United States would inevitably enter the war that he accepted appointment as regional director of Home Defense for New England, a post he could hold

101

while still serving as dean. Civilian defense was an old cause of his. As early as his Mercersburg schooldays in 1916 he had won the Junius S. Morgan award for an essay on "The Duty of a Private Citizen in the Matter of National Preparedness." In 1941 he worried about an enemy attack against New England. Predicting a London-like blitz, he declared that Massachusetts alone would need 100,000 men and women trained as enemy aircraft spotters. Heedless to charges of "warmongering," he rounded up volunteers to triple the manpower of local fire departments, double police forces, and provide one air-raid warden for every five hundred people in his region. "In time of trouble we want an army, not a mob," was his credo.[34]

From the start, administrative problems beset his operations. The national Office of Civilian Defense provided almost no financial aid and even less equipment, not even demonstrational gas masks. State governments balked at federal encroachment on local initiative through the civilian defense program, and municipal governments fought against state interference in their own affairs. Mayors refused to allow governors to take charge of their cities' professional police and firemen, needed for air-raid service. Even the Red Cross worried about losing its identity in civilian defense operations. To further complicate matters, Landis discovered that his region's Army and Navy commands maintained only perfunctory communications between them. He spent most of his time coaxing the various factions to sit down together and plan a unified defense.[35]

On Friday, December 5, 1941, he was in Washington testifying before Congress on new amendments to the Securities Act and working on the insurance program for the War Department. Saturday he returned to Cambridge and on Sunday afternoon was meeting in his study at home with a representative from the Securities and Exchange Commission when Stella rushed in to report a radio bulletin that the Japanese had bombed Pearl Harbor. As he hurriedly packed his briefcase to leave for civilian defense headquarters, Landis tossed the securities amendments they had been working on back to the SEC agent. "We'll take this up after the war," he said.[36]

8 | The Administrator at War

Boston's Back Bay railroad station served as the hub of a busy personnel interchange during the Second World War. Every arrival and departure of the Federal Express brought crowds of military officers, bureaucrats, lawyers, businessmen, and professors bustling through the terminal. Late on Sunday evening, January 11, 1942, a little over a month after Pearl Harbor, reporters gathered at the station to interview dignitaries bound for the 11:05 to Washington. Almost unnoticed in the crush, a small, tired-looking man in a dark overcoat and battered hat, carrying his own luggage, entered and took a seat, where he nervously chain-smoked cigarettes. "What's his name?" one reporter asked. "Landis," someone else replied. "Oh, yeah, Dean Landis, the guy who has something to do with this civilian defense business." If Landis had overheard their conversation, he would have been disappointed that after a decade of local and federal activity he remained such an unfamiliar face. But as director of the wartime Office of Civilian Defense, he would shortly gather national publicity in countless newsreels, pamphlets, and press releases revolving around his stormy agency.[1]

Operating an emergency government agency laid the severest burdens on an administrator. It required quick decisions, organizational innovation, ability to hurdle bureaucratic obstacles, and a thick skin. For those posts, Franklin Roosevelt called not upon his New Deal advisors but upon his long-time opponents, businessmen, bankers, and corporate lawyers. The ubiquitous "dollar-a-year men" moved into temporary office buildings that sprang up along the Mall, from which they directed a vast new partnership between government and private industry. In a "win the war" at-

103

mosphere, the government suspended antitrust actions and deemphasized its regulatory programs, to the point of moving an agency like the Securities and Exchange Commission to Philadelphia, to make room for more essential wartime operations within the capital.[2]

As the government deemphasized business regulation, Landis shifted his own talents to the civilian defense program. For the first two years of the war he no longer worried about security frauds and stock exchanges, and instead regulated the nation's preparations for enemy attack. Civilian protection and participation in the war were too important to leave to private groups, he believed, yet too dynamic to entrust to the established federal bureaus "with accustomed routines and paid employees, ill-adapted to deal with masses of volunteers." Like the regulatory commissions, the Office of Civilian Defense operated outside of the Cabinet departments and was responsible to both the President and Congress. But the agency differed from those of Landis' previous experience by its single administrator rather than a panel of commissioners. It also lacked any coercive powers, depending strictly on "persuasion and education" to achieve its objectives. Whether Landis could transform the much maligned OCD into an army of volunteers, whether he could create an organization to foster civilian discipline without trampling democratic rights, and whether he could quiet congressional criticism of the civilian defense program would rank among the toughest tests of his career.[3]

After Pearl Harbor Dean Landis almost completely abandoned the law school, supervising New England's civilian defenses seven days a week. On Christmas day 1941, while his family celebrated at home, Landis worked at his desk at the Boston civilian defense headquarters. The *Cambridge Chronicle,* which selected him as "Man of the Year" for the second straight year, reported him "frail, but there is a missionary fervor and a driving zeal about him that seems to give him the strength and endurance of ten normal men." By the end of December his efforts had made the New England organization stand out nationally from the other eight regions in the speed and efficiency with which its program had gotten under way. Massachusetts led every other state in aircraft observation posts, information and education services, blackout systems, and air-raid shelters.[4]

By contrast, the national Office of Civilian Defense was bogged down in administrative confusion. Back in May 1941, with much fanfare, President Roosevelt had appointed Fiorello LaGuardia as OCD director, as a political favor to help his reelection as mayor of New York. In principle, the colorful, energetic mayor should have made an excellent choice for booster of public morale, if only his numerous other responsibilities had not so distracted him from the nonsalaried OCD post. To keep the mayor interested in the job, Roosevelt invited him to attend regular Friday morning Cabinet meetings whenever he happened to be in Washington on civilian defense business. Soon LaGuardia was flying to the capital on Friday mornings, sitting in with the Cabinet, and then leaving immediately, usually without bothering to stop at OCD headquarters. Whenever he did stop by, he impressed the staff with his compulsion for acquiring fire-fighting equipment and with his interest in very little else.[5]

As far as LaGuardia was concerned, all volunteer activity except that of air-wardens and auxiliary firemen was "Y.M.C.A. stuff." That attitude led him to delegate all responsibility for other civilian efforts to his two assistant directors, an error that nearly destroyed the agency. To John B. Kelly, a Philadelphia Democratic politico and former Olympic athlete, LaGuardia assigned the physical training program. Full of grandiose plans, Kelly set up a "Hale America" program to improve national physical fitness in case of invasion. He surrounded himself with famous sports personalities, whom he appointed "coordinators" of every sport from boxing to bowling. More controversial than Kelly, the second assistant director was Eleanor Roosevelt, who took charge of volunteer participation. The President's wife had been publicly critical of lax federal attitudes toward civilian war efforts, and she accepted the post to correct that situation as well as to further her ideals of public service and social justice. Eleanor Roosevelt envisioned the marshaling of wartime patriotism to make the United States "the best possible country in which to live, so it's worthwhile to keep it from being attacked, worthwhile to defend it." But no matter how noble her intentions, by accepting the appointment she offered political opponents of the New Deal an easy means of indirectly attacking the commander-in-chief.[6]

The political onslaught began at once. Republicans and Southern Democrats ridiculed Mrs. Roosevelt for organizing lunch-time recreational dancing for OCD employees on the roof of the agency's headquarters at the Dupont Circle Building. When they discovered that she had also hired a friend, dancer Mayris Chaney, as a "recreational director for youth," they launched a congressional investigation. The dancer's $4,600 salary, critics pointed out, was equivalent to that of an Army major or Navy lieutenant commander. Other protégés of Mrs. Roosevelt's, including Joseph Lash on the Advisory Committee on Youth, came under fire as participants in a gigantic boondoggle. "Strike off the names of these leeches from the Treasury's payroll," demanded Representative John Taber. Normally sympathetic columnists like Raymond Clapper asked, "How can people take civilian defense work seriously when it is being cluttered at the top with this rhythmic dancing stuff?"[7]

The abysmal public image of the Office of Civilian Defense at the time the United States entered the war prodded the Roosevelt administration to overhaul the agency and to oust its director. Bureau of the Budget officials,

who prided themselves on their organizational orthodoxy, were shocked at
LaGuardia's sloppy leadership and called for someone who could do a
"cold, sober, solid planning job." Eleanor Roosevelt, keenly sensitive to the
internal problems at the OCD, suggested Dean Landis as the administrator
who might rescue the agency. Hearing that news, Treasury Secretary Morgenthau made one last attempt to secure Landis for his own department.
After interceding with the President to delay any OCD appointment, Morgenthau renewed his pleading with Senator Walsh to withdraw objection to
Landis' nomination. The senator would not be moved. In January, when
Landis called at the White House, he still had no idea about which job he
would get, until Roosevelt told him, "I want you to take OCD."[8]

Two obstacles remained in the way: Harvard University and Fiorello
LaGuardia. Harvard's long opposition to a leave of absence for the dean
melted more easily than Landis anticipated. The war was already draining
off students, and military units were taking their places in the law school's
classrooms. In 1942 President Conant announced demobilization of the
faculty for the duration of the war, with only a "corporal's guard" to stay behind and run the school. In fact, since December 1941 Conant had been
secretly devoting three quarters of his own time to coordinating the atomic
bomb project. At the law school other professors were delighted that Landis
had only asked for a leave instead of resigning outright, a possibility they
considered a "calamity." Edmund M. Morgan, who took over as acting
dean, informed Conant that Landis had "the respect, confidence, and affection of the entire faculty; the younger men who have been brought here by
him or consented to stay because of him cannot be equalled in any other
law school in the country." As additional insurance toward his return, the
school agreed to pay Landis the $4,000 difference between his salary as
dean and his new government wages.[9]

LaGuardia proved a more durable obstacle. The President simply could
not drop an old political ally so bluntly; he had to ease him out of office. On
January 2, 1942, during a meeting with the budget director and LaGuardia, Roosevelt told the mayor that he was overworked at the OCD job and
suggested that he devote himself instead to promoting "local morale
through visits and speeches in various parts of the country." To aid him,
Roosevelt would bring in James Landis as "executive" of the OCD to handle organizational matters. The odd title was the President's semantical
creation. He rejected "executive director" as demeaning to Director
LaGuardia, but he wanted something more independent-sounding for
Landis than "associate director." The title "executive" reminded Roosevelt
of a ship's executive officer and appealed to his nautical imagination. In
reality, Landis would come aboard as "special assistant to the President,"
since the OCD had no provision to pay his $10,000 salary.[10]

Publicly, LaGuardia welcomed the new arrangements and thanked Landis for lifting "the details of office administration off my shoulder." Privately, the reorganization left him gloomy over his future within the agency. After Landis became executive, LaGuardia rarely went back to OCD headquarters. Dorothy Brown, Landis' secretary, noted that LaGuardia's "pipe and tobacco were on his desk, but he never appeared for perhaps a month after we arrived."[11]

As administrators, the two men could not have been more different. A telephone conversation they held on the night after the bombing of Pearl Harbor best symbolized the gap between them. Landis had called LaGuardia to detail all his preparations for the New England region. LaGuardia responded: "Very fine, but I think you want to get them to march. Can you get a big parade going in Boston tomorrow?" Stunned, Landis answered: "Mayor, my men don't march. They don't know how to march. They're good at the various jobs they do. They're standing by and they're ready to move." LaGuardia persisted: "You ought to get them to march." "I can't get these men to march!" Landis shouted back. "They know marching isn't going to do anything here. They know exactly what their tasks are. They're ready to do them. I'm going to put out, in the next day or two, a test alert, just to see how well this thing works, and we will go through these exercises."[12]

Landis wanted no parades. He firmly believed that the Axis Powers would launch air attacks against major American coastal cities, and he hurried to provide those areas with warning systems, equipment, and trained air-raid personnel. But on January 8, the day before Roosevelt announced Landis' appointment as executive of the OCD, the House of Representatives voted 187 to 167 to transfer control of a $100,000,000 appropriation for civilian defense to the War Department and defeated by only one vote a bill to create an assistant secretary of war for civilian defense, abolishing the independent Office of Civilian Defense. Landis' appointment and Secretary of War Henry Stimson's opposition to burdening civilian defense on his department finally persuaded the Senate-House conference committee to return the appropriation to the OCD. In one last display of disapproval, Congress forbade the use of OCD funds for "instructions in physical fitness by dancers, fan dancing, street shows, theatrical performances or other public entertainment," and specifically earmarked the money for fire-fighting equipment, protective clothing, helmets, medical supplies, gas masks, and training facilities.[13]

In February, after a respectable interval had elapsed, LaGuardia "relinquished command" and Landis succeeded him as Director of the Office of Civilian Defense. The change stilled some congressional critics, but not all. "What will the American Legion and the Veterans of Foreign Wars say to

naming the man who whitewashed Harry Bridges from deportation proceedings?" asked Congressman Charles Faddis. "Dean Landis is 'pink,' "
concurred Congressman Leland Ford. "You would have a hard time getting someone 'pinker.' " To regain congressional confidence, Landis
adopted a hard-line administrative approach to his agency. He started by
shifting the controversial Physical Fitness Division out of the OCD to
another agency. Meeting late into the night with his aides, he next went
after Mayris Chaney. Telephoning her at the end of the meeting, at 3:00
a.m., he bluntly demanded her resignation. The startled dancer refused,
but after further pressure she agreed to resign to prevent "altercation which
might cause disunity and delay." Continuing to swing the axe, he abolished
the Division of State and Local Cooperation and the Office of Inspector
Generals, both of which had come under heavy fire for meddling in local affairs. Mayor LaGuardia had packed these divisions with fifteen former
mayors. Landis boasted that he "fired them all in one night."[14]

A month later, he accepted Mrs. Roosevelt's resignation. She had ten-
dered it on the day Landis became director, but he did not want her departure confused with LaGuardia's. Personally, Landis maintained excellent
relations with the First Lady. She never attempted to outrank him and insisted on holding all their conferences in his office, rather than requiring
him to come downstairs to her own office. She also drew away from him
most of the hostile fire from Congress and the press. Critics, for instance,
automatically blamed Mrs. Roosevelt for Landis' appointment of Melvyn
Douglas, an actor associated with numerous allegedly left-wing causes, as
head of the Arts Council. In spite of their ability to work together, Landis
realized that it was "a perfectly impossible situation, to have as an assistant
director the wife of the President of the United States."[15]

With the housekeeping accomplished, he set about reorganizing the
OCD into a "semi-military operation." Vowing that every employee and
volunteer would have a definite function directly related to the war effort,
he redivided the agency into six departments. Foremost were civilian protection, which prepared for air attack, and civilian mobilization, which replaced Mrs. Roosevelt's "volunteer participation." Other departments
handled information, interdepartmental problems, and a civilian air patrol
that flew the Atlantic Coast from Brownsville, Texas, to Bar Harbor,
Maine, in search of ships in distress and enemy submarines.[16]

Beyond internal reorganization, he was convinced that the agency could
achieve its maximum usefulness only through total integration into the
government's war program. He saw the OCD as a domestic coordinating
agency, and proposed an executive order for a civilian defense board to
oversee all civilian activities during the war. From his experiences in the
regulatory commissions, Landis believed that a collegial organization could

better deflect public criticism and handle complex problems. On first reading, however, President Roosevelt disapproved. "What is the matter with the Office of Civilian Defense continuing as it is?" he complained. "I hate setting up new agencies all the time." Only after the Bureau of the Budget altered the proposed board from an administrative to an advisory body would Roosevelt sign the order. In reality, the board's members, including several Cabinet secretaries, were far too busy with their own assignments, rarely met, and provided little advice and no protection.[17]

Throughout the war, the OCD lacked support from the established bureaucracies, which watched suspiciously over the development of a temporary rival. The Budget Bureau vetoed many of Landis' proposals, fearing that his elaborate reorganization plans would concentrate civilian defense work on the federal level rather than on the more easily dispersed state level. The War Department rejected Landis' requests for exclusive authority to issue regulations on civilian protection and to enforce penalties for violators. Even Henry Morgenthau protectively blocked OCD excursions into Treasury territory. When an aide informed him that the OCD wanted to take over war bond promotions and sales, Morgenthau replied, "Ask Landis how far it is from his office to the Potomac . . . Then tell him to take a swim."[18]

If he failed to expand his sphere of influence, Landis had more than enough trouble within his own domain. He found the OCD's administrative needs radically different from any he had dealt with before. To a large degree the agency was an information and publicity mill, producing thousands of pamphlets, newsreels, regulations, and instructions each month. From August 1942 until December 1943 it issued pamphlets in an estimated 116,000,000 copies. Since the OCD was well stocked with military officers, many of those leaflets read like military technical manuals, while others were couched in bureaucratic jargon. The Public Relations Office, under Frances Knight, struggled to rewrite the publications for the general public, and Landis himself tried to edit every document that crossed his desk. Eventually, the bulk of paperwork forced him to delegate that responsibility to others.[19]

With so many items released over his signature, errors were bound to appear. His worst moment came at a presidential press conference in March 1942, when Roosevelt read aloud an OCD pronouncement on blackout rules for federal buildings. "Such obscuration may be obtained whether by blackout construction or by terminating the illumination," the President stumbled over the words as reporters laughed. "The Dean of the Harvard Law School wrote this," Roosevelt explained with a grin. Then he turned to his press secretary and corrected the order to "turn out the lights." The incident received national press coverage and caused Landis, who had not written the offending document, no end of embarrassment. Later that day, the President called to invite him to dine at the White House. In an upstairs study that evening, FDR mixed several potent drinks before sheepishly apologizing. "I'm awfully sorry about that," he said, " . . . but I just couldn't help it."[20]

Other barbs came from Fiorello LaGuardia, who had never reconciled himself to his successor. A running battle in the newspapers over LaGuardia's charge that the OCD failed to give adequate equipment to New York ended in a burlesque public duel between the two men. LaGuardia objected to new civilian defense instructions for extinguishing incendiary bombs with direct jets of water and insisted that the New York Fire Department continue to use traditional spraying methods. Landis countered that new research into Axis incendiary bombs had prompted the change in orders and challenged LaGuardia to a demonstration. The two forces met at Randalls Island Stadium in New York. With Army sergeants manning the hoses, Landis' "jet" stream extinguished an incendiary bomb in fifteen seconds, while LaGuardia's "spray" took over a minute and used twice as much water. The mayor sighed, withdrew from the field of contention, and turned the matter over to his fire commissioner, who announced that New York City would accept the OCD order.[21]

Despite their feuding, Landis and LaGuardia shared some similar outlooks on civilian defense, especially their common premonition of air raids on American cities. Like LaGuardia, Landis concentrated first on civilian protection, to the exclusion of civilian mobilization. "Drill, drill and more drill is the answer," he told his audiences. "This is Civilian Defense, the defense of home, of ways of living, of the little luxuries that we prized and the great freedoms that are our heritage."[22]

On February 23, 1942, his arguments seemed vindicated when a Japanese submarine surfaced off the California coast near Santa Barbara and shelled an oil refinery. The attack caused little damage but threw the entire west coast into nervous apprehension. Two days later, antiaircraft batteries around Los Angeles opened fire on what they thought were Japanese planes. No planes ever appeared and no bombing took place; but fragments of antiaircraft shells damaged windows, roofs, and automobiles around the city, and five people died of heart attacks and traffic accidents during the blackout. "The Battle of Los Angeles" marked the most spectacular homefront debacle, but many other American cities underwent similar false alarms during the first few months of the war. In June, after the Doolittle raids on Tokyo, fears rose again in response to Secretary of War Stimson's warnings of possible Japanese retaliatory attacks on the United States.[23]

At night the Statue of Liberty was darkened. In Washington, the Park

Service turned off the spotlights on public monuments. Motorists taped their headlights and householders hung heavy drapes over their windows. Landis spent considerable time supervising blackout drills around the country. During one alert, he made an observation flight over the capital and was outraged to find that the only brightly lit building he could see from the air was his own civilian defense headquarters.[24]

In June Landis went to California to conduct similar tests. While in San Francisco, the commanding general of the Army on the west coast summoned him to the Presidio and outlined plans for the impending battle of Midway. If the Japanese won, they could move aircraft carriers to within striking distance of all bomber-producing plants from Seattle to San Diego. Sworn to military secrecy, Landis had to devise an alert without exposing battle plans. He ordered all civilian defense volunteers on twenty-four-hour alert for a week of "practice drill," during which he traveled along the coast inspecting procedures and making encouraging speeches. When the governor of California moved too slowly to issue blackout instructions, Landis ordered his regional directors to print, distribute, and post the regulations themselves. Although he lacked legal authority to make such an order, he did have the tacit approval of California's attorney general, Earl Warren. The frantic efforts ended after the resounding American victory at Midway, a turning point in the war for civilian defense as much as for the military. As the Allies advanced and the threat of homefront fighting diminished, Landis found his agency in the awkward position of having to keep civilians prepared for emergencies which few thought would ever occur.[25]

Improved war conditions turned Landis' attentions belatedly to civilian participation. Since Pearl Harbor there had been little problem with public morale, for the nation was more united than during any previous war. People volunteered faster than the OCD could create jobs for them. Sociologists warned that the government must meet those civilian needs, because volunteer activity helped overcome mass feelings of "helplessness, impotence, and unimportance" brought on by wartime restrictions. Officials also recognized that none of the wartime controls, fund-raising drives, and salvage operations could succeed without civilian support. Landis now perceived that the OCD could provide the organizational framework for volunteer efforts, and he began to preach that "*doing* in today's type of war is, in the true sense, fighting."[26]

During the summer of 1942 he personally moved to reorganize the OCD's volunteer program. Until then he had left that chore to Mrs. Roosevelt's successor, a North Carolina newspaper editor, Jonathan Daniels. A liberal Southerner, Daniels shared Mrs. Roosevelt's dream of using volunteers to improve the quality of American life and envisioned the OCD as a pioneer in such areas as minority rights. But after months of building back congressional support, Landis was not about to jeopardize it with any controversial racial programs. He retreated from Daniels' policy of employing race-relations advisors, which had angered Southern congressmen, and tried to emphasize the integration of the agency at all levels, at a slower rate. The only way to increase minority participation in civilian defense, he argued, was through "whites dealing with whites at the top," particularly in the South, "since state and local authorities through which we have to work refuse to deal directly with Negro representatives on our staff."[27]

Racial issues would not disappear solely because the OCD director chose to ignore them. Tensions rose over the most innocent events, such as a formal dance the OCD planned for its employees. Once congressional outrage over lunchtime recreational dancing had subsided, Mrs. Roosevelt urged Landis to sponsor a party for OCD personnel as a reward for their hard work and many hours on the job. The agency booked a hall at the Hotel Wardman Park, which followed the practice of most Washington hotels in admitting blacks only as waiters and bellboys. When black OCD employees purchased tickets to the dance, the hotel threatened to bar their admittance. Two days before the dance, a delegation of black employees marched to Landis' office and demanded that their tickets be honored or they would picket the affair. No matter which way he decided, some public uproar would result. In distress, Landis turned to Eleanor Roosevelt, who offered a compromise. White OCD employees went ahead with their dance at the Wardman Park, while Mrs. Roosevelt hosted a private party for black employees at the White House. Although unhappy with the segregated solution, black leaders cooperated out of respect for the First Lady. The incident went by without publicity but had an "impact on the entire staff," Landis conceded.[28]

Meanwhile, his relations with Jonathan Daniels steadily deteriorated. Daniels objected to his exclusion from congressional budget hearings for the OCD and to the scarcity of staff meetings at the agency. For his part, Landis dismissed his subordinate as a lightweight and distrusted him for contradicting his directives to the regional offices. By August he had decided to fire Daniels. To Mrs. Roosevelt Landis explained that the volunteer division lacked "(1) a sense of leadership . . . (2) a capacity to devise and operate programs that will go down to the grass roots, (3) tough, hard thinking on the things that communities should be doing that they are not yet doing, and (4) clear-cut decisive relationship with other federal agencies." ("Poor Jonathan Daniels," Mrs. Roosevelt confided to Joseph Lash. "He's up against an impossible situation, I fear—Landis is proving like LaGuardia and I know what he is going through.")[29]

Jonathan Daniels, however, had no intention of being kicked out. As the son of Franklin Roosevelt's old Navy boss, Josephus Daniels, he maintained valuable contacts in the White House and used them when needed. On August 17 Presidential Press Secretary Marvin McIntyre reported to Roosevelt that "Jonathan Daniels was due for a showdown with Landis" that morning but that he had talked them into keeping it quiet for a while. That maneuver gave the President time to reshuffle the deck. Word came from the White House that the President had an important (although unspecified) assignment for Daniels, who suddenly moved out of the OCD building and into a basement office in the State, War and Navy Building next to the White House. At the same time, Roosevelt issued directives to all his agency heads, including Landis, to refrain from publicly debating their administrative difficulties and to submit all internal disputes to the White House instead.[30]

In September 1942, with Daniels gone, Landis unveiled his master plan for organizing volunteer efforts. Already, ten million people had promised to serve. The ambitious program was a "Block Plan" for total coverage of all homes on a nationwide, block-by-block basis. Every neighborhood block would elect its own leader. Just as air-raid wardens were responsible for civilian protection in their sections, so the block leaders would handle all civilian information and participation, salvage drives, war savings campaigns, consumer education, day-care nurseries, and other services. Local defense councils would pass on all information from Washington to the block leaders for quick dissemination to all citizens. Landis wanted to be able to pick up his telephone and to issue an order that would set things in motion across the nation "immediately."[31]

The Block Plan was a purely administrative creation which lacked legislative mandate and legal sanction to control the activities of its millions of participants. One possible method of control might have been the withholding or withdrawal of federally-funded fire-fighting and air-raid protection equipment from any community that refused to follow national guidelines. But such an act would place the OCD in the villainous role of removing a city's "protection" from enemy attack. A far simpler and more effective means of control, the OCD discovered, was available through the distribution of insignia. Wartime patriotism and high esteem for the military had made civilians rank conscious. Volunteers clamored for ribbons and other commendations for their length and level of service. Landis ordered millions of ribbons and was amazed at the insistent demand for them. These insignia permitted the OCD to set standards of service on the local level, since only by following federal regulations could a block leader, air-raid warden, defense council member, or any other volunteer qualify for the coveted awards. The system brought maximum effort with minimum compulsion, allowing Landis to claim proudly that "no decrees fasten these duties on our people, no orders assign them to these manifold tasks."[32]

Some Republican congressmen were appalled with the Block Plan, which they suspected would put a New Deal agent in every neighborhood. They denounced the plan as a vehicle for creeping government intervention into home life, and a "diabolical scheme" for softening the voters "for the fourth-term blitz in 1944." While the storm in Congress never matched the outcry over Mayris Chaney nor seriously threatened the agency's operations, it did keep Landis on the defensive. "This civilian defense is based on the loyalty of the people," he protested, "and they would resent, as a people, politics being introduced into it." Minor manipulations might have occurred on the local level, as they did in Chicago, where Mayor Ed Kelly required Democratic precinct captains to submit recommendations for block leaders. But the OCD generally resisted political interference, and President Roosevelt refrained from making any partisan demands on its program.[33]

In the end, the Block Plan, like the civilian protection program, depended on civilian belief in the possibility of enemy attack. When no bombs fell, civilian defense shifted to rescue efforts in national disasters. During the autumn of 1942, when the Shenandoah and Potomac rivers flooded, civilian defense volunteers evacuated victims, repaired roads, and provided relief. But those services failed to impress the local and state officials who were eyeing civilian defense as an expendable item, ripe for budgetary pruning. Citizens grew tired of blackouts and air-raid drills. Block leaders and air-raid wardens were becoming nuisances rather than community leaders. The rate of volunteering declined and many posts, especially aircraft spotters, went unfilled. "There is no victory, no real security until the last battle is won," Landis warned, but to little avail. Surrender of the German army at Stalingrad, and the British and American victories in North Africa, made his precautionary tones sound absurd. One newspaper columnist reported that "Buster Keaton and Harold Lloyd themselves could not have been received with more laughter by the public than was Mr. Landis when he appeared on the screen, on a newsreel, to tell the public about the new air-raid signals." Stung by such ridicule, Landis continued to tour the country, where he gave pep talks, reviewed endless parades, and "bullied people into not leaving their jobs at this stage."[34]

By the summer of 1943 he reluctantly concluded that the OCD had outlived its usefulness. Therefore, he announced drastic cuts in the agency's budget and recommended that the administration parcel out the OCD's tasks to other federal agencies and local defense councils. "This job is one of the things I expect to chalk off as being finished, so far as my contribution is concerned, before I go," Landis informed President Conant at Harvard. But the Bureau of the Budget rejected his proposals as a "serious mistake." Budget officials worried that volunteer morale might collapse if the national organization disbanded. Landis agreed that the OCD's liquidation would dampen some enthusiasm but argued that the administration should control the dismantling process "rather than to have events drive us into action."[35]

He also let the White House know that he considered his own role in the OCD completed and desired another assignment closer to the "fighting' front." In August President Roosevelt offered him the new post of American minister for economic affairs to the troubled Middle East, which he accepted. As a temporary successor at the OCD, Roosevelt named Landis' deputy director, John B. Martin. For the next few months the President hunted unsuccessfully for a prominent appointee. Briefly, he even considered offering the post to the disgruntled James Farley in hope of winning back his support before the 1944 election. But the lack of any suitable candidate, together with the new Allied victories, made Landis' recommendation for dismantlement appear more realistic. "When no man of prestige will take it," advised Office of War Mobilization Director James Byrnes, "it is pretty good evidence it should be abolished."[36]

The OCD struggled on gamely until the end of the war. Finally, when Mrs. Roosevelt expressed her interest in seeing the agency continue its volunteer efforts in peacetime, she helped seal its doom. Budget Bureau officials hastily reversed their earlier stand and recommended abolition. Community spirit, they argued, stemmed from wartime patriotism and not from the OCD. The agency offered no solid foundation for long-range programs, and they doubted that Congress would continue its appropriations. On June 30, 1945, the Office of Civilian Defense turned over its remaining equipment to the Army and went out of business.[37] Thirty-one days later the explosion of an American atomic bomb over Hiroshima opened a new age of global paranoia. Soon the United States would require a new Civil Defense Administration to once again worry about air-raid sirens, wardens, and bomb shelters.[38]

"You cannot run a volunteer army of ten million people — about twice the size of our Army — without a lot of headaches, a lot of grumbling and a lot of disappointment," Landis wrote as he finished his seventeen months as OCD director. Yet, his reputation emerged enhanced from the job. The press, which plagued LaGuardia, credited Landis with cleaning up "the worst of all Washington's administrative messes." Opinion polls showed a substantial increase in public approval of civilian defense after he took charge, an increased confidence which manifested itself in burgeoning volunteer recruitments. It was a gratifying indication of success for Landis, given his own compulsion for public service.[39]

By the end of his civilian defense leadership, Landis had made himself nationally known as a hard-boiled and successful administrator. If he lacked the color of a Fiorello LaGuardia, he more than compensated by his firm handling of his once chaotic agency. Even his detractors acknowledged his dedication and stamina. In the highly charged circles of Washington he stood out as a man obsessed with his work, his career, and his loyalty to the President. There appeared few discernible signs that he was also undergoing a profound crisis in his personal life.

Some associates wondered if he had any private life at all. At the OCD he was seated at his desk in the morning when the staff arrived and was still there in the evenings when they left. Weekends and holidays rarely interrupted his routines. Few in Washington had ever seen him with his wife and children. Not many suspected that the small, thin, rumpled-looking man might possess a romantic side. Yet Landis was a deeply impassioned man who repressed emotions which could explode intellectually on a favored project or ferociously on those who disappointed him.

"Remember that I always have been an emotional creature," he once confided. "My capacities, my will to do things, depend so much upon the emotional side that underlies them." The whole of his life had dictated against emotional encounters and he had fiercely sought to suppress his passions. He refused to show any weakness, any deviation from his pursuit of excellence. His expectation that his staff keep pace with him made him a gruff, demanding, and unremitting executive who was impatient with sloppiness and surly in his relations with those closest to him, the very people who worked the longest and the hardest. One assistant who matched him hour for hour on the job recalled Landis throwing a report back with a growl, "This is garbage." Another aide found "not a speck of a snob in him," except for intellectual snobbery. One always had to measure up to his standards.[40]

His pattern of suppressed emotions lasted until the war and a woman changed his life. It began in 1941 when he accepted the post of regional director for home defense of New England and expanded his staff at the law school to meet his added responsibilities. When he advertised for a secretary, among the applicants was Dorothy Purdy Brown. She was thirty-two, married, and the mother of two boys. Having begun a family early, she had never lost her desire for a career, and when her sons were old enough she returned to college. The job at the Harvard Law School would help pay for her education. A sour-faced Dean Landis interviewed her and asked about her classwork. "I'm doing fine," she replied, "all A's and B's." "B's!" he snorted, "what good are they?" But he hired her and moved a desk into the corner of his office for her. Soon she was handling far more civilian defense work than Harvard assignments.

When Landis accepted the OCD post in Washington, he put together an office staff to bring with him. Stella planned to remain in Cambridge until their daughters' school terms ended in June. Accompanying him instead were Stanley Gewirtz, a promising law student, and Agnes Maher, Landis' secretary at the Boston civilian defense office. "I'd like very much for you to come to Washington with me," he also asked Dorothy Brown. She mulled over the opportunity: her husband was planning to enlist in the Navy; a relative staying at their home could take care of the children for a while; and a wartime job in Washington could be exciting and meaningful. After long discussions, her family agreed that she should take advantage of the offer.[41]

Dorothy Brown and Agnes Maher took an apartment together in Washington. Working for James Landis, both women were aware, would place oppressive burdens on them. The war had him going at full speed from eight in the morning until after midnight almost daily. To cope with such an untiring man, the women arranged a shift system, with one working mornings and the other taking afternoons and evenings. In passing they could outline for each other what business had transpired during their shifts and maintain the continuity of the office flow. At first, Landis seemed unaware when their shifts had changed and unable to distinguish between the two of them. But before long he began to notice Dorothy.[42]

A beautiful woman, she was full of gaiety and laughter, and her light-heartedness made the long hours in the office so much more tolerable. Once in a while even Landis had to stop. On February 10, 1942, the day LaGuardia "relinquished command," Landis invited Dorothy Brown out to dinner to celebrate. The next day he found himself looking forward to her arrival at work, and soon he was finding excuses to stay later and spend more time with her. One hot Sunday afternoon in May, he and Dorothy "cleaned up a good bunch of work" and then abandoned the stifling OCD offices for the coolness of the Potomac River banks. For the first time he admitted to Dorothy that he had fallen in love with her. Afterwards, they dated at the movies, at dinner, and on Sunday drives through the Virginia and Maryland countryside, retracing his favorite Civil War battlefields. "Gettysburg, Bull Run, Chancellorsville, Maryland with its twinkling lights — and there are times more," he later wrote. "It was, it is, joy inexpressible."[43]

Reminders that both were still married to others interrupted their idyll. That summer Dorothy's husband passed through Washington on his way to naval service and left their two sons to live with her. Then Stella appeared, bringing Ann and Ellen. Landis rejoined his family and took up residence in a crowded house which they shared with other boarders in the war-swollen capital. Time and Landis' neglect had altered the relationship between husband and wife. Stella was no longer the raven-haired, striking

117

Southern woman he had first met. A white streak now ran boldly through her hair and she had become overweight. The difference in their ages was never more apparent, and as Stella fretted over her husband's rumpled clothes and reminded him to take his pills, she made him feel old. He reacted by staying away from home, spending his time at the office or out of town on business, and drinking more heavily than usual. Not blind to events, Stella sensed that her marriage was crumbling and resorted to telephoning Agnes Maher at the office to ask indirect questions about her husband and Dorothy Brown.[44]

Like her husband, Stella Landis tried to forget marital troubles through war work. "Winning the war is the only thing that matters," she told one newspaper reporter. "Personal problems are entirely insignificant." With her husband absent, her children in school, and not even a home of her own, Stella turned to outside activities. At Mrs. Roosevelt's request she chaired a committee to study the needs of the women warworkers who had overfilled Washington since Pearl Harbor. Her committee found acute housing shortages, poor transportation, insufficient pay for the women, and an almost total lack of inexpensive recreational and entertainment facilities. Beginning where they could have the most effect, Stella launched a drive to create community centers and persuaded the wealthy Evelyn Walsh McLean to donate an old stable behind her Massachusetts Avenue mansion for the first center. Its Christmas Day opening in 1942 attracted local newspaper attention and praise for Stella's activities, always independent from those of her husband.[45]

The presence of Stella and the children, as well as Dorothy's children, greatly complicated Landis' life. By October he decided that he must ask for a divorce. "The answer is not the past," he wrote to Dorothy while on one of his many OCD journeys. "Despite the solace of time, the day of resurrections is over. I could never dig myself out of this landslide, nor do I have the slightest desire to do so." He could not deny his feelings. "I just cannot see life without living with you," he told her. "The only answer is marriage." He was relieved and gratified when Dorothy agreed and asked her husband for a divorce.[46]

Such decisions involved agonizing personal reevaluations, which had to take place amid a busy administrative schedule. "At 43 he is animated, eager, curious-minded, vibrant and a dynamo," the *New York Times* pictured Landis, "which his friends say is going to need some priorities or some replacement parts if he doesn't slow down." The dynamo was indeed slowing down. On his frequent nationwide civilian defense tours he found that he missed Dorothy painfully. "There is no dreaming when you are away and fears set in," he wrote her, "the old, eating ones that only you can drive away." Steeling himself against such "weakness," he returned to his familiar theme that "work is the only antidote and idleness would increase the sense of loneliness and absence." But this time the antidote failed; more work did not relieve the symptoms of self-doubt. Somewhere he had crossed a divide and was no longer the young man in a rush to success, the precocious scholar, the youthful administrator, the law school's youngest dean. "I am afraid of time without you," he wrote to Dorothy, "for I am too old to ever try to become young again."[47]

When the Office of Civilian Defense wound down in 1943, Landis saw the opportunity to break loose from his personal stalemate. His Harvard post still awaited him, but he was not ready to return. Harvard, he told Dorothy, had "an emotional drag that is very strong, but I don't believe it would be quite fair to throw you into the midst of that with all its past associations, its prejudices, its intrinsic smallness." Instead he accepted the Middle East assignment, which he hoped would give him enough distance and time to solve his problems. He asked Dorothy to join him there as his secretary and was stunned when she turned him down, reminding him that she had two sons to look after. In her place he asked Agnes Maher to take the job.[48]

Leaving Dorothy for so long disturbed Landis, but in a philosophical mood he decided that the separation would give each of them the freedom to make certain they had made the right decision. "And going away—I think you understand now. It really is the best thing," he wrote as he prepared to leave. "Not that we need to discover each other, but it's as good a way as I know to find a way of life."[49] He insisted that he was not running away, and yet the Middle East assignment would prolong his absence from Harvard and his avoidance of a confrontation with Stella. As the day of his departure arrived, he felt terrible ambivalence and depression, which he expressed in a farewell message to Dorothy:

> Ah God, the pain of knowing that my love
> Can never find a world for us to share,
> To know that years from now I still must move
> Ahead, but all alone without you there
> To make me laugh or cry, or still the waves
> Of bitterness that swell too often over me.
> These little things I dare not hope to save
> Outside the darkening niche of memory.
>
> And so the trail winds on. No stars now guide
> My faltering footsteps, and I cannot will
> To know just what the future may betide
> For this God must deny to man. But still
> One star is not too much to ask, one light
> To make less black the darkness of the night.[50]

9 | Middle East Odyssey

A rush of events preceded Landis' mission to the Middle East. Early in 1943 American forces had swept eastward from Algeria across North Africa to join the British, pressing westward from El Alamein. Together, the Allies cornered remnants of the Axis armies on the northwestern tip of Tunisia. By May two hundred thousand German and Italian troops had surrendered, making Anglo-American victory in the Middle East complete and unconditional. Within a month Allied troops landed in Sicily and the war's focus shifted to Europe and the Far East. Behind they left a vast region of displaced people, black markets, and raging inflation. British officials moved promptly to restore Great Britain's political and economic authority in the Middle East, but the United States was unwilling to abandon its own newly developed strategic and commercial interests there. With Washington's attention riveted to the warfronts, President Roosevelt sought an agent for the Middle East with administrative skills, economic foresight, and a capacity for independent action. The assignment fell to James Landis.

"This is a job to test the administrative abilities of any man," the *New York Times* wrote in endorsement, "and Mr. Landis, more than most men, knows the administrative field." The *Boston Globe* concurred: "Landis combines a talent for organization and a drive for getting things done with a positive genius for finding solutions to intricate problems."[1]

The new assignment meant a reversal in roles for Landis. He moved from overseeing the practices of American businessmen to assisting them in their rivalries with foreign competitors for overseas markets. He made the

120

transformation easily, largely because he found no reason to distinguish between the interests of the United States government and American business in a region where neither had ever held much sway. His democratic distaste for colonialism, and his distrust of Winston Churchill's postwar plans for a renewed British Empire, further assisted Landis in his relations with Arab leaders. In exchange, his Middle Eastern experiences reinforced his opposition to both corporate and government monopoly. He became more firmly convinced than ever of the necessity for a regulated private enterprise system.

"Forgive me for running out again," Landis apologized to acting dean Edmund Morgan at Harvard, "but I honestly think there is a job to do there and that I may make some contributions towards our general future." He had some financial reservations, however, since he had already gone into debt from the past two years of government service and the added diplomatic responsibilities would set him back further. "I am afraid that this job, like most jobs I have done for Uncle Sam, will cost me a little more than I will get paid," he explained as he made arrangements to borrow on his life insurance and sell a few stocks.[2]

There were other doubts in his mind, both personal and professional. He worried about how Dorothy would react to his long absence and whether she would still care for him when he returned. He could not shake those feelings during the last hectic month before his departure, which he spent at the Department of State being briefed on his mission and "getting shot in the arm for all sorts of dreadful diseases." From the onset, the diplomatic bureaucracy irritated him terribly. They shuffled him back and forth between the Middle East geographic desk for political discussions and an entirely separate economic desk for the same region, each with different perspectives on the same problems. Since he would also be representing the Lend-Lease Administration and the Board of Economic Warfare, they too required lengthy conferences. Fortunately, by the time of his departure the many parts of that complex machinery had simplified through their merger into a unified Foreign Economic Administration.[3]

During his rounds at the Department of State, Landis grasped the significance of his mission. He would be carrying American diplomacy into an area where the United States had maintained only perfunctory relations before the war. All that had begun to change in November 1942, when American troops came ashore at Oran and Casablanca. Afterwards, American military presence in North Africa warranted a greater diplomatic role for the United States, including membership in the Middle East Supply Centre, a British operation designed to maintain civilian production and control all importation of supplies. Although the Supply Centre supposedly became a mutual Anglo-American venture, its United States representatives, headed by Frederick G. Winant, adopted a decidedly deferential attitude toward their British counterparts. By 1943 the inequity of the arrangement had raised loud voices of protest from American exporters, who charged that the British were manipulating the Supply Centre to bolster their own trade. Under the rationale that imported materials should come from their nearest sources, the Supply Centre routinely forwarded all Middle East import requests to London, where British merchants "skimmed off the cream." Only those orders that the British could not fill went to the United States, where the Lend-Lease Administration took charge, again denying American merchants direct contact with Middle Eastern importers.[4]

Inevitably, oil also became a factor. Early in 1943 President Roosevelt sent Major General Patrick J. Hurley on a tour of the Middle East to determine "U. S. national interest" there. An Oklahoma oil man, Hurley concentrated his efforts on winning Saudi Arabian oil concessions. Meanwhile the Secretaries of State, War, Navy and Interior met in Washington to consider prospective shortages of domestic petroleum reserves and to study the Middle East as an alternative source of supply. But when the American minister in Cairo approached King Ibn Saud with an offer of direct United States Lend-Lease aid to Saudi Arabia to solidify relations with the oil-rich sheikdom, the British intervened. They demanded that Saudi Arabia channel all aid requests either through its legation in London or through the British legation in Jidda. The obvious strategic significance of the British middle-man position spurred the Department of State's efforts to revamp its Middle East division and to find a more forceful representative to the Supply Centre. After General Hurley and Ambassador William C. Bullitt rejected the post, FDR decided upon an agent with economic rather than diplomatic experience. James Landis thus became "American Director of Economic Operations in the Middle East and principal American Civilian Representative to the Middle East Supply Centre with the personal rank of minister."[5]

On September 21, 1943, Landis flew to London for two weeks of consultation with the British. Following so closely after his strenuous civilian defense performance, the new assignment allowed him no chance to rest in the interim. He felt bone tired, his body ached, and the long and arduous plane ride across the Atlantic did not help. Before departing, he had made a present of a bottle of Scotch to his secretary, Agnes Maher, who was accompanying him. Once in the air, however, he finished off the bottle himself in an attempt to get some much-needed sleep.[6]

Wartime London brought back memories of his unhappy stay there during the First World War. Once again, London gave him a keener sense of the immediacy and unpleasantness of the war than he had ever experienced in Washington. The bulk of his visit went to dinner engagements and meetings with Averell Harriman, Anthony Eden, and officials of the Colonial Office. British weather, combined with the lack of heat in his hotel room, led to a bad cold. After two weeks he left England, miserably ill and exhausted. Dulling his senses with whiskey, aspirin, and sleeping pills, he rendered himself unconscious until the plane landed in North Africa. At Marakesh there followed a day of talks with Robert Murphy and General Dwight Eisenhower before the flight on to Egypt.[7]

Twenty-four hours after his arrival in Cairo Landis was at his desk, sorting through stacks of reports and statistics on local economic problems. That same day he addressed his first press conference in the Middle East, where he portrayed himself as the representative of a new and permanent American interest in the region. "All policies must have long-range objectives," he asserted, "and these go beyond immediate war objectives and into a period of peace."[8]

The chief Middle Eastern role of the United States was as supplier of military materiel to the British and Russian forces. But the Allies could not ignore the eighty million people in the eighteen countries that made up the region. Concerned about the possibility of civilian disruption and unrest, the Middle East Supply Centre functioned as an unabashedly paternalistic agency, dispensing massive supplies of food and consumer goods. Landis' work at the Supply Centre involved such diverse tasks as salvaging Italian tractors in Ethiopia, encouraging the Ethiopians to produce grain for the Saudi Arabians, helping to control locust plagues in the grain-producing areas of Egypt, and providing pharmaceutical products for Iran.[9]

Among the first problems confronting him was a severe food shortage in Iran, a crisis compounded by the country's poor roads and transportation. Touring Teheran's slums, Landis was badly shaken at the sight of their squalor. Not even from the memories of his youth in the Orient could he recall such scenes of poverty and disease. In a sharply worded cablegram to the Department of State only two weeks after his arrival in the Middle East, he demanded that the United States show some concrete evidence of support for Iran. "Many prominent Iranians skeptical of us," he wired. "We talk big but produce little is their comment." Hesitation would be "suicidal." A month later, when no word had come in reply, Landis took his case directly to Franklin Roosevelt, who was attending the Cairo Conference. There he won presidential authorization for the first assignment of American personnel to build roads in Iran for the local population and the Russian supply routes as well.[10]

The Iranian incident demonstrated how poorly Landis fit into the State Department structure. He could never accommodate himself to its rigid bureaucratic procedures, and at the Cairo Conference he complained to the

President of the slowness and timidity of the State Department's hierarchy. "Well," Roosevelt suggested, "why don't you get a plane and go out there and talk this thing over." Without bothering to notify his superiors, Landis packed his bags and flew back to Washington, forcing the State Department to backdate its "request" that he return for talks. On still another occasion, when the department ignored his complaints about Russian army officers pilfering Lend-Lease tires for the Iranian black market, Landis again acted on his own. "These tires are designated for Stalingrad," he confronted the Russian ambassador in Cairo. "We want you to use them to kill Germans. We're not interested in these rich Iranians." The ambassador said nothing, but within days the Russian high command in Iran had changed and black market tire sales had ceased.[11]

His relations with the State Department deteriorated further over their differing opinions on Great Britain. As Landis saw it, his section chief, Assistant Secretary of State for Economic Affairs Dean Acheson, linked America's future too closely with the British, an emphasis that kept the department from paying sufficient attention to emerging nationalism in the Middle East and elsewhere. Repeatedly, Landis argued with Acheson for more long-range economic programs upon which the Middle Eastern countries could rely, and begged for the appointment of more "top-notch" ambassadors to the area. For the most part, however, he felt he received greater support from the political wing at the State Department than from Acheson's economic section.[12]

Both Acheson and Landis had imbibed English law under the anglophile Felix Frankfurter, who drew upon it often for his classroom examples and who considered Harvard the "center of Anglo-American law." Both men also had absorbed much of his admiration for the British. But Landis still harbored suspicions that dated back to his childhood in Japan. He contrasted the memory of his American neighbors, who had come with a "missionary drive" to build schools and hospitals, with his memory of the British, who seemed motivated solely by a "mercantile drive" to dominate Japan through trade. Later, reflecting the influence of Brandeis on his thinking, Landis equated the British Empire with a vast holding company controlling regional monopolies. In international trade he favored an open-door policy of free trade, which he frankly believed would favor American producers. National independence movements were an important corollary to his theory, for independence to him meant "a diffusion of power and a breaking up of the unnecessary bureaucracies of the world."[13]

When Landis arrived at the Middle East Supply Centre, he found Anglo-American partnership there little more than a euphemism. His American predecessors had underwritten British operations with scant knowledge of what many of the operations entailed. "I stuck my nose into it," said Landis as he demanded full information and equal treatment. Some issues were as petty as the British practice of charging Americans for air-mail deliveries, while the United States provided the same service to the British for free. Other issues were more fundamental, particularly British distribution of American Lend-Lease Administration goods, a system which misled local populations into assuming that the goods came from Britain. On Landis' insistence, all Lend-Lease contributions to nonmilitary activities became the joint project of an Anglo-American committee.[14]

It was apparent to Landis that the Supply Centre's controls favored the British exclusively. In January 1944 he returned to Washington to urge a complete reexamination of United States trade agreements in the Middle East. By relying on the British, he argued to Roosevelt and State Department officials, the United States was missing its chance to establish permanent trade ties with the Arabs, who were steadily accumulating capital through massive Allied military expenditures in their lands. After the war, he predicted, the Arabs would have oil to sell and the funds to purchase American raw materials, finished products, and technological skills.[15]

"This is a very hard job," he wrote to Dorothy in the spring of 1944. "I always have to be out on a limb, wondering whether I will get the support I need from home." In February he drafted a letter for Roosevelt to sign, outlining American goals for encouraging independent Arab economic policies. Harry Hopkins rewrote the letter, and Roosevelt gave Landis reason to believe he would endorse the antiempire program. But in March the State Department produced a much watered-down policy statement, which the President signed instead. Sadly, Landis concluded that the Skipper "changed his mind as a result of pressure from Churchill." It had not been a total defeat, since even the compromised letter promised that the nation would not retreat to its prewar isolation from the Middle East. On paper, the United States was "interested in seeing that itself and other nations should not be discriminated against in dealing openly and fairly with these territories in exchange of goods and resources." Landis also received authority to use all other American agencies in the Middle East to support his program. However, the State Department reminded him to "put first the strengthening in every way the warm and cooperative relations with our Allies, upon which our success in the war, and thereafter, so largely depends."[16]

The little lecture on British friendship, coupled with the weakness of the administration's stance, disheartened Landis. It seemed to underscore the department's lack of confidence in him. "I'm good, damn it," he privately complained, "and they won't admit it." He had no use for the professional foreign service officers in his command, and found it as difficult to work with them as they found it to work for him. "They haven't an idea about the

125

future of this area," he scoffed at the department, "and they won't accept any unless it comes from the sweet blue-shirted boys." After almost a year in the field he felt discouraged that he had so little to show for his efforts. In a fit of depression he typed out resignation letters to Acheson and to Leo Crowley, head of the Foreign Economic Administration, and sent them to Dorothy, who herself was working for the State Department, for her advice. She put the letters in her desk, and they went no further.[17]

In a sense, Landis had narrowed his vision solely to the Middle East and lacked a worldwide perspective. By contrast, the State Department's attitudes reflected concern for the broader war effort, the maintenance of the Grand Alliance, and preparations for the undoubtedly complicated postwar settlements, a vantage from which the Middle East appeared distant and obscure. So long as the British permitted American participation in the economic affairs of the region, State Department officials had no desire to disrupt existing political arrangements. But Landis' dealings on a daily basis with both British and Arab leaders convinced him that the situation was volatile and dangerous. The British, he decided, were determined to suppress Arab nationalism and to reestablish their domination over the region. It rankled him that the State Department chose to remain aloof in the interest of the alliance. "London is starting to get stiff," he commented, "and Washington is going soft."[18]

Nowhere did the British annoy him more than in their handling of Egypt's young king Farouk, for whom Landis came to develop great affection. The twenty-four-year-old monarch had first greeted the dour United States economic minister with sumptuous feasts and childish pranks. "Literally hundreds of retainers everywhere you turned," Landis described his first palace reception. "Eighteen courses to the meal. Trumpets, music—unbelievable but boring." Perhaps because Landis looked so uncomfortable in his formal regalia of dress suit, white tie, stiff collar, and red sash, Farouk had slipped behind him and poured a glass of champagne over his head. Not to be outdone, Landis waited for his opportunity and emptied his glass over the king. "There was dead silence, absolutely dead silence throughout the room," he shuddered. "I thought some big black guy with a scimitar would come in and really wreak vengeance on me." But the king took it as a grand joke and forgave him. Later that evening, Farouk pickpocketed Landis' car keys and hid his car. Afterwards, the king invited him to the royal estates for rounds of events, from early morning duck hunts to late evening luxurious dinners. Farouk came to like and trust James Landis.[19]

Late one night in April 1944 Farouk arrived unannounced at Landis' apartment, heavily guarded. The British had forced another prime minister upon him, and he wanted American assistance in taking a stand against

126

them. The young king reminded Landis of nothing more than a frightened law student seeking advice before the big exams. "I'm quite in sympathy with you," he replied, but he could promise nothing that would interfere with the Anglo-American alliance. Instead of leaving, Farouk stayed on long into the night, talking to Landis as a "father confessor" about his discouragements, his unhappy youth, and his thoughts of abdicating. "What can I do and why should these people rely on me?" Landis wrote to Dorothy after Farouk had left. "Why in hell should I have to carry this cross for something called the United States?"[20]

What was left of his tolerance for the British, after his evening with Farouk, evaporated with the brutal reoccupation of Greece. Liberated Greece was scheduled to come within Landis' sphere of responsibility as economic minister, and he had spent much time drafting recommendations with the aid of George Skouras, a Greek-American assigned to his staff. To counter British and Russian influence, Landis advised stationing American troops in Greece. It would be a "litmus test" for disengagement in all of Central Europe. But Roosevelt rejected the plan, stating flatly that "we have no business in the Balkans and the British have the Balkans."[21]

In April British forces suppressed a mutiny of Greek troops in Egypt. The following November and December British troops moved into Greece behind the fleeing Germans. Shortly afterwards fighting broke out between the British and antimonarchist resistance forces, whom Churchill called communists. Landis viewed them as democrats resisting a British-imposed king, and the slaughter dismayed him. By Christmas day 1944 Churchill had won a temporary truce, but Landis had had his fill of working with the British and notified Washington of his intention to resign. "Peace to me is a vision of free seas, free skies, free trade, and freedom in the development of ideas," he told the Royal Egyptian Society of Political Economy at that time. "It is not mercantilism, uneconomic and political subsidies, narrow nationalism, group preferences or the fascist conception of one race entitled to dominance over another."[22]

He regretted that events had thwarted his efforts "to build something that would outlast my stay," but believed he had made some impact. During his last trip back to Washington he convinced the State Department that rigid controls were no longer necessary for the Middle East Supply Centre. At his urging, Washington petitioned London to remove controls on all but a select list of commodities in short supply and to allow a resumption of normal trade agreements. Returning to Cairo via London, Landis negotiated the final agreement with the British. In his last press conference as economic minister, he emphasized that his mission had eliminated government procurement of consumer and industrial products, ended Lend-Lease aid and returned Middle Eastern imports to regular channels. It remained for American industry to take advantage of his opening the trade doors for them.[23]

His decision to leave the Middle East had been a complex matter. He had stuck to the post longer than he intended, strictly out of loyalty to FDR. But his mounting frustration, his distrust for the British, and his doubts about his personal future all dictated a return to the United States.[24]

At the start he had envisioned his Middle East assignment as a trial separation from Dorothy, to help them work out their feelings toward each other, and as a permanent separation from Stella. "The past is past," he said of his marriage. Stella remained in the crowded house on Q Street and spent her time managing a United Nations Service Center in the Capitol Park Hotel across from busy Union Station. There she directed some four hundred volunteers, who over a two-year span accommodated 1,500,000 military men and women who needed a place to stop, wash, and sleep over on their journeys through the capital. Although the job kept her more than busy day and night, she could not forget her personal problems. Stella pleaded with her husband to write and to show some sign of affection, once sending him a note with a single word in capitals: "WRITE." But all he could bring himself to send were postcards and letters to his daughters and an occasional message to Stella about family finances or other business.[25]

At the same time, Landis found that his separation from Dorothy hit him harder than he expected. He felt incredibly lonely, and the emotional drain reduced his capacity for work. "It seems as if I stepped off the end of the world and that nothing . . . exists anymore." True, Cairo offered a comfortable style of living. He shared a spacious apartment on the banks of the Nile with the diplomat Livingston Short. Three servants waited upon his demands. Next door, a country club offered golf, swimming, tennis, and riding. Diplomatic receptions and palace entertainments filled his evenings. Egypt's heat slowed down the tempo of his work and forced a leisurely four-hour lunch recess on him every afternoon. Yet, none of those comforts sustained him. If he read a story with the slightest sentiment, his eyes filled with tears. He could not sleep at night. He begged Dorothy for letters and cables and grew impatient over the three-week delay in correspondence from Washington. "You see," he explained, "I have nothing, absolutely nothing save the things of you I cherish. I live intentionally in a rough man's world where no confidences are exchanged, no sentiment betrayed."[26]

His continued isolation resulted in mounting paranoia. If the day's mail brought no letter from Dorothy, he worried that she had fallen ill, or worse, that she had stopped caring for him. He read intently between the lines of her letters and reacted with fits of jealousy and suspicion. Finally, when Dorothy could no longer tolerate his insinuations, she suggested that they break off their relationship. Her message horrified him. "Facts wrong, cable immediate, life death," he responded. He stopped working and took to bed for days. Agnes Maher, who had gone to great lengths to pretend she knew nothing of his affair, was forced to intervene. "Cable Jim immediately, effect devastating," she wired Dorothy. Hurriedly, a cablegram returned from Dorothy saying she was wrong and asking forgiveness. "Knees still weak but heart stout," he replied gratefully. "I have threatened suicide. I mean it when I say my life means nothing without you. But suicide today is out of the question. I shall live until I know definitely and absolutely that my cause is hopeless."[27]

The breakdown had been reminiscent of his physical and emotional collapse in England during World War I. On both occasions changes in his life had forced upon him personal decisions he was unwilling to face. Each time, he delayed making those decisions until they crashed down upon him. Earlier, it had been a rejection of his father's religion and career; now it was rejection of his wife and perhaps his career at Harvard. He found himself in a mental bind. No matter how desperately he loved Dorothy, he could not bring himself to ask Stella for a divorce. When he left for the Middle East, he had warned Stella only that "every probability" pointed to the fact that he would not return to her. He could not go any further.[28]

Dorothy's cable allowed him to resume his official duties in Cairo, but the crisis showed its effects. He grew more angry over bureaucratic problems and took out his frustrations on his staff, treating them more gruffly than usual. "I want to be alone, to brood, to swear at the world and the petty ambitions of people," he wrote. He escaped to "a lonely drink at the Auberge, a solitary drive to the Pyramids, a stroll beside the Nile." The lack of support from Washington, the prolonged absence from Dorothy, and the persistence of his indecisiveness plagued him. "I can't physically continue to take this punishment," read one of his daily letters to Dorothy, "and spiritually the unhappiness is beyond belief."[29]

Added to his burden were the heat, insects, and sickness of the Middle East, and a rising tide of violence that disturbed him. In November 1944 he narrowly escaped becoming a victim of that violence. One morning he had been conferrring with Lord Moyne, the resident British minister in the Middle East. When they broke for lunch, Moyne offered him a ride back to his apartment, but Landis had his car nearby and declined the offer. An hour later came the news that Zionist extremists from Palestine had ambushed and killed Moyne and his chauffeur. After the assassination the American Embassy in Cairo offered Landis a bodyguard, which he declined. He did agree to accept a pistol, but left it in a desk drawer in his office. The act of terrorism made no sense to Landis. "Considering our policy," he commented on American sympathy for an independent Jewish state, "it really seems more sensible for some Moslems to take a crack at us than for Jews to shoot the English." As he embarked for home, the Palestine question weighed heavily upon him.[30]

In January 1945, on his arrival back in Washington, Landis received his last assignment from the Skipper. Roosevelt was preparing for his Yalta trip and expected to pass through the Middle East on his return voyage. In the event that he met with Saudi Arabia's Ibn Saud, the President expected the Palestine issue to arise, and he asked Landis for a memorandum on a "possible rapprochement" on that subject. Until then Landis had carefully avoided taking a public stand, despite the efforts of Zionist friends to win his support. The two most influential men of his early life, Brandeis and Frankfurter, had been leaders in the American Zionist movement, but neither had much success in translating the "mystical emotion" of return to the Promised Land to their gentile students. In deference to their cause, Landis had at least sought to include Palestine representatives in nonpolitical agriculture and public health activities at the Supply Centre. But he worked far more closely with the British and Arabs. If the United States hoped to benefit from the Middle East's petroleum richness, he concluded, it would have to build good relations with such anti-Zionists as Ibn Saud.[31]

Landis wanted his report to relieve Roosevelt of any notion that he could reach a compromise with the Arab king. The controversy had a history far too long and bitter for the United States to intervene unless the President was prepared to make "some far-reaching proposals." Landis recommended that the United States oppose an independent Jewish state. "The political objective implicit in the Jewish State idea," he wrote, "will never be accepted by the Arab nations and is not consistent with the principles of the Atlantic Charter." Instead, a more limited concept of a "Jewish National Home" under Arab hegemony might prove feasible. Basically, he feared that "the economic absorptive capacity of Palestine has been grossly exaggerated" and the injection of the highly charged moral issue would severely disrupt budding Arab-American relations.[32]

As he prepared to return to Cambridge, after three years of wartime service, Landis made it clear he wanted no extended seclusion from public life. "I envy you on your trip to that area," he concluded the memorandum, "and only wish you had some need for someone to carry your seventeenth brief-case." A month later, after Roosevelt completed his journeys to Yalta and the Middle East, he invited Landis to the White House to hear of his meeting with Ibn Saud. In spite of Landis' warnings, Roosevelt had pressed the Saudi Arabian to admit more Jews to Palestine. Ibn Saud reacted exactly as Landis had predicted, and with such fervid conviction, Harry Hopkins observed, that he "made a great impression on the President that the Arabs meant business." Roosevelt emerged from the encounter a bit more respectful of Landis as a Middle East advisor.[33]

Landis had no premonition that the White House briefing would be his last meeting with Franklin D. Roosevelt. During their conversation, he could not help but notice that the President's color was gone, that he lacked the old *joie de vivre* characteristic of their many previous meetings. He simply thought that the President looked terribly tired. For twelve years James Landis had equated government service with working for Roosevelt. The President had used him, encouraged him, and inspired him. There had been fishing trips aboard the presidential yacht, and private conferences in the White House family quarters. Most importantly, the frequency of demands on his time and service made Landis feel that the President of the United States honestly needed and appreciated his talents. When Roosevelt died on April 12, 1945, Landis confessed that "in many ways his death has a closer feeling to me than that of my father's." He had lost an important touchstone in his life at a most crucial juncture.[34]

10 | The Discontented Dean

Harvard wanted Landis back badly. With the war churning to an end, the law school anticipated massive reconversion problems. Student enrollment, which had fallen from fourteen hundred down to eighty during the war, was expected to mushroom, with thousands of veterans wanting to complete their degrees as speedily as possible. Only ten law professors remained, and six of those were on part-time service to the government. The rest of the faculty was scattered about the globe, and the years of challenging war assignments had left more than a few of them disinclined to return to academic life. Housing shortages, budget deficits, teacher recruitment, and curriculum revision all awaited the dean. Members of his staff looked forward to his return and a resumption of "the excitement and stir that used to be in the office — the turning up of the unusual at any hour of the day (or night)." Landis was not as certain.[1]

Late in 1944 he heard rumors that Harvard President James B. Conant had "put the heat on" the Department of State to obtain his release from duty. Although Landis officially requested to leave the Middle East, he began having second thoughts about leaving so many issues unresolved. But Conant would accept no further delays and set January 1, 1945, as his deadline. As a final precaution, the law school announced Landis' resignation as Middle East minister six days before he made his own formal announcement.

Other Americans were traveling home, excited over the prospects of resuming their former lifestyles, but James Landis crossed the Atlantic with an anxious and agitated state of mind. He wanted to rejoin Dorothy, but in a year and a half he had made no headway in unraveling his tangled private life. Where should he go? What should he do? He had to convince Stella to file for divorce, but how would his Harvard colleagues react? Could he bring Dorothy to Cambridge as his wife? The scenario seemed impossible, and yet he could not conceive of an alternative.[2]

Divorce and a new start in life would require substantial funds, for alimony and child support among other items. Landis maintained that he had nothing, "in fact, less than nothing." He had always lived on his paycheck and had little in reserve to carry him through a period of unemployment. As a prominent lawyer, he could leave the law school and enter private practice. But he had never bothered to take a bar exam, and he remained skeptical of binding himself to full-time service for moneyed clients. In earlier years he might have sought another government post, but the recent frustrations of the Middle East had soured him on the bureaucracy. Temporarily, he toyed with the idea of entering business.[3]

A decade of association with businessmen convinced him that he could succeed in commercial enterprise. "I think I know quite a bit about running different types of business, and have some capacity for that sort of thing," he speculated while in the Middle East. "I'm a pretty fair 'trader' as my record here would demonstrate." He became intrigued with the business schemes of Dan Tyler Moore, Jr., an energetic fellow who had served on his staffs at the SEC and in the Middle East. Moore dreamed up a "Middle East Company" to tap Landis' expertise as a middleman between American manufacturers and Middle Eastern countries. A member of a prominent Cleveland family and brother-in-law of Drew Pearson, Moore had his own connections and made some early soundings of businessmen in 1944. He returned with positive responses. "There is something in Dan's idea," Landis confided to Dorothy.[4]

The Middle East Company promised "highly placed" agents in the field to watch over export-import trends, an arrangement that would have stationed Landis permanently in Cairo. If Dorothy agreed to join him there, they might escape the gossip and reaction that divorce and remarriage would surely stir in Cambridge and Washington. His plans, however, fell through, and once again Landis found the British at fault.[5]

It took little research to determine that British monetary policies would effectively bar American merchants from increasing their share of Middle Eastern trade. Since 1939, because of the need for large purchases of American goods, Great Britain had required all of its satellite states to turn in their American dollars. That policy converted the Middle East into an exclusively "Sterling bloc" and centralized United States trade in the region through London. The end of the war brought no indication that the British were ready to lift their dollar restrictions. Chances of American trade profits in the Middle East fell to a dismal low, and with them fell the prospects of the Middle East Company. Landis fumed over imperialistic and anti-free-trade policies and published a string of angry articles denouncing them, but he could not persuade the State Department to respond. "I'm afraid that I am a little cynical with regard to our policy which sacrifices legitimate enterprise of this character upon the altar of Anglo-American friendship," he commented. "We have paid a fearful price for that over the last half-century. We seem to be willing to continue to do so."[6]

Since the Middle East Company depended entirely upon Landis' reputation, he began to worry about risking so much on such a precarious venture. Dan Moore was a charming man with a "knack for getting people to do things," but Landis was not completely certain about the young man's business judgment. He also found himself growing "terribly tired" of the businessmen with whom he had to deal, and somewhat wistful over his academic career. "I have been trained to think and speculate," he said, "and not to wheedle and dicker." Although he agreed to serve as chairman of the board of the Middle East Company, his role would only be a subsidiary interest to his resumed duties as dean of the Harvard Law School.[7]

Initially, the decision to return to Harvard meant still another separation from Dorothy. She could not easily follow him to Cambridge without causing a scandal. His coming back to the United States would thus be harder on them than his absence in Cairo had been, for while they would be so much closer, they would have to maintain a pretense of distance. In January 1945 Landis left for Cambridge, with Stella remaining in Washington with the girls and Dorothy staying at her job in the State Department. For the next ten months he seized every opportunity to journey back to Washington on weekends to visit Dorothy, and in between he called her every night. His monthly telephone bills soon exceeded his Cambridge hotel bills. Stella generally knew of his trips to the capital only through third parties.[8]

For all of James Landis' adult life, Harvard had always provided him with a community, a place to come home to; now that was missing. When he stepped off the train, he was taken aback by the "essential ugliness of the place, covered as it is with a foot of dirty snow." The chilling weather made a harsh transition from the desert heat of Cairo. "And this is Cambridge in the wintertime —," concluded one of his verses, "Dreary beyond all measure."[9]

Like many others returning home from overseas, Landis found his old neighborhood unexpectedly provincial and cut off from the world that he had so recently experienced. His colleagues welcomed him back but asked all the wrong questions, about Stella and the children and when they would be rejoining him. "Does this place know anything else," he wondered, "nothing of adventure, of high beauty, of ecstacy such as which the great poets write . . . ? Cambridge was not built for those sorts of things."[10]

Living by himself in a small room at the Hotel Continental, he suffered acutely from loneliness. At least in Cairo there had been companions with whom to share meals and evenings. He had forgotten how central domesticity was to the community of scholars in Cambridge, and how much their entertaining was done in couples. He began to see how closely his past work had been tied to his concept of home. "My colleagues," he observed, "with rare exceptions think in the same terms. Most normal life runs in those channels — a job that is bearable, a wife, children, and a home and the fundamental comforts of life." While that pattern of existence had sustained him before, it was no longer enough.[11]

Always in the past Landis had avoided such fits of introspection and melancholia by throwing himself exclusively into his work. But his mounting personal crisis distracted him from administrative responsibilities. "The work thus far ceases to intrigue me," he puzzled. He could not rekindle his old enthusiasms nor brush up on the changes in law that had taken place during his absence. "There is no stir inside of me, not even enough to get initiated, and the tempo of things around here makes initiation an impossibility." He could only "fuss around" with the type of secondary problems he could handle mechanically. A mood of depression settled over him. "Sometimes I just go completely dead and nothing really rouses me out of that lethargy."[12]

He grew inward and began drinking heavily. His evenings were spent alone with a bottle of bourbon. When local civic leaders approached him with plans of resurrecting the old Plan E committee and running him for the City Council, he rebuffed their efforts.[13]

The specter of divorce, and all of its reverberations, paralyzed him. Painfully aware of his procrastination, he was helpless to do anything about it. He simply refused to make a firm decision, always hoping that given enough time a better alternative would develop. When Dorothy reminded him of the repeated postponements, he asked her to wait. "Time and the living of our lives," he promised, would solve their problems "without undue hurt to anyone." He set June 1945, when the first school term would be over, as the most reasonable date for confronting Stella with his final demand for a divorce.[14]

For those most intimately involved, the real tragedy was not Landis' divorce, one relative observed, but that he did it so badly. He could not make up his mind and "kept Stella on a string." Landis was haunted by guilt — for deserting his children, disappointing Stella, and rejecting the standards of his missionary parents. With anguish he realized that his wife continued to show "unutterably unselfish love" for him long after he had stopped loving her. She kept alive the myth of their marriage and refused to file for a divorce, although only she had the grounds to obtain a divorce in Massachusetts, based on her husband's desertion.[15]

Through a quirk of fate, Landis lost even the alternative of a Reno divorce. In June 1945 the United States Supreme Court upheld an adultery conviction of a North Carolina couple who married after divorcing their spouses in Nevada. "A man's fate often depends on far greater risks than he will estimate," wrote Mr. Justice Frankfurter for the majority. Although the North Carolina couple had believed themselves legally married, they were sentenced to prison because "mistaken notions about one's legal rights are not sufficient to bar prosecution for crime." The dean of the Harvard Law School certainly had no excuse at all. For the next three years Massachusetts' courts ruled against residents who obtained divorces out of state. Not until 1948, after it was too late for Landis, did the Supreme Court reverse itself and overturn the Massachusetts rulings.[16]

The June deadline Landis had set came and went without his persuading Stella to file for divorce. "I cannot conceivably tell you of the sense of loss that surrounds me day in and day out," he wrote to her ambiguously. "I am sorry to be so incapable of expressing anything." By placing the burden of the decision on Stella, he hoped to ease his own guilt, but his lack of resolve only encouraged Stella to hang on to the remaining shreds of their marriage. Nothing he tried seemed to work; he felt himself losing control of his life and verging on alcoholism. Finally, Landis sought psychiatric help. During the summer of 1945 he spent nine sessions with Donald MacPhearson, a Brookline psychiatrist, but without appreciable results.[17]

Years later, another psychiatrist, Dr. Lawrence C. Kolb, would diagnose Landis' problem as stemming from "an underlying sense of pathological guilt which drives him to excel as a means of obtaining a sense of satisfaction and acceptance by others to cover a deep seated insecurity and dependency." No matter how often he asserted his independence, Landis always turned to stronger figures for support. Now those men were gone. FDR had died, and Felix Frankfurter sat aloofly on the Supreme Court. Whatever dependency he had upon his own family was also stripped away. Landis was left with an overwhelming sense of failure, in his mission to the Middle East, in the lack of challenge from the law school, and in the collapse of his marriage, all of which contradicted inbred ideals of excellence and achievement. The outward symbol of his inner crisis, the psychiatrist later noted, was "his long-standing procrastination which contains an almost magical wish to avoid unpleasantness by not confronting others and frankly discussing unpleasant changes."[18]

As James Landis faltered, Stella took the initiative. During the summer of 1945 she had moved from Washington to their house in Newbury,

Massachusetts. Landis loved that house and its grounds more than any other place in the world because of its beauty and "because in no other place have I ever really worked the soil." Returning from Cairo, he drew pride in seeing the healthy growth of the trees and shrubs he had planted there. In spite of his attachment, he gave it all to Stella. "The place is hers, and so I have nothing to say." As a result, he somehow felt she would stay there with the children. But when autumn came, he was caught totally off guard when Stella sent the two girls to enroll in school in Cambridge. Suddenly they were moving into an adjoining room at his hotel. Ann and Ellen were teen-agers, quite different from the little girls he remembered. For some time he had worried that his estrangement from Stella would cost him his daughters' affection, but he was pleased by the evenings they now spent together. "I like them quite a bit and though we talk very little when we are together they seem to enjoy themselves," he reported to Dorothy. "It's a curious habit in my family to show no outward signs of affection to each other."[19]

No sooner had he adjusted to the presence of his children than Stella moved to Cambridge to join them. Resignedly, Landis decided he had only once choice of action, "and that is to move in with her to avoid open scandal, trust that the experiment will demonstrate its utter futility to Stella, and hope that somehow that when this shall have sufficiently broken all three of us, there will be enough left for Dorothy and me to build on." At least with the propriety of his household reestablished, he was able to persuade Dorothy to move back to Massachusetts and to rejoin him at the law school as his secretary.[20]

Setting up house again proved a difficult and heartbreaking chore. The large and drafty house on Highland Street that the family rented was so hard to heat that not even its two furnaces could combat the Cambridge winter, and it only added to their discomfort. The girls sensed that something was terribly wrong. Both their parents were drinking too much. Their father stayed away at the office, avoided meals at home, and shut himself up gruffly in his study for hours on end. Stella, too, found the experience of living together again more destructive than she had imagined. "Can't you look at me without hating me so?" she asked one day. Landis was shocked when he realized she was right. "For so long I haven't cared. I wanted to be kind," he wrote. "But no more." In December Stella left for a month-long visit to her childhood home in Mississippi. When she returned, Landis packed his bags and moved to the Harvard Club. They never lived together again.[21]

Meanwhile, with Dorothy back at her desk in his office, Landis tried to focus his attention once more on the law school. During that period he created the Harvard Law School Forum to foster wider discussion of contemporary world problems. His talent hunts added a number of attractive scholars to the faculty, including Archibald Cox. He tackled the multitude of veterans' problems and appointed a faculty committee to modernize the curriculum. "We have entered a period of more government management of our lives," he challenged them. "Some of the wartime controls will be liquidated; some of them won't. We must train men to handle the combination of law and government. We can't go on teaching law in the old-fashioned way." New students at the school found the dean extraordinarily eloquent and impressive. When he rose to welcome the incoming class, his jutting jaw, mannerisms, and long cigarette holder hauntingly reminded them of the late President Roosevelt.[22]

No matter how fervid his activities, it was a frustrating time for the dean. The continued absence of so many faculty members and the inability to predict when the government would release them from service stymied plans for the new curriculum. Pressures from the vast number of veterans applying to the school under the new GI Bill eroded the standards he had tried to set. To accommodate the veterans, the law school agreed to admit anyone with one year of military service and the equivalent of a college degree. A new schedule of three fifteen-week terms a year would enable them to complete all course work in a little over two years, just the opposite of Landis' proposals for extending and expanding legal study. His school was becoming an assembly line. The dean himself had to abandon his upper level administrative and labor law classes to help shoulder the first-year load. He went back to teaching contracts, where he had started twenty years earlier. The three-term schedule, he complained, was breaking his back and leaving him "too busy even to think."[23]

Some of Landis' friends feared that the law school was destroying him. Tommy Corcoran hunted for a new government post for Landis and found one, with the help of another Harvard classmate, Assistant Secretary of the Navy for Air John L. Sullivan. The chairman of the Civil Aeronautics Board had notified President Truman that he planned to resign. Corcoran and Sullivan spread the word in Washington that James M. Landis might be available. He was the nation's leading expert on federal regulation, they said, and had recently pioneered a new course in aviation law. In fact, the aviation law class was the only one on his schedule that recaptured his old flair and concentration. Typically, he had known next to nothing about the subject at the time he decided to master it. In preparing his class material he had to organize countless treaties and air conventions, state, national, and internaional laws, and the absence of laws, into some logical pattern. The challenge intrigued him so that he began planning a casebook on the subject. When President Truman called to offer him the CAB chairmanship, however, Landis the educator was again lured by the chance of becoming a shaper of policy and events. In April 1946 he accepted the appointment, to become effective that June.[24]

His planned departure from Cambridge also enabled him to convince Stella that their separation was irreconcilable. His action scandalized the community, for divorce within the proper atmosphere of Cambridge in the 1940s was still a shocking and socially unacceptable act. Almost all of his friends, law school colleagues, and even his own relatives sided with Stella. As the wife of the dean, she had been industrious, popular, and widely admired for her "gentle dignity and poise with a warmth and love of people." Landis' behavior seemed cruel and indefensible. Felix Frankfurter was especially outraged. His sympathies went entirely to Stella, and he expressed himself greatly pleased that Landis was stepping down as dean. "The evidence has been conclusive for me for some time that he was not fit for the headship of the school," Frankfurter wrote to Grenville Clark. Other colleagues followed Frankfurter in abruptly terminating their relationships with the wayward dean.[25]

Nor would Harvard tolerate another leave of absence. President Conant recommended that he resign as dean, although he could still retain his professorship. Landis resigned both posts. He fully realized that he could not bring Dorothy back to the lions' den as his wife. His departure from Harvard was "final and in sorrow."[26]

For his successor as dean, Harvard chose Professor Erwin N. Griswold, whose solidness stood in marked contrast to Landis' erratic behavior.[27] The interregnum was difficult for both men. Landis avoided the school as much as possible and came in only to teach his classes and sign the necessary documents. Griswold found the school's administration in shambles. With 1,400 students enrolled in the coming summer term, less than half of the teachers needed to cover their classes had been acquired. Weeks before he was scheduled to assume control, Griswold was recruiting summer school teachers and otherwise acting as de facto dean.[28]

One year later, Stella Landis filed for divorce on grounds of desertion. In October 1947 she won her suit and took custody of the children. For James Landis, the divorce and separation from Harvard meant a complete break with his past. Symbolically, he left his law books in Massachusetts and never returned to claim them. "You don't have to apologize to your world," he wrote to Stella. "I have to find a world that I don't have to apologize to."[29]

11 | Fair Deal Politics and Regulation

President Harry S. Truman considered it a "ten strike" when Dean Landis consented to join his administration as chairman of the Civil Aeronautics Board. Not only was Landis a talented administrator and recognized authority of federal regulation, but he had been a prominent New Dealer and confidant to FDR—important assets at the time when many liberals felt alienated from Roosevelt's successor. Landis took equal pleasure from the appointment. In June 1946 he resigned as dean of the Harvard Law School and came to Washington, with Dorothy Brown as his executive secretary and Stanley Gewirtz as his counsel and chief lieutenant. Remembering his satisfying experiences with the regulatory commissions in the 1930s, Landis anticipated the post as a vehicle for replacing unpleasant memories of his recent personal problems with a renewed sense of public mission. Unfortunately, the optimism of both men was grievously misplaced. In less than two years Truman would dismiss Landis from office.[1]

Washington had changed, but Landis returned too filled with enthusiasm for his new job to notice the differences. He saw only that the Civil Aeronautics Board was an ailing agency, its bureaucratic rigidity impeding growth and stifling innovation in the aviation industry. As he prepared a program of reform, his activities were controversial but his goals coincided with those of the administration. Only slowly did he discern a different atmosphere in the capital or feel any estrangement from the White House. The Truman administration, with unsteady public support and an uncertain election looming in 1948, proved more susceptible to industry influence and more given to political interference in the regulatory commissions than Landis suspected. Despite his most strenuous efforts, the combination of restrictive budgets, a distracted President, an inscrutable White House staff, a powerful airline lobby, and a politically hostile Congress frustrated Landis' programs and set the stage for his downfall.[2]

Before Landis' appointment as chairman, the CAB lacked strong leadership and a sense of direction. The board sat on years of backlogged cases while the aviation industry underwent unprecedented expansion. It pampered the larger airlines, ignored smaller lines, and created routes in a piecemeal fashion without sufficient regard for a coherent national air network. Growing public disenchantment with the airlines further reflected the CAB's poor performance. In one of the more irritating cases, a Texas businessman visiting Washington had to sign a month-long waiting list for a return flight to Dallas on American Airlines. At the same time, Washington newspapers were running American's advertisements for "A Flagship Every Day to London." Upon investigating, the businessman discovered he could fly overseas the very next day. Braniff Airways had long before petitioned to compete with American for the Washington-to-Dallas market, but the CAB had not yet reached a decision.[3]

Landis came to the CAB determined to reform its bureaucratic machinery and to clarify its economic goals. He wanted to accelerate procedures and cut workloads to give board members enough time to plan a new national route structure systematically. He also hoped to instill in the board a new respect for the values of competition, although he realized that the board was laboring under a congressional mandate to limit entry of new airlines into the field. Landis insisted that such protection was not "for the selfish benefit of the carriers involved" but for the public's benefit, through industry stability, reduced government subsidies, and maintenance of high safety standards. The CAB, he argued, must stimulate "intelligent and regulated competition" to improve services and techniques in air travel. His defense of competition and distaste for air cartels and monopolies echoed his earlier training under Justice Brandeis. In 1946 Landis believed those principles more vital than ever, but his message was one that the major airlines had no desire to hear.[4]

Institutional barriers made the tasks the new chairman set all the more difficult. His post carried little authority, allowing him to preside over meetings and act as the board's spokesman but denying him any control over appointments or delegation of duties. His colleagues were an unsympathetic and undistinguished lot: Oswald Ryan, former Republican congressman from Indiana, a staunch defender of the larger airlines; Harllee Branch, a Georgia newspaper editor who served as Postmaster General Jim Farley's assistant in charge of airmail; Colonel Clarence Young, once assistant secretary of commerce for aeronautics in the Hoover administration and a former official of Pan American Airways; and Josh Lee, one-time Democratic senator from Oklahoma who billed himself on the lecture circuit as a "rural philosopher and teller of tall tales." Only through the force of Landis' arguments and his capacity for mastering complicated technical data could he win a majority of the board's support. On a great many issues, however, the chairman voted in the minority.[5]

Structurally, the CAB dissatisfied Landis because of its statutory ties to the Commerce Department, which fostered unclear lines of authority and infringed upon the board's independent status. In 1938 Congress had created an independent Civil Aeronautics Authority composed of an administrator, a five-member quasi-judicial panel, and an Air Safety Board—a complex arrangement which had resulted from years of political struggle among Congress, the President, and the airlines. Two years later Franklin Roosevelt used his new executive reorganization powers to reshuffle the agency. He created a Civil Aeronautics Administration as a bureau of the Commerce Department to handle all executive functions, and merged the judicial panel and safety board into the Civilian Aeronautics Board (leaving considerable confusion over the exact boundaries of the two aviation agencies). The CAB regulated scheduled air carriers, supervised passenger and cargo rates, fixed mail payments, authorized routes, set safety standards, and investigated accidents. The Civil Aeronautics Administration operated control towers and other navigational facilities, promoted airport development, and enforced all CAB regulations. Under secretaries Henry Wallace and W. Averell Harriman, both presidential aspirants, the Commerce Department looked enviously on the policy-making powers of the CAB. Landis and his staff suspected Harriman of mistaking his "housekeeping responsibilities" for the CAB, which was physically housed in the mammoth Commerce building, for actual control over the agency.[6]

The board's secretary informed Landis that the Commerce Department acted as a channel of communications to the Budget Bureau, but that Commerce's assistance had been "so negligible as to be impossible of measurement." Ignoring tradition, Landis did not seek help from the Commerce Department. As one of his first acts as chairman, he communicated directly with the budget director and won a dramatic increase in funding for the CAB.[7]

An even more important maneuver for sidestepping the Commerce Department was Landis' effort to build direct contacts with the White House. By tapping his personal prestige, Landis hoped to overcome a peculiar quirk in the federal aviation laws: the President's authority to review all CAB decisions on overseas routes. Although he reluctantly conceded the national security justifications of such a unique executive power over an independent board, Landis worried that political rather than diplomatic considerations more often colored Truman's decisions. In the 1946 case of a Seattle-to-Honolulu air route, the White House had overridden a CAB certification for Northwest Airlines, claiming the route not economical enough to sustain profitable service. Before the CAB had a chance to revise its opinion, the White House reversed itself and approved the Northwest certification. Pan American Airways then protested, and a few weeks later the White House ordered certificates for both airlines on a route it originally rejected as too thin to support even one line. Such precedents, Landis thought, would shift industry attention from CAB hearing rooms to White House anterooms, where too many sympathetic listeners were available.[8]

To warn the President in advance of any airline lobbying pressures, Landis carried the most controversial CAB decisions to the Oval Office in person. But he found the atmosphere there startlingly different. No longer did a jovial Roosevelt wave him in, call him Jim, and gossip freely about other administrators. Behind the President's desk stood Harry Truman, deferentially greeting him as "Dean," and crisply inquiring about his business. A scheduled fifteen-minute interview with Truman was generally over in ten; and although more to the point than a meeting with Roosevelt, it was hardly as satisfying.[9]

In all of his dealings with Truman, Landis could never get over the feeling that the new President was a "small, small man" who lacked Roosevelt's aura of personal and political magnetism. The CAB chairman felt no inspiration from the chief executive and had to resort to gimmicks to catch Truman's attention. On his first trip to see the President he carried with him a large and colorful map illustrating the specific routes involved in a recent CAB decision. At the end of their meeting, Truman admired the map and asked to keep it. Landis cheerfully agreed, since he wanted the President to remember the case exactly as he had explained it. For his next visit he brought an even more elaborate map. "I had the seas colored blue, and dolphins and all that flying around, just like an old medieval chart — beautiful," he recalled. "I used that technique all the time."[10]

If Landis found it impossible to establish the same intimacy with Truman as he had enjoyed with FDR, at least he felt assured of the new President's confidence. Truman acknowledged his talents as a skilled if unorthodox administrator by designating him as his special representative to negotiate several complex international air treaties. The treaties reflected postwar commercial rivalries between nations in a world that aviation had made dramatically smaller. A prime stumbling block to negotiation was America's commitment to the "Fifth Freedom" of the skies: the ability of one nation's airlines to take on passengers in a second nation and to carry them to a third. United States airlines held that principle necessary for round-the-world coverage and Caribbean and South American service. Other nations were leery of American air superiority and preferred a system of dividing equally the passengers, cargo, and flights passing between two nations. Landis proclaimed himself firmly opposed to such efforts to "cartelize air traffic" as he flew to Rio de Janeiro to negotiate the United States-Brazilian air transport agreement in August 1946.[11]

Pan American Airways dominated Brazilian air traffic because of both its prewar pioneering and the collapse of German and Italian competition. In 1946 the CAB wanted to add Braniff Airlines as a competitor, much to the displeasure of both Pan American and the Brazilian government. Pan American also faced modernization problems. To accommodate seaplanes, the company's traditional routes had run along the Brazilian coast. Pan American hoped to retain those routes, but it also needed more direct inland paths for its newer aircraft. The Brazilians planned to terminate the sea routes and to restrict inland flights to a maximum of three a week. After a protracted stalemate, Landis decided to strike a compromise by unilaterally dropping United States demands for the obsolete sea routes in return for unrestricted overland flight, his prime objective. At the Department of State, surprised officials hurriedly contacted Pan American's president, Juan Trippe, who registered his disapproval. Pan American had substantial pride and money invested in the sea routes, and Trippe further emphasized the "complicated relationship of Pan American to the development by the United States of other airfields along this route." Nevertheless, Landis intended to sign the inland agreement, and the State Department, after some hesitation, gave its permission. Pan American, Landis noted, remained "extremely annoyed" over the deal.[12]

Seven months after settling the Brazilian pact, Landis flew to Argentina, where he faced even more obstinate negotiators. Arriving in Buenos Aires, he found the Argentine negotiating panel intractably dedicated to cartelization of air traffic as the only means of protecting their fledgling aviation industry against overwhelming American competition. Getting nowhere in the formal meetings, Landis consulted privately with Alberto Dodero, a powerful Argentine industrialist and close friend of President Juan Perón. On April 30, 1947, Perón invited Landis and United States Ambassador George Messersmith to his office, where he made it clear he desired an air transport agreement with the United States. "Well, I'm ready to meet any time with your people to see if it can't be smoothed out," Landis replied. "Can you meet now?" Perón asked. That afternoon the two delegations began a fourteen-hour session, deliberating continuously until early the next morning.[13]

Near midnight, with the Argentine delegates still demanding some form of cartelization and the Americans demanding unrestricted competition between each nation's designated airlines, Landis received an Associated

Press dispatch stating that Perón already had announced the signing of the pact. When the Argentine director of civil aviation launched into another discourse on his theories of divided traffic, Landis flew into a calculated rage. Gathering his papers he started to walk out of the chamber, feigning disgust. On the Argentine side of the table, a foreign ministry official slipped a note to the aviation director, who gestured disparagingly and abandoned his hard-line stance. Landis resumed his seat and at 8:30 a.m. the next morning signed an agreement largely embodying the American demands. He returned to Washington delighted with his triumph, although continued distrust and hostility between the United States and Juan Perón prevented his treaty from ever taking effect. The two nations failed to agree on any further routes or division of passengers and their airlines continued to operate under the Argentine system of unilateral permits.[14]

Landis' unorthodoxy and independence in international negotiations disturbed the Department of State and put him perpetually at loggerheads with the nation's leading overseas airline, Pan American. His feud with that airline reached its peak during the debate over Pan American's plan to monopolize all United States overseas air transportation. Before the war, Pan American had initiated transoceanic flying without any domestic competition. Then other American airlines gained experience transporting military passengers and cargo overseas and petitioned to challenge Pan American's hegemony. In response, Pan American proposed legislation to combine all United States overseas flights into a single "flag carrier." But in 1944, when Senator Pat McCarran introduced the measure, it evoked little support among the other airlines or in the Democratic Congress.[15]

As the war ended, the Civil Aeronautics Board granted certificates to Trans World Airlines and American Overseas Airlines for Atlantic routes, sent Northwest Air Lines across the Pacific, and Braniff into Latin America. By 1947 the CAB had authorized four times the mileage flown in 1939. Pan American still flew more than twice the combined mileage of all its competitors, but, finding its advantage insufficient, Pan Am resumed its campaign for a single company serving the nation as its "chosen instrument." If the new Republican Congress approved the monopoly, Juan Trippe promised, Pan American would abolish itself for "patriotic interests," although it would hold by far the largest share of the "chosen instrument's" stock. Britain, France, and other European nations had already nationalized their lines, and Trippe raised the specter of imminent airline competition from the Russians. In the first six months of 1946, he added, American lines carried ninety-four percent of all transatlantic passengers, while in the second six months they carried only seventy-seven percent.[16]

An intense congressional fight raged over the bill. Every airline opposed it expect for Pan American and United, which had no overseas routes.

Howard Hughes, then the major force behind TWA, complained that Maine's Senator Owen Brewster had tried to intimidate him into supporting the "chosen instrument." Other angry charges filled the newspapers. As CAB chairman, Landis appeared before Congress to testify that of the seventy-seven percent of transatlantic passengers American lines carried, more than half were citizens of other nations who declined to fly on their own governments' nationalized airlines. He looked upon British, Russian, and other lines as "infinitely inferior" to American service and expressed only the fear that "we won't get effective foreign competition." Landis believed that no single management, "however able, can have all the ideas and hunches that are needed in our international air effort." In addition, he warned that if the "chosen instrument" went into effect and failed, it would destroy any chance of restoring competitive enterprise in the field. "The only way would be a government controlled and government owned international air transportation system—the path to socialism."[17]

In his stand, Landis could count on complete support from the Truman administration. Truman's special assistant for air affairs, Edward Locke, Jr., endorsed Landis' position. The President's Air Coordinating Committee went on record against the "chosen instrument" and in favor of "regulated limited competition." Under Secretary of State Dean Acheson testified that the bill would "substantially affect our foreign relations," since other nations would interpret a single flag carrier as " 'imperialist' activities." With such solid administration opposition, the bill died; but for his effective campaigning Landis made an unforgiving enemy in Pan American.[18]

Competitive and anticompetitive movements in domestic aviation stirred equally heated debates. The postwar aviation field possessed airline executives "as colorful and as ambitious as any that our railroad history developed," Landis observed. Competition between the major lines was less among systems than among the personalities of men such as Juan Trippe, Howard Hughes, C. R. Smith, and Eddie Rickenbacker. United in the Air Transport Association, but varying in size and financial stability, the larger airlines were suspicious rivals. Challenging them were the smaller airlines specializing in charter and air cargo flights. Also looking to the CAB for protection were the aviation unions and the passengers who flew the lines. Together they made a divided and disruptive constituency for the regulatory board.[19]

Again, as economic difficulties mounted, industry demands for reduced competition and increased government subsidy ran into Landis' opposition. Long before the victories over Germany and Japan, the airlines had predicted a prosperous postwar future. They petitioned for new routes and ordered new equipment to meet the expected increase in public demand.

But when ticket sales multiplied, so did operating expenses. New equipment required heavier capital investment. Pilots struck for higher wages. Increased traffic resulted in increased accidents. As the long-awaited postwar era dawned, the airlines found themselves operating in the red. For the first six months of 1946 they suffered a combined loss of $1,634,000, compared with profits of $16,348,000 for the same six months a year earlier.[20]

The major airlines petitioned the CAB to relieve their financial burdens. They were the eighteen "grandfather" lines, which had been in scheduled operation before the CAB came into existence in 1938. Since then, they had been able to count on the board for protection against new carriers, extension of their own route patterns, and generous boosts in airmail payments to subsidize their operating deficits. As usual, they had no trouble finding champions on the CAB. In light of the downward financial trend, Commissioner Harllee Branch urged fellow board members to reconsider all pending cases that might authorize competition on established routes. Chairman Landis dissented. Although he agreed that the industry had entered "one of the gloomier periods" of its history, he still believed that increased competition was the key to stimulating industry development and reducing airline dependence on subsidies. "Aviation will not grow as private enterprise," he said, "unless, as Mr. Justice Brandeis taught me long ago, forces of competition are given full play and unless opportunities are created for the infusion of new men, like the returning G.I.'s with new ideas."[21]

In defending the influx of veterans into postwar aviation, Landis touched on the most highly charged, emotional issue then facing the board. Thousands of aviation-trained veterans, thrilled by the experience of flying and faced with bleak job markets, were coming home with dreams of building their own airlines. In 1945 and 1946, with the help of veterans' loans and Army surplus planes, 2,700 of them started independent ventures. Often they owned only a single plane, and pilots frequently had to pass the hat among their passengers to pay for refueling, but public sympathy went out to these former war heroes. Few had sufficient capital to warrant applying for a CAB certificated route, but they took advantage of a loophole in the law that permitted uncertified charter flights. Almost immediately, the grandfather lines protested that the "tramp ships of the air" were in reality scheduling "charter" flights for regular routes and departure times.[22]

In anticipation of a boom in nonscheduled flights, the CAB had launched an investigation and in June 1946 announced the findings of its two-year study. The report bluntly charged several veterans' airlines with violation of the Civil Aeronautics Act for operating scheduled flights, restricted all nonscheduled trips to a limit of ten per month between the same two destinations, and ordered all uncertificated airlines to register with the board. Resentment spread through the veteran-operated lines, and one "nonsked," as they were called, voiced their bitterness: "Well, the government sold us the airlines, had another government agency help us finance them and then had still another regulate us out of business."[23]

Reviewing the regulations, Landis frowned on their anticompetitive tendencies. Primary data for the report, he objected, was more than two years old and therefore obsolete in the fast-moving aviation industry. Nor did the report accurately reflect the "nonskeds' " role in air cargo. The grandfather lines still carried cargo in the holds of passenger planes as a decidedly secondary source of income. The nonscheduled operators, mostly cargo pilots during the war, concentrated on air freight and, for the first time, made air shipments economical and accessible enough for small businesses. Landis saw a profitable future for air cargo, but he believed its development would require full-time attention, far more concern than the grandfather lines were giving it. He announced his opposition to any regulations that might "kill or stifle the type of ingenuity which exists in the country and which can do a tremendous job in developing the imagination and benefits of air cargo transportation."[24]

He persuaded his colleagues to reevaluate nonscheduled operations and try to establish more sensitive regulatory policies. In June 1947, after another year of study, the board revised its regulations and certified all "nonsked" airlines, while concentrating only on the larger fifteen percent which controlled ninety percent of the nonscheduled traffic. The CAB allowed the larger lines to conduct scheduled cargo service, subject to a greater degree of regulation. Relaxing controls on the smaller lines, the board assumed they would fly, provide competition, and then merge or die. Landis had no desire to perpetuate any set number of airlines. He wished only to give the industry enough free play to allow its most efficient and economic units to prove themselves. Competition from the cargo lines would spur the grandfather lines to upgrade their own services, which "would drive the irregulars to the wall and . . . bankruptcies would relieve us of a substantial portion of the burden of enforcement." In the meantime, the public would enjoy lower freight rates resulting from the rivalry of scheduled and nonscheduled lines.[25]

Within the CAB, Landis generally defended the "nonskeds" but suffered no romantic illusions about them. The same "nonskeds" clamoring for the unrestricted ability to serve the public's needs were evasive on the question of continuing service of those needs. "Thus many of them seem to skim the cream of peak traffic potentials which may exist between points for limited periods of time," Landis charged, "while avoiding the burden of providing a service upon which the public can rely between the same points when the travel market appears less lucrative." He also worried about the safety of nonscheduled operations. Granted the competence of their pilots, the Army surplus planes were growing older and the small airlines lacked the funds for proper repair and replacement. He would accept no excuse for a "nonsked" operating below minimum safety requirements. "Our duty was to enforce safety whatever its costs," he maintained, even if those costs drove some smaller lines out of business.[26]

Landis' stand on the "nonskeds" was not hypocritical. He sincerely sought to evaluate all sides in the industry's debates and weigh their values and drawbacks. He never acted automatically against big business or in favor of small business. Nor did he ever hesitate to experiment. When the board rejected steamship lines' requests to examine combined air-sea service, Landis dissented. Without any fixed ideas on the subject, he could see no harm in at least studying the possibility. Again, when the board placed restrictions on short-haul "feeder-line" services, considering their profitability dubious, he recommended lifting the restrictions to "give management all the flexibility in operations that it needs" to prove its own profitability.[27]

Even on the questions of mergers, Landis remained undogmatic. Although he vehemently opposed mergers of strong lines, as in the "chosen instrument" case, or strong lines absorbing weaker ones, he considered mergers of the weaker lines to be entirely practical solutions. "Very often, just like in algebra, a minus and a minus becomes a plus," he explained. Looking over the eighteen grandfather lines, he singled out six of them as weak enough to warrant mergers: Colonial, Northeast, Capitol, Mid-Continent, Chicago and Southern, and National. Then he ordered financial studies of those lines, studies which he justified on the grounds that all received government subsidies. The CAB's infuriatingly slow machinery stalled the investigations and completed none during his tenure as chairman, but the eventual merger and disappearance of those lines remained a measure of his prescience. For raising the issue of mergers and seeming to take a dual stance, however, Landis confused many of the grandfather lines, who thereafter branded him as arbitrary and inconsistent.[28]

For the grandfather lines, Landis' open-mindedness and independence meant unpredictability, especially on such pressing issues as the continuation of government subsidies, then averaging forty-five million dollars a year. Since the 1920s the grandfather lines had depended on the beneficence of federal airmail payments. In 1946, when the scheduled lines requested hikes in the mail rates, the "nonskeds" protested that the CAB blocked them from bidding for mail contracts. They further charged that the government was paying exorbitant mail fees in order to underwrite the grandfather lines' operating losses. Landis sympathized with their complaints and held no brief for any airline unable "to pay its own way," but he despaired that the understaffed CAB could ever manage to segregate subsidies from airmail costs. On the other hand, he did object to continuing airmail payments for unprofitable routes. In March 1947 he dissented from a board decision on flights between New Orleans and Havana, saying, "I cannot be a party to inaction that continues the obligation of subsidy in behalf of Chicago and Southern, and that seeks to palliate by a temporary mail rate a situation where merger may be the only remedy." He went so far as to suggest that the CAB adopt the unprecedented move of revoking the airline's certification for its yet unflown routes to San Juan and Caracas, to save future subsidy payments.[29]

A tragic series of plane crashes triggered the final conflict between the CAB chairman and the grandfather lines. On Memorial Day weekend, 1947, a United DC-4 failed to lift off at LaGuardia Airport in New York, crashed through a barrier and across a busy highway into an embankment, where it burst into flames, leaving thirty-eight dead and ten others seriously injured. The next day the crash of an Eastern Air Lines DC-4 into a wooded area near Port Deposit, Maryland, killed all fifty-three aboard. Two weeks later, while Landis was at LaGuardia field investigating the first accident, he received word that a Capitol Airlines DC-4 had flown into the Blue Ridge Mountains, killing its fifty passengers and crew. The White House summoned him to an emergency meeting and the following day Truman appointed him to head a special board of inquiry. Noting Landis' multiple roles, *Aviation Week* dubbed him "the most important man in commercial aviation, the spearhead of the White House campaign."[30]

Instead of limiting his inquiry to the three most recent crashes, Landis insisted upon a full-scale investigation of all airline safety measures. In public hearings he showed open disdain for industry spokesmen and the "slide-rule engineering calculations" upon which they argued. "As I listened to the testimony, that plane should have gotten off," he remarked of the LaGuardia crash. "I got up thinking the accident hadn't occurred. But it had and that is what worries me." The airlines usually blamed major crashes on pilot error, an extremely difficult charge to disprove. In his examination of the LaGuardia accident, however, Landis discovered that the airlines and the Civil Aeronautics Administration had never set any optimum weight and temperature scales. The United plane that failed to take off had been dangerously overloaded for the weather conditions of the day. Rather than wait for months to release his complete report, Landis obtained permission from Presidential Assistant John R. Steelman immediately to announce his findings, which called for longer runways and standardized weight levels. Other interim reports followed regularly over the next few months. They called on Congress to restore budget cuts to federal aviation agencies, on the CAA to set higher flight patterns over mountainous regions, on the airlines to install new radar devices and to provide better working conditions for pilots, including higher salaries and retirement benefits.[31]

In advancing such innovations as the radar device, Landis showed unusual daring for a regulatory commissioner. Most of his colleagues claimed lack of technical knowledge and shied away from recommending major technical changes. Landis was a lawyer, and an aeronautics layman, but he had become intrigued with a "terrain proximity indicator" developed by the Hughes Tool Company. He ordered a test of the equipment on a Constellation which deliberately flew toward the Blue Ridge. When the radar correctly signaled the approaching mountains, Landis was convinced. His third interim report unqualifiedly urged the CAA to order installation of the instrument on all planes. Estimates of the projected costs boggled airline leaders, who protested that the indicator frequently broke down and was therefore untrustworthy. For the time being, the device proved unsuccessful. Only after years of further experimentation did an improved version become standard equipment on larger planes. In the meantime, Landis won recognition for his willingness to experiment with new methods of safety precautions.[32]

Loudest praise came from the pilots. They appreciated the CAB chairman's refusal to blame all accidents on "pilot error," and applauded his recommendations for better working conditions. "Unlike his predecessor and many others in government agencies," said Air Line Pilots Association President David Behncke, "he has shown a refreshing preference for firsthand information and down-to-earth realism over bureaucratic paperwork and flimsy theories." The only member of the board of inquiry to dissent from its final report was retired General Milton Arnold, representative of the Air Transport Association (the grandfather lines' trade association). "I cannot be party to opinions and recommendations concerning avaiation economic problems which have been presented to the Board under a 'cloak of safety,' " Arnold complained. To his mind, the inquiry had strayed into far too many irrelevant areas.[33]

The safety investigation completed the grandfather lines' alienation from Landis. He had sided with the pilots and his reports, if implemented, would cost the lines millions of dollars. Furthermore, they could not be sure if he would support increased subsidy payments to cover the extra costs. The grandfather lines pictured Landis as a "brilliant but dominant" man who generally voted in the minority on the board. But if he could influence the selection of new appointees, he might someday control the CAB's decisions. The airlines' financial woes bore heavily on their growing resentment of Landis. In 1947 the scheduled lines suffered a net loss of twenty million dollars. Passenger and cargo traffic reached new heights, but costs and accidents wiped out profits. "There is too much competition," complained

Eddie Rickenbacker of Eastern Air Lines. "We're all losing money and in trouble." Landis blamed their problems on over-expansion and poor management. The airlines blamed Landis for misrepresenting their case before Congress and the public. As the expiration of his first term on December 31, 1947, drew nearer, the airlines launched a behind-the-scenes lobbying campaign to remove him from office.[34]

With only a month remaining in his term, Landis had received no official word from the White House concerning his reappointment, other than general indications that the President was pleased with his work and wanted him to stay on the job. When stories to the contrary surfaced in the trade journals, Landis called his old friends on Capitol Hill, House Democratic leader Sam Rayburn and Senate Democratic leader Alben Barkley, to have them check on the rumors. Rayburn called back shortly and assured him: "There's no use worrying about the thing. The President's very happy that you will continue."[35]

Throughout December the stories persisted. *Aviation Week* reported a "Hate Landis Campaign" emanating from the grandfather lines. Spearheading the lobbying drive was former Assistant Secretary of War Louis A. Johnson, counsel for Pan American, who was soon to assume the duties of financial director of Truman's presidential campaign. Powerful support also came from Commerce Secretary W. Averell Harriman. The many vague divisions of power between Commerce's CAA and the CAB had caused Landis and Harriman to lock horns on a number of jurisdictional issues. To Harriman's displeasure, Landis fought constantly to preserve CAB independence from the empire-building Commerce Department. Harriman urged the President to replace Landis with Stanton Griffis, a former investment banker and ambassador to Poland. Another negative opinion came from Clarence Young, a retiring CAB member, who complained to Truman of Landis' dominating tendencies on the board.[36]

Landis also had his supporters. Besides Rayburn and Barkley, the Democratic National Committee hoped for his reappointment. With former Vice President Henry Wallace's preparations to challenge Truman in 1948 an open secret, party leaders feared repercussions from the firing of another New Dealer. The Air Line Pilots Association demanded his renomination, as did the American Federation of Labor and the Congress of Industrial Organizations in recognition of Landis' longstanding sympathies for labor. The *Washington Post* editorially challenged Truman to resist the "high pressure" campaign against Landis, whom it described as "the shining light on an otherwise mediocre board." The *Post* conceded that Landis had made many enemies through his own eccentricities. "His mannerisms have been irritating. Some of his decisions have seemed pedantic and excessively doctrinaire. Occasionally abrupt actions on his part have also caused more than necessary disruptions." But the airlines wanted him out for reasons of policy, not personality. It was Landis' opposition to monopoly and his championship of improved air safety that brought him the wrath of the grandfather lines and the praise of the *Post*.[37]

Unquestionably, Landis had become a difficult man to work with. The traumas of divorce and separation from his family and friends ate away at him. During the days, he worked feverishly at the CAB. After these long hours of toil he drank heavily to relax and required pills to put himself to sleep every night. His excessive off-hours drinking became common gossip in Washington, which his opponents turned to their own use. One false rumor to reach the smaller airlines was that Landis had become intoxicated at a cocktail party and vowed to wipe out all nonscheduled lines. Anti-Landis forces also reminded the moralistic Truman of Landis' divorce and intentions to marry his secretary. Privately, Truman remarked that Landis seemed unable "to get along with people," but, as a columnist for the *Nation* noted, that view overlooked the fact that "many of these same people had private axes to grind."[38]

The long silence from the White House ended on the day after Christmas, when Truman invited Landis to his office. "I have decided not to reappoint you," the President started off bluntly, explaining that he had promised the job to someone else. "Have I offended you in any way, Mr. President?" Landis asked. "No, you have done a good job," Truman replied. "In fact, I think it has been a magnificent job, but as you can see I am in a hell of a fix and there is nothing I can do about it." With some embarrassment, Truman added: "Shortly after I took over this job as President, Ed Flynn said to me 'you'll have to be a son-of-a-bitch half the time.' This is one of the times." Solicitously, Truman asked if he could be of any future help. Landis had heard rumors that he might be appointed ambassador to Guatemala, but declined any assistance, expressing instead how deeply it hurt him to leave the CAB. "I have worked harder in this job than on any other I ever held," he said. "I have given it everything I had."[39]

Thunderstruck, Landis left the White House and wandered about the city and its taverns for the rest of the day. At his apartment at the Dorchester, Stanley Gewirtz and Dorothy Brown waited for his return. Gewirtz had also called in Tommy Corcoran, whom Landis could always count on in an emergency. Later that evening, Landis stumbled into the apartment and recounted for them the whole sorry story. Corcoran immediately reached for the phone and called Joseph Kennedy in Florida. "Joe, you've got to take Jim on," he insisted. Kennedy agreed and promptly offered Landis a position with "Kennedy Enterprises." "What's that?" Landis asked. "Oh, we'll figure that out after you're down here," Kennedy assured him. "You'll need a rest for a while." Landis had no second thoughts about accepting. He could not go back to Harvard, nor even practice law until he passed a bar exam. With alimony and child support payments due, he was "tremendously embarrassed" financially. Whatever the new post, it came as a godsend.[40]

Sympathetic letters from pilots, small airlines, various government officials, and friends arrived to reassure him. As one CAB employee commented, "the thought that personal integrity, intellectual honesty, and fearless pursuit of statutory duty could be so rewarded came as a profound shock." The *Washington Post* decried Truman's "curt and ungracious way" of treating Landis, only months after the President had conferred upon him the Medal of Merit for "exceptionally meritorious conduct" during World War II.[41]

Some liberals interpreted the firing of Landis, and the demotion of Marriner S. Eccles from chairman of the Federal Reserve Board a month later, as part of Truman's political swing to the center in preparation for an uphill election fight in 1948. Idaho's liberal Democratic Senator Glen Taylor was on his way to a news conference to read his letter turning down the vice-presidential spot on Henry Wallace's Progressive Party when he spotted a morning newspaper with the Landis story. "When I saw that and started to think of all the other recent Truman dismissals and appointments," said Taylor, a Landis admirer, "I got so disgusted I changed my mind, tore up the letter I had written, and decided to wait a while." Two months later, Taylor accepted Wallace's offer and joined the Progressive campaign against Truman.[42]

Having removed Landis, Truman found it surprisingly difficult to replace him. Secretary Harriman's candidate, Ambassador Stanton Griffis, turned down the job. Tired of the Cold War and cold weather in Poland, Griffis had been anxious to leave his post, but he returned to the United States only to find himself the target of newspaper and radio criticism linking him to the lobbying that had ousted Landis. "I am allergic to airplanes, and had no desire to be involved in this particularly difficult job," Griffis later wrote to explain his retreat back into the diplomatic fold. "Even the dullness of life in Poland seemed preferable."[43]

Truman then named Major General Laurence S. Kuter, United States representative to the International Civil Aviation Organization, as the CAB head, also with an endorsement from Harriman. But twice the Senate rejected his nomination. The general refused to resign his military commission to accept the low-paying regulatory position, and Rayburn and Barkley, still smarting over Landis' dismissal, saw to it that the Senate Armed Services Committee prevented the general from holding another civilian post while still in uniform. It took the President three embarrassing months to find someone who would take the job and whom Congress would accept, Joseph J. O'Connell, Jr.[44]

The President's discomfort over the Landis affair was evident in his total lack of public explanation either at the time or in his memoirs. At one staff meeting, shortly after the Senate rejected General Kuter, Truman told his closest aides that he had not reappointed Landis because "he just could not get along with anybody." Landis, according to the President, was issuing and signing CAB orders without consulting with other board members or with Secretary of Commerce Harriman, the administration's chief aviation policymaker. However, Truman added that he personally liked Landis. In another private session, the President explained to Dean Acheson that he had not made the reappointment because of the "mess," presumably in Landis' personal life, and because the Senate would not have confirmed him. Acheson's report astonished Felix Frankfurter, who had learned from Chief Justice Fred Vinson of the President's promises to congressional leaders to make the reappointment. "Indeed, the only criticism that has come from Vinson's lips about Truman," Frankfurter noted in his diary, was "that he thought the Landis thing was pretty bad."[45]

As Landis cleaned out his desk, he regretted the unfinished business he was leaving behind. For the first time in years the CAB had begun to reduce its backlogs, but cases more than two years old still waited for decisions. He had overseen the delegation of more responsibility to the staff, streamlined accident investigations, simplified registration forms, and reduced financial reports from monthly to quarterly to speed up the board's work. Yet, the dockets remained filled with applications for new certificates, requests for mail rate increases, and unfinished investigations. On Landis' desk lay a comprehensive reorganization plan for the Civil Aeronautics Board which he had requested months earlier from the Bureau of the Budget but which he had never had the time to put into effect.[46]

The eighteen months Landis spent on the CAB, no matter how disappointing, had been a valuable experience for him. The deterioration he saw settling in at the regulatory commissions forced him to question many of his earlier assumptions about the administrative process. He had to reevaluate the relationship of the agencies to the chief executive and to the industries they regulated, their ability to handle increased workloads, their need for better appointees, and their lack of coordination with the programs of the other branches of the federal government. During the next decade Landis became a frequent critic of the process he had helped to shape, but thirteen years would pass before he could return to Washington to begin salvage operations.

12 | Kennedy Enterprises

January and February 1948 were wretched months for Landis. Fired from the Civil Aeronautics Board, divorced from Stella, and not yet married to Dorothy, he felt himself stripped of family, friends, status, and purpose. His life became a vacuum. "Before I can move in any direction I must find a way to live," he told Stella. "I must have a job before I can think of anything else." At Joseph Kennedy's insistence he checked into the posh Palm Beach hotel, The Breakers, but the forced vacation only gave him time to brood and drink. A robust and resourceful Joe Kennedy then stepped in to take charge. "I will have a talk with him and try to get him on a regular path," Kennedy promised in response to a private note from Stella. "He has lots and lots of ability; he will just need to settle himself down—that is what he needs more than anything."[1]

Physically and emotionally, James Landis had worn down. He arrived in Palm Beach feeling ill and spent days on the hotel's sundeck recuperating, tanning, and condemning himself for such an idle waste of time. The other guests, wealthy devotees of golf and fishing, made him feel awkwardly out of place. "This isn't my crowd anyway," he grumbled. "I know nobody nor care to." Although the Kennedys did their best to entertain him at their active home, he came away restless and dissatisfied. Nothing much interested him or gave him any sense of direction.[2]

Early each morning he awoke to troublesome thoughts. "I think only very insensitive people or people with clear consciences can sleep late," he said, "and obviously I fit neither category." In such moments he reached out to the two women of his past and future, Stella in Cambridge and

156

Dorothy in Washington. His poignant letters to Stella recounted the memories that still haunted him, how often his thoughts returned to their home in Newbury, his children, the garden, and the family dogs. "I would give everything in the world if I could get back to those days," he grieved.[3]

He wrote to Stella not to rekindle affection but because only she understood what he had lost. They each came from such difficult pasts, the isolated missionary compound in Japan and the poverty-stricken but proud Southern planters. Together they entered the prestigious and powerful society of Cambridge and conquered it. Coming from the outside, speculated their daughter Ann, made them "probably far more impressed with that society . . . than had they been born into it." But that also made the wrenching away of those bonds all the harder. From the astonishing successes of their early married years, they had become embarrassments for their Cambridge friends and associates.[4]

"I see myself as the most utter fool ever created," Landis wrote. "I have lost everything that I ever struggled for over so many years—literally everything. There is not only a home and family, character, health, friends, and all those by-products of living. I am close to being an alcoholic." He turned to Stella for empathy. "Do you understand how I have to live two lives?" he asked her. "I have to have something that will tie me in with the roots of my beginning. My life didn't begin in 1942."[5]

"All this writing seems so useless," he continued. "I go back in my mind and think of things I should have done but didn't, things—beautiful things—that have been lost forever. I never knew before what memories were. I would have been so much better if I had died." Death became a recurring theme in his letters. "I am afraid of death. But so many things are closing about me, and I am so tired." He felt that the future held no shape for him. "All the life I was bred to is in the past as you well know, and I am too old, too set to be reborn again."[6]

That Landis turned to his former wife in these dark moments was a sign of his lingering ambivalence; that Stella cared to respond was all the more remarkable. For her, the divorce had been devastating. She depended upon Landis for alimony and for the girls' tuitions, but typically he proved unreliable. His checks did not arrive for months, while bills accumulated and college bursars notified her of their lack of payment. Stella refused to beg or protest, and not until intermediaries reminded Landis of his obligations would he hurriedly send the back checks. His forgetfulness was curiously selective; on anniversaries he continued to send red roses. The combined effects of his insensitivity, Stella's own inability to accept the reality of the divorce, and the looks of pity she saw on the faces of her friends eventually drove her to alcoholism. Only after entering several institutions and joining Alcoholics Anonymous was she able to construct a a new life for herself. She took a post as secretary to the president of Smith College, then as a newspaper columnist in Cambridge, and finally as executive secretary to the Cambridge Art Association, raising funds, organizing exhibits, and attending to the local artists. "I wish I had had a job like this years ago," Stella wrote in later years to Marion Frankfurter. "I might have made a career of it."[7]

For James Landis the climb back was equally rigorous. It took all of his inner strength, Dorothy's love, and Joe Kennedy's force of authority to help him overcome his sense of degradation. Both his new job and new environment came from Kennedy. The millionaire financier wanted Landis to relocate himself in New York and sign onto the staff of Kennedy Enterprises, an organization designed to bolster the financial and political fortunes of Kennedy and his family. Landis, worried about attaching himself so closely to one man in such a vague capacity, sought Dorothy's advice before he acted. "You have been used to wild, teeming jobs ever since the beginning of the war—and before that, too—and this will be different," she wrote back from Washington (where she remained at the CAB to assist in the transition to a new chairman). The job promised to be challenging in its own right, yet the pace should be slow enough to allow for involvement in outside causes. "Anyway, darling," she encouraged him, "I think we can build an interesting life together so long as we both keep our spirit of adventure and our love for each other intact . . . This will be the beginning of a new era for us both."[8]

On July 3, 1948, James Landis and Dorothy Brown were married. Both Presbyterians, they found their church cold toward marriages between divorced persons, but a friend persuaded her minister to conduct the service in his Maryland home. When Dorothy went to apply for the Maryland marriage license and reported that Landis had been born in Tokyo, an outraged clerk replied, "You can't marry a Jap in this state!" Finally, the arrangements were completed and Landis telegraphed Stella that "the time has come." The ceremony took place on a Saturday morning and afterwards they held a wedding breakfast at the Carlton Hotel, where fifteen years earlier Landis and Ben Cohen had drafted the Securities Act. That afternoon, Boston newspapers featured photographs of Jim and Dorothy Landis, looking relaxed and happy as they boarded a plane for their Bermuda honeymoon.[9]

With moral support from his new wife, Landis managed to bridge the many gaps in his life. He returned to work, built a new career as a private attorney, and resumed his involvement in the federal regulatory process. And for at least the next few years Joe Kennedy provided the strength, financial aid, and employment that Landis so desperately needed. He moved his desk into Kennedy's office at the Hotel Marguery on Park Avenue in New York, and he and Dorothy took up residence in a large apartment just across the courtyard from the Marguery. In the heart of Manhattan he could stroll through the courtyard to work, come home for lunch, and return with clients for dinner. But the desk in Kennedy's office remained a symbol of Landis' lack of independence and caused considerable derision among his former friends. "I never liked Joe Senior," commented Felix Frankfurter. "Does anybody like Joe Senior? . . . Maybe Jim Landis. Sure, he was his bread and butter. Poor bread and poor butter."[10]

However much Frankfurter and others disapproved, Landis remained eternally grateful to Kennedy and his "Enterprises." He helped supervise the trust funds that Kennedy established for his children, worked to set up the Park Agency to handle his real estate investments, advised him on taxes, wrote his speeches, and began to ghostwrite his projected memoirs. At one point, Landis was able to convince Congress and the Internal Revenue Service to alter the tax codes to grant charitable tax status for Kennedy's Merchandise Mart in Chicago (by way of a lease-back arrangement with the Joseph P. Kennedy, Jr., Foundation). He came to be by far the brightest star in Kennedy's highly competent and well-paid circle of assistants. Kennedy the businessman had always been fascinated with men of intellect. He delighted in acquiring Landis among his advisors and placed him on a generous retainer. At Palm Beach Kennedy remarked that he earned more money in interest off his investments while sitting on the beach than he had in all his active days in the stock markets. "Now you just sit here and try it too!" he told Landis.[11]

Financially secure at last, Landis could not sit on the beach for long. He itched to return to the law, and Joseph Kennedy knew better than to bind him solely to his Enterprises. In August 1948, twenty-four years after graduating from law school, forty-eight-year-old James Landis flew to Washington to take his first bar examination. He stopped by the offices of his prospective law partners and asked to see their copies of the District of Columbia Code and the United States Code, casually mentioning that he had not had a chance to study for the exam. They set him up in the firm's library and found him there the next morning, sound asleep with his head down on the District of Columbia Code. He awoke, washed, and left for the exam totally assured, passing it without any trouble. Printed cards soon announced the establishment of Landis, Gewirtz, and Maclay. Joining him were his two former CAB associates, his executive assistant, Stanley Gewirtz, and the board's assistant general counsel, Hardy K. Maclay.[12]

For the most part, Landis remained in New York on full-time service to Kennedy, but he enjoyed occasional travel to Washington to assist his firm in regulatory matters. He played the "strategist" while his partners handled the daily mechanics of their cases. "We specialize in everything that provides a real fight," Landis said proudly. The only drawback, so far as he was concerned, was the need to bother with clients at all, although his income from Kennedy gave him the freedom to choose whom he would serve. "We're a small firm, and intend to remain so in order that we can do our own work," he explained. "That is real fun." The partners' common background in aviation regulation assured their demand among the airlines for cases before the CAB. Most of their work dealt with the smaller lines, reflecting the partners' sympathies and the larger lines' antagonisms. The exception was Landis' first big case, which involved him with the giant scheduled lines and brought him back into contention with Pan American in what he later termed one of "the most bitterly contested hearings ever held before the Civil Aeronautics Board." The dispute also gave the author of *The Administrative Process* a galling lesson in the deficiencies of the regulatory commissions.[13]

Early in 1949 the pilots and employees of American Overseas Airlines approached Landis and asked him to defend their interests in a proposed merger between AOA and Pan American. He accepted the case, partly out of sympathy with the employees who stood to lose their jobs but more out of suspicion that the merger of two of the three United States transatlantic competitors represented a covert attempt to revive the "chosen instrument" scheme. Landis considered Pan American unfit to operate the AOA routes and, to prove his point, petitioned the CAB for access to the board's records on Pan Am's past competitive and financial practices. Angrily, Pan American's counsel, Henry J. Friendly, accused Landis of poor ethics in using information he had obtained while still a board member. Friendly's brief charged Landis with turning the proceedings into a "trial of all his grudges against Pan American Airways." While elements of vendetta clearly existed in Landis' actions, his arguments were sound enough to convince the CAB's public counsel, who persuaded the board to widen its investigation into the merger.[14]

During the boisterous hearings that followed, Landis found himself the target of some surprisingly hostile publicity. The syndicated columnist Ray Tucker singled out Landis and former White House advisor Clark Clifford, counsel for Trans World Airlines, for exploiting their government connections for personal profit in the case. At a time when many New Deal and Fair Deal lawyers were becoming wealthy by defending business clients before the very regulatory commissions they had helped to create, Tucker described Landis and Clifford as "lined up against the consumers and masses they once championed." The airline merger, he contended, would save the government millions of tax dollars a year in mail subsidies and would lower passenger rates for travel abroad. The charge of self-interest was patently unfair and stung Landis. Unlike Clifford, who received a

160

$50,000 retainer from TWA, Landis accepted the AOA pilots as a "charity case" and charged them no fees other than his actual expenses. He believed that his position best served the public interest, that no public savings would accrue from the merger, and that Pan American's record of suppressing competition made the company dangerous "to be entrusted with great public responsibility." He denied that he had abandoned his New Deal liberalism. "I still dislike empires and all that they mean," he insisted, "whether it's steel, public utilities or aviation."[15]

Landis came close to winning his skirmish until Pan American changed the rules of the game. After the Justice Department's Anti-Monopoly Division protested that the merger would leave Pan American free to "concentrate its major resources on the remaining carrier," the CAB voted three to two to deny the merger request. The decision went to President Truman, who signed it. Immediately, airline lobbyists descended on the White House. At the CAB, Chairman Joseph J. O'Connell, Jr., Landis' successor, had already prepared mimeographed notices of the merger veto when he received a request from the White House to delay public announcement. On Sunday morning, July 2, 1950, members of Truman's staff called CAB Vice-Chairman Oswald Ryan, a supporter of the merger, to a closed-door meeting with airline representatives. Afterwards, Truman "recalled his approval" of the CAB decision. The uninvited O'Connell did not learn of the secret meeting at the White House until after he had returned the documents. By then, Truman had reversed his decision, eradicated his name from the documents, and approved the Pan American-AOA merger. O'Connell promptly resigned as CAB chairman.[16]

Truman tried to explain his reversal as an attempt to prevent monopoly rather than as a capitulation to industry. Admitting that he was permitting a decline in the number of transatlantic carriers, he compensated by placing the two remaining scheduled lines into direct competition at major European cities. TWA could compete with Pan American for the profitable London market, while Pan American could fly to Rome and Paris, previously TWA's domain. The CAB, less Chairman O'Connell, approved. But, as *Time* magazine pointed out, "neither the President nor the CAB had reckoned on the legal resourcefulness of James M. Landis."[17]

On the night before the merger decision's release, Landis received word of Truman's actions. Hastily he had his law partners draft an injunction, hunt up a notary public, and race to Chevy Chase, Maryland, to persuade Federal Judge Henry Schweinhaut to sign it. At 1:30 a.m. they roused the judge and got their restraining order. The victory enjoyed only a brief life. In court the next week, Assistant Attorney General H. Graham Morrison successfully argued that the President's signature on the CAB decision made it an accomplished fact, thereby invalidating the stay. Landis appealed to the Supreme Court, but the high court refused to review that aspect of presidential power. Pan American quickly effected the merger and absorbed American Overseas Airlines.[18]

Defeat left Landis with a bitter taste. Complaining of the "general stench attached to the President's action," he cynically suggested that "where we failed, perhaps, was in not having supplied the palace guard at the White House with adequate quantities of Bourbon." The long delays and expensive proceedings involved in the AOA and other regulatory cases also disturbed him. "Some years ago I wrote a fairly popular book defending the administrative process on the ground that it would be expeditious and less costly than going to court," he noted. "After this experience and several others with the CAB I almost feel it a moral duty to revise my estimate of that process made before my acquaintance with the organization."[19]

Back in New York, he apologized to Joseph Kennedy for stirring up such a "hornet's nest" in the Pan American case, which diverted his attentions from Kennedy's offices for so long. The truth was that Landis had become bored with his work for Kennedy and longed to devote himself completely to the practice of law. Leaving Kennedy would be no easy chore. Ahead lay the New York bar exam — the most difficult in the nation. Failure to pass would expose the former dean of the Harvard Law School to public ridicule and professional embarrassment. Landis first attempted to win exemption from the exam on the grounds of his many years of practical experience, but after losing that bid he bowed to the inevitable and signed up for a refresher course along with the greenest of law school graduates. In March 1949 he took the exam, and although some of the questions concerned laws he had helped to draft himself, he reported it the toughest test he ever saw. In May his name was posted among the 665 candidates who passed.[20]

New York newspapers now carried notice that Landis would join the Wall Street law firm of McGoldrick, Winn, Dannett and Burke. The prestigious firm included former New York City Comptroller Joseph McGoldrick and Milton Winn, Landis' general counsel at the Office of Civilian Defense. At the last moment, however, the deal fell through. Joe Kennedy disapproved, making Landis feel he would be "falling down" on his commitments to Kennedy Enterprises. Even though his association with the law firm as its Washington counsel would be largely nominal, Landis withdrew from the arrangement. He could never forget Kennedy's help when he had been "in the dog house and pretty much [up] against it."[21]

In 1949 and 1950 Joseph P. Kennedy had no plans to retire. Skillful in public relations, he kept his name politically alive through speeches and articles on the Truman Doctrine and other global policies. In the wake of his generous publicity, rumors spread that he still harbored dreams of a presidential nomination. But hanging in Kennedy's closet were the skeletons of his prewar isolationism and "America First" leanings, from which he sought vindication. For years, he toyed with the idea of publishing a grand memoir to tell the story of the war from his point of view. Something had always interfered with the project, but in 1948 he assigned Landis the task of organizing his massive collection of diplomatic dispatches, radiograms, and other correspondence for the book. At first, Landis found this "fascinating work" and produced copious notes and drafts of chapters. The result was not a Kennedy memoir but only a slim volume on *The Surrender of King Leopold,* published jointly over the names of Joseph P. Kennedy and James M. Landis. Culled from Kennedy's papers, the little book defended the Belgian King's surrender to the Germans, an act which Churchill and other Allied leaders had roundly criticized. Kennedy and Landis argued that by stalling for time, Leopold had actually protected the British evacuation at Dunkirk. The "revisionist" account puzzled many of Landis' friends but won him the award of "chevalier de l'Ordre de Leopold II" from the Belgians. Defying conventional wisdom, the book reflected Landis' distaste for Winston Churchill, which Kennedy freely shared, as well as his delight in intellectually shocking others by taking unpopular stands.[22]

The full-scale Kennedy memoir died in 1951 when Kennedy's oldest surviving son, John, decided to challenge Henry Cabot Lodge, Jr., for his Senate seat from Massachusetts the next year. With that news, the elder Kennedy bowed out of public life, ceased his speechmaking, and cancelled the memoir as potentially too controversial for his son's career. He no longer voiced any objection to Landis' desire to strike out independently. With his blessing, Landis organized his own New York law firm, with Telford Taylor and David Scoll, and merged his Washington firm to bring in Wallace Cohen, Seymour Rubin, and Abba Schwartz, to form Landis, Cohen, Rubin, Schwartz, and Gewirtz (which was known in Washington humorously as "four Jews and an Arab"). Separation from Joe Kennedy did not mean the end of either their personal or business associations. In addition to keeping Landis on annual retainer, Kennedy signed a promissory note for $20,000 to assist him in setting up his new law offices.[23]

Private law practice stirred mixed emotions in Landis. The academic within him complained that "the great tragedy of practicing law is that you have to have clients," while the public servant in him ruminated, "I shall make of myself the shrewd, amoral lawyer that I have always despised." He possessed a gifted legal mind that craved outlets but, except for a brief stint as chancellor of the financially troubled Asia Institute in New York, he never went back to teaching. Private practice was his only avenue to the law.[24]

His misgivings were lessened by three sources of income upon which he could regularly count. Annual retainers from Kennedy Enterprises, the

Skouras brothers' motion picture theater chain, and the Commonwealth Fund, a Boston mutual fund operation, gave him the financial independence to pick and choose among other clients. To the dismay of his law partners, Landis customarily chose cases out of sheer interest and often drastically undercharged his clients. He sometimes accepted what he called "Christ cases," defending those whose budgets could not otherwise have afforded his services. In contrast, he refused lucrative retainers if his principles clashed with the client's objectives. Wallace Cohen recalled how their Washington firm had once arranged to take the case of a major railroad for a large fee, but Landis refused to sign the documents supporting the line's contentions on barge shipments down the Mississippi River. Landis then went to the railroad's general counsel to outline what he considered the honorable position to take, and lost the client.[25]

Until 1958 Landis never bothered to keep a desk at any of his law offices, which were really just loose associations of individual lawyers who shared housekeeping expenses. His partners rarely saw him, except when a particular case caught his interest. Characteristically, when he decided to change those arrangements, he delayed telling his associates the unpleasant news until the last possible moment. One morning he arrived at his New York office to inform Taylor and Scoll that he planned to leave the firm to join a full income-sharing partnership. After discussing the matter for a few minutes he left, just before the same morning's mail brought an announcement of the new firm of Landis, Brenner, Feldman and Reilly. For the remainder of Taylor and Scoll's lease, however, Landis continued to contribute his share of the expenses.[26]

Another significant partner during the 1950s was not a lawyer but a colorful motion picture entrepreneur, George Skouras. Landis had met Skouras during the war in Cairo, where Skouras served as an Office of Strategic Services agent specializing in Greek affairs. The two men were avid democrats who shared a revulsion against British suppression of the Greek resistance forces. Each was a compulsive worker with a tough exterior that masked a romantic nature. They respected each other, enjoyed each other's company, and became warm friends. Skouras encouraged Landis to loosen up, play more golf, and join him for weekly private screenings at his home of the new films which would soon open in his family's theaters.[27]

Skouras had returned from the war to assume the presidency of the Skouras Theaters Corporation and later to head the United Artists Theater Circuit. In 1953 he joined with Broadway producer Mike Todd to form the Magna Theater Corporation to finance a new wide-screen projection process known as Todd-A.O., the latest and most spectacular Hollywood gimmick to lure television viewers back to the movies. Todd-A.O. and

"Cinerama" required special theaters and expensive equipment and necessitated a close working arrangement between the movie suppliers and the theater outlets. But federal antitrust regulations had forced the major studios to divest themselves of their theater chains. To steer the Magna Theater Corporation through its seemingly endless legal battles, Skouras recruited Landis. Besides his legal skills, the former Harvard Law School dean added a dividend of respectability to the board of directors of Magna and other Skouras projects. It was Landis who lobbied with Senator Lyndon Johnson, among other Washington contacts, to persuade the Justice Department to loosen its antitrust restrictions, and who defended the corporation in a round of lawsuits over the distribution rights of Cinerama. Always a risky business, Todd-A.O. was assured of its profitability only after the signing of contracts to produce movie versions of Rodgers and Hammerstein's "Oklahoma" and "South Pacific." The wide-screen process achieved its greatest success in 1956 when Mike Todd independently produced the immensely popular "Around the World in 80 Days." "Those were harassing days," Landis later recalled, "when you didn't know whether you were going to be bankrupt the next day or not, and whether people were going to run out on you."[28]

Landis was clearly an asset for Skouras and his retainer was lucrative and dependable, allowing him to accept less remunerative cases if they interested him. For example, during the 1950s he devoted himself with equal vigor to the Skiatron Electronics and Television Corporation, a small firm which offered more in potential than in immediate reward. Skiatron promoted a pay-as-you-see television system, which scrambled the picture and sound of its broadcasts. Unless the viewer used a decoder card, the reception looked distorted and sounded "like a cat wailing on a back fence." Of the five competing systems of pay-television being advanced, Skiatron's "Subscriber-Vision" was the simplest, requiring no elaborate outdoor wiring, telephone hookups, or coin boxes.[29]

The concept appealed to Landis, who had advocated educational broadcasting on radio during his law school years. Now television added a new dimension; it was a "beautiful instrumentality for bringing home . . . knowledge to the millions of people who are this society," people who deserved a more democratic choice over what was broadcast. With Subscriber-Vision the audience would decide by paying for the programs they wanted. Audiences could still enjoy sporting events and light entertainment, while more selective viewers could turn to opera and educational broadcasts which the sponsors generally shunned.[30]

Still in an experimental stage, pay-television could only be test-marketed with the authorization of the Federal Communications Commission. Skiatron had therefore hired as its attorney Telford Taylor, a former counsel to the FCC, but when Taylor returned to government service in 1951, Landis inherited his law partner's case. Of course Skiatron was delighted to obtain the former dean for its legal staff, since he added "the glamor of a familiar figure." The company planned to use him not only to argue its cases before the FCC and the courts but also to go on television and before congressional committees, and envisioned featuring him in its documentaries. "Lawyers of Mr. Landis' prominence and ability," Skiatron notified its board of directors, "are customarily compensated not merely for the time and labor devoted to the tasks in hand, but also for the responsibilities assumed and the magnitude of the issues involved." Actually, Landis took his first payments in Skiatron's stock, indicating his belief in its future. His later fees remained only a small portion of Skiatron's total legal fees.[31]

It was not an easy case. Landis had no experience with the FCC and at first found it difficult to fathom the technical data necessary to present his argument. He was aware that Congress had assigned the FCC to preserve and encourage competition in broadcasting, and that the commission had allocated VHF (very high frequency) stations to insure that as many cities as possible would have their own local stations. By 1948 the FCC had assigned most of the available VHF stations and not until 1952 did it lift its freeze on new UHF (ultra high frequency) stations. Alone among the competing pay-television systems, Skiatron then pegged its petition to the FCC to the use of UHF stations. The company asked only to establish a pilot program, which would give the commission time to examine its results before promulgating an industry-wide decision.[32]

The FCC hesitated to act. Should it permit all five pay-television systems to operate, or single out the most desirable system? Would such designation create a monopoly? Would viewers purchase expensive adapting equipment for systems that might fail? The three national broadcasting networks and most movie theater owners opposed any type of pay-television, as did many viewers, who feared they would lose their favorite programs from commercial television. The FCC preferred to delay—endlessly if necessary—until it had exhausted every effort to reach a compromise. But continuation of the status quo suited the commercial networks perfectly, while it left Skiatron and other pay-television systems shut out of the market.[33]

In February 1955 the FCC rejected petitions to establish immediate pay-television service and declined to act on the request for a pilot project. Instead it invited all interested parties, including the public, to submit their opinions, launching a "battle of the mimeograph machines" as pay-television advocates, commercial networks, actors' guilds, theater owners, and other interested groups rushed to provide documentary evidence supporting their positions. Tens of thousands of letters and postcards reached the FCC from television viewers, without indicating any clear trend of public sympathy. "Almost everyone is adamantly on one side or the other," said FCC Chairman George McConnaughey. During the fight, Landis pleaded Skiatron's case, explaining on one televised debate: "All we are asking for is the opportunity to go public. If the public doesn't like us we go broke."[34]

More than a year later, months after the many briefs and petitions had been filed, but with the FCC still silent, Landis testified before a Senate committee investigating pay-television. As a former regulatory commissioner, he said, he could sympathize with the FCC and the burden it bore; but the commission needed to realize how expensive its delay was to a small company like Skiatron, which was financed through public stock. Skiatron could sustain a few more months' wait, he suggested, "but what we fear is a delay of, say, 4, 5, 6 years, as happened in color television. By that time our tongues will be hanging so far out we will be completely parched."[35]

Not until September 1957 did the FCC vote to give television stations the option of adopting pay-television on a trial basis. That decision came under congressional attack from House Judiciary Committee Chairman Emmanuel Celler, who decried "gas-meter television" which would divide viewers by economic class, and from the House Interstate and Foreign Commerce Committee, which passed a resolution demanding that the FCC withdraw its authorization of any pay-television tests. Withering under the heat of congressional criticism, the commission again postponed action.[36]

Finally in March 1959 the FCC arrived at a compromise which would permit each pay-television system to test its method in one city. Such limited markets would prevent the spread of any system until it had won congressional approval. But the scheme was too little and too late for Skiatron, which no longer had the resources to launch its pilot program. When the company attempted to sell more stock to underwrite a test of its system, the Securities and Exchange Commission issued a stop order on the registration, charging that Skiatron had misled buyers on the extent of its financial standing. Landis argued Skiatron's case before the SEC, but there was little left to defend. Skiatron admitted to liabilities of $1,650,000 and assets of only $17,000. Trading on the stock terminated in December 1959 and never resumed. Landis had watched the bright hopes of a small company disappear in a maze of bureaucratic paperwork and delay.[37]

He was more successful in presenting other cases before the commissions, and lawyers and clients sought after him constantly. During those years, his wife recalled, "the phone never stopped ringing." His clients covered a wide territory: the Arabian-American Oil Company (Aramco), various small airlines, coal companies, railroads, unions, and disgruntled stockholders. During the 1950s his practice took him before each of the major federal regulatory commissions. Landis saw no conflict between his earlier service on the commissions and his regulatory law practice. "With all those years in Government," he explained, "I have gotten to know more and more about less and less so I can't be too selective." Within the sphere of the commissions his practice was diversified, financially rewarding, and intellectually stimulating. For all that, he still had unburnt energy, unsatisfied desires, and unachieved goals. His search for more out of life therefore brought him back repeatedly to the door of Joseph P. Kennedy.[38]

If Landis no longer worked exclusively for Joe Kennedy, he put himself wholeheartedly at the service of Kennedy's remarkable family. Ever since the 1930s he had enjoyed acceptance as something of an honorary uncle to Kennedy's children. At Harvard he had watched over the academic progress of Joseph, Jr., and John, sending periodic reports on them to their father at the American Embassy in London. Landis especially admired the aggressive and outgoing Joe, Jr. In his appraisal the young man had the grades, ambition, personality, and other earmarks of a first-rate lawyer and politician, perhaps a future president. Landis left his door open to him at all times, and Joe, Jr., never hesitated to take him up on the offer. In the spring of 1941 he discussed with Landis his indecision over joining the Naval Reserve or the Naval Air Corps and received from the dean a letter of recommendation to the commandant of the First Naval District. Three years later, in August 1944, Landis received the bad news. "Young Joe Kennedy's death has hit me hard," he wrote to Dorothy. As for the family's second son, Landis read the galley proofs of John Kennedy's *Why England Slept* and was "amazed at the quality." He discounted any future for John as a lawyer or politician but assured the ambassador that "he seems to have the makings of a good historian in him."[39]

No matter what the task, Landis always made himself available to the Kennedy family. When Eunice and Jean planned a trip to the Middle East, the former economic minister planned their itinerary. When Robert and Edward prepared to enter the University of Virginia Law School, the onetime Harvard dean provided each with impressive letters of recommendation. He advised them on domestic and foreign policy matters, assisted in their writing of magazine articles, and drafted some of their speeches. He tolerated Eunice's attempts to interest him in Catholicism ("I enjoy religious controversy as much as I enjoy most controversy," he wrote to her good-naturedly, "with one difference—I always have a respect for the feelings and faiths of others, whereas in political controversy, I always think that the man who differs with me is either immoral or corrupt"). In latter years, as the Kennedys gained political prominence, his tasks grew proportionally.[40]

Of all the Kennedys, Landis came to admire Robert the most, for qualities which reminded him strongly of the lost Navy pilot. When Robert Kennedy headed the Virginia Student Legal Forum, Landis spoke before it on "Vital Issues in the Middle East and Their Relationship to World Peace." Later, Landis sent him a lengthy critique of the Yalta Conference, which Kennedy used to write one of his law school papers. Fresh out of law school, the young man served a stint as the *Boston Post's* special correspondent at the signing of the Japanese peace treaty in 1951, with Landis, as usual, supplying him the necessary background reading material. "Bobbie is really growing up and thinking hard in this last article of his," he congratulated Joe Kennedy on the first fruits of the assignment. By 1954 Robert Kennedy was counsel to the Democratic minority during the Army-McCarthy hearings. At the conclusion of the hearings he approached Landis for help in preparing the minority report. Landis agreed, but only if Kennedy was willing to do a hard and thorough job. For three weeks the two men holed themselves up in a Cape Cod cottage, not far from the Kennedy compound in Hyannisport, and closely examined the record. When they emerged they had produced so superior an analysis of the hearings that the committee's Republicans adopted most of it for their own final report, less the conclusions. Robert Kennedy, said Landis with admiration, possessed "a very deep sense of public service," and the stamina to keep up with Landis' own standards of performance.[41]

Yet the bulk of Landis' assistance went to the family's sole elected officeholder during the 1940s and 1950s, John F. Kennedy. Soon after Landis joined Kennedy Enterprises, the freshman congressman began incorporating Landis' ideas into his own political program. In April 1948 Kennedy stood in the House of Representatives to demand fair play for his "fellow veterans of World War II" who were operating nonscheduled airlines. His denunciations of the Civil Aeronautics Board for mistreating the "nonskeds" and for excessive mail payments to the larger lines closely paralleled Landis' thinking. After leaving the CAB, Landis reversed his opposition to separating mail payments from subsidies and concluded that the subsidies had made it impossible to determine the efficiency or inefficiency of airline management by hiding their operating deficits. The Hoover Commission on government reorganization (which Landis advised) also endorsed separation of the subsidies and mail payments; and in 1949, Congressman Kennedy and Senator Edwin Johnson of Colorado sponsored legislation to enact that recommendation. Landis assisted Kennedy in the preparation of the bill, co-signed a letter of support with him in the *New York Times,* and testified in its behalf before the Senate. The Johnson-Kennedy bill set October 1, 1951, as the date for separation of subsidies and mail rates. Within two years, all but three of the leading domestic lines were operating without subsidies, greatly satisfying statistics for James Landis.[42]

John Kennedy may have provided Landis with a congressional forum, but his overall record in the House hardly was inspiring. In the middle of an active and promising first term, Kennedy had been stricken with Addison's disease, which terribly sapped his energy.[43] Soon, he was noticeable only for his absenteeism. The John F. Kennedy whom Landis knew at that time was a pale, gaunt, and sickly war veteran, a reluctant politician who seemed to lack the dynamism of his father and brothers. Occasionally, on a Sunday afternoon, Joe Kennedy would bring his son to Landis' apartment for political strategy sessions. There the congressman would stretch out exhaustedly on the couch while the two older men vigorously debated the issues. Not until he ran for the Senate did he impress Landis, who admitted, "I never saw a man work as hard as Jack Kennedy did, for his election in '52."[44]

Officially, twenty-seven-year-old Robert Kennedy served as his brother's campaign manager. But no one doubted Joe Kennedy's influence on the campaign. At the Boston Ritz-Carlton he set up camp and imported his New York staff to help run the operation. Landis worked on the campaign for over a year and spent several months in Massachusetts. An old hand at Bay State politics from his Cambridge years, he had a special feel for its affairs. He pointed to the migration of the textile mills and other industry out of Massachusetts to the South and urged Kennedy to hit hard at Senator Lodge for his international activities and comparative lack of concern for the New England economy. That strategy became the heart of Kennedy's "He Can Do More for Massachusetts" campaign.[45]

During the campaign, Landis played mediator between Joe Kennedy's conservative assistants and John Kennedy's more liberal supporters, forces which collided head-on over the issue of McCarthyism. When campaign workers demanded that their candidate denounce the rabidly anti-Communist senator from Wisconsin, Joseph McCarthy, Joe Kennedy went into a rage and heaped his celebrated verbal abuse onto the staff. The senior Kennedy made no secret of his admiration for McCarthy, since he had entertained him at home and had contributed financially to his reelection campaign. Landis considered John Kennedy a "realistic liberal," and worked to steer him on a moderate course between the two factions. At a tense strategy session of campaign directors, Landis defended the candidate's father's position, in less offensive language, and reasoned that the best time for moral crusades came after an election, not before one. If Kennedy attacked McCarthy during the campaign, he would lose votes in the Irish and Italian wards of Boston. The advice carried and John Kennedy remained silent on McCarthyism.[46]

Having convinced the candidate and his crew, Landis then tried to reduce the ill-will that Kennedy's noncommittal stance had created within liberal Democratic ranks. As a member of the domestic council of the

Americans for Democratic Action, Landis had access to many prominent Democratic progressives. He and his law partners attended the 1952 Democratic convention primarily to smooth over feelings for John Kennedy. But Kennedy's continued silence, followed by his absence during the Senate's censure of McCarthy in 1954, further hardened liberal estrangement from the freshman Massachusetts senator. In 1956, when Kennedy maneuvered for the Democratic vice-presidential nomination, Landis flew to the Chicago convention seated beside Eleanor Roosevelt and attempted to win over the widow of his political idol to Kennedy's candidacy. As eloquently as he could describe the senator's vote-getting appeal in the industrial states, Landis could not duck Mrs. Roosevelt's questions on why Kennedy had not declared himself against McCarthy. "It was always a little difficult matter to explain," he admitted; but he related how he had visited Kennedy in the hospital at the time of the censure vote, and how near death the senator had been. Far from persuaded, Mrs. Roosevelt at least agreed to talk with Kennedy at Chicago. But the face-to-face meeting in her Blackstone Hotel suite, filled with noisy Roosevelt grandchildren, was a disaster. She put the McCarthy question to Kennedy bluntly. "The answer he gave me just wasn't enough," Mrs. Roosevelt reported, and she refused to support Kennedy's candidacy.[47]

Passed over in 1956, John Kennedy set out to win the Democratic presidential nomination in 1960, and James Landis accompanied him along the entire route. During those years, Landis' regulatory practice brought him to Washington almost weekly, and he made it a point to stop by the senator's office for conversation and consultation. Through Joseph Kennedy's retainer, he served in effect as a paid member of the senator's staff. He submitted drafts of articles and speeches, studies for the senator's subcommittees, and advice on labor and economic problems, but not once presented a bill for his work on any legislative matter. In response to one of his many efforts, Senator Kennedy appreciatively called it "a real Landis job."[48]

Landis felt comfortable with John F. Kennedy and his political thinking. They shared a peculiar brand of iconoclasm, admiring those whom history and popular opinion scorned for courageous but unpopular acts. Following the death of the conservative Republican Senator Robert A. Taft, Landis helped prepare Kennedy's glowing eulogy of Taft as "Man of the Year" for 1953. During Kennedy's long convalescence after major surgery the following year, Landis supplied him with research material for his Pulitzer-Prize-winning book, *Profiles in Courage*. In his acknowledgments, the author gave credit to his "able friend, James M. Landis, who delights in bringing the precision of the lawyer to the mysteries of history." When literary gossip suggested that Landis and others had ghostwritten the book, he insisted that his role had been limited to that of research assistant. Kennedy, he said, reshaped and reworked the material into his own style and "didn't pick up everything that came along." Landis' contributions were limited mainly to the chapters on Taft and Daniel Webster, and perhaps influenced Kennedy's sympathetic treatment of Webster's financial difficulties. But on the qualities of "greatness" and "courage" they concurred.[49]

As the 1960 election approached, John Kennedy became far too preoccupied to notice signs of distress in an always reliable advisor. Outwardly, Landis' performance and powers of concentration seemed unimpaired and undiminished. Although his associates worried that he ordered too many drinks with his lunches, no one suspected the depth of his personal problems, both emotional and financial. Inexplicably, Landis had fallen years behind in filing his income tax returns. Anxiety over his secret led him to periodic bouts with alcoholism. As he felt himself losing control, he increasingly preferred to play a backstage role to avoid embarrassing the Kennedys and their candidate.[50]

Thus, when John Kennedy made his bid for the presidency, Landis joined Joseph P. Kennedy in keeping a low profile for the duration. He attended the Democratic convention in Los Angeles to work for Kennedy (and to urge the vice presidential nomination of Lyndon B. Johnson), but afterwards he studiously avoided taking an official role in the campaign. Only once did his name surface in the press, when a whispering campaign spread rumors that Joseph Kennedy as ambassador to Great Britain had sympathized with Nazi prejudices against the Jews. Because of Landis' familiarity with the Kennedy ambassadorial papers, the family asked him to head the efforts to clear Joe Kennedy of the charges. But Landis' own sympathies for the Arabs had made him vulnerable to charges of anti-Semitism, despite his relations with Brandeis, Frankfurter, and several Jewish law partners. There was also little he could say that would not further fan the controversy, so he decided to handle it gingerly and quietly, trusting Jewish voters' antipathy to Richard Nixon, the Republican candidate, to counteract rumors against the ambassador.[51]

Behind closed doors in the Kennedy camp, Landis' name came up more frequently. During the campaign, Democratic strategist James Rowe urged Kennedy to choose someone "in whom you have real confidence" to head the transition team to prepare for the budget and personnel decisions that a victory would immediately thrust upon him. Off-handedly, Kennedy suggested Landis for the job, but Rowe reminded him that Landis' experience was regulatory rather than executive, and the assignment went instead to Clark Clifford.[52]

Meanwhile, in 1960 Landis had begun his own quixotic presidential campaign, for the presidency of the Air Line Pilots Association. Dissident pilots from Eastern Airlines approached him with the suggestion that he enter the race. After taking bruising public criticism in their disputes with the Federal Aviation Administration over mandatory retirement ages, working conditions, and strikes, they blamed their union for failing to defend their public image. "We have come out on the short end of everything from court actions to press notices," one Eastern pilot charged, "and it's nobody's fault but the ALPA." Landis had won their confidence as a negotiator in the Eastern pilots' recent wildcat strike, and they remembered his past crusade for the American Overseas Airlines pilots. His law partners thought the whole idea insane, but Landis accepted the challenge. "I like flying and I like pilots," he stated. The race might also cover his absence from the front lines of the Kennedy campaign.[53]

James Landis was an odd bird among the aviators. A lawyer rather than a pilot, his candidacy broke all of the union's traditions, as well as its by-laws that union officials must come up from the ranks of the licensed pilots. Yet, Landis went to the union's convention in Miami Beach as an active and hopeful candidate. His platform promised decentralization of the union to give locals more authority in negotiations, higher salaries with cost-of-living adjustments, a campaign against technological unemployment, and better public relations for the profession. Against him stood an entrenched leadership, headed by the union's president, Clarence "Clancy" Sayen, who firmly controlled the convention's mechanisms. Unless he could win a rules change to permit a nonpilot to hold office, Landis did not stand a chance. Shuttling between the various convention caucuses, he did his best to persuade the delegates to vote for a rules change. At one caucus of United Air Lines pilots the questions harped on specific details of his general program. Landis finally resorted to a favorite quotation from Justice Oliver Wendell Holmes: "No man has earned the right to intellectual ambitions until he has learned to lay his course by stars he cannot see." The crew-cut engineers and practical-minded navigators in the audience stared at each other in bewilderment. "I think I blew it," Landis laughed when he telephoned his law partners after the session.[54]

The same month that Landis lost his race for the Air Line Pilots' Association presidency, John F. Kennedy won election as President of the United States. Twelve years of service for Kennedy Enterprises were about to reward Landis handsomely. For all practical purposes his return to the federal government was assured. No matter how strongly he protested, he would not be able to refuse the new President's offer. The stars upon which he charted his course had truly become those he could not see.

13 | The New Frontier

At his New York and Washington law offices and Westchester home the messages were all the same: the President-elect wished to speak with Dean Landis. The responses were also identical: Dean Landis was unavailable. A puzzled John F. Kennedy mentioned the unreturned calls to his father, and that brought an angry call from Joe Kennedy, who had no trouble getting through. "Look," he said, "the President of the United States wants to talk to you." Reluctantly, Landis agreed to speak with John Kennedy but protested that he did not want an assignment in the new administration. "I've no interest in a steady government job," he maintained. "The way I see it, I've already served my sentence in Washington."[1]

Kennedy indeed had an offer for him, to return to Washington in a position of authority and regain the public spotlight. He extended to Landis a chance that few men would ever have, to reevaluate his own life's work and to mold into policy the ideas he had developed over the length of his career. In Landis' case, that meant a chance to rehabilitate the federal regulatory commissions. Forgetting his personal problems and casting aside any instinct of self-preservation, he agreed to take on the task.

"For me to have watched the growth of the administrative process has been, perhaps, the most exciting chapter in my life," he explained in 1961. More than any of his contemporaries, James Landis had associated himself with the independent agencies, as a teacher, writer, practitioner, and critic. During the 1950s, cut off from direct access to the Truman and Eisenhower administrations, he had watched from the sidelines as a pallor spread across the commissions. Somehow they lost the sense of challenge they had

174

held in the 1930s. No longer did they attract the "race of giants" who once presided over their affairs, men of the stature of Joseph Eastman, Joseph Kennedy, and William Douglas. From his new functions as a private attorney appearing in behalf of clients at regulatory hearings, Landis also encountered the commissions' rigid and unrealistic regulations, their susceptibility to political pressure, and their maddening bureaucratic inertia. His dissatisfactions rose as the commissions were racked by conflict-of-interest scandals and sank into incompetence and indifference. He sorely felt his lack of influence to check their decline, and with whatever means were open to him he worked to further an atmosphere of regulatory reform.[2]

After his unceremonious departure from the Civil Aeronautics Board, Landis had reentered the regulatory scene on Joseph Kennedy's coattails. In 1947 Kennedy had accepted appointment to the Hoover Commission on government reorganization, but with "so many horrible problems facing the world" he preferred to concentrate his attentions on foreign affairs and foreign travel. The following year, when Landis joined his staff, Kennedy gladly turned over to him his related files and responsibilities, particularly those concerning his place on the subcommittee on regulatory agencies. To the Hoover Commission, through Kennedy, Landis presented a catalogue of correctable abuses in the administrative process. Recent appointments of commissioners had fallen below quality. Unnecessary red tape clogged procedures. Regular delegation of minor business to staff members was absent. Increased work loads distracted the commissioners from their planning and promotional duties. Leadership within the commissions and coordination with the executive branch were noticeably missing.[3]

To Chairman Herbert Hoover, those failings demonstrated inherent weaknesses in the independent agencies, and he pressed the commission to assign all regulatory duties to the Cabinet departments. But Landis counseled against such radical surgery and outlined a program of specific reforms that would preserve the commissions' independence. The real solution, he insisted, lay in attracting talented personnel and giving them power to carry out their tasks. To that end, Congress should raise their salaries substantially. The President should designate all commission chairmen and have the power to remove them from their chairmanships, although not from completing their full terms as commissioners. Chairmen should serve as more than presiding officers, should handle all administrative decision making, and should direct all delegation of workloads. Finally, to bring about continuing regulatory reform, he recommended creation of an Office of Administrative Procedures to study other means of improving commission performance. His suggestions persuaded even Chairman Hoover, who praised Landis' "painstaking" work. The Hoover Commission's final report incorporated the core of Landis' proposals, which later appeared in modified version as the Truman administration's regulatory reorganization program. Congress adopted reforms for the FTC, SEC, CAB, Federal Power Commission, and Federal Maritime Board but vetoed similar proposals for the Interstate Commerce Commission, Federal Communications Commission, and National Labor Relations Board, where interest-group lobbying was most intense. Looking back, Landis decided that his accomplishments had been mostly "those that kept things out rather than those that put things in" the Hoover Commission report, but all in all he considered it "a good job."[4]

At the same time, he seized another public forum as chairman of the Twentieth Century Fund's committee on cartels and monopoly, with its news releases, newsletters, and published monographs. There his prime target was the Federal Trade Commission, and his slashing attacks revealed no residue of sentimentality for his own eight months on the commission in 1933. "Like Sodom," he described the FTC, "there are not ten men worthy of saving in the entire outfit." The FTC lacked any coherent or consistent program for supervising national economic growth, and he accused the commission of wasting its time on irregular and arbitrary assaults on "bigness" instead of conducting research in those areas where economic concentration either aided or injured the public interest. "I dislike to carry the flag for any particular theory," he said to those who might have expected him to side automatically with the anti-big-business forces. Out of his own experiences with the stock exchanges and aviation he had concluded that economic and social circumstances would push some institutions toward growth and prominence. In those cases, close government regulation would prevent any recurrence of "the flagrant abuses of the nineteenth century." Properly conducted, federal regulation would serve as a middle ground between Robber Baron entrepreneurialism and state socialism. "I have always considered," he wrote in phrases which echoed those of Felix Frankfurter, "that my work with the Government was to try to make administrative regulation sufficiently effective so as to enable capitalism to live up to its own pretensions."[5]

Without a commission or a classroom for a pulpit, Landis had not much room for action. During the Eisenhower administration he served on the temporary Administrative Conference, and at the peak of the regulatory scandals in the late 1950s he wrote an occasional commentary for the *New York Herald Tribune*. But he lacked a real voice in policy making until 1960, when he answered John F. Kennedy's call.

At his first postelection press conference, Kennedy announced his first appointments to the new administration. Along with retaining J. Edgar Hoover at the FBI and Allen Dulles at the CIA, the President-elect commissioned James M. Landis to undertake a study of the regulatory commissions aimed at improving their performance. The press took note that Kennedy, eager to recapture the spirit of the New Deal, had singled out "an early and ardent New Dealer" to stand among his initial appointees. Accepting the assignment, Landis promised to try to stop the "downhill" trend of the commissions, and he sent shock waves through the regulatory agencies by threatening to "remove do-nothing dead wood that is afraid to show leadership," from the commissioners "down the line to staff membership."[6]

A month and a half later the Landis Report was completed. The speed, scope, and conciseness of the report surprised those who doubted him still capable of his old levels of performance. Some said that Landis' law partners had done the work, but they denied making any contribution other than providing him with office space and secretarial help. In fact, Landis wrote out the entire document, which came to eighty-seven printed pages, in his tight, precise long-hand, on legal-sized yellow pads. Employing old work habits, he buried himself in his material, so that on some nights he slept in his office on blankets on the floor. Landis saw no reason for surprise over his performance. "In a sense," he told reporters, "I've been working on this report all my life."[7]

The Landis Report summarized thirty years of experience. In sweeping statements it charged that the regulatory commissions affected "almost every significant aspect of our national being," and speculated that their economic responsibilities exceeded those of both the executive and legislative branches. If President Kennedy intended to redeem his campaign pledges to stimulate American productivity to meet the competition of Communist nations, he would have to begin with reforming the commissions. By 1960 they had become an anchor on the economy, falling hopelessly behind in their work, suffering under inadequate budgets and personnel, and lacking any coordination of policy between them. The Federal Power Commission, Landis' worst case example among the many, would need thirteen years just to complete its already-pending cases. "Good men can make poor laws workable," Landis asserted; "poor men will wreak havoc with good laws." He laid the largest share of blame for the regulatory decay on the low quality of Truman's and Eisenhower's appointees. Those commissioners lacked either the time or the competence to write their own case opinions, and instead unofficially passed that critical assignment off onto their staffs. Landis recommended giving commission chairmen authority to delegate routine and trivial business to staff members in order to clear commissioners' desks for decision writing and long-range planning. Finally, he called for more direct presidential leadership in coordinating the fragmented economic policies of the various agencies.[8]

Presidential involvement became the most controversial aspect of the

Landis Report. "We've allowed this situation to drift too long," he said in defense, "and it's time now that it be pulled together, and I think that the only way it can be very effectively pulled together is through strong executive leadership." Mindful of his own difficulties with Truman's interference in CAB decisions, Landis insisted that the President should never attempt to influence a pending regulatory decision, since White House meddling would place a premium on "lobbying in its worst characteristics." On the other hand, the chief executive had to be concerned with the efficiency of the commissions and their ability to handle the problems which Congress had delegated to them. Because of his responsibility to see that the laws were faithfully executed, and because of his authority to remove commissioners for neglect of their duty, the President had to keep abreast of the commissions' activities. To solve the paradox between presidential leadership and presidential politics, Landis suggested lengthening commissioners' terms in office as a means of insulating them, and recommended creation of an Office of Oversight of Regulatory Agencies in the White House. Such a permanent office would serve as a protagonist for the agencies before the President, the Budget Bureau, and the Congress, to offer "imaginative and creative" solutions to agency problems.[9]

On December 26, 1960, thirteen years to the day since Truman had dismissed him, Landis handed the President-elect his report. "This is a most important and impressive analysis of the regulatory agencies which deserves the attention of the members of Congress as well as the agencies themselves," Kennedy responded in endorsement. The new President's enthusiasm sent regulatory commissioners scrurrying to "scrounge up copies" of the privately printed booklet as best they could. Widespread newspaper and magazine coverage, with feature articles on the report in business, travel, television, and consumer publications, attested to the commissions' extensive influence on society. Not all were favorable, and the mixed bag of cheers and catcalls that greeted the report revealed how controversial the "dull, faceless agencies" had become. Professor Carl McFarland, chief author of the Administrative Procedure Act, hailed the Landis Report as "the voice of one crying out in the wilderness" and praised it for illuminating "an area which has been dim and confused for years." Reporters trailed behind former President Harry Truman, on one of his early morning walks, for his opinion. Truman recalled Landis as "one of the Harvard eggheads and a good one." He acknowledged the report's criticisms about the quality of some of his appointees but swiftly parried, "Jim ought to know something about it. He was one of the appointees."[10]

Critics across the political spectrum flailed at the report. From the conservatives came attacks in William F. Buckley's *National Review* and in the *New York Daily News* (bemoaning that any regulatory reform would burden taxpayers with "a bigger and more strongly entrenched bureaucracy than ever"). The columnist David Lawrence accused Landis of handing the President "dictatorial power over the commissions." Arthur Krock likened the goals of the Landis Report to those of the 1937 Brownlow Report: "Presidential domination of the so-called independent agencies that Congress refused to give to President F. D. Roosevelt." From the left, reformers disliked the report's moderation. Whereas the public debate over regulation in the 1950s had concentrated heavily on the failure to protect the public interest, Landis had emphasized the failure to serve the regulated industries efficiently. He played down the "industry orientation" of many commissions, which he explained as inescapable by-products of the day-to-day contacts between commissioners and businessmen, and the absence of effective citizens' lobbies. To correct that imbalance, the report suggested that each commission appoint a "public counsel," modeled after a post the CAB had long employed. "The rougher he is the better he is," Landis argued. "He may annoy you, and irritate you, but he brings you back to a sense of what the public interest is."[11]

Coming in the wake of Sherman Adams' resignation as White House chief of staff for tampering with regulatory decisions, and of congressional investigations into regulatory failings which ran the gamut from antitrust administration to television gameshow rigging, Landis' report struck some reformers as little more than cosmetics on a corpse. Louis J. Hector, who had just quit the CAB in disgust, laid regulatory problems to "basic and inescapable contradictions" in the commissions' structure. The commissions could not police and promote industry at the same time, Hector told Congress, and no amount of patchwork would repair that defect. Congress, he recommended, should abolish the independent agencies and turn their functions over to the executive branch and to a special administrative court. Landis strongly dissented from Hector's idea that only single-headed agencies could cope with modern economic challenges, and continued to defend the collegial bodies. "I just worry about these things — this single-minded genius," he said, pointing to such types as the arbitrary and irascible head of the Federal Aviation Administration, General Elwood Quesada. Landis also doubted that Congress would willingly shift so much of the regulatory process to the Cabinet. He expected rough congressional treatment for his own fairly modest proposals for presidential coordination, and doubted that Hector's plan stood any chance at all.[12]

By the end of December Landis hoped that his own role in the debate had ended. John Kennedy, however, pressed him to join the administration to carry out his report's recommendations. Unable to refuse the President — or the President's father — Landis agreed to serve as special presidential assistant in charge of regulatory policy for a period of six months. If he were lucky, he could do the job and be out of the administration before any of his personal problems came to light. As it was, he made good copy for the press. Stories pictured him as a "crusty New York lawyer" and a "sort of human barbed wire fence" who could not help but snag countless difficulties in his sensitive post. Both the "Today" show and Mike Wallace interviewed him on television, and he became the focus of considerable speculation in Washington. The press dubbed him "Regulatory Czar," but he declined the title, protesting that "the last thing I want is a czar in the field." He would rather foster a "quiet revolution" among the commissions themselves.[13]

For the old New Dealer, the New Frontier meant resurrection and vindication. During the Inaugural festivities, Landis' law partners honored him with a reception to welcome him back officially to the capital. Shortly afterwards came a special reunion with Felix Frankfurter. Friends invited both men separately to a luncheon without telling them of the other's attendance. Landis, who had just turned down an invitation to dine with the President-elect, arrived at the restaurant to find his former mentor waiting there. For years Frankfurter had not forgiven Landis for his diverted loyalties or for his divorce. Landis equally had been scornful of Frankfurter's conservative stance on the Supreme Court, which he rather unfairly attributed to the justice's desire to win social acceptance. "It's so easy, in this life, to associate with people who have prestige and money," Landis said of Frankfurter, ". . . you become a little loose in your thinking. The kind of things that you sweated for when you were twenty and thirty and forty, they get a little dim, and you start to compromise." But the warmth of their reunion melted the years of estrangement. They fell into animated and intimate conversation, reliving their years together at Harvard. Frankfurter confessed that of all the thousands of students he had taught, none had been "so congenial and intellectual a companion" as Jim Landis. The luncheon lasted over four hours, and when he left Landis broke down and wept. "I loved that guy," he told friends. "All those wasted years!"[14]

Business matters in New York kept Landis from joining the administration until February 1, 1961. When he arrived at the White House, he was immediately taken with the youth of the staff. The Kennedy men reminded him of himself as a novitiate in the New Deal, although at age sixty-one he found himself the old man of the group. His easy access to the President, and their similar attitudes on government reorganization, quickly made him feel at ease. During his first months in office, President Kennedy was dismantling the pyramid of interdepartmental committees that his predecessor had erected and was rechanneling all major policy decisions through his office. He ordered the executive departments to send him twice-weekly progress reports and requested that the independent regulatory commissions voluntarily file similar reports through Landis' office. With most of the commission chairmanships to fill, along with several other vacancies, Kennedy turned to Landis for advice on appointments. William L. Cary, a Columbia Law School professor who had worked under Landis at the SEC during the 1930s, took over as the new SEC chairman. Paul Rand Dixon, counsel to the Senate Anti-Trust and Monopoly subcommittee, moved to the FTC. Alan Boyd was elevated to CAB chairman. The Federal Communications Commission chairmanship went to thirty-five-year-old Newton Minow, a law partner of Adlai Stevenson. "Breaking through routines and getting new ideas requires a violent dash which only youth possesses," Landis remarked of that group with a hint of reminiscence.[15]

As special presidential assistant, Landis spent the lion's share of his time on the preparation of the administration's regulatory reorganization proposals. His program fell into two major parts: specific plans for each commission, and the creation of a coordinating body. It had already become apparent to Landis that his suggested "Office of Oversight" in the White House stood no chance of adoption. "Jim," Felix Frankfurter twitted him gently, "when you were Chairman of the Securities and Exchange Commission, how would you have liked to have one of these youngsters, one of these squirts, tell you . . . about things — and say you should do it the other way? You wouldn't have liked it, would you? So why do you think other people would like it?" Capping the decision to drop that plan was Landis' own refusal to accept a permanent post in the administration. If the most logical candidate would not take the job, Kennedy decided against creation of the office to avoid needlessly inflaming congressional sentiments. In its place, Landis, Judge E. Barrett Prettyman, and Nathan Nathanson, a Northwestern University law professor, drafted an executive order to create the Administrative Conference of the United States. By establishing standardized procedures and promoting the interchange of ideas and techniques, that body would "bring a sense of unity to our administrative agencies." At Landis' insistence, the Administrative Conference mixed lawyers, administrators, and political scientists, who he hoped would be more inclined to experiment and explore new approaches to regulation.[16]

On April 13 President Kennedy signed the executive order and appointed Landis to the executive council of the Administrative Conference. That same day, the President sent the first of his proposed regulatory reforms to Congress, which had sixty days to veto them under the provisions of the Executive Reorganization Act of 1949. The Landis-drafted program covered every major commission except for the politically enmeshed Interstate Commerce Commission. The heart of each plan was identical: increase the power of the chairmen, give them authority to delegate work to other commissioners and to the staff, and make them directly responsible to the President.[17]

"I like your Report — very much," the politically astute James Rowe had written to Landis. "Perhaps I am old and tired and cynical but I think you are going to have a helluva time getting it through Congress." Rowe was right. Both the President and his special assistant expected their program to encounter serious opposition but neither was prepared for the severity of the assault. They misjudged the depth of congressional opposition and the ferocity of lobbyist activities. Ominous words of disapproval were already rumbling through the Capitol. "We don't want a chief executive" for the agencies, stormed Representative Albert Thomas, whose committee controlled regulatory appropriations. Other legislators expressed fears that Landis might become "a super Sherman Adams." The House Legislative Oversight Subcommittee, which for two years had been investigating regulatory misadventures, issued a report insisting that only Congress had the power to supervise the regulatory process. Oren Harris, the subcommittee's chairman, termed the commissions "trustees of Congressional power." In the hostile atmosphere, lobbyists moved swiftly to help undermine any reforms that threatened to disrupt their clients' long-established ties with the commissions. Against them, the White House needed a monumental effort.[18]

In an unusual move, President Kennedy waived executive privilege and sent his special assistant to Capitol Hill to testify in defense of the plans.[19] The President's action reflected the confidence he placed in the man he deferentially called "Dean" (while Landis continued to refer to the President affectionately as "Jack"). "I have a great many friends in the Senate and the House," Landis assured the President, "and I can talk with them and explain what I am trying to do." He felt particularly close to Senator Warren Magnuson, chairman of the Commerce Committee, and Representative Emmanuel Celler of the House Judiciary Committee, and their influential staffs. He further counted on his friendship with House Speaker Sam Rayburn which dated back to the days when they worked together on FDR's securities legislation.[20]

Of all his proposals, Landis expected the least opposition for the reorganization of the Securities and Exchange Commission, and so had made it Plan #1. Landis' report directed only the mildest criticism against his step-child agency, blaming most of its defects on insufficient operating funds. Landis was also troubled with the vesting of undue policy-making power in the lower echelon of the SEC staff, a situation that had developed out of the need for rapid answers in securities cases, while at the same time less pressing and less significant business cluttered the commissioners' desks. A strong chairman with the power to delegate the workload could reverse that trend. He expected and received full support from the new SEC chairman, William Cary, sending him a copy of the plan just before it went to Capitol Hill, with no chance for Cary to comment upon it. The New York Stock Exchange, similarly unadvised, was furious. Exchange President Keith Funston called the plan a "blunderbuss," and warned the Senate Banking Committee that "the commission should not be permitted to delegate to anyone its legislative powers or its life and death authority over so important a segment of our economy." On the Senate floor, the New York liberal Republican Jacob Javits led the fight to kill the SEC proposal, arguing that it left unanswered too many disturbing questions about the delegation of legislative powers and could conceivably permit junior SEC staff members to gain "a hold on the jugular vein of the nation." The House passed Plan #1, but the Senate killed it by a vote of fifty-two to thirty-eight.[21]

More devastating was the defeat of his Federal Communications Commission plan. There, the same dynamic leadership that Landis considered so vital for the commission actually proved its undoing. The new chairman, Newton Minow, defended the Landis plan to increase the FCC chairman's power to delegate routine items to the staff. "It's really oppressive," Minow explained. "We sit here worrying about whether a shrimp boat's radio license should be revoked." But Minow had made powerful enemies among the broadcasters when he denounced television programing as a "vast wasteland" and threatened to deny license renewals to any station that failed to live up to its programing promises. The networks, the National Association of Broadcasters, and the federal communications bar turned loose their "enormous propaganda potentialities" on the plan. "The networks have vested interest in the status quo," Landis countered. "Their opposition stemmed not from a belief that the plan would not work, but from a fear that it might work too well."[22]

Leading those who protested that the FCC plan would turn other commissioners into "office boys" for the chairman was Commissioner Robert T. Bartley, nephew and former administrative assistant to Speaker Sam Rayburn. The House Government Operations Committee then rejected the plan. In the House chamber, Rayburn stepped down from the speaker's rostrum to criticize the FCC reorganization as an attempt to amend the original legislation, thereby infringing on congressional rights. "I was the author of the Federal Communications Act," Rayburn asserted, "and I think I know something about it." Without the speaker's support, the administration had no hope. On June 16 the House voted down the plan, 323 to 77.[23]

The columnist Tom Wicker called the FCC vote "the most complete rout the Kennedy administration has ever suffered in this Congressional session." A month later the House defeated Plan #5 for the National Labor Relations Board. Three rejections added up to a stunning setback for Kennedy. Angry White House aides contacted the regulatory chairmen to criticize them for not working hard enough for the plans. One aide called FTC chairman Paul Rand Dixon and told him, "Well, we're in trouble. It's embarrassing to the President now. We've got to win one and you're it." Eventually, the FTC plan did pass, and along with it Congress accepted plans for the CAB, the Federal Power Commission, and several minor agencies where industry opposition had not been effectively organized.[24]

The onus of the defeats fell on Landis. He hurried to Capitol Hill in search of an answer, and Senator John McClellan was more than happy to oblige him. As chairman of the Government Operations Committee, McClellan had shepherded the executive reorganization authority bill through the Senate, but then had voted against the SEC reorganization and sharply criticized the CAB plan. When Landis confronted him, the senator expressed annoyance that the administration had not bothered to consult with him on the drafting of any of the plans. McClellan admitted having had great trouble making up his mind over the SEC plan and said that he had decided to oppose it only thirty minutes before the vote. He found the Democratic leadership in the dark over the administration's intentions and thought that Majority Whip Hubert Humphrey "seemed to have been called in at the last moment" to defend the SEC plan. Even Humphrey suggested that the administration would have been wiser to consult with Congress in advance.[25]

Against such Democratic uncertainty, the Republicans presented a solid front. When Landis and his staff examined the congressional tallies, they found that only 85 members of the House of Representatives voted consistently for the first four reorganization plans, and all were Democrats. Of the 177 members who voted against all four plans, 162 were Republicans. Not counting the FCC plan which Speaker Rayburn opposed, 221 Democrats voted consistently for the other three plans while no Republicans had voted for all three. Only two Republicans defied their party policy committee's opposition to the plans and voted affirmatively on any of them: Albin Norblad of Oregon and Laurence Curtis of Massachusetts, both "Harvard law men."[26]

The administration never intended to try to ramrod its plans through Congress. Kennedy promised to cooperate fully with members of the House and Senate, but because the regulatory commissions touched upon such a range of interests, there were too many congressmen to see and too many lobbyists to compete against. Assessing his own role, Landis blamed his failure on the President's undeveloped staff system. Kennedy had grown used to a small, closely-knit staff during his years in the House and Senate and had not yet adjusted to the large-scale operations that a White House staff entailed. While the President made himself remarkably accessible, in

1961 he still dealt with his advisors on an individual basis and rarely called them together to enlist their common efforts behind a single project. Often only by accident, through table talk at the White House mess, did staff members discover they were working on related matters. The responsibilities that the President had placed upon him, Landis decided, had been "too much for one man." Nor had his programs stood alone in defeat. Despite heavy Democratic majorities in both houses, Congress rejected or delayed Kennedy-sponsored legislation for health, housing, and civil rights as well as the three reorganization plans.[27]

In retrospect, Landis erred tactically in planning the reorganization assault. The orderly and symmetrical flow charts and organization tables in his Executive Office Building suite hypnotized him and made him lose track of the human fears and sensitivities over organizational change. He presented his program as a unified package, with essentially the same plan for every agency. He also attempted to control the whole program himself, excluding both the regulatory commissioners and key congressional figures from the planning stages. It annoyed Newton Minow to receive his copy of the FCC plan only a day before the plan went to Congress. William Cary similarly had no opportunity to comment on the SEC plan. Frank McCulloch of the National Labor Relations Board received his agency's plan from Landis as a *"fait accompli."* [28]

The most serious mistake was his decision to present the entire program as an administrative act rather than as a series of bills. Each plan had to be referred to four committees (the House and Senate Government Operations committees as well as the committees in each body with specific jurisdiction over the substantive areas of the commissions). Either house could kill a plan by a majority vote of those present; and the leadership could not postpone voting until a more suitable time because of the constraints of the Reorganization Act. Finally, there was the "psychological reaction of the Congress against a reorganization plan," one of Landis' aides noted. Executive reorganization authority worked best for executive branch agencies and not for the independent commissions. Apparently, Landis had forgotten his own opposition to FDR's similar scheme for regulatory reorganization in 1937; a quarter of a century later the Kennedy administration suffered the same congressional rebuke. SEC Chairman Cary, who termed it "political ineptitude on the part of the White House," recounted how Senator Javits had telephoned him at the time of the SEC plan's defeat to promise, "I just want you to know you are going to get the same powers in the form of a bill. Senator Harrison Williams and I have agreed upon that." Other congressional actions further demonstrated that the administration had suffered defeat unnecessarily. Congressman Oren Harris introduced and passed legislation for the Federal Communications

Commission that differed only slightly from Landis' plan. A year later, Congress also passed its own version of the SEC plan. Landis had lost more over his methods than over his objectives.[29]

The dramatic defeats obscured some significant accomplishments. With the exception of the early New Deal period, the Kennedy administration sparked more positive change in the administrative process than had occurred in any other period to that time. Landis believed that he had instilled "a new fire" in the commissions and had helped restore "a sense of their own importance." The atmosphere of change and challenge, he hoped, would soon attract the same enthusiastic talent into the commissions as they had drawn in the 1930s. "If so," he promised, "it is certain to succeed in making more palatable, but, more important, more workable, the relationship of industry and the public to government; and in doing so will ensure the survival of the American idea, the concept of free but controlled enterprise."[30]

In June 1961, when the first stage of reorganization ended, Landis submitted his resignation to the President. He had done what he could and felt it was time for the commissions to prove themselves. He looked forward to a return to the privacy of his law practice and to Dorothy. Since his post in the administration was intended to be temporary, she had remained in New York at her job as an English teacher at Bronxville High. (At first Landis had been dubious when Dorothy enrolled at Columbia University to complete her bachelor's degree and then take a master's in education. But he studied every course along with her, and was enormously proud the day she made Phi Beta Kappa, calling all of his friends with the news and arranging a dinner party for her that night at the Plaza Hotel.) Throughout the spring of 1961, Landis flew to Washington on Sunday nights and back to New York on Thursday evenings. Although Dorothy was teaching, he never thought twice of asking her to pick him up at the airport, at any time of the day or night. It was, she understood, "just second nature for him to have service."[31]

Kennedy refused to accept his resignation. Rumors in Washington had it that the President was considering Landis for a Supreme Court appointment, when one became available. As the story went, Felix Frankfurter had privately indicated that his health might soon cause him to consider leaving the court, and that he would look favorably on Landis as a successor. But Landis dismissed the notion of a court appointment. Twenty years earlier he might have been interested, but he told his law partner Justin Feldman that he would not accept any position that required Senate confirmation. Feldman took the remark as a veiled reference to Landis' drinking problem and pursued the point no further. At that same time, Internal Revenue agents in New York were discovering some startling news about the special assistant to the President: they could find none of his income tax returns for the years after 1955.[32]

Unaware of these developments, President Kennedy asked Landis to stay on at the White House to handle negotiations with the Soviet Union to establish the first direct air service between New York and Moscow. Landis' last federal assignment reconfirmed his abundant abilities for handling any task, no matter how complex and controversial. In the midst of heightened Cold War tensions over the Bay of Pigs invasion in April, and Nikita Khrushchev's bellicose statements during his Vienna meeting with Kennedy in June, with both nations expanding their military forces for possible confrontation over Berlin, Landis conducted friendly and conciliatory negotiations. In a short time he reached accord on a commercial air treaty with the Russians. To his regret, the Department of State rejected the treaty in protest over the building of the Berlin Wall. However, Pan American Airways, whose representatives attended the negotiations in anticipation of gaining the Moscow route, did not fail to recognize the agreement as a testament to Landis' personal skill. Burying a fifteen-year feud, the airline offered Landis a retainer to handle some of its own legal problems.[33]

By then Landis needed the work. Unexpected events at last terminated his White House post. During the summer his letter of resignation had remained in the President's office without any acknowledgment. Unfortunately, Landis had written other letters. Always an incorrigible poet, he sent flirtatious rhymes to his White House secretary. When the poems fell into the hands of her husband, he named Landis as correspondent in their divorce suit. Reporters called Landis at his New York law office when the news broke on September 7, 1961. "My wife will never take this," Landis gasped, and left immediately for Washington, without calling Dorothy to explain.[34]

How could he explain? In a youthful administration, which intertwined political power and sexual allure, Landis found it painful to accept the mirror's image of a balding, paunchy, jowly man of sixty-one. Always having regretted not being tall and handsome, he more than ever needed to prove his attractiveness and virility. Now, realizing that his indiscretion had embarrassed his wife and his President, he shut himself up in his Washington apartment to drink. "I understand I have a problem," he meekly greeted Stanley Gewirtz, who came when he heard the news. As in past crises, Gewirtz telephoned the resourceful Tommy Corcoran, who reassured them, "You can get something on anybody." (Four months later the litigation against Landis was dropped.) Later that night, Justin Feldman drove to Washington to take him back to his home in Harrison, New York. At 3:00 a.m. a sorrowful James Landis arrived home. Dorothy asked no questions and told him to get some sleep and not to talk about it.[35]

The incident came as a shock at the White House. When Congressman Oren Harris visited the President, Kennedy wryly commented he thought it "rather ironical" that the distinguished dean of the Harvard Law School would be the first to leave his administration under such a cloud. But the President acted swiftly. "You kick them out as soon as you find them," John Kennedy explained to Ben Bradlee his policy for handling potential scandals. The same day, the White House released Landis' letter of resignation, dated August 1, and Kennedy's acceptance, dated September 1. Presidential Press Secretary Pierre Salinger assured reporters that the divorce suit and resignation had been purely coincidental. The President's letter graciously thanked Landis for his service. "Your efforts are reflected in the programs of this Administration for greater efficiency and protection for the public interest," he wrote, "and you can be justifiably proud of these accomplishments."[36]

Back in private life, Landis never again exerted a major influence on the federal regulatory commissions. On occasion he did speak out on the subject, and delivered what was to be his valedictory address to an audience of Chicago advertising executives in November 1962. That speech took on a more conservative tone than was usual for Landis, reflecting perhaps his age, his identification with the tribulations of his business clients, and his disappointment that the commissions were not responding more forcefully to his reforms. Having begun his career by battling unchecked business influence, he ended by denouncing the overextension of the federal government and the bureaucratic stifling of corporate creativity. The commissions should work "to allow the forces of competition to provide a free market, and to permit the entry into that market of new creative forces, as well as to keep that market reasonably clean so that seller and purchaser will deal fairly with each other at arm's length." The problem had become how "to keep the regulatory process within bounds." But for all their deficiencies, he still placed his faith in the long-range potential of the independent commissions. "What I seek for the regulatory process is not its abolition but its ascendancy," he concluded, "provided that it moors its activities to the message of Saint Paul in First Corinthians—faith in our system of private enterprise, hope in its inherent possibilities, and charity to the inevitable vicissitudes that attend those who have the courage to seek new horizons."[37]

14 | What Went Wrong?

Friday, August 2, 1963, James McCauley Landis appeared in the United States District Court in Manhattan to plead guilty on five counts of failure to file income tax returns between 1956 and 1960. He offered little explanation. "The taxpayer, being deeply engrossed in public affairs and the affairs of clients," his lawyer said, "neglected his own personal matters." United States Attorney Robert Morgenthau added that Landis offered the government "full cooperation" during the investigation. Landis had already paid more than $94,000 in back taxes but owed another $76,000 in additional taxes and delinquency penalties. The judge released him in his own custody and set sentencing for August 30. News of the guilty plea shocked everyone who knew him. David Lilienthal, for one, could hardly believe the front page story in the *New York Times*. He remembered his Harvard classmate as a man of "ardor and impetuousness," whose later career had been perpetually stormy. "But just blandly neglecting to report his income tax for five years," Lilienthal pondered, "how the hell can you explain that in a first-rate *lawyer?*" [1]

The tax case exposed only the surface of James Landis' tragedy. A man who had directed his entire life towards public service, he had never quite recovered his equilibrium after his dismissal from the Civil Aeronautics Board two decades earlier. Power never corrupted him, but absence from power thoroughly depressed and disoriented him. The 1950s offered Landis a happy marriage, close friends, a highly successful law practice, financial reward, and all other accoutrements of "the good life." Yet, private practice somehow lacked the same satisfaction and solace that public service

189

offered. In need of public gratification and recognition, Landis spent the decade of the 1950s searching, almost frantically, for tasks large enough to fit his abilities. Once he told his family that he had accepted an assignment to investigate a messy race track scandal in New York as his own way of avoiding depression. Other times he accepted his "Christ cases" at low or nonexistent retainers for their sheer personal stimulation. He even played intensely, devoting enormous amounts of time to card games, and entering newspaper contests on bridge hands, jingles, and anagrams.[2]

In 1952, at the urging of his friend George Skouras, Landis and his wife moved from their Manhattan apartment to a ten-room, Spanish-style house on the grounds of the Westchester Country Club in Harrison, New York. In that beautiful setting, Skouras assured him, he could find time to unwind and play a little more golf. For a while Landis settled into comfortable suburban living. He installed a swimming pool behind the house and planted a garden, where he could putter for hours on weekends. He and Dorothy assembled a small menagerie of nine cats, a Saint Bernard, and a Labrador, and took up horseback riding (where his "I can do anything" attitude prompted him to attempt jumps without the slightest experience or training, to the horror of his instructor).[3] But a leisurely life-style could not hold Landis for long. Within months he became embroiled in local politics.

His interest first became aroused when the Harrison Board of Education imposed a loyalty oath on all teachers and speakers at the town's schools. Ever since the Harry Bridges case, Landis had treated the communist issue with great caution. He declined to serve as a lawyer for communists indicted under the Smith Act and dutifully reported to the FBI any unsolicited radical literature he received. At the same time, he suspected that the anticommunist crusade was intent on discrediting old New Dealers, among them many of his friends, and none more prominently than his former law student Alger Hiss. So he joined the movement to revoke the loyalty oaths. As a result of the fight, he met Paul Bauman, counsel for the anti-loyalty-oath forces and a lawyer active in Westchester County's Democratic politics. Bauman shrewdly assessed Landis' political potential and cultivated his interest in the local minority party. In 1955 he proposed that Landis run for town supervisor, but Landis refused, citing his busy law practice. The next evening, Bauman returned with other Harrison Democratic leaders to renew the appeal and got Landis to accept. "It seems to me that a person should develop community roots politically as well as socially," Landis rationalized.[4]

The race seemed completely futile. Harrison, along with the rest of suburban Westchester, overwhelmingly voted Republican. Moreover, a majority of the town's population was of Italian origin, as was the incumbent Republican supervisor, Alfred F. Sulla, Jr. Still, Landis carried impressive credentials for the local race. His opponents, after surveying his long list of government and academic posts, had expected him to be a man in his seventies and were surprised to learn that he was only fifty-six. Their next reaction was to brand the former New Dealer as "a Red or a Communist," but Landis came prepared with a letter of endorsement signed by the minority counsel of the McCarthy committee, Robert F. Kennedy. Each evening, Landis left his Manhattan law practice, took the train to Harrison, and hit the campaign trail, talking to the voters on the streets or in small groups at friends' homes. He had learned much about ethnic politics from years of observing FDR and took care to read the local society and obituary pages, to attend funerals, appear at wedding receptions, and visit nearby hospitals on Sunday mornings. Before long he boasted that he could "drop into any place and everybody knows me." On election day the Republicans swept Westchester County with one exception: Landis' upset victory by 143 votes. Every other position in Harrison but the superintendent of highways went to the Republicans.[5]

"Other municipalities may have had more important elections today," a *New York Times* reporter wrote from Harrison, "but it is doubtful if any could equal the minor miracle accomplished by the voters from this town — the election of a staunch New Dealer in this long-time heart of Republican conservatism." Up in Boston, the *Globe* recalled Landis' civic activities in Cambridge and hailed him as an example for others "of capacity who deem local politics too far beneath them." The victory also inspired Westchester Democrats to dream of greater achievements. Bauman and others were soon telling Landis that a Democrat who could carry the suburbs would make an unbeatable candidate for the United States Senate in 1956 or 1958. Ten years earlier Landis had mused to Dorothy: "I love politics. If I had nothing else to do and plenty of money I would run for Senator just for the hell of it, and I think I could make it." Now he had the time, the money, and the reputation of a vote-getter in a Republican stronghold. About that time he also opened a local law office with Paul Bauman and former Westchester County Surrogate Judge George Brenner.[6]

For the next two years Landis used his part-time, $13,600-a-year supervisor's post to battle the entire Westchester Republican machine. As a member of the county's Board of Supervisors, he became a sharp-tongued foe of Republican plans for taxes, pipelines, airports, and highways, and kept his name constantly in the news. "We're scared to death of him," one Republican supervisor confided. Few Westchester politicians could call upon so many contacts in Washington and in the national news media. Landis needed all the advantages he could muster, for the Republicans held a two-thirds majority in the county and a four-fifths majority in his own town government, where they regularly vetoed his proposals and appointees. In 1956 Democratic leaders in Westchester proposed Landis for the party's Senate nomination, but state-wide party leaders wanted Mayor Robert F. Wagner of New York City to make the race. Wagner's defeat that year made James Landis a more attractive candidate for 1958.[7]

Because of his good record and favorable publicity, Landis expected to win reelection in 1957 in a rematch with former supervisor Sulla. He did not count on the blunderings of his own supporters. New York's Byzantine political traditions had spawned an intricate system of minor parties, such as the United Harrison Independent Party which Landis' supporters created to attract Republican voters who would not vote for him on the Democratic line. At the last moment before the filing deadline, Landis' campaign manager, Bauman, discovered that he had neglected to obtain enough signatures on their petitions to assure a place for the Independent Party on the ballot. In desperation he forged the required number of names and got Landis' young secretary, Joseph Straface, Jr., to sign the petitions as a witness. The Republicans were far too intent upon defeating Landis not to scour his petitions carefully. Early in October, the Republican district attorney indicted both Bauman and Straface for campaign violations.[8]

Candidate Landis, who had known nothing of the incident, immediately fired Bauman as his campaign manager and asked him to resign from his law firm. But he could not bring himself to desert Straface, assuming that the young man, only recently out of the Navy, had blindly followed orders. In defending his Italian aide as "morally innocent" while dismissing his Jewish law partner, Landis alienated many voters in the Jewish neighborhoods of Harrison. Although he fought an intense campaign, he could not overcome the scandal. In November 1957 he lost by twenty-two votes. With the loss of his supervisor's post went his reputation as a suburban vote-getter and any chance of the 1958 senatorial nomination. Landis insisted that he was relieved to return to his law practice, but his good friend Tommy Corcoran believed the defeat broke his heart.[9]

George Brenner accompanied Landis back to Manhattan, where they formed the firm of Landis, Brenner, Feldman and Reilly. Then Brenner also failed him. In 1959 the former county judge was arrested and convicted of counterfeiting stock certificates to obtain business loans. Before sending Brenner to prison, the judge described him as a man "with an insatiable appetite for worldly and material goods; with an elaborate thirst for power; with a foolhardy desire to maintain a public image which required ostentatious and extravagant living far beyond his means." Association with Bauman and Brenner caused Landis much embarrassment. To some, he was "guileless" and too trusting, a man of "bumbling innocence," his name and reputation easy prey for the exploitation of ambitious lawyers.[10]

The convictions of Bauman and Brenner also created mistaken impressions about Landis' later financial problems. On the surface, he appeared to have fallen victim to the same insatiable materialistic drives. Yet of all his failings, materialism counted the least. James Landis enjoyed good food, good drink, and a good life, but he rarely paid much attention to his possessions or his personal appearance. Nor did he devote much time to his own finances. In the 1920s, after his first marriage, he had kept an intricate ledger in two colors of ink for all family expenses. That project barely lasted a year. Afterwards, he concentrated on national finance to the exclusion of his own. Habitually he missed deadlines for filing his tax returns, beginning as early as 1934. "I should like to plead generally the press of government business in Washington during these extraordinary days," he wrote to the Internal Revenue that year. He filed late in 1935, and the next year, while chairman of the Securities and Exchange Commission, he sent in his check "late as usual." Periodically, he also forgot to pay his real estate taxes. When he did file, his returns were uncharacteristically careless and in error, showing hasty preparation. He regularly owed more than he paid, usually in small sums of less than one hundred dollars.[11]

By the 1950s his wealth had risen appreciably. In 1956 he had a taxable income of $60,000. In both 1957 and 1958 his annual income exceeded $100,000. But having passed the stage that permitted petty errors, he had not reformed his old habits. He allowed bills to collect on his desk for months until he finally would sit down and write checks for every bill in sight, sometimes paying the second and third notices for the same bill. When the companies returned his overpayments in the form of credit, he might send off a check covering the credit. That muddle provoked Dorothy Landis to take charge of all household bills. His law firm filed their business taxes, which left only personal tax returns to Landis' responsibility.[12]

In 1956 Landis requested one of his regular extensions for filing his returns, citing a major family crisis. During the previous summer both his daughter Ann and her husband had contracted paralytic polio. In his anguish, Landis felt considerable guilt as a father. Since his divorce he had neglected his children more shamefully than before. At times they might receive lengthy handwritten letters from him, and then another year could pass without further contact. The divorce, Stella's alcoholism, and the generally disturbed family life had been hardest on Ann, who had suffered a nervous breakdown while in college and then the polio attack. During one long night of fever when Ann was struggling to breathe and it seemed as though she might not live, Landis prayed for his daughter in the hospital chapel. "What a wonderful way to have your faith in God restored," Dorothy exclaimed the next morning when they heard that the fever had subsided. "God had nothing to do with it," Landis snapped back, "it was the

193

doctors." While his son-in-law's wealthy family took care of the medical bills, Landis' thoughts immediately turned toward physical rehabilitation. Independently, he arranged for Ann and her husband to undergo therapy at the Rusk Institute in New York, for which he would handle the expenses. While the costs were steeper than anticipated, his financial situation was sufficient to sustain them, requiring only that he liquidate some assets. In the process, he discovered that some of his records were incomplete.[13]

Back in the 1930s Landis had inherited a few stocks from his mother, which were now worth about $3,700. Since his mother had died without a will, he was unable to determine their initial value for the purpose of establishing a profit or loss on the sale. The stocks had originally come from his father's estate, and that would require digging further back through a tangle of financial records. It would have been easier to concede the whole sum a profit and to pay the small tax, but for Landis it became a matter of principle and he obtained an extension to complete his search. Later that year, in the heat of Harrison politics, he simply forgot about the unfiled returns. Not until the following spring when he began to prepare his next year's returns did he discover his neglect. At the top of the 1040 form there appeared an ominous question as to whether one had filed a return for the previous year.[14] Perhaps afraid of the political repercussions such a confession would cause, he deposited the money he owed into a checking account and hid the tax forms in his desk. Irrationally, year after year he continued the process, closing his mind to his dire situation. From time to time he would gather up his returns and tell his unsuspecting law partners that he planned to work on his taxes over the weekend, but he could never really face up to his predicament. For years he carried on the deception, while he served as Harrison supervisor, considered running for the United States Senate, accepted a post on the New York State Public Service Commission, campaigned for the presidency of the Air Line Pilots' Association, and joined the White House staff as special assistant to the President.[15]

His secret emerged accidentally during a routine check of all presidential appointees in the spring of 1961. The Internal Revenue agent who discovered the absence of Landis' returns did not launch a regular departmental investigation. To avoid a political scandal, he instead passed the word to the President's father. A disbelieving Joseph Kennedy traced Landis down by telephone, demanded the truth, and then flew into a whirlwind of activity to get the taxes paid, quickly and quietly. He ordered Landis to report to the attorney general at once and explain the whole sorry story.[16] Making that admission to Robert Kennedy was especially painful for Landis, who had long advised the thirty-five-year-old attorney general "like an old lawyer would help an aspiring lawyer." The attorney general could only advise him to see the commissioner of internal revenue, Mortimer Caplin, who in turn recommended that Landis file his back taxes as soon as possible. With a twenty-five percent delinquency penalty and six percent interest, the amount he owed totaled more than he had set aside in the checking account, but, with a loan from Joseph Kennedy, Landis paid $94,492 to the government. The IRS division in New York accepted the returns as a voluntary filing.[17]

The story did not end there. In Washington, top-ranking IRS officials had their doubts about the Landis case. The agency maintained a hard and fast rule that it would not bring criminal indictment if it received late returns before a formal investigation had begun; but once an investigation was underway, no filing could be "voluntary" and indictment would be mandatory. A special IRS agent arrived in New York to examine the case and to comb through Landis' personal and business transactions. Every client of his came under scrutiny, every dealing was reassessed. The agent questioned Landis about a Cadillac he had given away to a favorite bartender at Longchamps rather than trade it in and disallowed numerous deductions from his returns. Calculating the additional taxes and penalties, the IRS concluded that Landis still owed $76,401. As part of the investigation, agents called Landis in to explain his actions personally. He went to the New York IRS office without bothering to bring any counsel. When asked why he had finally decided to file his back taxes, Landis candidly admitted that Joseph Kennedy had told him to do so. "I think I've done a very stupid thing," he reported back to his law partners. His admission destroyed both the "voluntary" nature of his filing and any defense on the lack of willfulness in his failure to file.[18]

Owing to Landis' relationship with the President and the involvement of the President's father in the case, no official in Washington relished the responsibility of deciding whether to bring a criminal indictment. The IRS reported its findings to the Justice Department recommending prosecution, much to the attorney general's displeasure. Robert Kennedy forwarded the case to Louis Oberdorfer, chief of the Tax Division, but Oberdorfer felt personally indebted to Landis for helping him through his confirmation hearings, at no cost, and disqualified himself on grounds of conflict of interest. His disqualification was symptomatic of a major dilemma for Landis, whose extensive intimacy with those of high rank in the government and the courts worked to deny him leniency. Those friendliest toward him withdrew, leaving those with the least amount of sympathy to handle the case.

At the Justice Department, the case finally settled on the desk of Deputy Attorney General Nicholas Katzenbach, who set out to explore every way possible to avoid bringing an indictment. He called in a young lawyer from the Tax Division and assigned him the role of Landis' advocate, instructing him to write the best memorandum he could on why an indictment was unnecessary. Katzenbach also conducted meetings with the career attorneys of the Tax Division and the IRS and consulted with Landis' lawyer, Dean William C. Warren of the Columbia Law School, who argued that the failure to file had been psychologically motivated and that indictment would be unfair. But in the end, Katzenbach felt compelled to indict. The memorandum failed to convince him, as did the psychological defense. The IRS took the position that failure to file was almost always a psychological problem, since it inevitably led to detection and punishment. Conscious cheats would file fraudulent returns instead. Yet to decriminalize the failure to file might turn it into a loophole for future chiselers. The career attorneys at the Tax Division also held to that interpretation and were carefully observing how the political appointees handled the case. The final difficulty, as Katzenbach perceived it, was that Landis had also failed to file his New York State returns, and the administration of Governor Nelson Rockefeller, a potential candidate against John F. Kennedy in 1964, was watching and waiting. If the federal government did not press charges, then New York might act, which would have the same devastating effects on Landis plus more damaging political consequences for the Kennedy administration. Katzenbach could see no way out of it.[19]

As the Justice Department moved toward an indictment, Landis' lawyers tried to build his defense. Incompetency for psychological reasons seemed their best argument. Since the tax case had begun, Landis had sunk into depression, had trouble working, suffered from insomnia and excessive drinking, and was having thoughts of suicide. In June 1962 Dean Warren sent him to see Lawrence C. Kolb, chairman of the Department of Psychiatry at the College of Physicians and Surgeons of Columbia University and director of Psychiatric Services at Columbia Presbyterian Hospital and the New York State Psychiatric Institute. When Kolb first heard the details of the case, he assumed that Landis had become senile, but during their initial conversations he found him "clear as a bell." After a thorough neurological examination revealed a cardiac problem but no signs of brain damage, Kolb suggested that Landis undergo psychiatric evaluation. He began with a battery of tests, from the Rorschach and Bender-Gestalt to the Thematic Apperception (TAT) tests. The examiner, who knew nothing of Landis and tested him "blind," found the subject a man of "very superior" intellectual range who showed "no sign of loss of intellectual vigor."[20]

A portrait emerged from these tests of a fiercely competitive person whose dominant behavior masked a very serious lack of self-esteem. In his responses, Landis placed recurring emphasis on success and personal achievement, and yet most of his stories ended on unsatisfactory or unhappy notes. Shown a series of ambiguous TAT pictures, he saw in one a young boy "learning to play his violin and daydreaming about being a great performer," but "it could turn out the way my own violin playing did — no good." In other responses he denied vigorously that anything had ever held him back or that he had ever failed an examination of any kind. "In his attempts to compensate for his lack of genuine self-esteem," the examiner suggested, "the patient seems to have developed a grandiose self-image, with little recognition of realistic limitations."[21]

The tests further indicated "strong hostile and destructive impulses, which appear to be associated with pervasive, but denied, dependency needs." Lingering in Landis' personality was the youth from the missionary compound, deeply dependent upon his mother and competitive with his father. Shown a picture of an older and younger man together, he described a son "intent on getting the good end of the deal" from his father. In another picture of a postmortem operation he perceived that the son had murdered his father, although hastily adding that "the boy shot his father by accident." Tracing the root of his hostility to the subject's competitiveness with his father, the examiner noted that he "directs a considerable amount of hostility toward himself, to such an extent that self-destructive behavior, probably of an indirect nature, such as obviously indiscreet or inappropriate behavior, is a distinct possibility." The examiner also noted signs of withdrawal on the subject's part, as old age and personal failure clashed with grandiose goals. James Landis of Harrison, New York, ended one TAT story with a description of a character who would "go on living in a small village, and live out a very quiet life."[22]

The psychiatrist had no trouble charting Landis' episodes of procrastination: his twenty-four-year delay in taking a bar examination; the years of agonizing indecision leading to his divorce; his unpaid bills, unsent alimony checks, and unanswered mail.[23] In the 1960s the Securities and Exchange Commission had called Landis to task for failing to report certain stock transactions. Similarly, the New York State Bar Association's Ethics Committee had chastised him for not answering their repeated inquiries into a complaint of mismanagement of a case, although the complaint had no foundation in truth. Dr. Kolb concluded that behind Landis' procrastination lay a desired self-destruction. To Dean Warren, the psychiatrist wrote that he had found "a long standing personality disturbance in a man of high intelligence and moral conviction which impaired his capacity to conform to the income tax laws."[24]

The attorneys recognized the gamble in a psychological defense, but it was Landis' only alternative to pleading guilty. Dr. Kolb encouraged them to continue, not only because he considered his diagnosis correct but because he hoped the case could establish a new principle of "willfulness" and overturn New York State's reliance on the archaic M'Naghton Rules (which recognized a psychological defense only when the defendant could not distinguish between right and wrong).[25]

In July 1963 Nicholas Katzenbach journeyed to New York to meet with Landis' lawyers. At that time, Dean Warren and Justin Feldman spelled out their intentions to argue the case on grounds of incompetency. Feldman suggested that the United States attorney bring the case before the grand jury, even though it had not been a felony. He felt sure that they could convince the jury that Landis had been overwrought and neurotic, rather than willfully fraudulent, and that the closed-door grand jury proceedings would relieve the government of having to bring an indictment. But for Katzenbach the problem was one of public perception: the government must "play it absolutely straight" and not leave the slightest suggestion of political interference. The deputy attorney general doubted that a psychological defense could work or remain secret for long. He also did not believe that the lawyers were speaking for James Landis himself and challenged them to consult with their client first. When Landis joined the meeting, he agreed with Katzenbach. "I've embarrassed the Administration enough," he said. "Nick's quite right." A plea of not guilty by reason of incompetency would only reflect on his regulatory reorganization program. In any case, Landis considered "incompetency" as degrading as conviction.[26]

Given Landis' reputation and distinguished career, Katzenbach recommended that he get in and out of court quickly, plead, pay the penalties, and be done with it. United States Attorney Morgenthau provided the defense with a schedule of sitting judges and allowed the lawyers to select the most sympathetic judge and convenient time. They chose the Labor Day weekend for sentencing, trusting that the holiday would minimize the publicity. At the most they expected a fine and suspended sentence.[27]

The ultimate decision rested with Landis, and he agreed to plead guilty and throw himself on the mercy of the court. Unfortunately, the court showed no mercy. The friendly judge they had counted on considered himself too friendly to the defense and disqualified himself. In his place sat District Court Chief Judge Sylvester J. Ryan, well known for his sternness. Dean Warren asked the judge for "compassionate consideration" in light of his client's long and selfless public career. Judge Ryan responded that he was disturbed over reports that Landis had been a patient at the Columbia Presbyterian Neurological Institute since entering his plea earlier that month and wondered "whether this man was competent to enter a plea of guilty." Warren assured the judge of his client's competency, and Landis, who had been slumped in his chair, nervously clasping and unclasping his hands, rose to address the court. "I would like to express regret, indeed repentance, for the folly that led me to put off filing of those returns," he said. "At no time did I intend to deprive the government of any revenue."[28]

No one anticipated Judge Ryan's virtually unprecedented sentence of thirty days in prison and one year on probation. As he heard the sentence, Landis raised his hands before him in disbelief and then let them drop remorsefully to his sides. "You have formed a habit you found difficult to control," declared the judge, alluding to his alcoholism. "Men of my heritage often have had such difficulties." His purpose in imposing sentence, the judge explained, was "to give you an opportunity to reflect and straighten yourself out." Dean Warren begged for a "little time" for his client, but the judge was unmovable. "The sooner he serves the sentence, the better it will be for the defendant." Marshals escorted a frail and dejected-looking Landis from the courtroom to the Federal House of Detention. Later that day, citing health reasons, the government transferred him to the Public Health Service hospital on Staten Island and assigned him to the third floor ward where alcoholics were treated.[29]

"Ex-Harvard Dean Jailed"; "Jail for Landis on Tax Count"; "Landis Gets 30 Days on Tax Charge," read the headlines. Friends of Landis were saddened and bewildered. Felix Frankfurter became distraught over the news. Landis' six-year-old granddaughter asked her parents: "If grandfather is so close to President Kennedy, why didn't he stop the trial?" In Washington Attorney General Robert Kennedy was dumbfounded that the judge had jailed a man of such distinction on a tax charge. Nicholas Katzenbach also considered the ruling disgraceful and the judge's lecture to Landis merely publicity seeking. If Judge Ryan had not made a speech, Katzenbach thought, there might not have been so much of a story.[30]

At the Public Health Service hospital, Landis' mental and physical condition deteriorated rapidly. Since the previous March he had suffered from convulsive attacks, which made his doctors suspect the possibility of a brain tumor. Dr. Kolb visited him regularly and prescribed antidepressant drugs. The hospital, on the other hand, treated him as a potential suicide and removed his belt, razor, and, worst for a chainsmoker, his cigarettes. When Dorothy visited, she found him white and shaking. During a game of rummy with her the cards suddenly flew out of his hands while he was shuffling, and he fainted. Almost hysterical, Dorothy called his law partners to tell them he was not receiving proper medical care. They petitioned to transfer him to Columbia Presbyterian, but Nicholas Katzenbach refused to sanction the move. James Bennett, head of the Bureau of Prisons, assured Katzenbach that Landis had gotten special quarters and excellent medical treatment. The attorney general, however, personally overruled Katzenbach. It had been one thing not to shield a close friend who broke the law, but it was an entirely different matter to punish him as a means of protecting the President from adverse publicity. Disregarding the potential public reaction, Robert Kennedy ordered Landis transferred to the

Harkness Pavilion at Columbia Presbyterian. Two plainclothes guards sat outside his hospital door for the duration of his sentence.[31]

The fear of unfavorable publicity for the President proved groundless. Only one congressman publicly denounced the move. The conservative columnist David Lawrence, who rarely had a good word for Landis during his federal career, now wrote a compassionate column in his behalf. In private, some were less charitable. "I would be profoundly sorry for him and his pathetic performance," wrote Gardner Jackson, "if I hadn't been privy to his cruel indifference and worse to some of those once close and dear to him."[32]

Landis' own distorted comprehension of his plight contributed to the final disgrace. Released from the hospital after his completed sentence on Friday, September 27, he appeared at his law office on Monday, September 30. Naturally, the story that he returned so quickly to work made news, which helped undermine his case against disbarment. In New York a lawyer's conviction of a crime meant almost automatic disbarment, but Landis hoped that by demonstrating his crime had not involved moral or ethical failings, he could reduce the penalty to censure, or possibly convince the Appellate Division of the State Supreme Court to dismiss proceedings against him altogether. Both Attorney General Kennedy and Deputy Attorney General Katzenbach sent letters recommending against disbarment. Dr. Kolb testified that the judge had erred in ascribing his patient's failure to file to chronic alcoholism. Landis was a "symptomatic alcoholic" who drank to find relief during periods of stress, and his heaviest drinking had begun after his tax problems, not before. Instead, Kolb described Landis' problem as a "compulsive drive to excel" which devastated his private life but actually stimulated his professional competency. Furthermore, Kolb warned that should the court deny Landis the opportunity to continue his professional work, "the outlook would be very unfavorable, in terms of his physical and psychological life."[33]

Impressed by Dr. Kolb's testimony, the designated referee in the disbarment proceedings, State Supreme Court Justice Gerald Nolan, determined that Landis had not been guilty of fraud or deceit. Nor had the crime involved him as a lawyer or any of his relations with a client. Nolan could find no reason for Landis' action other than psychological, and accepted Dr. Kolb's interpretation that his problems had not affected his professional conduct. As further evidence of Landis' fitness to continue as a member of the Bar, Nolan cited his "splendid record of public service and devotion to the affairs of others" and the "great number of letters submitted by persons prominent in public and professional life" in his behalf. Nevertheless, on July 10, 1964, the New York Supreme Court suspended James M. Landis from practice for one year to uphold the dignity of the legal profession.

Forty years of devotion to the law came to an end.[34]

"The scars that this episode has inflicted on me," Landis wrote to Dr. Kolb, "are too deep to be readily healed." He brooded and worried over what he would do for the next year. His friends worked on several possibilities: a world tour for Pan American; a feasibility study of a merger between Pan Am and TWA; renewed interest in completing Joe Kennedy's memoirs. Robert Kennedy offered him the post of chairman of the review committee to declassify the records of the John F. Kennedy Presidential Library. At first Landis dismissed these efforts as charitable crumbs tossed in his direction. He could not stand to see himself as the object of pity. Eventually, Justin Feldman, Wallace Cohen, Stanley Gewirtz, and others persuaded him that he was still a functionally effective person with many years of public service ahead of him. At their urging, he agreed to accept Robert Kennedy's offer and made arrangements to fly to Washington during the first week in August to meet with representatives of the Kennedy Library at the National Archives.[35]

The Friday before that meeting, July 30, 1964, was a hot and humid day in New York. Landis spent the morning at his Manhattan law office and returned home ready for a swim in his backyard pool. The house was empty. Dorothy had taken her visiting father on a long drive to Staten Island and had been caught in commuter traffic coming back. Neighbors who often swam in the pool were home making preparations for a party that evening. Always an excellent swimmer, Landis dove into the pool alone. Shortly afterwards, two neighboring teenagers arrived to join him. They had a standing invitation to use the pool as long as adults were present, and they expected to find Mr. Landis swimming at that hour. When they reached the pool, they found him floating face down. All attempts at resuscitation failed. When Dorothy arrived back, she found the street jammed with police cars. Neighbors brought her the news that James Landis was dead.[36]

His death, coming so soon after imprisonment and disbarment, caused many friends, relatives, and the press to assume he had committed suicide. The coroner, however, ruled it accidental drowning, with the probability that he had suffered a heart attack in the pool. The autopsy revealed a ninety percent narrowing of his coronary arteries and signs of recent hemorrhage. There was also a considerable amount of alcohol in his blood, indicating that he had been drinking within hours of his death but not necessarily enough to cause intoxication. Landis' personal and professional wounds might have been self-inflicted, but he had not taken his own life.[37]

The funeral in Rye, New York, brought together a cross section of friends from his complex life — former Harvard students, regulatory commissioners, Washington and Wall Street lawyers, and Italian politicians from Harrison. Others were necessarily absent. Two towers of strength in his life, Felix Frankfurter and Joseph P. Kennedy, had suffered debilitating strokes. John F. Kennedy had died of an assassin's bullet. Robert Kennedy represented his family at the ceremony, where he quietly, but visibly, wept. There was no shortage of eulogies. Speakers recalled Landis' brilliant mind and dedicated career as a teacher, lawyer, and government official. Later, at a memorial service in Washington, the new attorney general, Nicholas Katzenbach, commended Landis for his decision to plead guilty in the tax case. "I think that was in a way one of the finest things Jim did, to judge himself in that way, and to go through all the horror of that experience." In a letter to the *Washington Post,* one of Landis' law partners added a final tribute. "The death of Jim Landis invokes all too automatically facile comparison to a Greek tragedy—the fatal flaw, the fall from greatness, the fascination and gossip of the mob," wrote Seymour Rubin. "He deserved better in his last years." Landis, in Rubin's words, had the look of "an untamed eagle" and the "lonely independence that justified that appearance." The nation had profited greatly of James Landis. "It can profit more, if we remember his quality of mind and spirit."[38]

Landis had wanted no burial or headstone. In a handwritten will he asked that his body be cremated and his ashes scattered over the garden he loved, a request with which Dorothy complied. Death did not end the family's difficulties, for the United States government continued to press its case against his estate to pay the additional penalties. Just before he died, Landis had declared the penalties miscalculated and exaggerated and talked of fighting the case in court. His widow was in no state to carry on that struggle. In a final irony, the government closed its case by taking Landis' home and property, with the pool in which he died and the garden which contained his ashes.[39]

Afterword

> History, as Carl Becker used to
> tell me, teaches nothing save
> the egotism of the historian,
> who by a judicious selection of
> the facts thinks that he has
> finally divined the Eternal Will.
>
> —James M. Landis, 1945

In the years following Landis' death, the regulatory process and its political underpinnings came under critical scholarly reappraisal. Writers assailed federal regulation for fostering a "broker state" and "interest-group liberalism." Widespread attacks on the various commissions drove their image, in the words of one congressional committee, "to an historic low."[1] While regulatory criticism was common during Landis' lifetime, much of the scholarly disaffection grew from events which took place in the decade after his death. The failure of the Great Society to live up to its promise, the trauma of the war in Vietnam, Watergate, inflation, and recession all called into question reliance on federal solutions for social and economic problems. Since the regulatory commissions often served as prime examples of federal mismanagement, they received extensive historiographic attention. James Landis' cynicism about historians notwithstanding, they leveled serious charges against the process which he had made his life's work and legacy.

Several major themes developed: that the New Deal had expanded and perpetuated federal regulation because of its lack of commitment to central planning and its reliance on ad hoc solutions; that the government adopted the role of broker between competing interest groups, but that instead of producing "countervailing forces" the broker state had led to a system of bargaining in which the best organized groups predominated; that regulatory commissions had become the captives of the industries they were assigned to regulate; and that the very impetus for federal regulation had originated with sophisticated businessmen rather than with reformers.

203

"The Conservative Achievement of Liberal Reform," Barton Bernstein's essay on the New Deal, summarized the revisionist approach of the 1960s. The New Deal's much lauded experimentalism, Bernstein commented, had been limited to means rather than ends. Its liberal reforms had conserved and protected corporate capitalism while failing to redistribute income, extend equality, or make business significantly more responsive to the general social welfare.[2] Paul Conkin expressed similarly negative opinions, concluding that the Roosevelt administration caused more problems than it solved, was erratic rather than pragmatic, and lacked any unified plan of action. The administration should have followed one of two paths, Conkin reasoned, either to adopt central planning or to win business confidence. Instead the New Dealers chose to weave a path between the two options, thereby leaving a society balanced between big business and big government, and "always, one or the other partner could try to gain too much power and upset the partnership."[3]

Echoing the themes of such earlier advocates of central planning as George Soule, Stuart Chase, Adolf Berle, and Rexford Tugwell, historians elaborated on the New Deal's failure to respond to the depression with concerted and rational federal planning. Otis L. Graham, Jr., portrayed the New Deal as fumbling its opportunity by adopting partial planning and by making only minor structural adjustments to the system through regulation of specific industries. Graham credited the broker state chiefly for its tenacity: "It gave the appearance of competent social management for many years. No major depression occurred; economic stability and growth came together under its regime . . . The post-New Deal system maximized the freedom of organized groups to pursue their own welfare through political channels." But by the 1960s the broker state had proved inadequate to handle racial discord, generational alienation, inflation, pollution, abuse of government power, and material shortages.[4]

From a different perspective, Charles A. Reich argued that the federal government from the New Deal to the Great Society was moving the United States toward a "highly organized, scientifically planned society of the future." The problem then was to preserve democratic participation in governmental decision making and to make planning and allocation more pluralistic and egalitarian. If individuals were to survive the pressures of a collective society, they could not entrust their rights and livelihoods to the discretion and largess of government authorities and commissions, which could act oppressively as well as benevolently. Reich warned that the regulatory commissions were eroding individual liberty and creating a "rigid managerial hierarchy" in which a small elite ruled the nation. The commissions had transferred power "from the man on the street to the man from the *Harvard Law Review*" (Reich taught law at Yale). What was necessary, he concluded, was "de-institutionalization" of the government and a raising of public consciousness to create a more humane society and a more liberated individual.[5]

The broker state also came under fire from scholars for its pluralistic assumptions. Grant McConnell observed that regulatory solutions by compromise and accommodation had been possible only because not all interests had equal representation before the commissions. Interest groups did not necessarily balance each other out, and many lacked countervailing opposites. Because of their independence from partisan politics, the regulatory commissions had grown to respond to small constituencies of special interests, which were carving up governmental authority for their own ends. Such fragmentation needed to be reversed, McConnell argued, by a return to a broader-based control of governmental processes through the presidency and national party politics.[6]

Most far-reaching of the critiques of the broker state was Theodore J. Lowi's *The End of Liberalism*. Like the advocates of central planning, Lowi also revived an old debate, although with arguments more reminiscent of those of Ernst Freund and Willis Van Devanter. Blaming the crisis of the 1960s on the interest-group liberals who dominated American politics, Lowi accused them of creating a gigantic but impotent and amoral government, one which could neither plan nor achieve justice. The New Dealers' pluralistic ideology had caused them to supplant economic competition with group competition, which enabled powerful interest groups to force government to accommodate their needs, a situation amounting to oligarchy. Symptomatic of the government's capitulation was the "regulatory revolution," with its excessive delegation of power from elected representatives to appointed commissioners. Liberals, he charged, had enacted statutes without standards of implementation, relied on policy without law, and worshiped process as distinguished from form and procedure. Thus "liberalism had become a doctrine whose means are its ends, whose combatants are its clientele, whose standards are . . . those the bargainers can fashion to fit the bargain." Lowi called for a return to stricter standards and a harkening back to the "still valid but universally disregarded *Schechter* rule."[7]

Lowi's arguments were ones with which the author of "Statutes and the Sources of Law" could not have been wholly unsympathetic. Landis, however, had concluded from experiences with Congress during the drafting of the securities legislation that statutes with specific standards were easier to advocate than to implement. During the 1940s he strongly opposed the efforts of the American Bar Association to impose stricter form and procedure on the commissions, a movement which resulted in the Administrative Procedure Act of 1946.[8] Bascially a conservative backlash, the

Administrative Procedure Act made little improvement. "The act forced the regulatory agencies to adopt more the ways of the courts and thereby slowed them down," wrote Louis M. Kohlmeier, Jr. "It allowed more industries and companies to participate in formal agency hearings . . . Thus it encouraged the delays for which the agencies are now famous."[9]

Undeniably, opponents of the broker state had made valid criticisms of the New Deal and its successors. The Roosevelt administration, with its many camps of advisors, did lack a single-minded, uniform plan of action, and it did not radically alter the nature of the American capitalistic system. Mostly, it suffered from an ambiguity over large-scale economic power, an ambiguity shared by the society as a whole. "The search in twentieth century America," wrote Ellis Hawley, in one of the most balanced analyses of liberal economic thinking, "was for the solution that would reconcile the practical necessity [of big business] with the individualistic ideal, some arrangement that would preserve the industrial order, necessarily based upon a high degree of collective organization, and yet would preserve America's democratic heritage at the same time."[10] For men like James Landis, the solution was the regulatory process.

Beyond focusing on the New Deal, scholarly analysis of federal regulation has frequently emphasized a "capture" theory of the commissions. The most prominent proponent of the capture theory was Gabriel Kolko, who argued that the commissions were not reform vehicles but instruments of the status quo, fostering corporate power rather than checking it. Although Kolko dealt with the Progressive era origins of the Interstate Commerce Commission, the Federal Trade Commission, and the Federal Reserve Board, he was expansive in his conclusions. The triumphant businessmen "permitted political capitalism to direct the growth of industrialism in America, to shape its politics, to determine the ground rules for American civilization in the twentieth century.[11] An auxiliary theory held that those reformers who endorsed the regulatory process had been co-opted by shrewd business leaders. "Corporate liberalism," as James Weinstein defined it, was the "product, consciously created, of the leaders of the giant corporations and financial institutions."[12]

Neither theory satisfactorily applies to James Landis' career. There were elements of corporate encouragement for securities and exchange regulation, for example. In his study of securities regulation during the New Deal, Michael Parrish detailed the efforts of the Investment Bankers Association to establish some form of federally endorsed self-regulation to prevent stock fraud. But the bankers became estranged from the New Deal as the regulatory legislation emerged from Congress. What they received was far more than they had bargained for.[13]

There were also aspects of Landis' career which fit the "corporate liberal" image, particularly his belief that government should promote business development at home and expansion overseas. But the label would distort his record more than clarify it. Throughout his federal service Landis was more often at odds with corporate leaders than in alliance with them. His views were too independent to reassure businessmen, no matter how conciliatory his approach. In the 1930s he helped force regulation on the stock markets; in the 1940s he worked to wean airlines away from over-regulation; and in the 1960s he proposed reforms to strengthen the regulatory commissions. In each case he was out of step with prevailing corporate sentiments. In the larger sense Landis, Roosevelt, Truman, Kennedy, and the predominant banking, business, and labor interests of their time all operated under the same tent and did not entertain noncapitalistic alternatives. But while Landis believed in capitalism and held ideas and objectives similar to those of business leaders, he reached his positions without co-option, coercion, or collusion.

Political scientists proposed a less ideological "capture" theory, most comprehensively presented by Marver H. Bernstein. Bernstein theorized that all regulatory commissions went through a "life cycle." In youth the agencies attracted public and political support, enabling them to pursue aggressive agendas and attract talented personnel. In maturity the agencies' popular support would wane, causing them to seek the support of the regulated industries, which would temper their policies and their personnel, who would move easily between employment in the commissions and the regulated industries. In old age the agencies would become more bureaucratic and complacent, rigid in procedure, and protective of industry, with whom they had established "special relationships." In the post-New Deal years Bernstein's thesis seemed almost self-evident, explaining the lethargy of the once crusading commissions. Even Landis, whose own life cycle resembled that of the commissions, talked nostalgically about their youthful past.[14]

Later quantitative analysis by Kenneth J. Meier and John P. Plumlee failed to substantiate Bernstein's "life cycle" theory. Over time, Meier and Plumlee found, the interchange of personnel between commissions and industries actually decreased. Their data also indicated, contrary to Bernstein's predictions, that "aging agencies do not have increased turnover, decreased expertise, increased backlogs, or decreased efficiency." Most significantly, they found that new political demands placed on an agency could reverse its life cycle, and cited the revitalized Federal Trade Commission as an example.[15]

Paradoxically, for all the scholarly attack on the regulatory process and political demands for "de-regulation," the commissions continued to expand in size and responsibility. While persistently opposing presidential attempts to bring the commissions under executive authority, Congress steadily added to the roster of commissions, creating among others the Equal Employment Opportunity Commission in 1964, the Occupational Safety and Health Administration and Environmental Protection Agency in 1970, the Consumer Product Safety Commission in 1972, the Commodities Futures Exchange Commission in 1974, and the Nuclear Regulatory Commission in 1975.[16] Many of these new commissions broke sharply with past regulatory practice by concerning themselves with single issues, whether racial and sexual equality, worker safety, or consumer protection, that cut across industry in general. Therefore they face no single identifiable corporate interest. In the future they should furnish new material with which to further test the "capture" and "life cycle" theories.

The literature on the regulatory process has kept pace with the swelling volumes of the *Federal Register* and the *Code of Federal Regulations*. Important contributions to the field have also been made by Louis Jaffe, Henry Friendly, and William Cary, men personally associated with Landis, and by numerous others.[17] In a careful dissection of their many conflicting theories, Thomas K. McCraw found some fault with all the arguments, in part because regulation itself was "an instrument capable of serving diverse, even contradictory ends, some economic, some political, some cultural."[18] The debate, like the commissions, will continue. However, the "outstanding theoretical elaboration of administration regulation," as McCraw described it, remains *The Administrative Process* by James M. Landis.

Manuscripts

ALUMNI RECORDS CENTER, PRINCETON UNIVERSITY.

AYERS, EBEN A. Papers. Harry S. Truman Library, Independence, Missouri.

BUREAU OF THE BUDGET. Record Group 51. National Archives.

CHAFEE, ZECHARIAH. Papers. Harvard Law School Library.

CIVIL AERONAUTICS BOARD. Chairman's Correspondence and Minutes. Record Group 197. National Archives.

CIVIL AERONAUTICS BOARD. Commissioners' Speeches. CAB, Washington, D.C.

DEPARTMENT OF LABOR. Secretary's File. Record Group 174. National Archives.

FEDERAL TRADE COMMISSION. Securities Act of 1933, Press Releases. Library of Congress.

FELDMAN, MYER. Papers. John F. Kennedy Library, Waltham, Massachusetts.

FENBERT, DOROTHY BROWN LANDIS. Private collection. Scarsdale, New York.

FRANKFURTER, FELIX. Papers. Harvard Law School Library; Library of Congress.

GRIFFIS, STANTON. Papers. Harry S. Truman Library.

HART, HENRY M. Papers. Harvard Law School Library.

HUMPHREY, WILLIAM E. Papers. Library of Congress.

JACKSON, GARDNER. Papers. Franklin D. Roosevelt Library, Hyde Park, New York.

KATZ, MILTON. Papers. Harry S. Truman Library.

KENNEDY, JOHN F. Campaign File, Central Name File, President's Office File. John F. Kennedy Library.

KOLB, LAWRENCE C. Private collection. New York.

LANDIS, JAMES M. Papers. Harvard Archives; Harvard Law School Library; John F. Kennedy Library; Library of Congress.

LOWELL, A. LAWRENCE. Papers. Harvard Archives.

McKEE, ELLEN LANDIS. Private collection. Chevy Chase, Maryland.

McLaughlin, Ann Landis. Private collection. Chevy Chase, Maryland.

Morgenthau, Henry M., Jr. Diaries, Presidential Diaries. Franklin D. Roosevelt Library.

Office of Civilian Defense. Record Group 171. Federal Records Center. Suitland, Maryland.

Pound, Roscoe. Papers. Harvard Archives; Harvard Law School Library.

Records of Foreign Missions of the Presbyterian Church of the U.S.A. Presbyterian Historical Society, Philadelphia, Pennsylvania.

Richberg, Donald. Papers. Library of Congress.

Roosevelt, Eleanor. Papers. Franklin D. Roosevelt Library.

Roosevelt, Franklin D. Official File, Personal File, President's Secretary's File. Franklin D. Roosevelt Library.

Rosenman, Samuel I. Papers. Franklin D. Roosevelt Library.

Securities and Exchange Commission. Chairman's Correspondence and Minutes. SEC, Washington, D.C.

Securities and Exchange Commission. Commissioners' Speeches. Library of Congress.

Taft, William Howard. Papers. Library of Congress.

Thompson, Huston. Papers. Library of Congress.

Truman, Harry S. Official File. Harry S. Truman Library.

Interviews and Oral Histories

BOSWORTH, FRANCIS. Oral history. Research Center for the Federal Theatre Project. George Mason University, Fairfax, Virginia.

COHEN, BENJAMIN V. Interview on 9 January 1974.

COHEN, WALLACE. Interview on 18 September 1974.

CORCORAN, THOMAS G. Interview on 21 March 1974.

DIXON, PAUL RAND. Oral history. John F. Kennedy Library, Waltham, Massachusetts.

DOUGLAS, WILLIAM O. Oral history (RFK). John F. Kennedy Library.

DOWLING, EDDIE. Oral history. Columbia University, New York.

FELDMAN, JUSTIN. Interview on 11 June 1975.

FENBERT, DOROTHY BROWN LANDIS. Interviews on 5 April 1974 and 9 June 1975.

FRANKFURTER, FELIX. Oral history. John F. Kennedy Library.

GEWIRTZ, STANLEY. Interviews on 6 March 1974 and 12 June 1975.

GLADIEUX, BERNARD L. Oral history. Columbia University, New York.

GRISWOLD, ERWIN N. Interview on 3 June 1975.

HARRIS, OREN. Oral history. John F. Kennedy Library.

JACKSON, GARDNER. Oral history. Columbia University.

KATZENBACH, NICHOLAS D. Interview on 19 March 1977.

KNIGHT, FRANCES G. Interview on 16 December 1975.

KOLB, LAWRENCE C. Interview on 8 September 1975.

KROCK, ARTHUR. Oral history. Columbia University.

LANDIS, JAMES M. Oral history. Columbia University.

LANE, CHESTER T. Oral history. Columbia University.

LOCKE, EDWARD A. Oral history. Harry S. Truman Library, Independence, Missouri.

McCULLOCH, FRANK. Oral history. John F. Kennedy Library.

McKee, Mr. and Mrs. William, and Mr. and Mrs. Charles McLaughlin. Joint interview, 27 February 1974.

McLaughlin, Ann Landis. Interviews on 20 January 1974, 10 April 1974, and 5 July 1975.

Maher, Agnes. Interviews on 13 October 1975 and 6 December 1975.

Martin, John B. Interview on 7 March 1974.

Regulatory Agency Panel. Oral history (Alan Boyd, William Cary, Newton Minow, Joseph Swindler, and William Tucker). John F. Kennedy Library.

Sacks, Albert M. Interview on 13 June 1975.

Scott, Austin Wakeman. Interview on 13 June 1975.

Smith, Jean P. Interview on 18 July 1975.

Solomon, George. Interview on 11 June 1975.

Spaulding, Charles. Oral History. John F. Kennedy Library.

Taylor, Mary Walker. Interview on 6 March 1974.

Taylor, Telford. Interview on 6 March 1974.

Throop, Allen. Interview on 21 March 1974.

Walker, Eleanor Landis. Interview on 26 February 1974.

Notes

Introduction

1. The classic account of the early development of the regulatory process is Robert E. Cushman, *The Independent Regulatory Commissions* (New York, 1941).

2. Nationalization was the chief alternative to regulation of private enterprise in the debates of the 1930s. Other government options for supervising and maintaining competitive markets included antitrust prosecution, taxation, and changes in liability rules. See Stephen Breyer, "Analyzing Regulatory Failure: Mismatches, Less Restrictive Alternatives, and Reform," *Harvard Law Review*, XCII (January 1979), 578-584.

3. James M. Landis, "The President's Reorganization Program for the Regulatory Agencies: Gains and Losses," address delivered before the Southeast Regional Meeting of the ABA, Birmingham, Alabama, 9 November 1961, James M. Landis Papers, Library of Congress.

4. Arthur E. Sutherland, *The Law at Harvard: A History of Ideas and Men, 1817-1967* (Cambridge, Mass., 1967), 300; Landis, draft for an article, 1938, Landis Papers; *New York Times,* 31 July 1964.

5. *New York Post,* 4 December 1960; Landis to Evans Clark, 28 July 1950, Landis Papers.

6. See, for example, Marver H. Bernstein, *Regulating Business by Independent Commission* (Princeton, 1955); Theodore J. Lowi, *The End of Liberalism: Ideology, Policy, and the Crisis of Public Authority* (New York, 1969); and Louis L. Jaffee, "The Effective Limits of the Administrative Process: A Reevaluation," *Harvard Law Review,* LXVII (May 1954), 1105-1135, "James Landis and the Administrative Process," *Harvard Law Review,* LXXVIII (December 1964), 319-328, and "The Illusion of the Ideal Administration," *Harvard Law Review,* LXXXVI (May 1973), 1183-1199.

7. James M. Landis, *The Administrative Process* (New Haven, 1938), 46; Landis, *Report on Regulatory Agencies to the President-Elect, Submitted by the Chairman of the Subcommittee on Administrative Practice and Procedure to the Committee on the Judiciary of the United States Senate,* 86th Congress, 2nd sess., December 1960, 70-72.

8. Howard C. Westmore to Landis, January 1948, Landis Papers.

1. A Demand for Excellence

1. Interview with Dorothy Landis Fenbert, 9 June 1975; Terrance Rattigan, *The Winslow Boy* (London, 1946).

2. "Henry Mohr Landis," *Necrological Reports and Annual Proceedings of the Alumni Association of Princeton Theological Seminary,* V (Princeton, 1922), 187-188; A. K. Reischauer, "Rev. Henry Mohr Landis," clipping, George P. Pierson to James M. Landis, 31 August 1933, James M. Landis Papers, Library of Congress; interview with Eleanor Landis Walker, 26 February 1974; George Landis to author, 10 March 1974.

3. Landis oral history, 4-5, Columbia University; Henry M. Landis to John M. Gillespie, 5 February 1899, 2 April 1890, Henry Landis to Theodore McNair, 18 January 1898, East Japan Mission, Record Group 93, Records of the Foreign Missions of the Presbyterian Church of the U.S.A., Presbyterian Historical Society, Philadelphia.

4. Z. Goshi, "An Appreciation of Rev. Mr. H. M. Landis," clipping, Landis Papers.

5. "The Legend of Landis," *Fortune,* X (August 1934), 44.

6. Interview with Mary Walker Taylor, 6 March 1974; Henry Landis to John Gillespie, 22 April 1893, Records of Foreign Missions; Landis oral history, 7-10.

7. John Gillespie to Henry Landis, 19 June 1890, Harvey Brokaw to Robert Speer, 21 December 1918, Brokaw to A. J. Brown, 13 September 1921, J. K. Kimum, medical certificate, 10 December 1918, D. MacDonald, M.D., to Board of Foreign Missions, 21 January 1896, J. C. Ballagh to John Gillespie, 29 January 1896, Emma Landis to Robert Speer, 9 April 1904, Records of Foreign Missions; interview with Eleanor Landis Walker, 26 February 1974; George Landis to author, 10 March 1974.

8. Emma Landis to Robert Speer, 9 April 1904, Records of Foreign Missions.

9. Emma Landis to Robert Speer, 21 February 1906 and 29 January 1915, Records of Foreign Missions; "Legend of Landis," 44-45.

10. Interview with Dorothy Landis Fenbert, 5 April 1974.

11. "Legend of Landis," 45; Landis oral history, 15; George Landis to author, 10 March 1974.

12. William M. Coats to Landis, 21 October 1935, Landis to Coats, 21 October 1935, Landis Papers; Emma Landis to Robert Speer, 29 January 1915, Records of Foreign Missions; *Mercersburg Academy Alumni Quarterly,* 1934, 49-51.

13. Landis oral history, 276-284.

14. Ibid., 20-21, 27; Henry Landis to Robert Speer, 15 August 1917, Records of Foreign Missions; "Legend of Landis," 45.

15. Mary Shipman Andrews, *The Three Things: The Forge in Which the Soul of a Man Was Tested* (Boston, 1915); Landis diary, 12-15 May 1917, Landis Papers.

16. Landis diary, 19 September 1917, Landis Papers; Landis oral history, 21-24.

17. Landis diary, 17 November 1917, poem, "Despondency," summer 1917, Landis Papers; Landis oral history, 13.

18. Henry Landis to Robert Speer, 15 August 1917, Records of Foreign Missions.

19. Harvey Brokaw to Robert Speer, 21 December 1918, William Imbrie to Speer, 17 July 1919, Records of Foreign Missions.

20. A Meiji Gakuin teacher attributed Landis' decision not to become a missionary to his "grief or indignation at the treatment your father received"; George P. Pierson to Landis, 31 August 1933, Landis Papers. Landis oral history, 13, 23-24; F. Scott Fitzgerald, *This Side of Paradise* (New York, 1920), 282; George Kennan, *Memoirs, 1925-1950* (Boston, 1967), 4; *Newsweek,* III (12 May 1934), 15.

21. John H. Leh to author, 23 May 1975; Francis B. Bowman to author, 15 June 1975; Gordon H. Curtis to author, 14 June 1975; Robert Denniston to author, 7 June 1975; Landis oral history, 3; *New York Sun,* 9 November 1920; interview with Dorothy Landis Fenbert, 9 June 1975.

22. John H. Leh to author, 23 May 1975; "Legend of Landis," 46. After graduation, Landis sold the Syllabi Company, but his successor ran afoul of the administration by predicting exam questions, and Princeton outlawed the whole business.

23. New York *Sun,* 9 November 1920; news release, 9 January 1942, Alumni Records Center, Princeton University; "Legend of Landis," 46; Robert W. McLaughlin to author, 26 August 1975.

24. *Mercersburg Academy Alumni Quarterly,* Summer 1936, in Landis Papers; *Nassau Herald* (1921), 174-175, Alumni Records Center, Princeton University; Landis, "The Commerce Clause as a Restriction on State Taxation," *Michigan Law Review,* XX (November 1921), 50-85.

25. Landis oral history, 8; Landis to Jean P. Smith, 1 November 1924 and 20 January 1925, Landis Papers, Harvard Law School; Landis to L. Robert Driver, 31 December 1937, Edward S. Corwin to Landis, 8 January 1938, Landis Papers, Harvard Archives.

26. Theodore P. Walker to William Imbrie, 30 June 1919, George P. Pierson to Robert Speer, 31 March 1920, Harvey Brokaw to Speer, 21 January 1921, Brokaw to A. J. Brown, 13 September 1921, A. J. Brown to Japan Mission, 13 October 1921, Brokaw to Brown, 2 November 1921, *Japan Advertiser,* 7 September 1921, Records of Foreign Missions.

2. Frankfurter and Brandeis, Mentors

1. Arthur E. Sutherland, *The Law at Harvard: A History of Ideas and Men, 1817-1967* (Cambridge, Mass., 1967), 250-259; Joseph P. Lash, ed., *From the Diaries of Felix Frankfurter* (New York, 1975), 31-34; Jerold S. Auerbach, *Unequal Justice: Lawyers and Social Change in Modern America* (New York, 1976), 130-157.

2. Lyttleton Fox, Jr., "The Incubator of Greatness," *Forum,* LXXXIX (May 1933), 288-293; Walter Johnson, ed., *The Papers of Adlai Stevenson,* I (Boston, 1972), 112; Archibald MacLeish and E. F. Prichard, eds., *Law and Politics: Occasional Papers of Felix Frankfurter, 1913-1938* (Boston, 1939), xx.

3. "The Legend of Landis," *Fortune,* X (August 1934), 46; interview with Austin Wakeman Scott, 18 June 1975; Landis oral history, 31-32.

4. Landis to Jerome Shestack, 4 March 1949, Landis Papers; W. Barton Leach, "Landis: Roommate and Dean," *Harvard Law School Bulletin,* XIX (March 1968), 16; interview with Dorothy Landis Fenbert, 9 June 1975.

5. Leach, "Landis: Roommate and Dean," 16-17; Erwin N. Griswold, "James McCauley Landis—1899-1964," *Harvard Law Review,* LXXVIII (December 1964), 313. When the top students were earning combined grades in the 460s, 470s, and possibly the 490s, under the Harvard Law School system, Landis scored a phenomenal 505 in his second year. Roscoe Pound to A. Lawrence Lowell, 6 August 1923, A. Lawrence Lowell Papers, Harvard Archives.

6. Landis to Jerome Shestack, 4 March 1949, Landis Papers; Liva Baker, *Felix Frankfurter* (New York, 1969), 103-106; Arthur M. Schlesinger, Sr., *In Retrospect: The History of a Historian* (New York, 1963), 82-83.

7. "Legend of Landis," 46-47; interview with Austin Wakeman Scott, 18 June 1975; Roscoe Pound to A. Lawrence Lowell, 21 March 1924, Lowell Papers; Sutherland, *The Law at Harvard,* 233. Others who held the research fellowship after Landis included Thomas G. Corcoran, Henry M. Hart, and Paul Freund.

8. Landis to Jean P. Smith, May 1925, Landis Papers, Harvard Law School. Lewis S. Feuer noted the relationship between travelers to the Soviet Union in the 1920s and New Deal advisors in the 1930s, in "American Travelers to the Soviet Union, 1917-1932: The Formulation of a New Deal Ideology," *Marx and the Intellectuals: A Set of Post-Ideological Essays* (Garden City, N.Y., 1969), 100-140.

9. Landis oral history, 98-100, 107.

10. Ibid., 100-102; *Baltimore Sun,* 16 October 1924, 24 November 1924.

11. Landis oral history, 102-106; *Baltimore Sun,* 24 November 1924; Landis to Learned Hand, 1 February 1946, Landis Papers, Harvard Archives.

12. Landis oral history, 107-110. In an account of his life published shortly after he joined the federal government, Landis felt it impolitic to mention his Russian trip and reported instead that during the summer of 1924 he had "toured Cornwall and Devon on bicycle"; see "Legend of Landis," 47.

13. Interview with Jean P. Smith, 18 July 1975; Jean P. Smith, "Frankfurter's Apprentice: Echoes from the '20s from Letters to a Friend," Landis Papers, Harvard Law School. "Frankfurter's Apprentice" is a typescript of Landis' correspondence with the young woman he had met on shipboard. Subsequently, Jean Smith donated the original letters to the Library of Congress.

14. Landis to Jean P. Smith, 1 November 1924, March 1925, Landis Papers, Harvard Law School.

15. Landis oral history, 126-127; Landis to Jean P. Smith, 8 January 1925, Landis Papers, Harvard Law School.

16. Landis to Jean P. Smith, 20 January 1925, Landis Papers, Harvard Law School; Felix Frankfurter and James M. Landis, *The Business of the Supreme Court: A Study in the Federal Judiciary System* (New York, 1928; rpt. 1972).

17. Erwin Griswold, "James McCauley Landis," 314; Landis oral history, 36; Landis to Ernst Freund, 27 November 1929, Landis Papers.

18. Frankfurter to Landis, 5 July 1932, Landis Papers; Frankfurter to Stella

McGehee, 13 August 1926, Ellen Landis McKee Collection; Landis to Jean P. Smith, 30 June 1925, 15 July 1925, 2 August 1925, Landis Papers, Harvard Law School.

19. Landis to Marion Frankfurter, 2 July 1925, Marion Frankfurter to Felix Frankfurter, 6 July 1925, Felix Frankfurter to Marion Frankfurter, 8 July 1925, Felix Frankfurter Papers, Library of Congress.

20. Landis, "Mr. Justice Brandeis: A Law Clerk's View," *Publications of the American Jewish Historical Society,* no. 936 (June 1957), 2, 5-7.

21. Ibid., 2-3; Landis to Frankfurter, 1 November 1925, Frankfurter Papers.

22. Landis, "Brandeis: A Law Clerk's View," and Landis, "Mr. Justice Brandeis," address delivered at the 10th Anniversary Celebration of the Brandeis Youth Federation and the Brandeis Camp Institutes, 6 June 1950, Landis Papers.

23. Melvin I. Urofsky, *A Mind of One Piece: Brandeis and American Reform* (New York, 1971), 71-92; George Rublee, "The Original Plan and Early History of the Federal Trade Commission," *Proceedings of the Academy of Political Science,* XI (January 1926), 114-120; Felix Frankfurter, "Brandeis," in MacLeish and Prichard, eds., *Law and Politics,* 108-112.

24. *Myers v. U.S.,* 272 U.S. 56 (1926); William Howard Taft to Thomas W. Shelton, 9 November 1926, Taft to Casper S. Yost, 1 November 1926, Taft to Horace D. Taft, 28 October 1926, and Taft to J. C. C. Black, 5 November 1926, William Howard Taft Papers, Library of Congress. For the background of the *Myers* case see U.S. Congress, Senate, *The Power of the President to Remove Federal Officers,* S. Doc. 174, 69th Congress, 2nd sess., 1926.

25. *Myers v. U.S.,* 272 U.S. 135; see also Charles A. Miller, *The Supreme Court and the Uses of History* (New York, 1972), 52-70.

26. *Myers v. U.S.,* 272 U.S. 241-243 (Brandeis, J., dissenting).

27. Alpheus Thomas Mason, *William Howard Taft, Chief Justice* (New York, 1964), 226; Landis oral history, 38-41; Landis, "Brandeis: A Law Clerk's View," 8-9.

28. Landis, notes for a speech, "Mr. Justice Brandeis," Landis Papers.

29. Landis to Frankfurter, 27 January 1926, Frankfurter Papers; Landis to Jean P. Smith, 11 March 1926, Landis Papers, Harvard Law School; Frederick M. Kerby to Landis, 2 May 1927, Landis Papers.

30. Landis to Jean P. Smith, 15 February 1926, November 1925, Landis Papers, Harvard Law School; interview with Eleanor Landis Walker, 26 February 1974; M. P. Walker to Guido Gores, 15 March 1924, Emma Landis to Paula L. Gores, 4 March 1925, Landis Papers.

31. Landis to Jean P. Smith, 15 July 1925, Landis Papers, Harvard Law School.

32. "Legend of Landis," 47; Landis to Jean P. Smith, 11 January 1926, 11 March 1926, Landis Papers, Harvard Law School; Oliver Knight, ed., *I Protest: Selected Disquisitions of E. W. Scripps* (Madison, 1966), 97; "Madrillon—A Restaurant," 25 January 1926, Ann Landis McLaughlin Collection.

33. Landis to Jean P. Smith, 11 January 1926, Landis Papers, Harvard Law School; Landis to Stella "Magee," 25 January 1926, Ann Landis McLaughlin Collection.

34. Landis to Stella M. Landis, c. 1928, Jackson, Miss., *Daily News,* October

1922, Ann Landis McLaughlin Collection. For Stella's background see John H. Napier, III, "Judge Edward McGehee: Cotton Planter, Pioneer Manufacturer and Mississippi Philanthropist," *Cotton History Review,* I (January 1960), 27-28; and *Biographical and Historical Memoirs of Mississippi,* I (Chicago, 1891), 1191-1198.

35. Emma Landis to Guido Gores, May 1926, Paula L. Gores to Landis, c. summer 1926, Landis Papers.

36. Interview with Eleanor Landis Walker, 26 February 1974; Emma Landis to Paula L. Gores, c. September 1926, Emma Landis to Guido Gores, c. May 1927, Landis to Paula Gores, 2 February 1933, Landis Papers.

37. Landis to Jean P. Smith, 20 January 1925, Landis Papers, Harvard Law School; Pound to Frankfurter, 26 December 1925, Roscoe Pound Papers, Harvard Law School; Pound to A. Lawrence Lowell, 6 January 1926, Lowell Papers. Considering Landis' appointment, one member of the Harvard Corporation wrote: "Ideally we ought to farm him out to some law firm with an active practice, to take him back after the experience, but if the choice is necessary now, I am for taking him"; Charles P. Curtis, Jr., to Lowell, 1 February 1926, Lowell Papers.

38. Landis, "Mr. Justice Brandeis and the Harvard Law School," *Harvard Law Review,* LV (December 1941), 189-190; Louis D. Brandeis to Frankfurter, 25 July 1926, Frankfurter Papers. For years Brandeis also made financial contributions to Frankfurter for "political purposes" and to help pay family medical expenses; see Nelson L. Dawson, "Louis D. Brandeis, Felix Frankfurter and the New Deal" (Ph.D. diss., University of Kentucky, 1975), 13-14.

39. Frankfurter to Stella Landis, 6 August 1964, Frankfurter Papers, Harvard Law School; Landis to Jean P. Smith, 5 February 1925, Landis Papers, Harvard Law School. Landis was referring to his first teaching experience as a substitute for Frankfurter while a research fellow in 1925.

3. Harvard Law and the Making of a New Dealer

1. Harry S. Coleman to Landis, 29 January 1930, Landis Papers; Louis D. Brandeis to Frankfurter, 30 December 1926, Frankfurter Papers; Landis oral history, 136; interview with Telford Taylor, 6 March 1974; interview with Wallace Cohen, 18 September 1974.

2. For general surveys of legal realism see Edward A. Purcell, Jr., "American Jurisprudence between the Wars: Legal Realism and the Crisis of Democratic Theory," *American Historical Review,* LXXV (December 1969), 424-446; Grant Gilmore, "Legal Realism: Its Cause and Cure," *Yale Law Journal,* LXX (June 1961), 1037-1048; and Wilfred E. Rumble, *American Legal Realism: Skepticism, Reform and the Judicial Process* (Ithaca, N.Y., 1968).

3. Herman Oliphant, "The New Legal Education," *Nation,* CXXI (5 November 1930), 493-495; Arthur E. Sutherland, *The Law at Harvard: A History of Ideas and Men, 1817-1967* (Cambridge, Mass., 1967), 174-183; Joel Seligman, *The High Citadel: The Influence of Harvard Law School* (Boston, 1978), 20-51; Henry Steele Commager, *The American Mind: An Interpretation of American Thought and Character since the 1880s* (New Haven, 1950), 374-390; see also Morton White, *Social Thought in America: The Revolt against Formalism* (Boston, 1949).

4. Roscoe Pound, "Mechanical Jurisprudence," *Columbia Law Review,* VIII

(December 1908), 605-623; Thurman Arnold, *Fair Fights and Foul: A Dissenting Lawyer's Life* (New York, 1967), 20-22, 57-70; Liva Baker, *Felix Frankfurter* (New York, 1969), 45-47; Barbara Frank Kristein, ed., *A Man's Reach: The Philosophy of Judge Jerome Frank* (New York, 1965), 272-288; Karl N. Llewellyn, *Jurisprudence: Realism in Theory and Practice* (Chicago, 1962); and Llewellyn, *The Bramble Bush: On Our Law and Its Study* (New York, 1951), 12.

5. Roscoe Pound, *Interpretations of Legal History* (Cambridge, Mass., 1923), 1-2, 19-21; and Pound et al., *Federalism as a Democratic Process* (New Brunswick, N.J., 1942), 9-10; David Wigdor, *Roscoe Pound, Philosopher of Law* (Westport, Conn., 1974), 255-267.

6. Landis to Felix Frankfurter, 29 July 1929, Frankfurter Papers; Landis to Karl Llewellyn, 12 April 1932, and Young B. Smith to Landis, 14 May 1929, Landis Papers; Felix Frankfurter, "The Task of Administrative Law," in Archibald MacLeish and E. F. Prichard, Jr., eds., *Law and Politics: Occasional Papers of Felix Frankfurter, 1913-1938* (New York, 1939), 236.

7. Landis, "Constitutional Limitations on the Congressional Power of Investigation," *Harvard Law Review,* XL (December 1926), 153-221; see also discussion of *McGrain v. Daugherty* in Arthur M. Schlesinger, Jr., and Roger Bruns, eds., *Congress Investigates, 1792-1974* (New York, 1975), xi-xx.

8. Benjamin Cardozo to Landis, 18 February 1927, John Dickinson to Landis, 3 January 1927, Landis Papers; *Boston Herald,* 18 January 1927; New York *World,* 19 January 1927; Landis oral history, 123; Frankfurter had made similar arguments in "Hands Off the Investigations," *New Republic,* XXXVIII (21 May 1924), 329-331.

9. Henry Friendly to Landis, 7 April 1928, Stella Landis to James Landis, summer 1929, Landis Papers; Stella Landis to Frankfurter, 14 August 1964, Frankfurter Papers, Harvard Law School; Joseph P. Lash, ed., *From the Diaries of Felix Frankfurter* (New York, 1975), 54.

10. Baker, *Frankfurter,* 87-141; Felix Frankfurter and James M. Landis, "Bankers and the Conspiracy Law," *New Republic,* XLI (21 January 1925), 218-220; Landis, "Labor's Day in Court: The Supreme Court Vindicates Jury Trials in Contempt Cases," *Survey,* LIII (15 November 1924), 175-177; and Landis, " 'By the Artificial Reason of Law': An Experiment in Compulsory Arbitration Comes to an End," *Survey,* LIV (15 May 1925), 213-214.

11. Arthur Sutherland to Landis, 30 April 1927, William L. Marbury to Landis, 17 June 1927, Landis Papers; Landis to Jean P. Smith, May 1927, Landis Papers, Harvard Law School; *Boston Herald,* 20 April 1927; David Felix, *Protest: Sacco-Vanzetti and the Intellectuals* (Bloomington, Ind., 1956), 182-183.

12. Roscoe Pound to Richard Washburn Child, 3 January 1927, Pound to Walter Lippmann, 26 February 1927, Pound to Edwin S. Lines, 29 April 1927, Pound to H. F. Day, 5 May 1927, and Pound to Eustace Seligman, 23 May 1927, Pound Papers, Harvard Law School; Paul Sayer, *The Life of Roscoe Pound* (Iowa City, 1948), 219-224; Wigdor, *Roscoe Pound,* 249-250; Baker, *Frankfurter,* 121-123; Sutherland, *The Law at Harvard,* 269-272; Theodore Miner to Landis, 6 March 1928, Landis Papers. Pound did write one letter to the *Boston Herald,* 4 June 1927, on the Sacco-Vanzetti case. Perhaps the most telling evidence of his feelings about

Frankfurter's involvement in the case and its effect on the law school was his response to a letter from an editor of the *Boston Evening Transcript* asking for a formal denial that Frankfurter would be asked to resign from Harvard because of his defense of Sacco and Vanzetti. The letter, in Pound's manuscript collection, shows evidence of having been crumpled into a small ball — better to hurl at a wall — and is affixed to his terse reply: "It seems to me that the wisest course is to say nothing"; Harlan R. Radcliffe to Pound, 12 September 1927, Pound to Radcliffe, 13 September 1927, Pound Papers, Harvard Law School.

13. President Lowell wrote Dean Pound: "I have been looking over your proposed list of increases of salaries and I do not see why we should increase those of men who we wish would leave. I am referring to Professors Frankfurter and [Thomas Reed] Powell"; Lowell to Pound, 13 March 1927, also Lowell to Pound, 15 March 1927, Lowell to Eugene C. Upton ('81), 26 April 1927, Lowell Papers; Harlan B. Phillips, ed., *Felix Frankfurter Reminisces* (New York, 1960), 202-217.

14. Phillips, ed., *Frankfurter Reminisces,* 167-170; Baker, *Frankfurter,* 100-102; William T. Ham, "Harvard Student Opinion of the Jewish Question," *Nation,* CXV (6 September 1922), 225-227; Nathan R. Margold to Landis, 18 February 1928, Landis Papers; Frankfurter to Pound, 27 February 1930, Roscoe Pound Deanship Papers, Harvard Archives; Frankfurter to Walter Lippmann, 28 April 1933, Frankfurter Papers.

15. Phillips, ed., *Frankfurter Reminisces,* 19; Frankfurter to Charles W. Clark, 18 July 1929, Frankfurter Papers.

16. Landis to Jerome Shestack, 4 March 1949, Landis to H. Nelson Gay, 29 February 1928, Landis to Salvatore Galgano, 29 February 1928, Landis Papers; Landis to Jean P. Smith, 15 February 1925, Landis Papers, Harvard Law School; interview with Austin Wakeman Scott, 18 June 1975; Landis, "The Study of Legislation in Law Schools: An Imaginary Inaugural Lecture," *Harvard Graduate's Magazine,* XXXIX (June 1931), 433-442.

17. Robert Dechert, "Francis Hermann Bohlen, 1868-1942," *Shingle,* January 1943, 11-14; Robert Dechert to Landis, 29 October 1928, Landis Papers; Frankfurter diary, 27 April 1928, Frankfurter Papers; interview with Mr. and Mrs. Charles McLaughlin and Mr. and Mrs. William McKee, 27 February 1974.

18. Frankfurter diary, 27 April 1928, Frankfurter Papers; Landis oral history, 150.

19. Roscoe Pound to A. Lawrence Lowell, 26 May 1928, Pound Deanship Papers, Harvard Archives.

20. "Legend of Landis," *Fortune,* X (August 1934), 47; Lowell to Pound, 11 June 1928, Lowell Papers; Frankfurter diary, 3 May 1928, 14-30 June 1928, Frankfurter to John M. Maguire, 29 June 1928, Frankfurter Papers; Zechariah Chafee to Pound, 25 June 1928, Pound to Frankfurter, 2 July 1928, Pound Papers, Harvard Law School; Landis to Chafee, 2 July 1928, Zechariah Chafee Papers, Harvard Law School.

21. Landis to Alpheus Thomas Mason, 5 May 1930, Landis to Guido Gores, 10 December 1929, Thomas P. Fry to Landis, 14 January 1931, H. H. Harley to Burton K. Fiske, 18 April 1931, and Landis to Alice H. Palache, 15 April 1932, Landis Papers.

22. Landis, "Statutes and the Sources of Law," in *Harvard Legal Essays: Written in Honor of and Presented to Joseph Henry Beale and Samuel Williston by Their Colleagues and Students* (Cambridge, Mass., 1934), 213-246; Sutherland, *The Law at Harvard,* 291-292; Harlan F. Stone to Landis, 8 June 1936, Landis Papers; William O. Douglas, "The Brandeis Tradition," *The Record: Publication of the Jewish Historical Society of Greater Washington,* IV (May 1969), 4; Erwin N. Griswold, "James McCauley Landis — 1899-1964," *Harvard Law Review,* LXXVIII (December 1964), 314.

23. Landis, "Mr. Justice Louis D. Brandeis," address delivered at the 10th Anniversary Celebration of the Brandeis Youth Federation and the Brandeis Camp Institutes, 6 June 1950, Landis Papers; Landis, "The Challenge to Traditional Law in the Rise of Administrative Law," *Mississippi Law Journal,* XIII (September 1941), 724-731.

24. Charles E. Clark to Frankfurter, 2 August 1929, Frankfurter Papers; Young B. Smith to Landis, 28 April 1929, Landis to Smith, 2 May 1929, Smith to Landis, 4 May 1929, Landis to Smith, 12 May 1929, Landis Papers.

25. Roscoe Pound, *Jurisprudence,* I (St. Paul, Minn., 1959), 250; Landis to Philip E. Wheelwright, 8 May 1930, Landis Papers; Frankfurter to Charles E. Clark, 22 July 1929, Clark to Frankfurter, 20 July 1929, Frankfurter to Clark, 22 July 1929, Clark to Frankfurter, 8 January 1930, Frankfurter to Karl N. Llewellyn, 10 October 1930, Frankfurter Papers.

26. Landis to Frankfurter, 29 July 1929, Frankfurter Papers; Landis to Arthur Drinkwater, 15 June 1937, Landis to Young B. Smith, 12 May 1929, Landis Papers.

27. Franklyn C. Setaro to Landis, 28 September 1935, Landis Papers; "Legend of Landis," 47.

28. Frankfurter diary, 9 January 1931, Frankfurter Papers; Philip La Follette to Frankfurter, 22 January 1931, Landis to Malcolm P. Sharp, 2 March 1931, Landis to Philip La Follette, rough draft, January 1931, Landis Papers.

29. V. L. Collins to Landis, 29 April 1927, Collins to Landis, 26 April 1929, Landis to George Landis, 26 January 1926, Landis to Guido Gores, December 1928, Landis to Paula L. Gores, 2 February 1933, Stella Landis to James Landis, 6 August 1929, Landis Papers.

30. Nationally, from 1929 to 1933, real income declined thirty-six percent. See Milton Freeman and Anna J. Schwartz, *The Great Contraction, 1929-1933* (Princeton, 1965), 5; Seymour E. Harris, *Economics at Harvard* (New York, 1970), xxxvii; Guido Gores to Landis, 17 September 1931, John W. Ames to Landis, 10 April 1931, Landis Papers.

31. See "Herter" and "Russell" files, Landis Papers; "Legend of Landis," 47; *Boston Herald,* 21 October 1932; Landis to Roscoe Pound, 26 October 1932, Pound Deanship Papers, Harvard Archives.

32. As another sign of his casual approach to politics, Landis registered as a Republican for the purpose of voting against the incumbent, Senator William M. Butler, in the 1926 primary; but by 1932 he still had not changed his registration. Landis to Robert F. Bradford, 11 July 1932, Landis Papers; interview with Ann Landis McLaughlin, 10 April 1974.

33. Phillips, ed., *Frankfurter Reminisces,* 248; Frankfurter memorandum, 11 May 1933, Landis Papers.

34. Pound to Lowell, 28 November 1932, Lowell to Pound, 9 December 1932, Lowell Papers.

35. Landis memorandum, 10 May 1933, Landis Papers; Roscoe Pound to Lowell, 29 April 1933, Lowell Papers.

36. Robert Houmans to Lowell, 2 May 1933, Henry L. Shattuck to Lowell, 2 May 1933, Thomas Nelson Perkins to Lowell, 2 May 1933, Charles P. Curtis, Jr., to Lowell, 5 May 1933, Lowell Papers.

37. Frankfurter diary, 8 May 1933, Frankfurter Papers.

38. Ibid.; Landis to Roscoe Pound, 9 May 1933, Frankfurter memorandum, 11 May 1933, Landis Papers; Lowell to Frankfurter, 10 May 1933, Lowell Papers.

39. Frankfurter memorandum, 11 May 1933, Roscoe Pound to Landis, 11 May 1933, Landis Papers; Lowell to Charles P. Curtis, Jr., 11 May 1933, Lowell Papers.

4. The Happy Hotdogs

1. Raymond Clapper, "Felix Frankfurter's Young Men," *Review of Reviews,* XCIII (January 1936), 27-29, 57; *Time,* XXII (12 September 1938), 22-24; and Raymond Moley, *27 Masters of Politics, in a Personal Perspective* (New York, 1949), 151-164.

2. Thomas G. Corcoran to Felix Frankfurter, 22 April 1933, Frankfurter Papers. Frankfurter disagreed with the "two New Deals" thesis, and wrote to historian Arthur Schlesinger, Jr., "I must reject your assumption that there was a real clash of views between Moley-Tugwell and FF-Brandeis. This assumes that the respective parties had coherent and systematic views on some of the problems that are involved in Roosevelt's policies." Max Freedman, ed., *Roosevelt and Frankfurter: Their Correspondence, 1928-1945* (Boston, 1967), 24-26. Landis also showed confusion over the "two New Deals" concept, in his oral history, 212-213, 304-305.

3. For further information see Donald A. Ritchie, "The Pecora Wall Street Exposé, 1934," in Arthur M. Schlesinger, Jr., and Roger Bruns, eds., *Congress Investigates: A Documented History, 1792-1974,* IV (New York, 1975), 2555-2578.

4. Raymond Moley, *After Seven Years: A Political Analysis of the New Deal* (New York, 1935), 75-79; Moley, *The First New Deal* (New York, 1966), 306-311; Huston Thompson diary, 13, 19 March 1933, Thompson to Franklin D. Roosevelt, 4, 11 June 1932, 7 July 1932, Huston Thompson Papers, Library of Congress. Two useful histories of the New Deal securities legislation are Ralph F. DeBedts, *The New Deal's SEC: The Formative Years* (New York, 1964); and Michael E. Parrish, *Securities Regulation and the New Deal* (New Haven, 1970).

5. Louis D. Brandeis, *Other People's Money, and How the Bankers Use It* (New York, 1914, rpt. 1932); U.S. Congress, House of Representatives, Committee on Interstate and Foreign Commerce, *Hearings on Federal Securities Act,* 73rd Congress, 1st sess., 1933, 9-69, 137-138; Moley, *First New Deal,* 312. For the "blue sky" laws, see Parrish, *Securities Regulation,* 5-7.

6. U.S. Congress, House of Representatives, Interstate and Foreign Commerce Committee, *Stock Exchange Regulation,* 73rd Congress, 2nd sess., 1934, 8; interview

with Benjamin Cohen, 9 January 1974; interview with Thomas Corcoran, 21 March 1974; Landis to Frankfurter, 6 March 1934, Frankfurter Papers; Landis to Hollis R. Bailey, 26 October 1932, Landis Papers; Landis oral history, 158, 160-161.

7. Frankfurter to Landis, 23 March 1933, Frankfurter Papers; "The Federal Securities Act," *Fortune,* VIII (August 1933), 55, 108; interview with Benjamin Cohen, 9 January 1974; Ernst Freund, "Historical Survey," in Freund et al., *The Growth of American Administrative Law* (St. Louis, 1923), 9-41.

8. Landis oral history, 139-140; Landis, "Legislative History of the Securities Act of 1933," *George Washington Law Review,* XXVIII (October 1959), 34-35; note Malcolm A. MacIntyre, "Criminal Provisions of the Securities Act and Analogies to Similar Criminal Statutes," *Yale Law Journal,* XLIII (December 1933), 270.

9. Landis, "Legislative History of the Securities Act," 34; Thompson diary, 7 April 1933, Thompson Papers; Landis oral history, 157, 161.

10. Landis oral history, 161-162; Landis, "Legislative History of the Securities Act," 36.

11. Landis to Frankfurter, 6 June 1936, memo of a telephone call from Benjamin Cohen to Frankfurter, 13 April 1933, Frankfurter to Cohen, 14 April 1933, Frankfurter to Roosevelt, 14 April 1933, Frankfurter to Sam Rayburn, 14 April 1933, Frankfurter to Raymond Moley, 15 April 1933, Frankfurter Papers; *Washington Post,* 5 March 1977.

12. Landis oral history, 164.

13. *New York Times,* 30 May 1933; *Business Week,* 26 April 1933, 20; Moley, *First New Deal,* 311-312; Landis oral history, 164-167.

14. *New York Times,* 3, 6 May 1933; Benjamin Cohen to Landis, 5 May 1933, Landis Papers.

15. Moley to Frankfurter, 9 May 1933, Landis Papers; Landis, "Legislative History of the Securities Act," 44-49; Parrish, *Securities Regulation,* 70; Frankfurter to Moley, 16 May 1933, Frankfurter Papers; Samuel I. Rosenman, ed., *The Public Papers and Addresses of Franklin D. Roosevelt,* II (New York, 1938), 213-214.

16. Sam Rayburn to Frankfurter, 26 May 1933, Frankfurter Papers; Otis B. Johnson to Landis, 21 June 1933, Cohen to Landis, 7 June 1933, Landis Papers.

17. Landis oral history, 40-41, 172-173; William E. Humphrey, undated memorandum, "Changes Made in the Federal Trade Commission since Mr. Humphrey Became a Member," William E. Humphrey Papers, Library of Congress; Raymond Stevens to Roosevelt, 26 August 1933, Official File-100, Franklin D. Roosevelt Library; interview with Erwin Griswold, 3 June 1975; see also William E. Leuchtenburg, "The Case of the Contentious Commissioner: Humphrey's Executor v. U.S.," in Harold M. Hyman and Leonard W. Levy, eds., *Freedom and Reform: Essays in Honor of Henry Steele Commager* (New York, 1967), 276-367.

18. Humphrey to Roosevelt, 11 August 1933, Humphrey Papers; *Humphrey's Executor (Rathbun) v. United States,* 295 U.S. 602 (1935); Landis oral history, 41; Landis, "Mr. Justice Brandeis: A Law Clerk's View," *Publications of the American Jewish Historical Society,* no. 936 (June 1957); Landis, The Administrative Process (New Haven, 1938), 115-116.

19. *New York Times,* 7, 8 June 1933, 6, 8 July 1933; *Time,* XXII (17 July 1933)

38; Landis oral history, 173, 175-176; Federal Trade Commission, "Securities Act of 1933," release 6 (8 July 1933).

20. Landis oral history, 173-174; *New York Times,* 8 July 1933; FTC, "Securities Act of 1933," release 23 (12 August 1933), release 37 (31 August 1933).

21. Landis to Maurice Merrill, 3 April 1933, Landis Papers; Brandeis to Frankfurter, 15 September 1933, Corcoran to Frankfurter, 8 September 1933, Frankfurter Papers.

22. Stella Landis diary, 6 October 1933, McLaughlin Collection; T. R. Powell to Frankfurter, 10 October 1933, Grenville Clark to Frankfurter, 11 October 1933, Calvert Magruder to Frankfurter, 2 November 1933, 4 December 1933, Julian W. Mack to Frankfurter, 20 November 1933, Frankfurter Papers.

23. Landis oral history, 176; *Wall Street Journal,* 31 October 1933; *New York Times,* 2 April 1933. The I.B.A. had earlier advocated federal regulation; see Parrish, *Securities Regulation,* 7-41.

24. J. C. Muirhead to Baldwin Bane, 14 September 1933, E. G. Parsley to Bane, 15 September 1933, Dudley Henderson to Landis, 20 March 1934, Frederick A. Ballard, "The Federal Securities Act of 1933," Landis Papers; *New York Times,* 13 September 1933, 15, 30 October 1933.

25. FTC, "Securities Act of 1933," release 93 (23 December 1933), release 111 (4 February 1934); *Time,* XXII (25 December 1933), 31; *New York Times,* 1, 4, 17 October 1933; *New York Herald Tribune,* 6 February 1934; *Business Week,* 23 September 1933, pp. 20-21, 30 September 1933, p. 18, 21 October 1933, p. 21, 9 December 1933, p. 16; Edward Aswell to Frankfurter, 6 December 1933, Frankfurter Papers; William O. Douglas, "Protecting the Investor," *Yale Review,* XXIII (March 1934), 529-530.

26. Memorandum, W. D. B. to Henry Bruère, 26 October 1933, Henry Bruère and Fred N. Oliver, memorandum to Franklin D. Roosevelt, 27 October 1933, Roosevelt to Landis, 14 November 1933, Landis Papers; Bernard Flexner to Frankfurter, 5 December 1933, Frankfurter Papers; Homer Cummings to Roosevelt, 4 December 1933, Landis Papers, Harvard Law School; Adolph Berle, Jr., to Roosevelt, 4 December 1933, Roosevelt to Berle, 15 December 1933, Official File-242, Roosevelt Library.

27. Corcoran to Frankfurter, 13 December 1933, John T. Flynn, "Other People's Money," *New Republic,* LXXV (2 August 1933), 315-316; *Time,* XXII (30 October 1933), 43; Cohen to Frankfurter, 9 October 1933, Frankfurter Papers.

28. Moley to Frankfurter, 16 December 1933 and 27 March 1934, Frankfurter Papers. In *After Seven Years* and *The First New Deal,* Moley portrayed his relations with the Frankfurter group as far more aloof than his contemporary correspondence reveals. Corcoran attributed Moley's eventual break with them to "battle-weariness" and personality differences rather than to any clash of ideologies. See Corcoran to Frankfurter, 11 May 1934, Frankfurter Papers.

29. Calvert Magruder to Frankfurter, 4 October 1933, Landis to Frankfurter, 27 January 1934, Corcoran to Frankfurter, 11 December 1933, Cohen to Frankfurter, 1 January 1934, Frankfurter Papers.

30. Corcoran to Frankfurter, 13 October 1933, Frankfurter Papers.

31. Stella Landis to James Landis, undated correspondence, summer and

autumn of 1933 and 27 October 1933, Landis Papers; Landis to Frankfurter, 6 March 1934, Frankfurter Papers; Stella Landis diary, 9 December 1933, 30 January 1934, 10 March 1934, 2 April 1934, 9 June 1934, McLaughlin Collection.

32. Max Lowenthal to Frankfurter, 26 October 1933, Frankfurter Papers; "Mr. Roosevelt's Men," *Fortune*, IX (April 1934), 148.

33. "The Wonder Boys in Washington," *Fortune*, VIII (July 1933), 119; *Time*, XXIII (19 March 1934), 62-63; George L. Haskins, "John Dickinson, 1894-1952," *University of Pennsylvania Law Review*, CI (October 1952), 1-25; John Dickinson, *Hold Fast the Middle Way: An Outline of Economic Challenges and Alternatives* (Boston, 1935); T. R. Powell to Frankfurter, 20 March 1934, Frankfurter Papers; U.S. Congress, Senate, Banking and Currency Committee, *Stock Exchange Regulation*, 73rd Congress, 2nd sess., 1934.

34. Landis, "Comments on the Proposed Report to Secretary Roper on Stock Exchange Regulation," Landis Papers; Landis to Frankfurter, 27 January 1934, Corcoran to Frankfurter, 13 October 1933, Lowenthal to Frankfurter, 17 April 1934, Calvert Magruder to Frankfurter, 17 February 1934, Frankfurter Papers; *Literary Digest*, CXVII (10 February 1934), 37.

35. Joseph Alsop and Robert Kintner, "The Battle of the Market Place," *Saturday Evening Post*, CCX (11 June 1938), 75; Frankfurter to Lowenthal, 23 January 1926, Frankfurter Papers; Landis oral history, 197-199; interview with Benjamin Cohen, 9 January 1974; interview with Telford Taylor, 6 March 1974.

36. Alsop and Kintner, "Battle of the Market Place," 75; John T. Flynn, "The Marines Land in Wall Street," *Harper's*, CLXIX (July 1934), 150; *New York Times*, 10 February 1934; *Wall Street Journal*, 10 February 1934; interview with Thomas Corcoran, 21 March 1974.

37. Landis oral history, 199; *New York Times*, 8 February 1934; U.S. Congress, House of Representatives, Interstate and Foreign Commerce Committee, *Stock Exchange Regulation*, 73rd Congress, 2nd sess., 1934, 148; *Business Week*, 3 March 1934, p. 36, 17 February 1934, p. 8; *Wall Street Journal*, 14, 15 February 1934.

38. Landis oral history, 201; Landis to Frankfurter, 13 December 1933, Frankfurter Papers.

39. C. Dwight Dorough, *Mr. Sam* (New York, 1962), 243; Richard Whitney to the presidents of all listed corporations, 14 February 1934, petition on behalf of the floor traders of the NYSE, 24 March 1934, Landis Papers; *New York Times*, 15, 16 February 1934, 11 March 1938, 28 April 1938; *USA before SEC in the Matter of Richard Whitney* (Washington, D.C., 1938).

40. Landis to Frankfurter, 6 March 1934, Dickinson to Frankfurter, 6 March 1934, Frankfurter Papers; *Wall Street Journal*, 9 March 1934; House Interstate and Foreign Commerce Committee, *Stock Exchange Regulation*, 506-514.

41. Interview with Benjamin Cohen, 9 January 1974; Raymond Moley to Frankfurter, 27 March 1934, Frankfurter Papers; Rosenman, ed., *Public Papers and Addresses of Franklin D. Roosevelt*, III (New York, 1939), 169-170.

42. *New York Times*, 4, 10, 12 April 1934; *Business Week*, 14 April 1934, p. 39; Parrish, *Securities Regulation*, 131-136.

43. *Congressional Record*, 73rd Congress, 2nd sess., 7693-7696, 7943-7944, 8013; *Time*, XXIII (14 May 1934), 66.

44. *Congressional Record,* 73rd Congress, 2nd sess., 8110-8111.

45. Landis to Frankfurter, 6 March 1934, Frankfurter Papers; Landis oral history, 196-197.

46. Landis, "Should the Federal Securities Act of 1933 Be Modified?" *Congressional Digest,* XIII (May 1934), 141-143; *Congressional Record,* 73rd Congress, 2nd sess., 8667-8669; Lawrence Stein, "New Financing Unshackled," *Magazine of Wall Street,* LIV (23 June 1934), 232-233, 267; Landis oral history, 196.

47. *Wall Street Journal,* 14-17 May 1934; *New York Times,* 16, 17, 21, 27 May 1934; *Business Week,* 19 May 1934, p. 20, 26 May 1934, p. 37; *Time,* XXIII (28 May 1934), 11; Flynn, "Other People's Money," *New Republic,* LXXIX (13 June 1934), 127-128; interview with Benjamin Cohen, 9 January 1974; interview with Thomas Corcoran, 21 March 1974.

48. *Wall Street Journal,* 2 June 1934; *New York Times,* 2 June 1934; *Chicago Tribune,* 6 June 1934; Hillel Black, *The Watchdogs of Wall Street* (New York, 1962), 233-234.

49. *Business Week,* 9 June 1934, pp. 10-11; *Time,* XXIII (11 June 1934), 62; Auville Eager to Landis, 10 May 1937, Landis Papers; Corcoran to Frankfurter, 11 May 1934, Frankfurter Papers.

50. Corcoran to Frankfurter, 22 April 1933, 11 May 1934, and 30 May 1934, Frankfurter to Corcoran, 7 May 1934, Frankfurter Papers; Moley, *After Seven Years,* 286-289, and *First New Deal,* 517-519; George Wolfskill and John A. Hudson, *All but the People: Franklin D. Roosevelt and His Critics, 1933-39* (New York, 1969), 65-92. Benjamin Cohen adamantly denied that he ever sought or had any interest in the post; interview with Benjamin Cohen, 9 January 1974.

51. Landis oral history, 191; Flynn, "Other People's Money," *New Republic,* LXXIX (18 July 1934), 265; Theordore M. Knapper, "The Rulers of the Stock Market," *Magazine of Wall Street,* LIV (21 July 1934), 329; Roosevelt to Herbert Bayard Swope, 2 July 1934, Official File-1062, Roosevelt Library.

52. Landis oral history, 192-193.

53. *New York Times,* 3, 4 July 1934; *New York Herald Tribune,* 3, 4 July 1934.

5. Wall Street's Policeman

1. *New York Times,* 1 July 1933.

2. *Business Week,* 14 July 1934, p. 20, 21 July 1934, pp. 13-14; Calvert Magruder to Frankfurter, 11 May 1934, Frankfurter Papers; Auville Eager to Landis, 10 May 1937, Landis Papers.

3. Landis to Sam Rayburn, 20 August 1934, Landis Papers, Harvard Law School; Landis to Frank L. Scheffey, 25 January 1939, Landis Papers, Harvard Archives; Landis, "Excessive Speculation: The Regulation of the Exchanges," *Vital Speeches of the Day,* II (9 March 1936), 374-376; Joseph P. Kennedy, "Shielding the Sheep," *Saturday Evening Post,* CCVIII (18 January 1936), 64-69.

4. U.S. Congress, House of Representatives, Subcommittee of the Committee on Appropriations, *Urgent Supplemental Appropriations for 1935,* 74th Congress, 1st sess., 1935, 3; "Mr. Kennedy, the Chairman," *Fortune,* XVI (September 1937), 57.

5. Securities and Exchange Commission minutes, 26 July 1934, 23 August 1934, 11 October 1934, SEC, Washington, D.C.; Frankfurter to Landis, 18 December 1935 and 11 January 1936, Frankfurter Papers; Landis to Frankfurter, 10 January 1936, Chairman's Correspondence, SEC; Landis oral history, 565-566.

6. Landis oral history, 261; memorandum of a telephone call between Landis and Frankfurter, 8 July 1934, Frankfurter Papers; Landis to Sam Rayburn, 20 July 1934, Landis Papers, Harvard Law School; Stella Landis diary, 12 July 1934, McLaughlin Collection; Marvin McIntyre to Roosevelt, 12 July 1934, Official File-1060, Roosevelt Library; *Washington Herald,* 1 October 1934. Benjamin Cohen insisted that he was uninterested in any official position with the Securities and Exchange Commission; interview with Benjamin Cohen, 9 January 1974.

7. Cohen to Frankfurter, 2 October 1934, Frankfurter to Landis, 9 October 1934, Frankfurter Papers; Jonathan Daniels, *White House Witness, 1942-1945* (Garden City, N.Y., 1975), 38; "Legend of Landis," *Fortune,* X (August 1934), 47. Afterwards, Landis cultivated Drew Pearson's friendship and provided the columnist with material. When Pearson was writing his book on the Supreme Court, *Nine Old Men,* Landis supplied information that helped shape the book's favorable interpretation of Justice Brandeis; interview with John B. Martin, 7 March 1974.

8. Landis oral history, 249; see also Eddie Dowling oral history, 255, 366-367, Columbia University; Arthur Krock oral history, 1-2, Kennedy Library; Richard J. Whalen, *The Founding Father: The Story of Joseph P. Kennedy* (New York, 1964); and David E. Koskoff, *Joseph P. Kennedy: A Life and Times* (Englewood Cliffs, N.J., 1974).

9. Landis oral history, 252-253; see also Charles Spaulding oral history, Kennedy Library.

10. Joseph P. Kennedy, address at the National Press Club, Washington, D.C., 25 July 1934, SEC; *New York Times,* 27, 31 July 1934, 14 August 1934, 9 February 1935; *Time,* XXIV (6 August 1934), 55-56.

11. Whalen, *Founding Father,* 148; Theodore N. Knappen, "S.E.C. Surprises Both Friend and Foe," *Magazine of Wall Street,* LVI (14 September 1935), 539; *Business Week,* 21 July 1934, p. 22, 1 September 1934, p. 29, 8 September 1934, p. 37, 15 September 1934, p. 33; *New York Times,* 25 August 1934, 13 September 1934.

12. Kennedy, "Shielding the Sheep," 66; *Business Week,* 13 October 1934, p. 12; SEC minutes, 25 September 1934; *New York Times,* 17 November 1934.

13. Kennedy, "Shielding the Sheep," 64; "Why Bankers and Businessmen Hesitate," *The Commercial and Financial Chronicle,* CXL (23 March 1935), 1893-1894; *Time,* XXVI (22 July 1935), 41-42; Milton V. Freeman, "A Private Practitioner's View of the Development of the Securities and Exchange Commission," *George Washington Law Review,* XXVIII (October 1959), 18.

14. SEC minutes, 8 November 1934, 18 December 1934; Landis to Franklin Roosevelt, 4 May 1936, Landis Papers; Raymond Gram Swing, "Soft Pedal at the S.E.C.," *Nation,* CXL (19 June 1935), 706-708; Michael E. Parrish, *Securities Regulation and the New Deal* (New Haven, Conn., 1970), 200-208.

15. Landis oral history, 193-194; *New York Herald Tribune,* 21 September 1935; Whalen, *Founding Father,* 174-177.

16. Joseph Kennedy to Franklin Roosevelt, 20 September 1935, Official File-1060, Roosevelt Library; see also Parrish, *Securities Regulation,* 145-178; and Ralph F. DeBedts, *The New Deal's S.E.C.: The Formative Years* (New York, 1964), 112-143.

17. *New York Herald Tribune,* 24 September 1934; *Nation,* CXL (2 October 1935), 365; John T. Flynn, "Other People's Money," *New Republic,* LXXXV (8 January 1936), 253.

18. Stella Landis diary, 28 September 1935, McLaughlin Collection.

19. *Washington Post,* 24 September 1935; *New York Times,* 24 September 1935.

20. *New York Times,* 6 October 1935; *Boston Evening Transcript,* 24 January 1937; Landis to John Carson, 25 January 1936, Landis Papers.

21. Ellis Hawley, *The New Deal and the Problem of Monopoly: A Study in Economic Ambivalence* (Princeton, 1966), 329-333; interview with Benjamin Cohen, 9 January 1974.

22. TRB, "Funny Business in Baltimore," *New Republic,* LXXXV (20 November 1935), 35-37; John T. Flynn, "Other People's Money," *New Republic,* LXXXV (30 October 1935), 33-35; William H. Harbaugh, *Lawyer's Lawyer: The Life of John W. Davis* (New York, 1973), 365-372.

23. Landis, address over the nationwide hook-up of the Columbia Broadcasting System, 28 September 1935, SEC; Theodore M. Knappen, "Are the Utility Companies Inviting Trouble?" *Magazine of Wall Street,* LVII (23 November 1935); Chester T. Lane oral history, 247-250, Columbia University; Landis to Lothrop Withington, 8 November 1935, Chairman's Correspondence, SEC; SEC minutes, 21 November 1935.

24. Landis oral history, 220-224; *Newsweek,* VI (7 December 1935); *Time,* XXVIII (23 November 1936), 75-76.

25. Sidney Olson, "Wall Street Watchdog," *Financial Observer,* 23 February 1937; DeBedts, *New Deal's S.E.C.,* 173-183.

26. Landis to Edward A. Pierce, 7 October 1935, Landis to Helen Rogers Reid, 30 September 1935, Chairman's Correspondence, SEC; Landis oral history, 227-228; SEC minutes, 15 May 1935. The differences between Whitney's faction and the commission houses were summarized by Joseph Alsop and Robert Kintner in "The Battle of the Market Place," *Saturday Evening Post,* CCX (11 June 1938), 74-75: "Whitney's followers were the floor traders, the specialists, and others concerned in the actual buying and selling of stocks on the Exchange floor. These men were the old guard, the direct descendants of the intimate community of beaver-hatted bulls and bears who first gathered under Wall Street's buttonwood tree. They thought of the Exchange as being the same family affair it had been when trading 'in the stocks' was confined to a small group of experts in New York's financial community. The commission houses, on the other hand, knew the public's interest in the Exchange. Their network of wires brought the public's business in, from their branches on hundreds of Main Streets to the traders on the Exchange floor. Therefore, they saw the Exchange as a national institution, and were all for compromise and co-operation with a Government they distrusted less than they did the Whitney tactics."

27. "S.E.C.," *Fortune,* XXI (June 1940), 92, 124-126; *New York Times,* 11 October 1935.

28. SEC minutes, 25 October 1935; Eddie Dowling oral history, 335-336, Columbia University; Rudolph L. Weissman, *The New Wall Street* (New York, 1939), 134.

29. "In the Matter of Michael J. Meehan," *Securities and Exchange Commission Decisions,* II (Washington, D.C., 1939), 240, 593-619.

30. Oil royalties were investments in land from which developers hoped to

pump oil. Investors who purchased the oil royalties on the promise of immediate dividend payments generally did not realize that the depleting oil wells would eventually run dry and leave their holding worthless. The SEC considered oil royalties the "biggest racket in the country" and estimated three thousand dealers in New York alone, many of whom carried their offices under their hats. *New York Times*, 2, 26 May 1935.

31. Chester T. Lane oral history, 272; SEC minutes, 13 December 1934, 21 January 1935; *New York Times*, 19 June 1935; *Jones v. Securities and Exchange Commission*, 298 U.S. 1 (1936); see also J. Edward Jones, *And So — They Indicted Me! A Story of New Deal Persecution* (New York, 1938).

32. Landis to Roosevelt, 6 April 1936, Chairman's Correspondence, SEC; *New York Times*, 1 July 1935; see "The S.E.C. and the Rubber Hose," in Jerome Frank, *If Men Were Angels: Some Aspects of Government in a Democracy* (New York, 1942), 316-331.

33. Eugene L. Garey, "Wall Street Looks at the Securities and Exchange Commission," address before the Legal Institute on Modern Federal Administrative Law, Richmond, Virginia, 28 April 1939; Landis, *The Administrative Process* (New Haven, 1938), 136-139; Landis to Frankfurter, 11 March 1936, Frankfurter Papers.

34. Landis to Frankfurter, 6 June 1936, Chairman's Correspondence, SEC; *Nation*, CXLIV (23 January 1937), 86-87.

35. John T. Flynn, "The S.E.C. Unmasks the Brokers," *New Republic*, LXXXVIII (8 July 1936), 260; Flynn, "Other People's Money," *New Republic*, LXXXV (8 January 1936), 253; *New York Herald Tribune*, 4 February 1937.

36. Landis to Roosevelt, 20 June 1936, Official File-1060, Roosevelt Library; "S.E.C. Bombshell," *Literary Digest*, CXXII (4 July 1936), 38; Flynn, "S.E.C. Unmasks the Brokers," 261; *New York Herald Tribune*, 4 February 1937; *New York Times*, 21 June 1936.

37. "S.E.C. Bombshell," 38; Flynn, "S.E.C. Unmasks the Brokers," 261.

38. Landis to Frankfurter, 6 June 1936 and 6 July 1936, Landis to Bruce Bliven, 3 July 1936, Chairman's Correspondence, SEC; Frankfurter to Landis, 9 June 1936, Frankfurter Papers; John T. Flynn, *The Roosevelt Myth* (New York, 1948), 60.

39. *New York Times*, 16 March 1937, 5 October 1937; *New York Herald Tribune*, 4 February 1937.

40. Landis to Franklin C. Setaro, 28 October 1935, Chairman's Correspondence, SEC; Calvert Magruder to Frankfurter, 12 May 1934, Frankfurter to Landis, 17 March 1934, Frankfurter Papers; "The Legend of Landis," *Fortune*, X (August 1934), 120; interview with Ann Landis McLaughlin, 20 January 1974; interview with Mr. and Mrs. William McKee and Mr. and Mrs. Charles McLaughlin, 27 February 1974.

41. Stella Landis diary, 27 June 1934, 12 July 1934, McLaughlin Collection;

42. Edmund M. Morgan to Landis, 7 November 1936, Roscoe Pound Deanship Papers, Harvard Archives; Landis to Edmund M. Morgan, 22 January 1937, Landis to R. E. Gardner, Jr., 1 February 1937, Landis to Charles E. Clark, 6 March 1937, Chairman's Correspondence, SEC.

43. Landis to Henry J. Friendly, 1 February 1937, Landis to Marion Tomlin-

son, 22 October 1935, Chairman's Correspondence, SEC; Chester T. Lane oral history, 239, 285-288; interview with Allen Throop, 21 March 1974. Landis was alluding to the Harvard law library's "red set" of crimson-bound copies of works by faculty members.

44. Landis oral history, 187, 238-239, 242; interview with Mary Walker Taylor, 6 March 1974.

45. Landis oral history, 242-244.

46. Roosevelt to James Conant, draft, 5 January 1937, Landis to Roosevelt, 13 January 1937, 11 September 1937, Landis Papers; telephone conversation, Landis and Henry Morgenthau, Jr., 20 May 1937, Morgenthau Diaries, vol. 69, Roosevelt Library; *Complete Presidential Press Conferences of Franklin D. Roosevelt, 1937* (New York, 1972) 9:383-384; William O. Douglas, *Go East, Young Man: The Early Years* (New York, 1974), 281.

47. William E. Leuchtenburg, *Franklin D. Roosevelt and the New Deal* (New York, 1963), 243-246; *Christian Science Monitor,* 5 May 1937; *Newsweek,* X (20 September 1937), 28; *Wall Street Journal,* 15, 16 September 1937; *New York Herald Tribune,* 16 September 1937; *New York Times,* 15, 16 September 1937.

48. Landis oral history, 232-234; Landis to Herman Oliphant, 7 January 1933, Landis to Roosevelt, 20 December 1935, William O. Douglas to Landis, 5 October 1937, Landis Papers; Landis to Frankfurter, 6 March 1934, Frankfurter Papers; Landis to William Rosenblatt, 26 November 1935, Chairman's Correspondence, SEC.

49. William O. Douglas to Frankfurter, 14 January 1938, Landis Papers; *Time,* XXX (11 October 1937), 61-62.

50. Joseph Alsop and Robert Kintner, "The Battle of the Market Place," *Saturday Evening Post,* CCX (25 June 1938), 10-11, 78-82; Fred Rodell, "Douglas over the Stock Exchanges," *Fortune,* XVII (February 1938), 64, 116-126, James Allen, ed., *Democracy and Finance: The Addresses and Public Statements of William O. Douglas* (New Haven, 1940), 79-91; Douglas, *Go East, Young Man,* 283-285, 289-292.

51. Alsop and Kintner, "Battle of the Market Place," 81-82; *New York Times,* 11 March 1938, 28 April 1938; see also *United States of America before the Securities and Exchange Commission In the Matter of Richard Whitney, et al.* (Washington, D.C., 1938).

52. *Boston News Bureau,* 26 February 1937; Landis, "The Securities and Exchange Commission and How It Operates," address before the Stock Exchange Institute, 10 October 1935, SEC; *St. Louis Post-Dispatch,* 14 January 1962; Hurd Baruch, *Wall Street: Security Risk* (Baltimore, 1971), 298-322; Landis to Gerhard Gesell, 6 December 1940, Landis Papers.

6. Dean of the Harvard Law School

1. Stella Landis diary, 13 January 1937, McLaughlin Collection; *Boston Herald,* 12 January 1937.

2. *Washington Daily News,* 25 January 1937; *Boston Evening Transcript,* 12 January 1937.

3. Landis to Frankfurter, 27 January 1934, Calvert Magruder to Frankfurter, 17 February 1934, Frankfurter Papers; Landis to Edmund Morgan, 21 October 1933, Landis to George K. Gardner, 22 October 1935, Landis to James B. Conant,

14 March 1936, Landis to Austin Wakeman Scott, 23 March 1936, Chairman's Correspondence, SEC.

4. Frankfurter diary, 14 March 1930, 1 April 1930, 6 May 1930, Frankfurter to Grenville Clark, 4 December 1933, Frankfurter to Conant, 11 September 1936, Frankfurter Papers; Landis oral history, 150-151; Arthur E. Sutherland, *The Law at Harvard: A History of Ideas and Men, 1817-1967* (Cambridge, Mass, 1967), 288-289; David Wigdor, *Roscoe Pound: Philosopher of Law* (Westport, Conn., 1974), 248-254; James B. Conant, *My Several Lives: Memoirs of a Social Inventor* (New York, 1970), 109-110.

5. Conant, *My Several Lives,* 112-113; Pound to William M. Chadbourne, 24 October 1935, and Pound to William Thomas, 17 October 1935, Pound Papers. Pound retired at 66 and died at 93 in July 1964, the same month that his young successor, James Landis, died at 64.

6. W. Barton Leach, "Landis: Roommate and Dean," *Harvard Law School Bulletin,* XIX (March 1968), 17; Frankfurter, memorandum of a conversation with President Conant, 30 September 1935, Robert K. Lamb, memorandum of a conversation with President Conant, 23 March 1936, Frankfurter Papers.

7. Frankfurter to Grenville Clark, 4 December 1933 and 4 April 1946, Frankfurter to Conant, 26 May 1936, Frankfurter, memorandum of a conversation with President Conant, 30 September 1935, Frankfurter Papers; Gardner Jackson oral history, 396, Columbia University; Stella Landis diary, 28 September 1935, McLaughlin Collection; Landis oral history, 303-304; Leach, "Landis: Roommate and Dean," 17-18.

8. Interview with Austin Scott, 18 June 1975; interview with Erwin N. Griswold, 3 June 1975; Frankfurter to Landis, 5 January 1937, Landis Papers. Frankfurter later described his ideal Harvard law dean in a letter to McGeorge Bundy, 28 May, 1963, Frankfurter Papers. Among other criteria, he wrote: "As for stimulating contributions by members of the Faculty, the Dean makes all the difference, just as it makes all the difference whether Toscanini or Koussevitzky or Howard Mitchell conducts an orchestra. The properly equipped leader of an orchestra can bring out all the music that is in his orchestra, unlike a commonplace fellow like Howard Mitchell, not to mention others."

9. Landis oral history, 68.

10. For the background of the Supreme Court Packing Plan see Joseph Alsop and Turner Catledge, *The 168 Days* (New York, 1938); Leonard Baker, *Back to Back: The Duel between F.D.R. and the Supreme Court* (New York, 1967); and William E. Leuchtenburg, "The Origins of Franklin D. Roosevelt's 'Court-Packing' Plan," *Supreme Court Review,* IV (1966).

11. Landis oral history, 45; John J. Burns to Frankfurter, 29 May 1935, Frankfurter Papers; A. Moran to Landis, 23 March 1937, Landis Papers; Landis to Frankfurter, 11 March 1936 and 12 May 1937, Landis to Benjamin Cohen, 2 June 1936, Chairman's Correspondence, SEC; *Newsweek,* V (18 May 1935). Earlier, Landis had suggested that better retirement pay for the justices might help reform the court. See Landis to Donald R. Richberg, 29 May 1935, Donald R. Richberg Papers, Library of Congress.

12. *Washington Post,* 23, 28 February 1937; *Chicago Tribune,* 11 March 1937.

13. Harold L. Ickes, *The Secret Diary of Harold L. Ickes: The Inside Struggle, 1936-1939,* II (New York, 1954), 100; Homer Cummings to Landis, 11 March 1937, Landis to Roosevelt, 3 March 1937, Jerome Frank to Landis, 28 March 1937, Thurman Arnold to Landis, 23 March 1937, Landis Papers; Landis oral history, 45.

14. Landis, address before the Third Annual Eastern Law Students Conference, Catholic University, Washington, D.C., 20 March 1937, Thomas L. Elder to Landis, 21 March 1937, Landis Papers; *New York Times,* 21 March 1937; *Washington Evening Star,* 25 March 1937; *New York Herald Tribune,* 6 April 1937; see also Irving Bernstein, *Turbulent Years: A History of the American Worker, 1933-1941* (Boston, 1971), 488-501.

15. *Princeton Alumni Weekly* (9 April 1937), *Harvard Alumni Bulletin* (May 1937), 887, anonymous to Landis, 31 March 1937, Lawrence G. Brooks to Landis, 20 March 1937, Landis Papers; Landis to Reginald H. Smith, 21 April 1937, Chairman's Correspondence, SEC.

16. Charles E. Clark to Landis, 9 December 1935, Landis to Clark, 18 December 1935, Landis to Clark, 6 March 1937, Landis Papers.

17. Samuel Rosenman, ed., *The Public Papers and Addresses of Franklin D. Roosevelt,* I (New York, 1937), 239; Daniel C. Roper with Frank H. Lovette, *Fifty Years of Public Life* (New York, 1938), 268; for the impact of the Brownlow Report see Richard Polenberg, *Reorganizing Roosevelt's Government: The Controversy over Executive Reorganization,* 1936-1939 (Cambridge, Mass., 1966), 3-51.

18. Landis to Jean P. Smith, 10 November 1924, Landis Papers, Harvard Law School; Landis to Frankfurter, c. 1926, Frankfurter Papers; Landis to Kenneth C. Sears, 17 December 1932, Landis Papers; Landis, "States Rights and the Colorado Project," *New Republic,* XLII (20 April 1925), 265-266; Landis, *The Administrative Process* (New Haven, 1938), 1-46.

19. Landis, *The Administrative Process,* 24, 155; Landis, "The New Responsibility of the Professions (Law, Engineering, Banking) in their Inter-Relationship with Business Management," 6 April 1939, Landis Papers; Raymond Clapper, "Felix Frankfurter's Young Men," *Review of Reviews,* XCIII (January 1936), 28.

20. Landis, *The Administrative Process,* 4, 46-47, 89-155.

21. Landis to Sam Rayburn, 9 September 1938, Rayburn to Landis, 26 September 1938, Landis Papers, Harvard Archives.

22. A. H. Feller, "The Quasi-Judicial, Quasi-Legislative Agencies," *Survey Graphic,* XXVII (December 1938), 620-621; Thomas T. Cooke, review of *The Administrative Process* in *Yale Review,* XLVIII (March 1939), 925-929; George K. Gardner, review in the *Harvard Law Review,* LII (December 1938), 336-342; Edward S. Corwin to Landis, 25 October 1938, Landis Papers, Harvard Archives.

23. Louis L. Jaffee, "James Landis and the Administrative Process," *Harvard Law Review,* LXXVIII (December 1964), 319-328; Milton Katz to Landis, 18 October 1938, Landis to Katz, 26 November 1938, Katz Papers, Truman Library, Independence, Missouri.

24. Landis to Raymond C. Wass, 9 February 1938, Landis Papers, Harvard Archives; *Washington Post,* 6 June 1937; *Boston Evening Transcript,* 18 September 1937; *New York Times,* 28 November 1937, 13 August 1939, 30 June 1940.

25. Landis, "The Harvard Law School Curriculum—1938," *Bulletin of the Harvard Business School Alumni Association,* XIV (February 1938), 77-80; Sidney Post Stimson, "The New Curricula of the Harvard Law School," *Harvard Law Review,* LI (April 1938); *New York Times,* 10 January 1939, 19 May 1940; Sutherland, *The Law at Harvard,* 306-307; Landis oral history, 461-464.

26. Interview with Erwin Griswold, 3 June 1975; *New York Times,* 28 November 1937; *Washington Post,* 6 June 1937.

27. Sutherland, *The Law at Harvard,* 304-305; Erwin Griswold, "James McCauley Landis—1899-1964," *Harvard Law Review,* LXXVIII (December 1964), 315-316; Landis to Francis Bohlen, 24 February 1941, Landis Papers; Landis to Frankfurter, 14 March 1939, Frankfurter Papers; Landis to Milton Katz, 24 April 1939, Katz Papers; Landis oral history, 467-476; interview with Benjamin Cohen, 9 January 1974.

28. Memorandum, 24 May 1937, Henry Morgenthau Diaries, vol. 69, Roosevelt Library; *New York Times,* 9 June 1939; Landis oral history, 303; interview with Stanley Gewirtz, 6 March 1974; interview with Mary Walker Taylor, 6 March 1974.

29. Harvard news release, 8 June 1939, Faculty Dossiers, Harvard Archives; Landis, "Fact, Fancy and Reform in Administrative Law," speech at the University of Wyoming, 7 February 1941, Landis Papers.

30. *Washington Post,* 6 June 1937; *Life,* III (1 November 1937), 42; remarks by Stanley Gewirtz at Landis Funeral, 2 August 1964, Frankfurter Papers, Harvard Law School.

31. *Boston Evening Transcript,* 18 September 1937; Jerome D. Greene to Landis, 27 November 1942, Josephine L. Bailey to Landis, 30 September 1937, Landis Papers; interview with Ann Landis McLaughlin, 20 January 1974.

32. Interview with Ann Landis McLaughlin, 20 January 1974; Ann Landis McLaughlin to author, 11 January 1973; Wiley D. Noyes to Edward Whitley, 13 November 1940, Landis Papers.

33. Landis to Jean P. Smith, 2 August 1925, Landis Papers, Harvard Law School; Landis to Lispenard B. Phister, 26 May 1941, Landis Papers.

34. Landis to Stella Landis, "Sunday afternoon," c. 1947-1948, McLaughlin Collection.

7. Freelance New Dealer

1. *Boston Evening Transcript,* 11 September 1937; Landis to James P. Kranz, 9 July 1938, Landis Papers, Harvard Archives; interview with Agnes Maher, 6 December 1975.

2. "Cambridge Committee for Plan E," news release, August 1938, "How Landis Became Head of the Plan E Group in Cambridge," newspaper clipping, c. 1940,

3. "How Landis Became Head of the Plan E Group in Cambridge," Landis Papers; *Time,* XXIII (31 October 1938), 30; *Cambridge Sentinel,* 2 November 1940.

4. *Boston Post,* 10 November 1938; *Cambridge Chronicle,* 7 November 1940, 9 January 1941, 6 February 1941; *Christian Science Monitor,* 6 October 1941.

5. Landis made contact with the Federal Theatre Project through its director, Hallie Flannegan, whose husband he had once roomed with at Harvard. Flannegan

approached Landis in 1935 for advice on how to sidestep government prohibitions against paying royalties to playwrights for their plays. Landis introduced her to Justice Brandeis, who found the perfect solution: instead of paying royalties, they should rent the plays on a weekly basis. Francis Bosworth oral history, Research Center for the Federal Theatre Project, George Mason University, Fairfax, Virginia.

6. Landis oral history, 128-129, 271-272, 276-280; Landis, "Labor's New Day in Court: The Supreme Court Vindicates Jury Trial in Contempt Case," *Survey,* LIII (15 November 1924), 175-177; Landis, *Cases on Labor Law* (Chicago, 1934); Landis to Francis E. Frothingham, 22 July 1940, Landis Papers.

7. Joseph Eastman to M. A. LeHand, 2 January 1941, Samuel Rosenman Papers, Roosevelt Library; *New York Times,* 30 April 1938, 25 September 1938.

8. Landis to William M. Leiserson, 15 September 1938, Leiserson to Landis, 16 September 1938, Roosevelt to Landis, 27 September 1938, Landis Papers, Harvard Law School.

9. Railway Labor Act, Chapter 691, 48 Stat. 1185 (1934); Landis to William T. Faricy, 5 November 1938, Landis Papers, Harvard Law School; *New York Times,* 28 September 1938, 1, 7, 8, 15, 30 October 1938.

10. Landis oral history, 51-52, 264-266.

11. Ibid., 52, 266-268; *Report of the Emergency Board to the President* (Washington, D.C., 1938); *New York Times,* 30 October 1938, 1, 5 November 1938; Gardner Jackson to Landis, 31 October 1938, Gardner Jackson Papers, Roosevelt Library.

12. Frances Perkins to Landis, 12 May 1939, Gerald D. Reilly to Landis, 23 May 1939, Landis Papers; James L. Houteling to Hamilton Fish, 26 February 1938, Department of Labor, Office of the Secretary, Box 53, RG-174, National Archives. For the story of the Bridges case, see Charles P. Larrowe, *Harry Bridges: The Rise and Fall of Radical Labor in the U.S.* (New York, 1972).

13. Landis was not Secretary Perkins' first choice. She originally assigned the case to Donald Hiss, but during the long wait for a Supreme Court ruling, Hiss transferred to the State Department. The Labor Department then turned to Grenville Clark, but Clark was counsel to the American-Hawaiian Steamship Company, which had long been battling Bridges. Clark declined and suggested Landis in his place. See Frances Perkins to Francis B. Sayre, 22 April 1938, Department of Labor, Office of the Secretary, Box 74, RG-174, National Archives; and Norman Cousins and J. Garry Clifford, eds., *Memoirs of a Man: Grenville Clark* (New York, 1975), 125-126.

14. Landis, *In the Matter of Harry R. Bridges: Findings and Conclusions of the Trial Examiner* (Washington, D.C., 1939), 49-52; Frances Perkins, *The Roosevelt I Knew* (New York, 1946), 315-317; J. R. Steelman to Perkins, 12 November 1937 and 8 September 1937, Department of Labor, Office of the Secretary, Box 28, RG-174, National Archives.

15. Walter Goodman, *The Committee: The Extraordinary Career of the House Committee on Un-American Activities* (Baltimore, 1969), 46-48; *Kessler v. Strecker,* 307 U.S. 22 (1939).

16. Estalov E. Ward, *Harry Bridges on Trial: How Union Labor Won Its Biggest Case* (New York, 1940), 20-23; Landis to Gerald D. Reilly, 28 May 1938, Landis to

Walter Birmingham, 28 June 1939, Landis Papers; *Boston Globe,* 30 December 1939.

17. Landis oral history, 53-55; Ward, *Bridges on Trial,* 225; Thomas B. Shoemaker, memorandum, 21 July 1939, C. E. Potts to Shoemaker, 2 August 1939, Landis Papers.

18. Landis oral history, 54-56; Landis, *In the Matter of Harry Bridges,* 12-86; Larrowe, *Harry Bridges,* 138-175.

19. Landis oral history, 57; Landis, *In the Matter of Harry Bridges,* 122-133; Larrowe, *Harry Bridges,* 176-216; interview with Ann Landis McLaughlin, 20 January 1974.

20. Ward, *Bridges on Trial,* 222-223.

21. Landis to Gerald Reilly, 26 September 1939, Landis to Harry C. Lang, 2 October 1939, Landis to Frances Perkins, 26 September 1939, Landis Papers.

22. Landis, *In the Matter of Harry Bridges,* 131-133; Henry Morgenthau presidential diaries, memorandum of a telephone conversation with FDR, 12 June 1941, vol. 4, Roosevelt Library; *Boston Globe,* 30 December 1939, *New York Times,* 31 December 1939.

23. New York *Sun,* 30 September 1941; *Los Angeles Times,* 17 December 1940; Larrowe, *Harry Bridges,* 217-249.

24. Statement of J. Edgar Hoover before a subcommittee of the House Appropriations Committee, 22 February 1941, Landis memorandum, 5 April 1941, J. Edgar Hoover to Landis, 11 April 1941, Landis to Hoover, 15 April 1941, Landis to Robert Jackson, 15 April 1941, Hoover to Landis, 25 April 1941, Landis to Hoover, 30 April 1941, Landis to Jackson, 30 April 1941, Landis to Gerald Reilly, 28, 30 April 1941, Landis Papers.

25. *Bridges v. Wixon,* 326 U.S. 135 (1945); Francis Biddle, *In Brief Authority* (Garden City, N.Y., 1962), 296-307; Landis to Dorothy Brown, June 1945, Landis Papers; Landis oral history, 58-63.

26. William Allen White to Landis, 2 October 1939, Landis to White, 3 October 1939, Landis Papers, Harvard Archives; Landis to Harry C. Lang, 2 October 1939, Hugh Moore to Landis, 7 October 1939, "Statement by Non-Partisan Committee of New England," October 1939, Landis address to the Non-Partisan Neutrality Committee of New England, 27 October 1939, Landis Papers.

27. Rosalind H. Greene to Landis, 3 December 1940, Landis to Claude Pepper, 24 June 1940, Landis Papers.

28. Landis to James Rowe, Jr., 6 June 1940 and 13 March 1941, John L. Sullivan to Landis, 16 March 1940, Paul McNutt to Landis, 30 September 1940, Landis Papers; *New York Times,* 17 January 1940.

29. Landis to David Glick, 8 December 1939, Landis Papers, Harvard Archives; Landis to Charles W. Cross, 30 September 1940, Landis, speech over WNAC, 14 October 1940, Landis Papers; Landis, "I Vote for Roosevelt," *Atlantic,* CLXVI (November 1940), 542-544.

30. Henry Morgenthau diaries, memorandum, 10 June 1941, vol. 406, telephone conversation with Frankfurter, 8 July 1941, vol. 419, telephone conversation with Grace Tully, 8 July 1941, vol. 419, Roosevelt Library.

31. Morgenthau diaries, telephone conversation with Landis 19 June 1941, vol. 410, also note 6 January 1936, vol. 15, Roosevelt Library.

32. Morgenthau diaries, telephone conversation with Landis, 19 June 1941, memorandum, 21 June 1941, vol. 410, Roosevelt Library; Landis to Morgenthau, 19 June 1941 (not sent) and 21 June 1941, Landis Papers; Landis to Frankfurter, 6 July 1941, Frankfurter Papers, Harvard Law School; James B. Conant to Roosevelt, 30 June 1941, President's Personal Files-91, Roosevelt Library.

33. David I. Walsh to Landis, 13 December 1940, Walsh to Alexander Cochrane, 24 December 1940, Landis to Morgenthau, 21 June 1941 and 3 July 1941, Robert Patterson to Landis, 18 January 1941, Howard C. Peterson to Landis, 28 January 1941, Landis Papers; Morgenthau diaries, telephone conversation with Landis, 24 June 1941, vol. 413, Roosevelt Library.

34. *Mercersburg Academy Alumni Quarterly,* 1934, 49-51; Frank H. Meloon to Landis, 27 September 1941, Landis to Meloon, 29 September 1941, Landis Papers; *Boston News Bureau,* 27 September 1941; Landis, "Organized Civilian Defense," *Postmaster's Gazette,* XIX (December 1941), 11-12, 34-35; newspaper clipping, 14 December 1941, McLaughlin Collection.

35. Landis oral history, 307-311; newspaper clipping, 14 December 1941, McLaughlin Collection.

36. Landis to Edward S. Greenbaum, 3 December 1941, Landis Papers; Landis oral history, 311.

8. The Administrator at War

1. *Cambridge Chronicle,* 15 January 1942.

2. See Richard Polenberg, *War and Society: The United States, 1941-1945* (Philadelphia, 1972); John M. Blum, *V Was for Victory: Politics and American Culture during World War II* (New York, 1976); Richard R. Lingerman, *Don't You Know There's a War On? The American Home Front, 1941-1945* (New York, 1970); and Adolph A. Hoehling, *Home Front, U.S.A.* (New York, 1966).

3. Landis, address to the Advertising Club of Boston, 24 November 1942, McLaughlin Collection.

4. *Cambridge Chronicle,* 1 January 1942; newspaper clipping, 14 December 1941, McLaughlin Collection.

5. *New York Times,* 21 May 1941; Robert McElroy, "Narrative Account of the Office of Civilian Defense," November 1944, Reports and Awards Office, Office of Civilian Defense, RG-171, Federal Records Center, Suitland, Maryland. McElroy's typescript history of the OCD was written while the agency was still in existence and includes portions of documents not otherwise preserved.

6. Bernard L. Gladieux oral history, 174, Columbia University; S. Howard Evans to John B. Kelly, 27 September 1941, in McElroy, "Narrative of the OCD"; Eleanor Roosevelt to Jonathan Daniels, 23 February 1942, Eleanor Roosevelt Papers, Roosevelt Library; *New York Times,* 2, 3 August 1941, 14 September 1941.

7. Joseph P. Lash, *Eleanor and Franklin: The Story of Their Relationship Based on Eleanor Roosevelt's Private Papers* (New York, 1971), 634-653; Roland Young, *Congressional Politics in the Second World War* (New York, 1956), 47-49; *New York Times,* 6-8 February 1942; *Boston Traveler,* 7 February 1942.

8. Gladieux oral history, 176, 293-294; Wayne Coy and Harold Smith memorandum to Roosevelt, 13 December 1941, Official File-4422, Roosevelt Library; Eleanor Roosevelt to Landis, 16 December 1941, Landis Papers; Henry

Morgenthau diaries, telephone conversation with Senator Walsh, 16 December 1941, vol. 473, telephone conversation with Landis, 18 December 1941, vol. 474, Walsh telegram to Morgenthau, 27 December 1941, vol. 478, telephone conversation with Landis, 6 January 1942, vol. 482, Roosevelt Library.

9. Barton Leach, "Landis: Roommate and Dean," *Harvard Law School Bulletin,* XIX (March 1968), 20; James B. Conant to the members of the Two Governing Boards, 25 August 1945, Edmund M. Morgan to Conant, 2 February 1942, Landis Papers, Harvard Archives.

10. Roosevelt to Landis, 2 January 1942 and 12 January 1942, Official File-4422, Roosevelt Library; Landis oral history, 314-315.

11. McElroy, "Narrative of the OCD," OCD news release, 9 January 1942, RG-171, Federal Records Center, Suitland.

12. Landis oral history, 312-313.

13. *New York Times,* 9, 15 January 1942, 7, 10, 18 February 1942.

14. *PM,* 11 January 1942; *Congressional Record,* 77th Congress, 2nd sess., 259; *New York Times,* 11, 12, 19 February 1942; Fiorello LaGuardia to Roosevelt, 10 February 1942, Official File-4422, Roosevelt Library; Mayris Chaney to Landis, 17 February 1942, Eleanor Roosevelt Papers, Roosevelt Library; Landis oral history, 315; interview with John B. Martin, 7 March 1974.

15. Landis oral history, 335-336; *New York Times,* 12 February 1942.

16. Landis oral history, 317; *New York Times,* 4, 12 February 1942; Landis to Paula Gores, 8 January 1943, Landis Papers.

17. Harold Smith to Roosevelt, 2 April 1942, Roosevelt to Smith, 6 April 1942, Smith to Roosevelt, 15 April 1942, Official File-4422, Roosevelt Library; McElroy, "Narrative of the OCD"; *New York Times,* 17 April 1942.

18. Bureau of the Budget staff memorandum, March 1942, in "Civilian Defense in the United States, 1940-1945," Reports and Awards Office, OCD, RG-171, Federal Records Center, Suitland; Morgenthau diaries, staff meeting, 9 July 1942, vol. 548, Morgenthau presidential diaries, memorandum, 10 July 1942, vol. 5, Roosevelt Library.

19. Landis to Jonathan Daniels, 22 July 1942, Landis memorandum to Mr. Scotten, 20 August 1942, Headquarters, OCD, RG-171, Federal Records Center, Suitland; interview with Frances Knight, 16 December 1975.

20. *Complete Presidential Press Conferences of Franklin D. Roosevelt, 1942* (New York, 1972) 19:187-188; Landis oral history, 246-247; Landis to David Glick, 21 February 1951, Landis Papers.

21. *New York Times,* 14, 27 April 1942, 7 May 1942, 24, 30, 31 July 1942; Office of Civilian Defense, *Fire Protection in Civilian Defense* (Washington, D.C., 1941), 4, 32; OCD newsletter, 15 August 1942, Official File-4422, Roosevelt Library, *Newsweek,* XX (10 August 1942), 35.

22. Landis address to civilian defense rally, Cleveland, Ohio, 21 May 1942, McLaughlin Collection.

23. *New York Times,* 24, 26 February 1942; Hoehling, *Home Front, U.S.A.,* 29-31; Landis oral history, 321-322.

24. Interview with Dorothy Landis Fenbert, 5 April 1974; interview with John B. Martin, 7 March 1974.

25. Landis oral history, 322-323; *Time,* XXXIX (15 June 1942), 15.

26. Ellsworth Faris, "The Role of the Citizen," in William Fielding Ogburn, ed., *American Society in Wartime* (Chicago, 1943), 118-142; Landis, radio address, Mutual Broadcasting System, 23 February 1942, McLaughlin Collection.

27. *Washington Afro-American,* 22 August 1942, Jonathan Daniels to Eleanor Roosevelt, 28 August 1942, Eleanor Roosevelt Papers, Roosevelt Library; Landis oral history, 335-337.

28. Interview with Dorothy Landis Fenbert, 9 June 1975; Landis oral history, 356-357.

29. Jonathan Daniels, *White House Witness, 1942-1945* (Garden City, N.Y., 1975), 5-15, 27-28; Landis to Jonathan Daniels, 22 July 1942, Headquarters, OCD, RG-171, Federal Records Center, Suitland; Landis to Eleanor Roosevelt, 24 August 1942, Eleanor Roosevelt Papers, Roosevelt Library; Lash, *Eleanor and Franklin,* 653.

30. Marvin McIntyre, memorandum to Roosevelt, 17 August 1942, file memorandum, 25 August 1942, Official File-4422, Roosevelt Library; interview with Frances Knight, 16 December 1975. Daniels never forgave Landis, whom he described as a "man with foxes in his vitals." His memoir, *White House Witness,* which misses no opportunity to criticize Landis, begins with Daniels' transfer out of the OCD, but offers no explanation for the shift.

31. Landis to Malvina C. Thompson, 25 September 1942, Eleanor Roosevelt Papers, Roosevelt Library; OCD, *The Block Plan of Organization for Civilian War Services* (Washington, D.C., 1942); Landis, "What Can I Do To Help?" *New York Times Magazine,* 6 September 1942; Landis, "Block by Block," *Victory: The Official Weekly of the Office of War Information,* III (22 December 1942), 3.

32. OCD, *Organization Outline for Local Defense Councils* (Washington, D.C., 1942); *New York Times,* 3 May 1942; C. C. Sisson, memorandum to Landis, 26 July 1943 and 26 August 1943, Reports and Awards Office, OCD, RG-171, Federal Records Center, Suitland; interview with John B. Martin, 7 March 1974; Landis, Labor Day address, Kansas City, Missouri, 7 September 1942, McLaughlin Collection.

33. *Congressional Record,* 78th Congress, 1st sess., 2818-2825, 6130-6131, A1633; McElroy, "Narrative of the OCD"; Hoehling, *Home Front, U.S.A.,* 44-45.

34. Landis, "We Have Become a Team," *New York Times Magazine,* 6 December 1942; *Newsweek,* XXI (22 February 1943), 37-38; Landis, address at the United-for-Victory Parade, St. Paul, Minn., 30 January 1943, Igor Cassini column, "The Charming People," c. March 1943, McLaughlin Collection; Landis to Samuel I. Rosenman, 8 September 1943, Landis Papers.

35. Landis to James Conant, 16 August 1943, Landis to Samuel I. Rosenman, 19 August 1943, Landis Papers; Landis, memorandum on the organization of civilian defense within the War Department, August 1943, Samuel I. Rosenman Papers, Roosevelt Library; Rosenman to Roosevelt, 19 August 1943, Official File-4422, Roosevelt Library.

36. Landis oral history, 372; Roosevelt memorandum to Rosenman, 7 September 1943, Roosevelt to Frank Walker, 15 September 1943, Roosevelt to Harry Hopkins, 19 October 1943, James Byrnes to Roosevelt, 30 September 1943 and 1 March 1944, Official File-4422, Roosevelt Library.

37. Roosevelt, memorandum to Eleanor Roosevelt, 8 January 1945, with

enclosure: Harold Smith to Roosevelt, 4 January 1945, Official File-4422, Roosevelt Library.

38. "I have been awe-stricken by this news of the atomic bomb," Landis wrote in August 1945. "I just about agree with the editorial in the Papal paper tonight to the effect that the persons who discovered the secret should best have forgotten about it. No man and no nation can be entrusted with the possession of that much destructive power. It makes the whole idea of defense ludicrous." A few days later he added: "I cannot have any jubilation over the wholesale slaughter of over 100,000 people, most of them innocent, many of them children." Landis to Dorothy Brown, August 1945, and 9 August 1945, Landis Papers; see also Landis letter to the editor of the *New York Times,* 6 August 1950.

39. Landis to Paula Gores, 8 January 1943, Landis Papers; "Civilian Defense in the United States," OCD, RG-171, Federal Records Center, Suitland; *Time,* XL (10 August 1942), 70.

40. Landis to Dorothy Brown, 22 August 1943, Landis Papers; interview with Frances Knight, 16 December 1975; interview with Stanley Gewirtz, 6 March 1974; interview with Agnes Maher, 6 December 1975.

41. Interview with Dorothy Landis Fenbert, 9 June 1975.

42. Interview with Agnes Maher, 13 October 1975.

43. Landis letters to Dorothy Brown, c. May 1943, Landis Papers. My research in this period greatly benefited from the receipt of a large box of Landis' correspondence, 1942-1948, from his widow, Mrs. Dorothy Landis Fenbert. The letters were handwritten on yellow legal paper and were often undated. Subsequently, Mrs. Fenbert deposited the letters with the rest of Landis' papers at the Library of Congress.

44. Elizabeth B. Schlesinger eulogy of Stella Landis, 14 November 1967, McLaughlin Collection; interview with Mr. and Mrs. Charles McLaughlin and Mr. and Mrs. William McKee, 27 February 1974; interview with Agnes Maher, 6 December 1975.

45. *Christian Science Monitor,* 20 March 1942; Stella Landis, memorandum to Eleanor Roosevelt, 26 January 1943, report of the Committee on Club Centers for War Workers, undated clippings, McLaughlin Collection; *Washington Post,* 26 February 1943, 19 March 1943.

46. Landis to Dorothy Brown, c. October 1942, Landis Papers; interview with Dorothy Landis Fenbert, 9 June 1975.

47. *New York Times,* 31 May 1942; Landis to Dorothy Brown, c. 1943, Landis Papers.

48. Landis to Dorothy Brown, Easter morning, 1943, and c. summer 1943, Landis Papers; interview with Dorothy Landis Fenbert, 5 April 1974; interview with Agnes Maher, 6 December 1975.

49. Landis to Dorothy Brown, 12 August 1943 and c. autumn 1944, Landis Papers.

50. In his last note before his departure, Landis also wrote: "I have a curious feeling that I am going to die soon. It does not distress me for I have been happy these last few months. I may be wrong in my presumption, but if I am not, remember that I have loved you"; Landis to Dorothy Brown, 23 August 1943, Landis Papers.

9. Middle East Odyssey

1. *New York Times,* 11 September 1943; *Boston Globe,* 14 August 1943.

2. Landis to Edmund M. Morgan, 20 September 1943, Landis to Marion Tomlinson, 16 August 1943, Landis Papers.

3. Landis to Samuel I. Rosenman, 6 August 1943, Rosenman Papers; Landis oral history, 373-375.

4. *Newsweek,* XXII (25 October 1943), 43-45; Landis oral history, 380-381; *New York Times,* 5 December 1943, 16 January 1944; see, in general, Martin W. Wilmington, *The Middle East Supply Centre* (Albany, N.Y., 1971).

5. Russell D. Buhite, *Patrick J. Hurley and American Foreign Policy* (Ithaca, N.Y., 1973), 110, 117-118; Cordell Hull to Admiral Leahy, 25 May 1943, in U.S. Department of State, *Foreign Relations of the United States, 1943: The Near East and Africa,* IV (Washington, D.C., 1964), 1-2; Cordell Hull et al. to Roosevelt, 26 June 1943, President's Secretary's File, State Department, Roosevelt Library; Landis to General Lucius D. Clay, 1943, Landis Papers; *New York Times,* 11 September 1943.

6. Landis to Dorothy Brown, 20, 22 September 1943, Landis Papers; interview with Agnes Maher, 13 October 1975.

7. Landis to Dorothy Brown, 22, 25 September 1943, 6 October 1943, Landis Papers.

8. *New York Times,* 6, 7 October 1943; *Time,* XLII (18 October 1943), 20.

9. Landis, "Middle East Challenge," *Fortune,* XXI (September 1945), 161; Landis oral history, 375-380, 448-449.

10. Landis to Dorothy Brown, October 1943, Landis Papers; Landis oral history, 430; Landis memorandum, 25 October 1943, in *Foreign Relations, 1943,* IV, 549; Cordell Hull to General Lucius D. Clay, 1 December 1943, in *Foreign Relations, 1944,* V (Washington, D.C., 1964), 308.

11. Landis oral history, 111, 428-429; interview with Dorothy Landis Fenbert, 5 April 1974.

12. Landis oral history, 423-427; Acheson, memorandum for Secretary of State, 9 October 1945, in *Foreign Relations, 1945,* VIII (Washington, D.C., 1969), 43-44.

13. Landis, "Anglo-American Co-operation in the Middle East," *Annals of the American Academy of Political and Social Science,* CCXL (July 1945), 70; Landis oral history, 418-420; Landis, "Middle East Challenge," 188.

14. Landis to Dorothy Brown, 29 October 1943, Landis Papers; *Boston Globe,* clipping, c. 1945, McLaughlin Collection; Landis oral history, 380-384.

15. *Newsweek,* XXIII (10 January 1944), 38-40; *New York Times,* 16, 24 January 1944; *Washington Evening Star,* 30 July 1944.

16. Landis to Dorothy Brown, c. spring 1944, Roosevelt to Landis, 6 March 1944, Landis Papers; Wilmington, *Middle East Supply Centre,* 186-187.

17. Landis to Dorothy Brown, 19 March 1944, 14, 16 May 1944, Landis to Leo Crowley, 19 March 1944 (unsent), Landis to Dean Acheson, 19 March 1944 (unsent), Landis Papers. Dorothy Landis Fenbert described these letters as "written in a depressed mood. Needless to say, I did not mail them" (personal communication).

18. Landis to Martin W. Wilmington, 12 July 1951, Landis to Dorothy Brown, 13, 20 May 1944, September 1944, Landis Papers; see also Phillip J. Baram, *The Department of State in the Middle East, 1919-1945* (Philadelphia, 1978), 157-170.

19. Landis to Dorothy Brown, 8 October 1943, Landis Papers; Landis oral

history, 393-394.

20. Landis oral history, 389-397; Landis to Dorothy Brown, 19 April 1944, 20 May 1944, Landis Papers; see also Barrie St. Claire McBride, *Farouk of Egypt* (London, 1967); and William R. Polk, *The United States and the Arab World* (Cambridge, Mass., 1975), 152-164.

21. Landis oral history, 361-362, 456-458; Cordell Hull memorandum to Roosevelt, 24 September 1943, Official Files, Roosevelt Library; Morgenthau diaries, staff meeting, 1 January 1944, vol. 689, Roosevelt Library.

22. U.S. Office of War Information, press release, text of address of James M. Landis before the Royal Society of Political Economy in Cairo, Egypt, 22 December 1944, McLaughlin Collection; see also Gabriel Kolko, *The Politics of War, the World and United States Foreign Policy, 1943-1945* (New York, 1968), 172-193; and Christopher M. Woodhouse, *The Struggle for Greece, 1941-1949* (London, 1976), 111-138.

23. *Foreign Relations, 1944,* V, 41-42; news release, 2 January 1945, "Landis Summarizes Work of American Economic Mission," McLaughlin Collection; *New York Times,* 3, 5, 10 January 1945. Landis was seconded by the Culberton Mission Report; see John A. DeNovo, "The Culbertson Economic Mission and Anglo-American Tensions in the Middle East, 1944-1945," *Journal of American History,* LXIII (March 1977), 913-936.

24. Landis to Dorothy Brown, 21 May 1944, Landis Papers.

25. For Stella Landis' war work, see copies of "Flags Abreast," newsletter of the United Nations Service Center, McLaughlin Collection; Landis to Dorothy Brown, 4, 13 November 1943, and 29 April 1944, Landis Papers.

26. Landis to Dorothy Brown, 27 September 1943, October 1943, 8, 14 November 1943, Landis Papers.

27. Interview with Dorothy Landis Fenbert, 9 June 1975; interview with Agnes Maher, 6 December 1975; Landis cablegrams to Dorothy Brown, 13, 16, 18 November 1943, Agnes Maher, cablegram to Dorothy Brown, 13 November 1943, Landis to Dorothy Brown, 13 November 1943, Landis Papers.

28. Landis to Dorothy Brown, 4 November 1943, Landis Papers.

29. Landis to Dorothy Brown, 22 February 1944, 3, 10 March 1944, Landis Papers.

30. Landis to Dorothy Brown, 7 November 1944, Landis Papers; Landis oral history, 406-409; *New York Times,* 7 November 1944; interview with Agnes Maher, 9 December 1975.

31. Roosevelt to Landis, 11 January 1945, Susan Brandeis to Landis, 16 August 1943, Landis Papers; Landis oral history, 385, 400-401; Dean Acheson, *Present at the Creation: My Years in the State Department* (New York, 1969), 169.

32. Landis to Roosevelt, 17 January 1945, in *Foreign Relations, 1945,* VIII, 680-682.

33. Ibid., 682; Robert E. Sherwood, *Roosevelt and Hopkins: An Intimate History* (New York, 1948), 871-872; Landis oral history, 404.

34. Landis oral history, 405-406; Landis to Dorothy Brown, 18 April 1945, Landis Papers.

10. The Discontented Dean

1. Edmund M. Morgan to James B. Conant, 2 February 1942, Landis Papers,

Harvard Archives; *Harvard News Service,* 7 April 1944, Marion Tomlinson to Landis, 7 April 1944, Landis Papers.

2. Landis to Dorothy Brown, 2 December 1944, 9 December 1944, Landis Papers; *New York Times,* 29 December 1944, 3 January 1945.

3. Landis to Dorothy Brown, 3 December 1944, Landis Papers.

4. Landis to Thomas G. Corcoran, 19 March 1944 (unsent), Landis to Dorothy Brown, September 1944, Landis Papers.

5. *Newsweek,* XXVI (17 September 1945), 72. The Middle East Company never made any pretenses about its dependency on Landis: "Your company was organized as an export-import company to capitalize on the personal contacts made by James M. Landis and Dan T. Moore," read one statement to the stockholders; Board of Directors to stockholders of the Middle East Company, 25 October 1950, Landis Papers.

6. Landis, "Anglo-American Co-operation in the Middle East," *Annals of the American Academy of Political and Social Science,* CCXL (July 1945), 64-72; Landis, "Middle East Challenge," *Fortune,* XXI (September 1945), 178; Landis to Jerome Frank, 7 January 1946, Landis Papers, Harvard Archives.

7. Landis to Dorothy Brown, 3 December 1944, 13 June 1945, 9 July 1945, Landis Papers.

8. Landis wrote Dorothy regularly during his absences, poignantly expressing his feelings. One series of letters starting in January 1945 described his reestablishment in Cambridge and his arrangement for frequent trips to Washington; Landis Papers.

9. Poem by Landis to Dorothy Brown, 21 February 1945, Landis Papers.

10. Landis to Dorothy Brown, January 1945, Landis Papers.

11. Landis to Dorothy Brown, 25 January 1945, 21 February 1945, Landis Papers.

12. Landis to Dorothy Brown, 25 January 1945, 13 February 1945, Landis Papers.

13. Landis to Dorothy Brown, 29 May 1945, Landis Papers.

14. Landis to Dorothy Brown, 8 March 1945, 10 March 1945, 28 March 1945, Landis Papers.

15. Interview with Mary Walker Taylor, 6 March 1974; Landis to Dan Tyler Moore, Jr., 12 October 1945, Landis Papers.

16. *Williams v. North Carolina,* 325 U.S. 238 (1945); Nelson Manfred Blake, *The Road to Reno: A History of Divorce in the United States* (New York, 1962), 61, 182-183.

17. Landis to Stella Landis, 22 May 1945, McLaughlin Collection; Donald J. MacPhearson to Lawrence C. Kolb, 7 November 1962, Lawrence C. Kolb Collection, New York.

18. Lawrence C. Kolb to William C. Warren, 9 April 1963, Kolb Collection.

19. Landis to Dorothy Brown, 1 April 1945, June 1945, October 1945, Landis Papers; Landis' daughter Ann remembered it as "a terrible period, fraught with frightening silences and awkwardnesses"; Ann Landis McLaughlin to author, 11 January 1977.

20. Landis to Dan Tyler Moore, Jr., 12 October 1945, Landis Papers.

21. Interview with Ann Landis McLaughlin, 5 July 1974; Landis to Dorothy Brown, November 1945, Landis Papers.

22. Arthur E. Sutherland, *The Law at Harvard: A History of Ideas and Men, 1817-1967* (Cambridge, Mass., 1967), 307-311; *New York Times,* 17 March 1946; "Landis Adjusts Law School for Influx of Soldiers," newspaper clipping, c. 1945, McLaughlin Collection; *Cambridge Sentinel,* 10 February 1945; interview with Albert Sacks, 13 June 1975.

23. Landis oral history, 460, 470-472; Landis to Jerome Frank, 7 January 1946, Landis to Felix Frankfurter, 6 March 1946, Landis to Lon L. Fuller, 1 December 1945, Landis Papers, Harvard Archives; Landis to Milton Katz, 7 November 1945, Milton Katz Papers, Truman Library; *New York Times,* 17 March 1946, 16 February 1945; Landis to Henry M. Hart, 19 November 1945, Hart Papers, Harvard Law School.

24. L. Welch Pogue to Harry Truman, 5 March 1946, 9 May 1946, Official Files, CAB, Truman Library; Landis oral history, 482; Landis to Dorothy Brown, 7 July 1945, 26 July 1945, Landis Papers; interview with Dorothy Landis Fenbert, 9 June 1975.

25. Interview with Ann Landis McLaughlin, 20 January 1974; interview with Mary Walker Taylor, 6 March 1974; interview with Eleanor Landis Walker, 26 February 1974; *Cambridge Chronicle,* 22 June 1967; Frankfurter to Grenville Clark, 4 April 1946, Frankfurter Papers.

26. Interview with Dorothy Landis Fenbert, 9 June 1975; Milton Katz, "James M. Landis," *Harvard Law Review,* LXXVIII (December 1964), 318.

27. After Griswold became dean there were no more divorces at the Harvard Law School, so the story went, "because no one would have dared." Joel Seligman, *The High Citadel: The Influence of Harvard Law School* (Boston, 1978), 72.

28. Interview with Erwin N. Griswold, 3 June 1975.

29. Richard Russell to Landis, 13 September 1947, Landis Papers; *Boston Traveler,* 24, 25 April 1947. Stella charged that Landis deserted her in Washington in September 1943 and did not return to her. Commonwealth of Massachusetts, Probate Court, decree of divorce, 13 October 1947, Landis Papers; interview with Mr. and Mrs. Charles McLaughlin and Mr. and Mrs. William McKee, 27 February 1974; Landis to Stella Landis, 22, 27 May 1948, McLaughlin Collection.

11. Fair Deal Politics and Regulation

1. Harry S. Truman, memorandum to Robert E. Hannegan, 7 February 1946, Official File, Civil Aeronautics Board, Harry S. Truman Library, Independence, Missouri.

2. For a detailed discussion of federal regulation under Truman, see Gale E. Peterson, "President Harry S. Truman and the Independent Regulatory Commissions, 1945-1952" (Ph.D. diss., University of Maryland, 1973).

3. "What's Wrong with the Airlines?" *Fortune,* XXIV (August 1946), 73-78, 190; A. L. Reed to Burton K. Wheeler, 28 January 1946, Office of the Chairman, Civil Aeronautics Board, RG-197, National Archives; *New York Times,* 11 August 1946.

4. Landis, "The Job Ahead for the Civil Aeronautics Board," 14 October 1946, Speech File, Civil Aeronautics Board, Washington, D.C.

5. Interview with Stanley Gewirtz, 6 March 1974; *Time,* XLIX (17 March 1947), 86-88; *New York Times,* 11 August 1967.

6. Landis oral history, 568-569; for the history of the Civil Aeronautics Act see

Robert E. Cushman, *The Independent Regulatory Commissions* (New York, 1941), 389-416; Charles S. Rhyne, *The Civil Aeronautics Act, Annotated* (Washington, D.C, 1939); and Henry Ladd Smith, *Airways: The History of Commercial Aviation in the United States* (New York, 1965), 239-310.

7. M. C. Mulligan to CAB members, 13 August 1946, Landis to James E. Webb, 12 September 1946, Office of the Chairman, CAB, RG-197, National Archives; Landis to Webb, 14 September 1946, Webb to Landis, 11 December 1946, Department of Commerce file, fiscal year 1948, vol. 5, series 39.5b, Bureau of the Budget, RG-51, National Archives.

8. Landis, "Meddling from the White House," *New York Herald Tribune,* 20 March 1958; Landis oral history, 515-518; CAB, *Economic Decisions of the Civil Aeronautics Board, June 1946 to March 1947,* VII (Washington, D.C., 1948), 83-131.

9. Landis oral history, 242-245.

10. Ibid., 556.

11. William E. O'Connor, *Economic Regulation of the World's Airlines: A Political Analysis* (New York, 1971), 1-46; Landis, "Progress in International Aviation," Landis Papers; Landis oral history, 512-515; *Time,* XLVIII (26 August 1946), 81-82.

12. Landis oral history, 522-524; Department of State, *Foreign Relations of the United States, 1946: The American Republics,* XI (Washington, D.C., 1969), 470-482.

13. Landis oral history, 526-527; *Foreign Relations, 1947,* VIII (Washington, D.C., 1972), 239-241.

14. Landis' detractors blamed the treaty's failure on his boasting of "slipping one over" on the Argentinians. *Newsweek,* XXXI (12 January 1948), 16; *Foreign Relations, 1947,* VIII, 246-251; Landis oral history, 527; *New York Times,* 2, 10 May 1947.

15. *New York Times,* 19 January 1947, 19 August 1947; see also Matthew Josephson, *Empire of the Air: Juan Trippe and the Struggle for World Airways* (New York, 1944); and Arch Whitehouse, *The Sky's the Limit: A History of the U.S. Airlines* (New York, 1971), 204-223.

16. *New York Times,* 29 April 1947, 19 August 1947, 2 October 1947.

17. Ibid., 5 April 1947, 17 May 1947, 4 June 1947, 7, 16 August 1947; *Time,* L (25 August 1947), 84.

18. Edward A. Locke, Jr., oral history, 46, Truman Library; *New York Times,* 19 April 1947, 3 May 1947.

19. Landis, "Air Routes under the Civil Aeronautics Act," speech before the Association of the Bar of the City of New York, 12 April 1948, Landis Papers.

20. Chief, Accounting and Rates Division, to Director, Economic Bureau, 28 February 1947, Office of the Chairman, CAB, RG-197, National Archives; Landis to William A. M. Burden, 27 January 1949, Landis Papers; *New York Times,* 29 August 1946.

21. Harllee Branch, memorandum to CAB members, 9 December 1946, Office of the Chairman, CAB, RG-197, National Archives; Landis, "The Problems of Air Transportation with Particular Reference to New England," speech before the Connecticut Chapter of the National Aeronautics Association, 10 December 1947, Speech File, CAB; *New York Times,* 3 January 1948.

22. Kenneth R. McDonald, "Soldier Beware," *Aviation,* XLV (July 1946), 38-41;

Newark Sunday Star Ledger, 22 October 1947; Philip B. Schary, "The Civil Aeronautics Board and the All-Cargo Airlines: The Early Years," *Business History Review,* XLI (Autumn 1967), 272-284.

23. Landis to Warren Magnuson, 13 August 1947, Office of the Chairman, CAB, RG-197, National Archives; *Time,* XLVII (17 June 1946), 87-88; *New York Times,* 6 June 1946, 28 July 1946.

24. Landis to Edwin C. Johnson, 28 April 1949, Landis Papers; Landis oral history, 687-689; Landis, speech at the Harvard Club, 18 December 1946, Speech File, CAB.

25. Landis to Johnson, 28 April 1949, Landis Papers; Landis testimony before the Air Policy Commission, 27 October 1947, President's Air Policy Commission, Truman Library; Landis to Garrison Norton, 14 October 1947, Office of the Chairman, CAB, RG-197, National Archives; *New York Times,* 5 July 1947, 1, 6 August 1947, 3, 4, 8 October 1947.

26. Landis to Jerry Voorhis, 27 September 1946, Office of the Chairman, CAB, RG-197, National Archives; Landis, "The Job Ahead for the Civil Aeronautics Board," 14 October 1946, Speech File, CAB.

27. CAB minutes, exhibit E-5662a, vol. 77, E-6018z, vol. 81, and E-6733a, vol. 87, Landis to James E. Webb, 15 April 1947, Office of the Chairman, CAB, RG-197, National Archives; Landis, "Air Routes under the Civil Aeronautics Act," 12 April 1948, Landis Papers; *New York Times,* 28 September 1946, 7 November 1947.

28. CAB minutes, exhibit E-5505, vol. 75, RG-197, National Archives; *New York* 13 February 1947, Speech File, CAB; Landis, "Air Routes under the Civil Aeronautics Act," Landis Papers; interview with Stanley Gewirtz, 6 March 1974. Five of the six lines merged within a few years of Landis' prediction. The merger of National with Pan American was in the process of being approved at the time of this publication.

29. *Aviation,* XLV (August 1946), 121; Landis, "Mutual Problems of Air Transportation Service," speech before American Municipal Associations, New Orleans, 6 November 1947, speech at Harvard Club, 18 December 1946, Speech File, CAB; CAB minutes, E-5975b and E-6018a, vol. 81, RG-197, National Archives; *Time,* XLIX (17 March 1947), 86-88. Landis' stand caused his estrangement from Carleton Putnam, president of Chicago and Southern, who later characterized the CAB chairman as "irresponsible, inconsistent and unsound"; Carleton Putnam to Harry S. Truman, 12 January 1948, Official File, CAB, Truman Library.

30. *New York Times,* 30, 31 May 1947, 15 June 1947; Truman to Landis, 15 June 1947, Official File, Special Board of Inquiry on Air Transport Safety, Truman Library; *Aviation Week,* XLVII (7 July 1947), 7.

31. *Aviation Week,* XLVII (21 July 1947), 55, XLVII (15 September 1947), 7; CAB minutes, Safety Bureau Accident Investigation Report, File 1-0064, vol. 81, RG-197, National Archives; Landis to John R. Steelman, 23 December 1947, Official File, Special Board of Inquiry on Air Transport Safety, Truman Library; *New York Times,* 29 June 1947, 3, 8 July 1947.

32. Landis oral history, 488-490; Landis to Robert Sibley, 31 July 1950, Landis Papers; *New York Times,* 8 July 1947.

33. *Aviation Week,* XLVII (21 July 1947), 57, XLVIII (17 November 1947), 11; *New York Times,* 3 January 1948; *American Aviation Daily,* 5 January 1948.

34. *New York Times,* 18 September 1947, 2, 8 January 1948; *New York Herald Tribune,* 10 May 1949; Carleton Putnam, "Airline Outlook," *Air Affairs,* II (Winter 1949), 491-504.

35. Sam Rayburn to Harry S. Truman, 30 December 1947, Official File, CAB, Truman Library; Landis oral history, 548-549; interview with Stanley Gewirtz, 6 March 1974; *American Aviation Daily,* 5 December 1947.

36. *Aviation Week,* XLVIII (15 December 1947), 11, XLVII (6 October 1947), 15; *American Aviation Daily,* 30 December 1947; *Newsweek,* XXXI (12 January 1948), 16; *U.S. Air Services* (January 1948), Landis Papers; interview with Thomas C. Corcoran, 21 March 1974. In September 1948, with Truman's reelection campaign at a nadir, Louis Johnson took over as Democratic Finance Committee chairman and signed a personal note for $250,000 to underwrite initial campaign expenditures. The following year Truman appointed Johnson secretary of defense.

37. William Green to Truman, 30 December 1947, Philip Murray to Truman, 29 December 1947, Walter Reuther to Truman, 31 December 1947, David Behncke to Truman, 23 December 1947, Official File, CAB, Truman Library; Peterson, "Truman and the Regulatory Commissions," 283; *American Aviation Daily,* 22 December 1947; *Washington Post,* 29 December 1947.

38. Interviews with Dorothy Landis Fenbert, 5 April 1974 and 9 June 1975; Tyler Abell, ed., *Drew Pearson, Diaries, 1949-1959* (New York, 1974), 238; John C. Senour to Landis, 14 January 1948, Landis Papers; Robert H. Estabrook, "Last of the Brain-Trusters," *Nation,* CLXVI (3 January 1948), 68.

39. Landis, memorandum of conversation with President Truman, 26 December 1947, Landis Papers; Landis oral history, 549-552. Landis repeated this conversation to several acquaintances at the time, made a memorandum on it, and repeated it in his oral history twenty years later. It left a searing mark on his memory. I found no evidence to contradict his version of the conversation.

40. Interview with Stanley Gewirtz, 6 March 1974; interview with Dorothy Landis Fenbert, 5 April 1974; interview with Thomas G. Corcoran, 21 March 1974; Landis oral history, 552-553.

41. Nate Calkins to Landis, 31 December 1947, Landis Papers; *Washington Post,* 2 January 1948; Estabrook, "Last of the Brain-Trusters," 68-70.

42. Helen Fuller and William Walton, "Eccles, Landis and Truman," *New Republic,* CXVIII (9 February 1948), 10-11; F. Ross Peterson, *Prophet without Honor: Glen H. Taylor and the Fight for American Liberalism* (Lexington, Ky., 1974), 101-103; see also Alonzo Hamby, *Beyond the New Deal: Harry S. Truman and American Liberalism* (New York, 1973).

43. Stanton Griffis, letter to friends, 11 March 1948, Radio Reports, "Pan American Airways Operates Lobby against Landis Reappointment," 28 December 1947, Stanton Griffis Papers, Truman Library; Stanton Griffis, *Lying in State* (New York, 1952), 175.

44. Landis oral history, 554-555; *New York Times,* 9, 10, 14, 17, 21 January 1948. CAB members received $10,000 in annual salary during the 1940s.

45. Eben A. Ayers diary, 14 January 1948, Eben A. Ayers Papers, Truman

Library; Joseph P. Lash, ed., *From the Diaries of Felix Frankfurter* (New York, 1975), 342.

46. Memorandum, "Contention that Board's Organization is to Be Blamed for Delays," c. January 1948, Office of the Chairman, CAB, RG-197, National Archives; Landis to Paul Appleby, 11 July 1946, W. H. Rommel, memorandum, "Organization Survey of the Civil Aeronautics Board," 10 July 1947, Arnold Miles, memorandum to Charles B. Stauffacher, 15 October 1948, series 39.32b, T12-41/46.1, Bureau of the Budget, RG-51, National Archives.

12. Kennedy Enterprises

1. James Landis to Stella Landis, c. 1948, Joseph P. Kennedy to Stella Landis, 21 January 1948, McLaughlin Collection.

2. Landis to Dorothy Brown, 30 January 1948, 2, 3 February 1948, Landis Papers; Landis to Stella Landis, c. 1948, McLaughlin Collection.

3. Landis to Stella Landis, a series of undated letters, internal evidence indicates they were written early in 1948, McLaughlin Collection.

4. Ann Landis McLaughlin to author, 11 January 1977.

5. Landis to Stella Landis, c. 1948, McLaughlin Collection.

6. Ibid.

7. Stella Landis died in her sleep in June 1967. *Boston Herald,* 16 June 1967; interview with Ann Landis McLaughlin, 20 January 1974; Ann Landis McLaughlin to author, 11 January 1977; Stella Landis to Marion Frankfurter, 27 March 1960, Frankfurter Papers.

8. Dorothy Brown to Landis, 23 March 1948, Landis Papers.

9. Interview with Dorothy Landis Fenbert, 9 June 1975; Landis telegram to Mrs. Thomas Reed Powell, 3 July 1948: "Dear Molly, Please tell Stella I have been trying to reach her for two days. She knows that the time has come. Tell her I am sorry. Please be good to her"; Landis Papers; *Boston Herald,* 3 July 1948.

10. Landis oral history, 581-585; Landis to Joseph Kennedy, 28, 30 June 1949, 14 May 1950, 13, 20 September 1950, Landis Papers; interview with Dorothy Landis Fenbert, 9 June 1975; Felix Frankfurter oral history, 5, John F. Kennedy Library, Waltham, Massachusetts.

11. Landis to Congressman Jere Cooper, 13 September 1950, Landis Papers; Victor Navasky, *Kennedy Justice* (New York, 1971), 379; Charles Spaulding oral history, Kennedy Library; David E. Koskoff, *Joseph P. Kennedy: A Life and Times* (Englewood Cliffs, N.J., 1974), 326-327; *New York Post,* 4 December 1960.

12. Interview with Wallace Cohen, 18 September 1974; *New York Times,* 18 August 1948.

13. Landis to John H. Leh, 7 March 1949, Landis Papers; Landis oral history, 538.

14. *AOA Employees Newsletter,* 29 April 1949, Landis Papers; Landis oral history, 537-539; *New York Times,* 13 December 1948, 22, 29 March 1949, 11 April 1949.

15. Ray Tucker, "National Whirligig: News behind the News," 17 April 1950, *Tarrytown Daily News;* Landis to Ray Tucker, not sent, 26 April 1950, Landis to Douglas Amann, 7 March 1949, Landis Papers; see also Joseph C. Goulden, *The Superlawyers: The Small and Powerful World of the Great Washington Law Firms* (New York, 1972), 90, 116-179.

16. *New York Times,* 7 February 1950, 9, 13, 15 July 1950; *Washington Post,* 2 November 1951; Landis, "Meddling from the White House," *New York Herald Tribune,* 20 March 1950; Landis to Victor C. Netterville, not sent, 4 August 1953, Landis Papers; Landis oral history, 541-542.

17. *New York Times,* 13-15 July 1950; *Time,* LVI (24 July 1950), 70-72.

18. *Time,* LVI (24 July 1950), 70-72; Landis oral history, 543-546.

19. Landis to Hubert A. Schneider, 28 July 1950, Landis to Charles F. Banfe, 17 November 1950, Landis to Edward H. Collins, 20 February 1952, Landis to Jack A. Haner, 8 February 1952, Landis Papers.

20. Landis to Joseph P. Kennedy, 23 February 1949, Landis to Judge Stanley Fuld, 29 November 1949, Landis Papers; *Boston Herald,* 9 March 1949, 17 May 1949; *New York Times,* 18 May 1949.

21. Milton Winn to Landis, 7 January 1949, Landis to Joseph P. McGoldrick, 19 October 1949, Landis Papers.

22. Koskoff, *Joseph P. Kennedy,* 340-370; Joan Blair and Clay Blair, Jr., *The Search for JFK* (New York, 1976), 107-109; Joseph P. Kennedy and James M. Landis, *The Surrender of King Leopold* (New York, 1950); *New York Times,* 8 March 1950.

23. Koskoff, *Joseph P. Kennedy,* 369-371; Blair and Blair, *Search for JFK,* 403; Joseph P. Kennedy, promissory note, 15 August 1951, Landis Papers; Stanley Gewirtz to author, 6 November 1979.

24. Landis to Morris L. Ernst, 12 June 1951, Landis Papers; Landis to Stella Landis, 27 June 1948, McLaughlin Collection. In 1953 Landis briefly served as chancellor of the Asia Institute, with novelist James Michener as president. The advanced-degree granting school had fallen into financial troubles, and his assistance was part of a last-ditch salvage operation. At the same time, Landis was also chairman of the Executive Committee of the International Conference on Asian problems and a member of the Council on Foreign Relations. See Landis to the Members of the Board of Trustees of the Asia Institute, 26 June 1953, Landis papers; Landis to Eleanor Roosevelt, 29 September 1953, Eleanor Roosevelt Papers, Roosevelt Library; *New York Times,* 2 April 1953.

25. Interview with Justin Feldman and George Solomon, 11 June 1975; interview with Wallace Cohen, 18 September 1974; interview with Mr. and Mrs. Charles McLaughlin and Mr. and Mrs. William McKee, 27 February 1974.

26. Interview with Mary Walker Taylor, 6 March 1974; interview with Telford Taylor, 6 March 1974.

27. Landis to Dorothy Brown, 5 March 1944, 13 December 1944, George Skouras, memorandum to Landis, 21 August 1952, Landis Papers; interview with Dorothy Landis Fenbert, 9 June 1975.

28. Landis to Lyndon B. Johnson, 14 July 1953, Landis to Rodgers and Hammerstein Pictures, Inc., 13 October 1954, Landis Papers; Landis oral history, 409, 594-601; Art Cohn, *The 9 Lives of Mike Todd* (New York, 1958), 339-341.

29. Landis to Joseph P. Kennedy, 24 October 1951, Landis Papers.

30. Landis to Ralph Kaltenborn, 29 March 1954, and Landis to Edgar Fuller, 23 October 1951, Landis Papers; *Washington Post,* 6 September 1954.

31. Telford Taylor, memorandum to Landis et al., 16 October 1951, Skiatron Board of Directors Agenda, 23 January 1953, Landis to Arthur Levey, 17 July 1953, Levey to Landis, 3 June 1953 and 10 October 1953, Kurt Widder, memoran-

dum to Levey, 1 November 1954, memorandum, Subscriber-Vision expenses, April-November 1954, Landis Papers.

32. F. V. Quigley, memorandum to W. J. Shanahan et al., 4 August 1954, Landis memorandum, c. 1953, Landis Papers; Roger G. Noll, Merton J. Peck, and John J. McGowan, *Economic Aspects of Television Regulation* (Washington, D.C., 1973), 98-102.

33. *New York Times,* 14 June 1953; Noll, Peck, and McGowan, *Economic Aspects of Television Regulation,* 124-126.

34. *New York Times,* 12, 20 February 1955, 2, 15, 30 May 1955.

35. U.S. Congress, Senate, Committee on Interstate and Foreign Commerce, *Subscriber Television,* part III (Washington, D.C., 1956), 1076, 1079.

36. *New York Journal-American,* 29 June 1955; *New York Times,* 20 June 1955, 20 September 1957, 7 February 1958.

37. Years earlier Landis had warned Skiatron's president against overly optimistic statements. "My general feeling is that in light of the fact that the Company is publicly owned, we should be restrained in our representations rather than otherwise," he cautioned. Landis to Arthur Levey, 3 April 1953, Landis Papers. *New York Times,* 4 October 1960, 2 February 1963; Securities and Exchange Commission, "In the Matter of Skiatron Electronics and Television Corporation," *Decisions and Reports of the Securities and Exchange Commission* (Washington, D.C., 1960), 236-251.

38. Interview with Dorothy Landis Fenbert, 9 June 1975; Landis to John H. Leh, 7 March 1949, Landis Papers.

39. Landis to Joseph P. Kennedy, Jr., 26 March 1937, Chairman's Correspondence, SEC; Joseph P. Kennedy, Jr., to Landis, 13 April 1941, Landis to Joseph P. Kennedy, Jr., 27 May 1938 and 28 July 1941, Landis Papers, Harvard Archives; Landis to Joseph P. Kennedy, Sr., 17 July 1940, Landis to Dorothy Brown, August 1944, Landis Papers.

40. Jean Kennedy to Landis, c. December 1950, Eunice Kennedy to Landis, 1950, Landis to Eunice Kennedy Shriver, 1 March 1954, Landis Papers.

41. Robert Kennedy to Landis, 15 February 1951, 25 April 1951, and 16 April 1957, Landis to Robert Kennedy, 28 March 1951, Landis to Joseph P. Kennedy, Sr., September 1951, Landis Papers; U.S. Congress, Senate, Committee on Government Operations, *Report Submitted by Senator Mundt,* 83rd Congress, 2nd sess., 1-76; Landis oral history, 612-617; Koskoff, *Joseph P. Kennedy,* 378.

42. *Congressional Record,* 80th Congress, 2nd sess., 5025, A4312-4315; Landis to Robert H. Wood, 26 April 1949, John F. Kennedy to Landis, 13 July 1950, Landis to Robert Johnson, 19 September 1950, Landis Papers; *New York Times,* 25 February 1949, 8 June 1952; Donald R. Whitnah, *Safer Skyways: Federal Control of Aviation, 1926-1966* (Ames, Iowa, 1966), 266-268.

43. Kennedy denied that he had Addison's disease, but Joan and Clay Blair, Jr., make a convincing case to the contrary in *Search for JFK,* 556-579.

44. Interview with Mr. and Mrs. Charles McLaughlin and Mr. and Mrs. William McKee, 27 February 1974; Landis oral history, 255.

45. Landis oral history, 587-591; Landis to Ted Reardon, 29 August 1952, Landis to Joseph P. Kennedy, Sr., 22 December 1952, Landis Papers.

46. Landis to Eleanor Roosevelt, 3 August 1956, Eleanor Roosevelt Papers;

Richard J. Whalen, *The Founding Father: The Story of Joseph P. Kennedy* (New York, 1964), 426-429; interview with Wallace Cohen, 18 September 1974; Landis oral history, 607-608.

47. Hubert Humphrey to Landis, 17 February 1949, Landis Papers; Landis to John F. Kennedy, 15 July 1952, Campaign File, Kennedy Library; Landis to Eleanor Roosevelt, 3 August 1956, Eleanor Roosevelt Papers; Landis oral history, 604-607; Ralph G. Martin, *Ballots and Bandwagons* (Chicago, 1964), 415-416.

48. Landis oral history, 714; Landis, "Report on the Capital Transit Company," 1952, Landis to Theodore Sorenson, 25 August 1953, John F. Kennedy to Landis, c. June 1952, Landis Papers.

49. Landis to John F. Kennedy, 30 November 1953, Landis Papers; John F. Kennedy, *Profiles in Courage* (New York, 1956), xx, 54-55; Landis oral history, 712-713.

50. See chapter 14 for Landis' income tax problems.

51. Landis oral history, 623-631; *New York Times,* 1 September 1960.

52. Arthur M. Schlesinger, Jr., *A Thousand Days: John F. Kennedy in the White House* (Boston, 1965), 117-118.

53. Michael Yaffee, "Landis Stumps for ALPA Decentralization," *Aviation Week,* LXXIII (12 September 1960), 43; *New York Times,* 3 September 1960; *Christian Science Monitor,* 8 September 1960; interview with Justin Feldman and George Solomon, 11 June 1975. Landis came to have second thoughts about the union election. "Thank God I didn't win!" he said in 1963. Landis oral history, 580.

54. David H. Hoffman, "Landis Fails in ALPA Presidential Bid," *Aviation Week,* LXXIII (28 November 1960), 40; interview with Justin Feldman and George Solomon, 11 June 1975. The Holmes quote was a lifelong Landis favorite; see Landis to Jean P. Smith, March 1925, Landis Papers, Harvard Law School.

13. The New Frontier

1. Interview with Wallace Cohen, 18 September 1974; interview with Justin Feldman and George Solomon, 11 June 1975; *New York Post,* 4 December 1960.

2. Landis, "Perspectives on the Administrative Process," *Administrative Law Review,* XIV (Fall 1961), 66-74.

3. David E. Koskoff, *Joseph P. Kennedy: A Life and Times* (Englewood Cliffs, N.J., 1974), 345; Joseph P. Kennedy to Henry Cabot Lodge, Jr., 25 July 1947, Kennedy to Jim Brogan, 25 July 1947, Landis, memorandum to Joseph Kennedy, April 1948, Landis Papers.

4. Landis, "Report on the Independent Regulatory Commissions," January 1949, Landis to Joseph Kennedy, 4 October 1948, 5 January 1949, 21 February 1949, Landis to Herbert Hoover, 17 February 1949, Hoover to Landis, 3 January 1949, Landis to James H. Rowe, Jr., 28 April 1949, Landis Papers; U.S. Commission on Organization of the Executive Branch of Government, *The Hoover Commission Report on Organization of the Executive Branch of Government* (New York, 1949), 429-440; Congressional Quarterly Service, *Congress and the Nation, 1945-1964: A Review of Government and Politics in the Postwar Years* (Washington, D.C., 1965), 1458-1463.

5. Landis to Evans Clarke, 28 July 1950, 5 October 1948, Twentieth Century

Fund news release, 15 January 1951, Landis Papers; George W. Stocking and Myron W. Watkins, *Monopoly and Free Enterprise* (New York, 1951), 541-547.

6. *New York Times,* 11, 13, 14 November 1960.

7. Interview with Mary Walker Taylor, 6 March 1974; interview with Wallace Cohen, 18 September 1974; interview with Justin Feldman and George Solomon, 11 June 1975; *New York Times,* 27 December 1960; *New York Post,* 4 December 1960.

8. Landis, *Report on Regulatory Agencies to the President-Elect, Submitted by the Chairman of the Subcommittee on Administrative Practice and Procedure to the Committee on the Judiciary of the United States Senate,* 86th Congress, 2nd sess., December 1960, 18, 66, and passim. Because of his urge for speedy publication of the report, Landis had the first edition privately printed at the expense of his law firm; later the official government publication appeared.

9. Ibid., 18, 66, 77, 86-87; recording of "Today Show" interview with Landis, 3 January 1961, McLaughlin Collection; Landis to Edward H. Collins, 20 February 1952, Landis Papers; Landis, "Pressures Tend to Develop," *New York Herald Tribune,* 16 March 1958.

10. *New York Times,* 27 December 1960; *New York Herald Tribune,* 28 December 1960; *Newsweek,* LVII (2 January 1961), 56-59; *Time,* LXXVII (6 January 1961), 16; Carl McFadden, "Landis Report: The Voice of One Crying Out in the Wilderness," *Virginia Law Review,* LXVII (April 1961); *New York Journal-American,* 27 December 1960.

11. *National Review,* X (14 January 1961), 9; *New York Daily News,* 28 December 1960; *New York Herald Tribune,* 28 December 1960; *New York Times,* 29 December 1960; *New Republic,* CXLIV (16 January 1961), 6-7; "Interview with James M. Landis: What's Right and What's Wrong with Government Regulation," *U.S. News and World Reports,* V (27 March 1961), 84.

12. *Christian Science Monitor,* 3 January 1961; *New York Times,* 14 November 1960, 2 December 1960, 3 January 1961; see also Bernard Schwartz, *The Professor and the Commissions* (New York, 1959), 193-237; and Eric F. Goldman, *The Crucial Decade — and After: America, 1945-1960* (New York, 1960), 315-325.

13. *Detroit News,* 31 December 1960; *Time,* LXXVII (6 January 1961), 16; *New York World-Telegram and Sun,* 28 December 1960; Deane Heller and David Heller, *The Kennedy Cabinet: America's Men of Destiny* (New York, 1961), 154; Landis to Philip Graham, 24 June 1961, Landis Papers, Kennedy Library.

14. Landis oral history, 95-96; Felix Frankfurter to Edward Costigan, 12 February 1964, Frankfurter to Stella Landis, 6 August 1964, Frankfurter Papers, Harvard Law School; interview with Wallace Cohen, 18 September 1974.

15. Landis oral history, 704, 709, 717; Helen Fuller, *Year of Trial: Kennedy's Crucial Decisions* (New York, 1962), 45-50; *Washington D.C. Record,* 23 February 1961, McLaughlin Collection.

16. John F. Kennedy to Landis, 1 February 1961, Myer Feldman Papers, Kennedy Library; Felix Frankfurter oral history, 34, Kennedy Library; E. Barrett Prettyman, "The Administrative Conference of the United States," address, 7 August 1961, Landis Papers; Landis to E. Barrett Prettyman, 21 April 1961, Landis Papers, Kennedy Library. The Administrative Conference became a permanent federal agency in 1964 and remains a mechanism for the study and reform of the regulatory process.

17. Landis memorandum to John F. Kennedy, 9 February 1961, President's Office File, Kennedy Library; Executive Order 10934 (13 April 1961); "Special Message to the Congress on the Regulatory Agencies," 13 April 1961, in *Public Papers of John F. Kennedy, January 20 to December 31, 1961* (Washington, D.C., 1962), 267-276.

18. James Rowe to Landis, 9 January 1961, Frederick G. Dutton to Landis, 16 March 1961, Landis Papers, Kennedy Library; *New York Post*, 5 January 1961; *Newsweek*, LVII (9 January 1961), 23-24; *Washington Post*, 20 March 1961; U.S. Congress, House of Representatives, *Report of the Special Subcommittee on Legislative Oversight of the Committee on Interstate and Foreign Commerce*, 86th Congress, 2nd sess., 1961.

19. The general rule against presidential aides testifying before Congress was really only one of convenience, the general counsel of the Budget Bureau advised. Such voluntary appearances made it difficult for other aides to refuse to testify. Landis discussed all aspects of his reorganization plans, but when Congressman William Springer (R-Ill.) asked him to reveal the substance of his conversations on the subject with the President, he refused. Chairman Oren Harris upheld Landis on his disinclination to testify. See Carlile Bolton-Smith memorandum to Landis, 8 May 1961, and Landis memorandum to Myer Feldman, 2 May 1961, Landis Papers, Kennedy Library; and Harold Seidman, *Politics, Position and Power: The Dynamics of Federal Organization* (New York, 1970), 51.

20. Frankfurter oral history, 31-32, Kennedy Library; Landis to Myer Feldman, 3 April 1961, Feldman Papers.

21. Landis, *Report to the President-Elect*, 45-48; *Congressional Record*, 87th Congress, 1st sess., 8025; *New York Times*, 3, 22 June 1961.

22. *New York Times*, 24, 26 May 1961, 9 August 1961.

23. Ibid., 16, 18 June 1961; Robert T. Bartley to John L. McClellan, 4 May 1961, Landis Papers, Kennedy Library; *Congressional Record*, 87th Congress, 1st sess., 10456. Rayburn was dying of cancer, which may have affected his ill temper at the time. "I have rarely seen Sam Rayburn blow off as much as he did this morning, and about minor things," Landis commented to Ralph Dungan, 29 March 1961, Landis Papers, Kennedy Library.

24. *New York Times*, 18 June 1961; Paul Rand Dixon oral history, 15-16, Kennedy Library; see also Congressional Quarterly Service, *Congress and the Nation*, 1468-1470, for a summary of the Kennedy administration's reorganization program.

25. Landis memorandum for Lawrence O'Brien and Mike Manatos, subject: conversation with Senator McClellan regarding reorganization plans, 24 June 1961, Landis Papers, Kennedy Library; *New York Times*, 22 June 1961.

26. Carlile Bolton-Smith memorandum to Landis, 13 July 1961, Landis Papers, Kennedy Library.

27. Landis oral history, 705-706; see also James MacGregor Burns, *The Deadlock of Democracy: Four-Party Politics in America* (Englewood Cliffs, N.J., 1963), 309-311.

28. Most helpful in evaluating the Landis program was a round-table oral history which Dan Fenn of the Kennedy Library conducted with Alan Boyd (CAB), William Cary (SEC), Newton Minow (FCC), Joseph Swindler (FPC), and William

Tucker (ICC); also the Frank McCulloch oral history, 6-8, Kennedy Library.

29. Carlile Bolton-Smith to Landis, 31 July 1961, Landis Papers, Kennedy Library; Regulatory Agency Panel, 13-15, Kennedy Library; William L. Cary, *Politics and the Regulatory Agencies* (New York, 1967), 21-31.

30. Landis, "The President's Reorganization Program for the Regulatory Agencies: Gains and Losses," address before the Southeast Regional Meeting of the A.B.A., Birmingham, Alabama, 9 November 1961.

31. Landis oral history, 470; interview with Agnes Maher, 6 December 1975; interview with Dorothy Landis Fenbert, 9 June 1975.

32. Victor Navasky, *Kennedy Justice* (New York, 1971), 379-380; interview with Justin Feldman and George Solomon, 11 June 1975. There were also rumors that Attorney General Robert Kennedy had attempted to persuade Justice William O. Douglas to become ambassador to India to make a seat on the Court available for Landis. Douglas later denied ever talking with Kennedy or anyone else about the matter. William O. Douglas oral history (RFK), 8, Kennedy Library.

33. *Aviation Daily,* CXXXV (7 July 1961); *New York Times,* 16, 18, 29 July 1961; Landis oral history, 112-113, 479-480; Landis was also working on general transportation matters, the New Haven Railroad case, telecommunications, natural gas, and Atomic Energy Commission problems; see Mitchell S. Cutler to Myer Feldman, 12 September 1961, Feldman Papers, Kennedy Library.

34. *Boston Traveler,* 8 September 1961; *New York Times,* 8 September 1961; interview with Dorothy Landis Fenbert, 9 June 1975.

35. Interview with Dorothy Landis Fenbert, 9 June 1975; interview with Stanley Gewirtz, 6 March 1974; interview with Wallace Cohen, 18 September 1974; *New York Times,* 20 January 1962. An interesting study of power and sex in Washington is Myra McPherson's *The Power Lovers: An Intimate Look at Politics and Marriage* (New York, 1975).

36. Oren Harris oral history, 35, Kennedy Library; Benjamin C. Bradlee, *Conversations with Kennedy* (New York, 1975), 81; *Boston Traveler,* 8 September 1961; White House press release, 7 September 1961, Landis to Kennedy, 1 August 1961, Kennedy to Landis, 1 September 1961, Feldman Papers, Kennedy Library.

37. Landis, "Private Enterprise and the Federal Regulatory System: Co-Existence or Capitulation," address before the AGATE Club, Chicago, 19 November 1962, Landis Papers; see also Landis' review of Henry J. Friendly, *The Federal Administrative Agencies,* in the *University of Chicago Law Review,* XXX (Spring 1963), 599-601.

14. What Went Wrong?

1. Less kindly, Yale Law School professor Fred Rodell wrote: "I still can't help wondering where all that Harvard Law School education and those associations with Harvard's greats went wrong; you'd think, wouldn't you, that if he was going to cheat he'd have learned enough to do it right"; *Washington Post,* 24 September 1967; *New York Times,* 3 August 1963; David E. Lilienthal, *The Journals of David E. Lilienthal: The Harvest Years, 1959-1963,* V (New York, 1971), 494.

2. Interview with Mr. and Mrs. Charles McLaughlin and Mr. and Mrs. William McKee, 27 February 1974; Landis' papers at the Library of Congress con-

tain many of his newspaper contest entries.

3. Interviews with Dorothy Landis Fenbert, 5 April 1974 and 9 June 1975.

4. Landis oral history, 693; "Harrison Loyalty Oath Fund," 1953, Landis to Paul Bauman, 8 May 1953, Gus Hall to Landis, 31 August 1950, Elizabeth Gurley Flynn to Landis, 17 April 1953, Landis to J. Edgar Hoover, 27 August 1954, Landis Papers; *New York Times,* 17 October 1955.

5. *New York Herald Tribune,* 22 September 1955; *New York Times,* 17 October 1955; Port Chester, New York, *Daily Item,* 9 November 1955; Landis oral history, 694.

6. *New York Times,* 9 November 1955; *Boston Globe,* 2 November 1955; Landis to Dorothy Brown, 9 March 1945, Landis Papers.

7. Landis, remarks of supervisor at Town Board Meeting, 2 January 1956, clipping, "Harrison Town Board at Peace after Sharp Landis-Condon Tilt," c. January 1956, Dorothy Landis Fenbert Collection; Port Chester *Daily Item,* 3 January 1956; *New York World-Telegram and Sun,* 25 February 1956; Landis to Herbert Lehman, 5 July 1956, Landis to John J. Rooney, 5 July 1956, Landis to Philip Graham, 10 July 1956, Landis Papers; *New York Times,* 28 August 1956.

8. Landis to Nathan Straus, 16 October 1957, "The People of the State of New York against Paul Bauman and Joseph R. Straface, Jr.," Landis Papers.

9. Landis, "An Open Letter to the People of Harrison," 1957, Landis Papers; Port Chester *Daily Item,* 2 November 1957; *New York Times,* 11, 24 October 1957, 1, 7 November 1957, 1 April 1958; Landis oral history, 695-697; interview with Thomas C. Corcoran, 21 March 1974.

10. *New York Herald Tribune,* 19 March 1961; *New York Times,* 20 January 1959, 14 January 1960, 25 February 1960; interview with Ann Landis McLaughlin, 20 January 1974; interview with Wallace Cohen, 18 September 1974; interview with Stanley Gewirtz, 6 March 1974.

11. Landis to Income Tax Director, Boston, 15 March 1934, Landis to William J. Shea (collector of taxes, Cambridge), 11 September 1935, Andrew P. Carroll (city treasurer) to Landis, 25 August 1938, Internal Revenue Service to James M. Landis and Stella M. Landis, 22 March 1940, Landis Papers.

12. *New York Times,* 31 August 1963; interview with Dorothy Landis Fenbert, 9 June 1975.

13. Interview with Ann Landis McLaughlin, 20 January 1974; interview with Dorothy Landis Fenbert, 9 June 1975; Ann Landis McLaughlin to author, 27 September 1979.

14. Shortly after the Landis case, the IRS removed that question from the 1040 form, to prevent others in similar circumstances from falling into the same bind.

15. Interview with Justin Feldman and George Solomon, 11 June 1975. Landis' 1955 taxes were not included in the indictment because the statute of limitations had expired on them by 1963.

16. Victor S. Navasky, *Kennedy Justice* (New York, 1971), 378-391. Navasky presented the first detailed account of Landis' tax case. My subsequent research and interviews with participants in the case confirmed the general substance of Navasky's account.

17. Landis oral history, 616-618; Edwin Gutman, *We Band of Brothers* (New York, 1971), 151-152, *New York Times,* 31 August 1963.

18. Interview with Nicholas Katzenbach, 19 March 1977; interview with Justin Feldman and George Solomon, 11 June 1975; interview with Wallace Cohen, 18 September 1974; Navasky, *Kennedy Justice,* 383.

19. Interview with Nicholas Katzenbach, 19 March 1977; Navasky, *Kennedy Justice,* 384-385. See Arthur M. Schlesinger, Jr., *Robert Kennedy and His Times* (New York, 1978), 418-421.

20. Interview with Lawrence C. Kolb, M.D., 8 September 1975; Lawrence C. Kolb to Dean William C. Warren, 4 October 1962 and 9 April 1963, Lawrence C. Kolb Collection.

21. William N. Thetford, M.D., "Psychological Evaluation of James M. Landis," 17 July 1962, Kolb Collection.

22. Ibid.

23. Interview with Lawrence C. Kolb, 8 September 1975.

24. Kolb to Dean Warren, 9 April 1963, Kolb Collection.

25. Interview with Lawrence C. Kolb, 8 September 1975. The M'Naghton Rules date back to a British parliamentary inquiry in 1843. Since then, medical authorities have denounced the "right and wrong" test as unrealistic and unenlightened. See Thomas S. Szansz, *Law, Liberty, and Psychiatry: An Inquiry into the Social Uses of Mental Health Practices* (New York, 1963), and Szansz, *Psychiatric Justice* (New York, 1965).

26. Interview with Nicholas Katzenbach, 19 March 1977; interview with Justin Feldman and George Solomon, 11 June 1975; interview with Telford Taylor, 6 March 1974; Navasky, *Kennedy Justice,* 387.

27. Interview with Nicholas Katzenbach, 19 March 1977.

28. *New York Times,* 31 August 1963.

29. Ibid.; *Boston Globe,* 29 September 1963.

30. *Boston Traveler,* 30 August 1963; *Boston Globe,* 30 August 1963; *Washington Post,* 31 August 1963; interview with Ann Landis McLaughlin, 20 January 1974; interview with Nicholas Katzenbach, 19 March 1977.

31. H. Houston Merritt to Lawrence C. Kolb, 9 April 1963, Kolb Collection; interview with Lawrence C. Kolb, 8 September 1975; interview with Dorothy Landis Fenbert, 5 April 1974; interview with Nicholas Katzenbach, 19 March 1977; Navasky, *Kennedy Justice,* 388-389.

32. *Congressional Record,* 88th Congress, 1st sess., 18395; *Washington Evening Star,* 3 September 1963; Gardner Jackson to Abba Schwartz, 9 September 1963, Gardner Jackson Papers, Roosevelt Library.

33. *New York Times,* 2 October 1963; Lawrence C. Kolb, affidavit, 1964, testimony before the Appellate Division, First Department, *In the Matter of James M. Landis,* 16 March 1964, Kolb Collection.

34. Gerald Nolan, decision *In the Matter of James M. Landis,* 5 May 1964, Kolb Collection; *New York Times,* 10 July 1964.

35. Landis to Lawrence C. Kolb, 13 May 1964, Kolb Collection; interview with Stanley Gewirtz, 6 March 1974; interview with Wallace Cohen, 18 September 1974; interview with Justin Feldman and George Solomon, 11 June 1975.

36. Interview with Dorothy Landis Fenbert, 5 April 1974 and 9 June 1975; *New York Times,* 31 July 1964; *Washington Post,* 31 July 1964.

37. Autopsy 6186, case 2095, James M. Landis deceased, Office of the Medical Examiner, Westchester County, New York. I am indebted to Joseph Bono, M.D.,

of Roanoke, Virginia, for his interpretation of the autopsy report.

38. Interview with Ann Landis McLaughlin, 20 January 1974; *Harrison Independent,* 6 August 1964; Port Chester *Daily Item,* 3 August 1964; *New York Times,* 3 August 1964; *Washington Post,* 3 August 1964; eulogies at the memorial service for James McCauley Landis, offered at the Cosmos Club, Washington, D.C., 14 August 1964, McLaughlin Collection. The *Harvard Law Review* published its tribute to Landis in the December 1964 issue.

39. Interview with Dorothy Landis Fenbert, 9 June 1975. After the shock of Landis' imprisonment and death, friends urged Dorothy either to see a psychiatrist or to buy a horse. She bought the horse, and through two young women riding companions at her riding club she met their father, Lee Fenbert, a man who loved horses and theater, who did not drink, and who had a great admiration for James Landis. After a year they married quietly at Stratford-on-Avon.

Afterword

1. U.S. Congress, House of Representatives, Subcommittee on Oversight and Investigation of the Committee on Interstate and Foreign Commerce, *Federal Regulation and Regulatory Reform,* 94th Congress, 2nd sess., October 1976, 1-2.

2. In *Towards a New Past: Dissenting Essays in American History* (New York, 1968), 263-288.

3. *The New Deal* (Chicago, 1967), 11-15, 39, 72, 77-81, 106. Much of the literature of the 1960s reflected the authors' frustration with contemporary events. Thus Conkin wrote of the New Deal's launching of "the American welfare state, a brand new, large, ungainly infant, destined to survive all the hazards of childhood and maladjusted adolescence, eventually to mature in the Great Society, still ugly but increasingly popular" (54).

4. *Toward a Planned Society: From Roosevelt to Nixon* (New York, 1976), 1-68. Graham also concluded that the New Frontier's program had amounted to "just a hair more than nothing in the effort to bring some rationality to regulatory policy" (134).

5. "The New Property," *Yale Law Journal,* LXXIII (April 1964), 733-787; "The Law and the Planned Society," *Yale Law Journal,* LXXV (July 1966), 1227-1270; *The Greening of America* (New York, 1970), 7-8, 41-58, 93-94, 97-101.

6. *Private Power and American Democracy* (New York, 1966), 280-368.

7. *The End of Liberalism: Ideology, Policy, and the Crisis of Public Authority* (New York, 1969), 68-97, 125-132, 146-147, 287-314.

8. Landis, "Critical Issues in Administrative Law: The Walter-Logan Bill," *Harvard Law Review,* LIII (May 1940), 1077-1102.

9. *The Regulators: Watchdog Agencies and the Public Interest* (New York, 1979), 267-269.

10. *The New Deal and the Problem of Monopoly* (Princeton, 1966), 473.

11. *The Triumph of Conservatism: A Reinterpretation of American History, 1900-1916* (New York, 1963), 305. A more generally accepted interpretation was Robert H. Wiebe's *Businessmen and Reform: A Study of the Progressive Movement* (Cambridge, Mass., 1962), which also concluded that "the business community was the most important single factor — or set of factors — in the development of economic regulation,"

but emphasized the wide diversity of opinion within the business community, its disagreements over regulation, and its more subtle responses to progressive reforms (217 and passim). See also Kolko, *Railroads and Regulation, 1877-1916* (Princeton, 1965).

12. *The Corporate Ideal and the Liberal State: 1900-1918* (Boston, 1968), xv.

13. *Securities Regulation and the New Deal* (New Haven, 1970), 5-41.

14. *Regulating Business by Independent Commission* (Princeton, 1955), passim. Bernstein also criticized Landis' defense of the independence of the commissions, arguing that regulatory commissioners occupied lower positions in the government hierarchy than did bureau chiefs, who had proved adept at resisting direction from their department heads. "The deficiencies which Landis has ascribed to the bureau chiefs," Bernstein wrote, "might more appropriately describe the role and position of the commissioners of an independent commission" (140-141).

15. "Regulatory Administration and Organizational Rigidity," *Western Political Quarterly*, XXI (March 1978), 80-95.

16. In a letter to President Jimmy Carter on 16 December 1977 a group of Senate Democratic chairmen and ranking Republican committee members wrote: "Congress, and not the Executive, controls the guidelines for the independent regulatory agencies. Congress created these agencies. Congress provided for their organization. Congress adopted their statutory mandates. Congress controls their budgets and oversees their performance. Congress specifies agency procedures"; *Congressional Record*, 95th Congress, 2nd sess., 5 April 1978, S4863-4864.

17. Louis L. Jaffe, "The Illusion of the Ideal Administration," *Harvard Law Review*, LXXXVI (May 1973), 1183-1199; Henry J. Friendly, *The Federal Administrative Agencies: The Need for Better Definition of Standards* (Cambridge, Mass., 1962); William L. Cary, *Politics and the Regulatory Agencies* (New York, 1967); Albro Martin, *Enterprise Denied: Origins of the Decline of American Railroads, 1897-1917* (New York, 1971); and Stanley P. Caine, *The Myth of a Progressive Reform: Railroad Regulation in Wisconsin, 1903-1910* (Madison, 1970).

18. "Regulation in America: A Review Article," *Business History Review*, XLIX (Summer 1975), 159-183; see also McCraw, "The Controversial World of the Regulatory Agencies," *American Heritage*, XXVIII (April 1977), 41-47.

Index